One Woman Against War

The Jeannette Rankin Story

Kevin S. Giles

Copyright © 2016 Kevin S. Giles

ISBN: 978-1-63491-706-3

All rights reserved. No part of this publication may be reproduced, stored in a retrieval system, or transmitted in any form or by any means, electronic, mechanical, recording or otherwise, without the prior written permission of the author.

Published by BookLocker.com, Inc., St. Petersburg, Florida.

Printed on acid-free paper.

www.kevinsgiles.com/kevin@kevinsgiles.com
2016

The previous edition of this book, originally entitled, *Flight of the Dove: The Story of Jeannette Rankin*, was published in 1980 by Touchstone Press of Portland, Ore.

On the cover: The oil painting of Jeannette Rankin that appears on the cover was created by New York artist Sharon Sprung, who granted permission for its use. She was commissioned to paint Congresswoman Rankin's portrait for the US House of Representatives collection. All of her work can be viewed at www.sharonsprung.com.

To Becky and our girls.

Other books by Kevin S. Giles:

Jerry's Riot: The True Story of Montana's 1959 Prison Disturbance

Summer of the Black Chevy

Details at Booklocker.com.

Contents

1 ~ Thousands of voices, speaking as one 1
2 ~ Born in Montana Territory 21
3 ~ Awakening to national reform 39
4 ~ Suffrage, one vote at a time 49
5 ~ Barnstorming Montana for suffrage 73
6 ~ Campaigning for U.S. House, 1916 91
7 ~ Mr. Speaker, the Lady from Montana 107
8 ~ A symbol for women, then comes war 127
9 ~ First woman in Congress, first vote 139
10 ~ A pacifist is born 147
11 ~ Social legislation in a War Congress 157
12 ~ Overcoming objections to national suffrage 187
13 ~ Weathering an assault on civil liberties 201
14 ~ Turning to Georgia for world peace 213
15 ~ One woman against war 233
16 ~ Lobbying Congress for peace 255
17 ~ The lonely dissenter 283
18 ~ An eerie echo of history 313
19 ~ Learning from Gandhi 347
20 ~ The Jeannette Rankin Brigade 371
21 ~ Voice for women and peace 387
22 ~ Government by the people 405
23 ~ Jeannette Rankin's legacy 417
Acknowledgements and Sources 431
Selected Bibliography 435
Citations 447

"War is the slaughter of human beings, temporarily regarded as enemies, on as large a scale as possible."

"Killing more people won't help matters."

Jeannette Rankin

Jeannette Rankin, the first American congresswoman.
(Bain Collection, Library of Congress)

1 ~ Thousands of voices, speaking as one

'We are unarmed and not at all threatening'

It wasn't a convenient morning. Snow had fallen overnight, filling the streets surrounding the United States Capitol with slush and mud. Several thousand women wearing boots and overcoats gathered around an old woman in the gray light outside Union Station. She stood shivering, hardly resembling a historical figure, at first appearing long past her prime. Eyeglasses loomed over her wrinkled face. The old woman watched the milling crowd while organizers called activists into place, state by state, and handed them protest banners. They would march on the Capitol to protest the war in Vietnam. They would decry the slaughter of young men, profiteering by corporations with fat defense contracts, congressional neglect of social and economic needs at home. They would take to the streets to beseech their government to listen to their grievances. They wanted change. They wanted peace. It all seemed hauntingly familiar to this diminutive octogenarian named Jeannette Rankin.

Half an hour before noon, the procession filed silently onto Louisiana Avenue. Rankin, standing all but a whisper past five feet tall in overshoes, walked at the middle of a banner that stretched thirty feet wide. "End the War in Vietnam and the Social Crisis at Home!" it commanded. Holding one end was Coretta Scott King, spouse of the crusading Martin

Luther King, Jr., the civil rights leader who just weeks earlier had announced plans for a massive Poor People's Campaign in the very streets where Rankin and nearly ten thousand other women now walked. Police estimated five thousand. They were notoriously bad at counting participants at public demonstrations. Surely it was ten thousand, Rankin surmised, because the procession stretched for several city blocks. She had some impressive experience with protests long before almost everyone walking with her. She knew a crowd when she saw it.

It was January 15, 1968, the opening day of the second session of the 90th Congress. President Lyndon Johnson enjoyed Democratic majorities in both the Senate and the House but national unity evident in those first weeks after the Christmas holidays soon would fade. Despite the president's "Great Society" domestic accomplishments with Head Start and Medicare and his leadership in civil rights, Democrats backed away in increasing numbers from his enthusiasm for United States military intervention in Vietnam. The war and its companion difficulties in the streets of America would figure strongly into Johnson's decision to leave the presidency when his term ended later in the year.

That day in Washington would replay dramatic scenes in Jeannette Rankin's mind. In the back pages of her memory she heard legions of feet shuffling, thousands of women's voices calling for the right to vote. In those rustling calendar pages of time she would remember exuberant soldiers and somber protests and stern faces in Congress. She would reflect on a lifetime of passion for peace. That day at Union Station came nearly fifty-one years after Rankin's first vote in Congress against war with Germany and more than twenty-six years after her landmark vote against war with Japan. Now, the Jeannette Rankin Brigade was taking the first step into one of the most tumultuous years in American history. A national protest in Rankin's name was of no little significance even if many Americans didn't remember her. History isn't especially fond of dissenters, often perceived as agitators, but Rankin had earned her reputation as one of the Twentieth Century's most notable women.

That year, 1968, would become memorable for its fashion chaos as go-go boots, bell bottom trousers, miniskirts and peasant dresses appeared everywhere. Peace signs, love-ins and psychedelic rock already ruled university campuses from Berkley to Columbia and counterculture meccas such as Haight-Ashbury in San Francisco. Flower children blossomed on street corners coast to coast after the Summer of Love. The King of Rock and Roll, Elvis Presley, would manage a musical comeback after making low-budget movies for seven years. The innovative television news magazine, *60 Minutes*, would redefine broadcast journalism. The Beatles would begin their final round of chart-topping songs with Paul McCartney's *Hey Jude*, a sad premonition of their band's dissolution as much as John Lennon's failing marriage and his son Julian being caught in the middle. One of the most memorable statements in popular culture, "Book 'em, Dano," would be introduced into American living rooms on color television. Hippies challenged Establishment America, while "Love It or Leave It" became the siren slogan for conservative Americans distressed over their crumbling conventional way of life.

Even as many of the nation's youth proclaimed Free Love and rocked to the psychedelic Doors and Jefferson Airplane and other signature bands rooted in the drug culture, 1968 would be remembered more for its history-altering tragedies. Three months after the march of the Jeannette Rankin Brigade, a white supremacist would shoot and kill Martin Luther King, Jr., as he stood on a Memphis motel balcony. The nation's cities, already edgy over racial strife, would erupt in flames and violence. More dreams of peace would wilt on a hotel kitchen floor after presidential candidate Robert Kennedy's assassination by a Palestinian Arab, Sirhan Sirhan, angry over Kennedy's support for Israel. A generation would reel in despair.

Republicans would nominate Richard Nixon, a moody and vengeful California conservative and President Eisenhower's vice president, as their presidential candidate at the Miami convention. The Democratic convention in Chicago would turn violent when police and protesters clashed in a nearby park, supplying vivid images of bloody beatings for the nation's television audiences. Hubert H. Humphrey, a Minnesota liberal and Lyndon Johnson's vice president, would emerge as the Democratic presidential nominee. In the South, voter support would grow for segregationists George Wallace and Lester Maddox. To the political left, minority militants such as Black Panthers, Chicano Brown Berets and the American Indian Movement would emerge. Students would seize five buildings at Columbia University for two months, showing in their "Strawberry Statement" how campuses could become centers for political protest. In a prologue to the eventual darkest chapter in presidential history known as Watergate, Nixon would ascend to the Oval Office after a razor-thin victory over Humphrey in November.

The backdrop to 1968, good and bad, was the cursed, deepening Vietnam conflict, not even recognized formally as a war. The mammoth surprise assault on American troops, known as the Tet Offensive, would impress on people back home the true misery of a little-understood Asian culture. The United States would lose its 10,000th helicopter in Vietnam. Coincidentally, an identical number of American troops would fall in combat that year. By year's end, United States troop presence in Southeast Asia would exceed half a million. More than 300,000 men would be drafted into the military in

1968, the peak year of the buildup. Many Americans were denouncing the military's demands for more troops to throw into the maw of Vietnam, where a jungle war supposedly would arrest the spread of communism.

The United States was fractured in 1968 and about to get worse. A resurgent Republican conservatism would challenge Democratic dominance. To the other extreme, legions of college kids embraced "message" musicians like protest-singer Country Joe MacDonald who mocked Middle America's baleful reluctance to view war as a grim horror with his lyrics, *Be the first one on your block/To have your boy come home in a box*. Vietnam had become a killing field for American boys. More than 11,000 died in 1967, the highest body count yet in the undeclared war. The bloodshed inspired a flurry of correspondence to Jeannette Rankin from young Americans anxious for activism to oppose the war. One letter that year came from Linda Goodman, a nineteen-year-old student at Stanford University in California. "I have come to believe now that perhaps the only way to stop the war in Viet Nam would be to have large masses of women act out against it," Goodman wrote Rankin. "I am frightened by the war, and all wars, and at the brutality and insensitivity which I see it breeding."[1]

For twenty-six years after Jeannette Rankin's second term in the US House of Representatives had ended, she disappeared from the American peace movement, preferring to occupy herself with world travels and quiet summers at her family's Avalanche Ranch in Montana. Public knowledge of the once-legendary Rankin, a hero to many people in her younger years but vilified by others as a traitor, had shriveled to a footnote in passing time. Many Americans had forgotten her. On the day that she joined thousands of like-minded women marching to the Capitol, the confluence of old guard First Wave suffragists and contemporary Second Wave feminists gave her a pulpit to revive her reputation. She was, again, a public figure.

Her comeback started inauspiciously enough. In May 1967, a Georgia pacifist and civil rights activist named Nan Pendergrast invited Rankin to Atlanta to speak about Vietnam to members of Atlantans for Peace. Pendergrast and Rankin were longtime friends and shared strong opinions against war. Many times Rankin stayed with Nan and her husband Britt, a conscientious objector during World War II, while visiting in Atlanta.

Rankin hadn't delivered a speech on peace for at least twenty-five years. Pendergrast was intimately familiar with Rankin's long history of pacifism and persuaded her friend to share her views on war and peace. That night, for a meeting at her house involving about twenty disciples of Atlantans for Peace, Nan invited an *Associated Press* reporter to visit with Rankin. Never short of drama, Rankin told the reporter she had read in a newspaper that very morning that 10,000 American men had died since the war began. Whether she knew how substantially that number would grow in the final months of 1967 remains a matter of speculation, but she clearly was alarmed at mounting casualties. Rankin told the reporter that if 10,000 women were prepared to march in memory of those dead men, they could stop the war. Women should commit to acts of civil disobedience and even jail, she said, showing her immersion in the teachings of pacifists Mohandas Gandhi and Henry David Thoreau in the years she had been out of the public eye. "The time has passed for us to be nice. The army isn't polite when it selects a young man and says, 'Come on and fight,'" she said.

That night, *Associated Press* distributed the story on its national wire. Rankin's pithy statement became an overnight sensation. "It must have been a slow news day," Pendergrast would relate years later. "Suddenly she was all over the newspapers nationally."[2] It appeared that many people remembered Jeannette Rankin after all. Illustrative of responses to the story was one from Edith Newly of New Mexico, who wrote Rankin to thank her "for being the courageous American, the magnificent woman you are. That you go on in spite of the past is in itself stupendous bravery."

Rankin received hundreds of similar letters. Struck by her antiwar comments and seeking leadership as news about Vietnam crowded the headlines, women across the country began to rally around her. Rankin tried to answer every letter, including one from Betty Meredith, who ran a nursery school for twenty-eight children in her house in a San Francisco suburb. Meredith had read Rankin's comments in the morning *Chronicle* and, stirred by the old suffragist's passion, showed the story to her friend Vivian Hallinan.

Protesters came and went in the 1960s, their numbers swelling and deflating as causes rose and fell, but Hallinan was no ordinary dissenter. She was a rich and persistent benefactor of liberal causes, drawing from a fortune she had accrued buying and selling apartment buildings during the Great Depression. She also had practical protest experience, having been sent to jail for participating in a civil rights demonstration in 1964. Hallinan was the elegant matriarch of a legendary and radical San Francisco family. Her husband was socialist attorney Vincent Hallinan, a 1952 presidential candidate on the Progressive ticket. Neither of the Hallinans was short of audacity when it came to funding political causes.

After Vivian read Rankin's story, she boarded a plane for Georgia. Some hours later, she found Rankin awaiting her at the airport in Atlanta. They made a contrasting pair, as *Ramparts* magazine later described them: the striking young California activist and socialite, dressed in a camel-colored zipper suit, fishnet stockings and an orange sweater; the spunky octogenarian wearing oversized glasses and a mundane dress that most respectfully could be described as stylishly earth-toned.³ As they bounced along for sixty miles on the Georgia countryside — Rankin squeezing the gas pedal of her Chevrolet to the floorboard with a high-heeled shoe, it was reported — Hallinan asked whether Rankin would allow 10,000 women to march on the United States Capitol in her name. They would be known as the Jeannette Rankin Brigade.

Being a longtime pacifist, Rankin found the military term "brigade" distasteful. For eighty years she had disliked everything about war, including words used to describe it, but in the new course of events she considered the objection insignificant. She didn't want to organize the march or recruit women because she had buried that brand of activism in her past. Hallinan assured her that other women would manage the details. Rankin would lend her name and help the coalition plan logistics.⁴ By the time Rankin braked her car to a stop outside the patched-up sharecropper's shanty she called home, she had agreed to participate in such a march. "She really did feel like she was beginning her life all over again," Nan Pendergrast would recall of that moment as Rankin confided it to her.

From the beginning, the Jeannette Rankin Brigade had deep roots in Women Strike for Peace, a national mass movement that began in 1961 to ban nuclear weapons. By the fall of 1967, members of the potent antiwar coalition began meeting almost daily to organize the brigade and a second action, a Congress of American Women, that would be held after the march to put "woman power" on display. More than a figurehead, Rankin was in the middle of the planning, even traveling to New York to participate in strategy sessions. Women Strike for Peace, of which Hallinan was a member, quickly backed away from Rankin's initial suggestions of civil disobedience and jail. Their notion was to recruit large numbers of church women to the brigade. These women, more conservative overall but increasingly vocal about their desire for peace, would unite forces with African American leaders and Second Wave feminists in 1968 to campaign against members of Congress who supported the war. The popular front that resulted, driven by feminist Ann Bennett and supported by acclaimed black civil rights leaders such as Rosa Parks and Fanny Lou Hamer, would converge peace and poverty into a single cause and bridge racial and social classes of people.[5]

For Jeannette Rankin, appealing for peace in Washington, DC, amounted to more than a protest of war. It would be symbolic of her life since she had joined the suffrage campaigns in 1910. Improving the welfare of women had been, to her, the all-inclusive reform that would establish government programs for mothers and children, help secure a more judicious manner of electing a president, clean up decadent social conditions and most of all, stop wars.

In 1918, Rankin had read *The Science of Power*, a book by British sociologist Benjamin Kidd. It fortified her belief that men wouldn't end war if women didn't make them do it. The book had become her peace bible. Rankin talked about the book, decades after her first reading of it, on national television talk shows. She carried a worn copy that she mailed to anyone who volunteered to read it.

Just as Rankin had learned from Gandhi and Nehru in her journeys to India that uncompromising support of women was essential to peace, Kidd awoke her to the philosophical differences between men and women on issues of war. To him, men were eternal aggressors, dueling like gladiators because of their obsession with material goods. This is what Kidd called *force*. He saw women as eternal procreators, looking after quality of life. This is what he called *power*.

Coincidentally, Kidd's theories paralleled the structures of Rankin's family. Her father, John Rankin, had stood for land, money and pride. He built his reputation and fortune as an influential community leader in frontier western Montana. Her mother, Olive Rankin, shaped her life around her seven children. The family lived far westward from the excesses of the *Gilded Age*, when a wave of wealth for some and poverty for many grew out of the post-Civil War industrial economy. Behind the curtain of national prosperity hid the omnipresent threat of war and other maladies Jeannette would come to hate, such as child labor and legal discrimination against women. Olive Rankin would not appear to lend much influence to Jeannette's political beliefs, but in outliving her husband by more than forty years, she would represent the maternal influence of which Kidd spoke. John Rankin impressed on Jeannette his gift for rugged individualism.

Rankin had made *The Science of Power* her workbook for involving women in the peace movement. Kidd wrote that women had the power to develop what he called *the emotion of an ideal*. This meant they could pursue an idea because they had a stirring love for it. Kidd concluded that a woman "is the creature to whom the race is more than the individual, the being to whom the future is greater than the present."

From Kidd's writings and Gandhi's teachings, Rankin shaped her pacifist philosophy about the future of world civilization, believing women who carried children in their bellies for nine months had more concern for their welfare than men, whom she saw as being forever preoccupied with combat. Rankin's ideas about force and power surfaced anew in 1967 when war again gripped the United States — and more evidence emerged that it wasn't going well. At age seventy-seven, the pacifist Gandhi had been walking to villages and townships to share his vision of civil disobedience. Rankin, at eighty-seven, decided she could perform a similar feat, even if more symbolic.

Throughout Rankin's long and often stormy life, critics accused her of pursuing a fairy tale in thinking that women could, or would, stop war. Rankin held fast to her belief that women had been frightened into silence by the "war habit," as she called it. To her, Americans had fallen to a mistaken belief that war was a patriotic obligation. To her, that belief was cemented in all strata of society.

In 1968, as opposition to the war in Vietnam mounted, Rankin stuck to her faith that women would lead the peace movement just as they had fought for their right to vote by federal amendment and finally won it in 1920. She had suffered many doses of bad luck in her campaigns to persuade women to quiet the motors of war. Many people ridiculed her as a bombastic tool of insurgents. They judged her quest for peace as political heresy in a land birthed from violent revolution. Conversely, many other Americans applauded her courage and vision. They saw her as a leader far ahead of the times, proposing ideas that seemed enduringly prudent but politically premature. As with any controversial figure in history, self-doubt tormented Rankin more than most anyone knew. After the Korean Conflict she had suffered bouts of depression, confiding to close friend and writer Katharine Anthony that despite a lifetime of effort she had failed to rally women against war. "I am not going to allow you to say that you are a futile person," Anthony shot back. "That just isn't true. And you mustn't ever say it again. With all that you have accomplished in life you should never let such a thought enter your mind."[6]

By 1968, principles and causes Rankin had embraced since before World War I were accepted to a great degree across the United States. Numerous federal and state laws had been enacted to protect workers and prohibit forced labor of children. Women had won the right to vote. More Americans understood that wars didn't come without a price paid in blood. Anger against the Vietnam conflict had stirred protests in cities nationwide. It was the kind of street-level protesting that Rankin had known from her early days in New York when she worked for social and political reform. Many so-called radical reforms were widely accepted if not widely tolerated. A notable exception was Rankin's quest to outlaw war. Throughout the decades, reasons given for United States intervention in foreign conflict echoed those of previous wars. On that point, Rankin hammered away that wars unfailingly produced predictable miserable results. She hadn't stood alone in her determination for permanent peace but to her, eight decades into her life, time was running out. In her single-minded effort to fight her private war against international war, she sometimes seemingly contradicted her own beliefs to make a point. Just why she voted in 1964 for presidential candidate Barry Goldwater wasn't clear to anyone who knew her. The Arizona senator was a noted war hawk and social conservative, an authentic antithesis to the longtime peace dove, but she liked him because he condemned US policy in Vietnam during his acceptance speech at the Republican National Convention.

The massive peace movement that Rankin coveted grew daily after President Johnson in 1966 increased American military troops in Vietnam to 375,000. Revelations abounded. Explosives dropped on North Vietnam eventually would quadruple the bomb tonnage rained on Germany and Japan during World War II. American taxpayers were paying twenty-five billion dollars a year for human destruction, reported graphically in newspapers and magazines: Vietnamese children scarred by napalm, appalling death tolls in firefights, machine gunning civilian peasants, killing American soldiers by their own misdirected "friendly fire," and even exploitation of Vietnamese coastal waters by

Standard Oil and other conglomerates.

As Vietnam's casualty figures sailed upward, voices of female protest grew louder. By 1967, more American women than ever demanded an end to the war. The massive "March to the Pentagon" in October reflected the growing national dissent, as did a series of anti-draft demonstrations in December.[7] Rankin had denounced war for decades but she hadn't persuaded enough people to stop it. She was an icon of pacifism during two world wars, a hero to many and a reprehensible traitor to others, but now thousands of activist women promised to join her in peaceful protest. Two voices were stronger than one, three stronger than two. To Rankin's delight, the march in Washington would satisfy Kidd's ideal of women using their power to secure their destinies. Growing discontent over Vietnam had made people eager for leaders. Rankin rode its crest to national prominence. She would become significant national news for the third time.

That very morning of the Jeannette Rankin Brigade, all over the country, Federal Bureau of Investigation agents began dispatching alerts to J. Edgar Hoover's office concerning alleged subversive activity. Any talk of dissent worried Hoover, and the attention he paid to Rankin suggested fear of her message and the merging of the peace and civil rights movements. Censors would black out substantial portions of memos containing apparent intelligence-gathering into the Rankin Brigade's activities. Information came from "sensitive sources," the FBI said, "the compromise of which would be detrimental to the U.S."

Agents were dutiful in watching the makings of the protest. In Philadelphia on the morning of January 15, they reported that dozens of "white, middle-aged women" wearing Women Strike for Peace buttons boarded three cars of *The Congressional* train bound for Washington, DC. From New York, 1,400 more came on a charter train for a roundtrip fare of $7.50 each. In St. Louis, marchers of "the white race" circled the county courthouse. One of the women carried a sign that read, "Jeannette Rankin Brigade Stop the War in Vietnam," in support of the larger demonstration in Washington. One woman brought two small children. "At one time two negro males observed the marchers and joined them," the agent wrote. "After about five or ten minutes they apparently learned what the demonstration was about and left."[8] In San Francisco, Atlanta, Chicago, Seattle and Phoenix, agents dutifully counted and observed protests planned in coordination of the large march in the nation's capital.

In a bizarre bit of irony that day, several activist women from California watched a movie, *Panic in the Streets*, on their transcontinental flight. The movie portrayed a villain who had built a nuclear bomb in the basement of a house in Los Angeles. In the words of Marion Beardsley, representing Women Strike for Peace: "The intrepid FBI scurried around everywhere including some swanky swimming pools with babes in bikinis lying around," until finally the hero found the bomb and hauled it to the ocean and dumped from a helicopter where "it went up in a mushroom cloud of glory." Wrote Beardsley, who made the journey to join the Rankin Brigade with leaders from several women's organizations: "It struck me that moving a bomb might be a lot simpler and easier than moving some of the minds in Washington."[9]

Hoover's FBI viewed the brigade as a public safety threat, linked to communists in a fantasy of true Hoover fashion. "The brigade has been founded as a response to a statement made by former Congresswoman Jeannette Rankin to the effect that if large numbers of women protested the war and were arrested, it would bring the war machine to a halt in this country," the Seattle office wrote Hoover. The memo also linked the Jeannette Rankin Brigade with groups such as Women Strike for Peace, the Society of Friends (Quakers) and

Seattle Women Act for Peace. Also under scrutiny were the publications *People's World* and the *National Guardian*, both of which the FBI surmised were communist.

Given the FBI's responsibility "to identify subversive elements," field agents were ordered to begin investigations of the old woman who would lead the march. Jeannette Rankin's pacifist history was noted, as were her congressional votes against two world wars. "She has stated that she is willing to stay in jail until the bombing in Vietnam is stopped," according to FBI records.

The FBI then dictated how it would canvass the Jeannette Rankin Brigade: Identities of participants, known subversives, would be sent to Hoover's office first by teletype and then by full memorandum. Each field office would document who was financing groups in the march. Special attention would be paid to Rankin and anyone else sponsoring the brigade. The *People's World* newspaper reported many of those sponsors: Jane Cheney Spock, wife of the famous pediatrician and author Benjamin Spock; the legendary Rosa Parks from the Montgomery, Alabama, bus boycott; authors Jessica Mitford, Susan Sontag and Kay Boyle; Coretta Scott King representing the Southern Christian Leadership Conference; actress Ruby Dee, known best for the film, *A Raisin in the Sun*, and Julie Belafonte, spouse of Caribbean singer Harry Belafonte. The story also quoted Rankin: "This is no time to be polite. The army isn't polite when it selects a young man and says, 'come and fight.' They don't take the politicians and decision-makers to fight." The march was timed to coordinate with the opening day of Congress.

That winter day in the nation's capital, Swedish film actress Viveca Lindfors would read a petition explaining that women marching in the Jeannette Rankin Brigade represented millions of people opposed to the war and suffering from neglect of human needs in the United States.

Marchers had attended a briefing the evening before they took to the streets. They were told that the presence of such a large group of protesters would violate Section 193 (g) of title 40 of federal law, which read: "It is forbidden to parade, stand, or move in processions of assemblages in said United States Capitol Grounds...." The evening before the march, radical feminists began agitating for civil disobedience confrontations that in their estimation would leave a stronger impression than women fulfilling expectations by abiding by rules and laws governing marches on the Capitol. To many people, the rift that resulted would become more memorable than the march itself.

Rankin and other march leaders thought the federal law violated the First Amendment's pledge that said: "Congress shall make no law ... abridging ... the right of the people peaceably to assemble, and to petition the government for a redress of grievances." They had gone to court six days before the march to seek an injunction against the law but failed, forcing them to assemble at Union Station rather than on Capitol grounds. Police appeared in large numbers.

The procession stepped softly into the snow to begin the half-mile march up Louisiana Avenue. As many as ten thousand women dressed in mourning black, carrying placards and banners imploring Congress to end the war in Vietnam, tromped silently. Their sometimes vocal, sometimes silent, procession extended for several city blocks. Hundreds of police officers stared from the sidewalks.

Despite disagreements from the start, the Jeannette Rankin Brigade transcended race, age and wealth. White-skinned women linked arms with black-skinned, red-skinned with yellow, some eyes brimming with anticipation, others showing tears. White-haired grandmothers shared the street with chic suburban housewives and teenage hippies. Youngsters strapped papoose-style to their mothers eyed the cavalcade with bewilderment. Celebrities mingled in the crowd. Mothers of men already killed in Vietnam walked stonily. Two marchers were World War II "Red Cross girls" who told the *Washington Post* they had witnessed war and wanted no more of it. Another marcher was Mabel Vernon, who had "worked for peace since 1917." Activists of national repute, like Rankin, closed ranks as they pressed forward. At times the march resembled a political convention as delegations raised their state banners. Many of the women wore lapel buttons. Some were tiny plastic doves. Other labels read, "Bring the Boys Home" and "End the War." Many women wore campaign buttons supporting Eugene McCarthy, the antiwar candidate for president. To Jeannette Rankin, the scene would look hauntingly familiar, similar in so many ways to the great suffrage demonstrations in the years preceding World War I.

At the forefront of this river of women, undaunted, was Rankin, the wily veteran of protest. She fixed her bespectacled eyes calmly on the Capitol dome and pushed ahead, invigorated with her excitement over taking to the streets. Her winter coat concealed barely a hundred pounds of body, shriveled from time. A brown wig covered what was left of the crisp white hair that marked the lonely dissenter during the World War II Congress. She didn't look the same but she was a symbol, an inspiration, for all the younger women surrounding her. Rankin looked to her left and to her right. The women closed around her, all of them matching her pace as they approached the Capitol dome. Rankin's black-gloved hands, gnarled as they were, gripped the banner as if she was embracing a lifetime of pacifism.

Historically, Rankin had walked a long way. Many of her parade companions hadn't been born even by the time of the second vote; few were alive at the time of the first. Other women looked at Rankin with astonishment, as she did at them. How could she explain to them her experiences of fully half a century? Lonely vigils to distribute suffrage literature on street corners? Arguments on Capitol Hill over war profiteering? Allegations of communism from the American Legion, boos and hisses from the House of Representatives gallery at a vote cast against war, her thrill at hearing Hindu villagers talk of their love for the peace-seeking Gandhi? To Jeannette Rankin all of these experiences meant a lifetime commitment to peace. A street march through wet snow by women dressed in black represented a new wave of activism. To Rankin, those women embodied the promise of a world free from war.

As the Jeannette Rankin Brigade swept toward the Capitol, a young police officer scooted into the front line. He gripped Rankin's arm, presuming to escort her, but she shook free. "Do you think this frail old woman isn't capable of good behavior on the Capitol grounds?" she asked him.

"She can walk. You don't need to help her!" someone shouted.

The officer, uncertain now, flashed a smile. "Don't deprive me of that pleasure," he said.

Offended, Rankin lashed out: "You don't need to worry about us. We are unarmed and not at all threatening."

Lyndon Johnson, knowing the war had become his worst political nightmare, feared war protests. Bad news from Vietnam kept the big Texan awake at night. The women knew that the large police force would jail them if they tried to break the law. Detention centers had been prepared to imprison five hundred of the demonstrators; a cordon of police was ready for mass arrest. Standing at the foot of the Capitol, shivering in the raw wind, Rankin again asked why so many people were needed to threaten people exercising their democratic rights: "There is no reason why old ladies should be denied the right to go into the Capitol and have policemen on every corner to see that we don't hurt you."[10]

Rankin and other march organizers had hoped to lead the full procession to the Capitol steps to present their petitions to House Speaker John McCormack. The 1882 law that prohibited mass demonstrations on Capitol grounds disrupted their plan, even if it seemed a clear contradiction to the First Amendment right to peaceful assembly. At the Capitol, Rankin and sixteen demonstrators, including Coretta Scott King, broke away from the main body. Reporters and photographers, watching their ascent to the Capitol, huddled deeper in their overcoats. As the remainder of the brigade moved to Union Square near the Ulysses Grant memorial, where Judy Collins sang *This Land is Your Land*, Rankin and her delegation found McCormack and presented him with a petition that read:

"We, the United States women, who are outraged by the ruthless slaughter in Vietnam, and the persistent neglect of human needs at home, have come to Washington to petition the Congress for the redress of intolerable grievances, to demand that:

"Congress, as its first order of business, resolve to end the war in Vietnam and immediately arrange for the withdrawal of American troops.

"Congress use its power to heal a sick society at home.

"Congress use its power to make reparation for the ravaged land we leave behind in Vietnam.

"Congress listen to what the American people are saying and refuse the insatiable demands of the military-industrial complex."

McCormack wasn't sympathetic but he promised to refer the petition to the appropriate House committee. He did, and it became known as Petition 219. Representative William Fitts Ryan, a Democrat from New York and an early opponent of the war, introduced the petition in the House three days later.

After Rankin talked with McCormack she turned her attention to Senate Majority Leader Mike Mansfield. He was a powerhouse in Congress, known for plain talk as much as his extraordinary leadership. Mansfield began his congressional career in 1943 when Rankin retired after one term and he was elected to her House seat from the western district of Montana. Like Rankin, he opposed the war in Vietnam. History would show that he privately told a succession of presidents that fighting in Vietnam was wrong and futile.

As the women outside sang *We Shall Overcome*, the gracious Mansfield tried to woo Rankin with a silver tea set. Thinking his hospitality was a gimmick to distract from the urgency of the peace protest, Rankin talked quickly, not giving him a chance to offer her a cup.

"We must bring the boys home from Vietnam," she told the lanky granite-faced senator.

"How are we going to do this?" he reportedly asked her.

"The same way we got them there. By planes and ships," she replied. When she left Mansfield's office, news reporters rushed her. What did the first woman elected to Congress more than fifty years earlier have to say about the most powerful man in Congress in 1968?

"He was very pleasant," Rankin told them. "You know how politicians are."

2 ~ Born in Montana Territory

'A rebel, more or less, always'

Eighty years before the old Jeannette Rankin marched to stop the Vietnam War, she was a young girl in Montana Territory, seemingly taking command of everyone around her, including her sisters.

The young Rankin girls tell of the day they cowered in their upstairs bedroom closet after they saw the doctor, black bag in hand, walking toward the porch of their house. Frontier medicine often meant a surprise visit to the front door. Mary, Grace and Edna didn't know what was coming but they suspected trouble. The doctor waited in the parlor, instruments in hand, to extract their tonsils and adenoids. The girls listened for Jeannette's footsteps on the stairs from their hiding place in the two-story house.

Afraid to argue with their unrelenting older sister, they submitted. The misery that followed was even worse than the day Jeannette marched the girls downtown for small pox vaccinations. To hear the Rankin girls tell it, Jeannette behaved as if she were their mother. "She was the decision maker, always," Edna would recall years later of Jeannette Pickering Rankin.

From the start, Jeannette Rankin was anything but a pampered child. Hard work was demanded of her as a means of helping to sustain her family's financial wealth. The seven children of John and Olive Rankin shared chores on their ranch and in their lavish city house in rustic western Montana, far from troubling class conflicts emerging in the East. Jeannette, a practical girl, wouldn't ever resemble the well-heeled society women seen in magazines cavorting with bicycles, cigarettes and Lillian Russell-style audacity. She was made from different cloth. As a girl from the West she knew nothing of Second Industrial Revolution excesses that ushered legions of poor immigrant women into factory sweatshops and even put young children to work on dangerous machines.

During Rankin's first ten years of life, major new inventions would arrive on the marketplace: George Eastman's Kodak cameras, Thomas Edison's incandescent light bulb, and big thundering machines known as Linotypes that launched printed newspapers into an era of faster mass production. During those years the Brooklyn Bridge opened, the Statue of Liberty was unveiled, and thirty-six years of construction ended at the Washington Monument. Booker T. Washington founded Tuskegee Institute in Alabama for young black teachers. Civil War nurse Clara Barton, the "Angel of the Battlefield," organized the American Red Cross. With the good came the bad. An assassin felled a second American president, James Garfield, just months after his election. That first decade of Rankin's life would close with more bad news for American Indians already reeling from westward expansion and broken treaties. Bowing to land developers, the United States government paid tribes in Oklahoma a comparative pittance, then opened the first public land rush. By nightfall in a single day, white settlers swarmed over Indian land like fire ants, seizing nearly two million acres.

Jeannette Rankin's young life started far from the centers of American power, as the beginnings of famous people often do, but it wasn't without early signs that she would mature into a complicated woman with political ambitions.

Born June 11, 1880, to an ambitious father from Canada and a withdrawn mother from New Hampshire, the girl who would rise to national fame was different. Like anyone who emerged a leader for a cause she someday would be applauded and vilified, embraced and shunned, magnificent and disappointing. She would pass into history as the Twentieth Century's most enduring symbol for women and peace, yet the footnotes would hardly remember her. In most of her ninety-three years she would voice consistent criticism of powerful men without fear. They, in turn, would ridicule her ideas for women's rights and international peace as foolishness from a mere woman. Jeannette Rankin would become a heroic figure to many people and to others, a tragic one. She would stand as a lonely voice of reason to some. To others, she represented a strong voice of treason. One thing was clear from the beginning: she was an uncommon leader.

Montana Territory in Rankin's childhood was a wide reach of thick timber and empty prairie. The last free Indians camped in the sleeves of mountain ranges. A year after her birth, it was reported that Missoula had 226 children, of which 174 were between the ages of four and twenty-one. New buildings of commerce, including gambling houses and hotels, appeared in the midst of liveries and blacksmith shops. The Northern Pacific trains arrived in Missoula in 1883, the same year voters approved a charter for the new town. A new City Hall would follow. Then came a telephone exchange and a library. Horse-drawn streetcars began operating. The growing town incorporated as a city. By 1895 the state's first university opened in Missoula with fifty students.

Montana Territory became the nation's forty-first state in 1889. As the great Eastern cities struggled with corruption, crime and poverty, most of Montana's pioneer communities were founding city governments. National news was slow to reach the newborn camps and towns. Young Jeannette Rankin, as many other Montanans, would know little about the class struggle nationwide.

In Jeannette's first years, John and Olive Rankin and their growing family lived at their ranch six miles northwest of Missoula until John finished building a house at 134 Madison Street in the young city. It was topped with a glass-enclosed Burmese-style cupola with a widow's walk and had rare amenities in a frontier outpost: hot and cold running water, a wood-burning, forced-air stove and a zinc bathtub. When Jeannette began school she brought gawking new friends home with her but she didn't regard the house as novel. Later in life, she spoke of the neighborhood with some awe because she discovered that explorer Meriwether Lewis had camped at nearby Rattlesnake Creek on his return from the Pacific Ocean. When Indians moved their camps and passed the Rankin house in sad processions, Jeannette and her siblings stood at the windows to watch them. Horses dragged travois poles loaded with possessions. "I can remember we were trying to frighten ourselves saying they would come and get us," Rankin would recall years later. "We knew they wouldn't, but we pretended they would. It was just a game. I'm sure we all knew it was a game, that the Indians would never attack us. We'd see the Indians passing day after day. They were friendly but we were so dumb."[11] The Rankin house was one of the busiest and most remembered in Missoula until the Rankin children left home. Decades later it was torn down to clear a path for a paved highway.[12]

Summers at the ranch appealed more to Jeannette than life in town. The Rankin children loved loading their belongings into a surrey and riding west into the country. The ranch was in a steep canyon, and from the porch, the family had a panoramic view of the majestic Bitterroot Mountains, crowned with snow. Jeannette's imagination flourished in this wide open country. It was a place of bounty. The ranch had cattle and hay, and the family grew apples and sometimes sold butter and milk.

As the oldest of seven children, Jeannette knew well an adult's world of sacrifices. Following her in the birth order were Philena, Harriet, Wellington, Mary, Edna and Grace. A few days before Thanksgiving in 1891, Philena died of an apparent ruptured appendix at age nine. Her death devastated Olive Rankin. For a while, Jeannette became the surrogate mother and housekeeper. Having assumed motherly care of her siblings at such a tender age, Jeannette was acquainted with child care in an era before washing machines and other modern conveniences.

On the Grant Creek Ranch, her childhood years were remembered for her love affair with the interests of men. She had inherited, in many respects, the tough and colorful personality of her father, a hot-tempered, influential man. To Jeannette, John Rankin was distinguished and clever. He amassed a small fortune from the profits of his land holdings, his ranch and his water-powered sawmill on Grant Creek.

Jeannette's father was a fighter who worked hard for what he wanted. Born in 1841 in Appin, Ontario, the fourth son of Scottish immigrants Hugh and Jeannette Rankin, he learned early in life that he could relieve the financial burden of his parents by putting himself to work. He dropped out of school after only three grades to learn carpentry.

Joining up with brother Duncan, John Rankin set out in 1869 for Fort Benton, Montana Territory, driven by rumors about gold strikes in the Rocky Mountains. They traveled along the fabled Missouri Breaks, navigating a river that roamed the flood plains of a vast prairie. The brothers found themselves stranded when their boat ran aground on a sandbar forty miles from Fort Benton, the town from where adventurers launched their overland travels. As John Rankin would tell his children, he heaved his tool chest onto his back and walked to the pioneer town.

Hearing that fire had destroyed much of Helena, the Rankins bought a team of oxen and headed south, hoping to profit from the rebuilding. When they arrived, most of the work had been done. Helena again was a busy hub of activity. The Rankin brothers, known as the "Canada Boys," wasted no time. They moved four miles up Last Chance Gulch to the village of Unionville where gold had been discovered. They built a stamp mill to crush ore but John Rankin tired quickly of his investment, driven to discover whether life had anything more appealing to his sense of adventure. He traveled westward across the Continental Divide to Missoula, where at twenty-nine he established himself as an architect, logger, carpenter and artisan. In only a few years he figured prominently in city politics and, through his business investments, began to make money.

Many years in the future, after Jeannette left Missoula and joined the nation's movement to reform dastardly working conditions, she would confess conflicted emotions over the family's wealth. She wanted to erase miseries afflicting the poor and oppressed. Her father's reward for his hard labor was material wealth that prevented a life of economic misery. A student of geometry, he emerged in reputation in his community when he built the Methodist Church in 1872. He also constructed the first bridge across the Clark Fork River, which had divided Missoula. He was a founder of the Western Montana Fair and served three years as a county commissioner, elected as a Republican. John Rankin became a rich man by Western standards even before the woman who was to become his wife made her way west. He also was a man of influence; landowners traveled to Missoula to seek his advice on cattle deals. He was elected to the local government two years after Crazy Horse and Gall and their warriors annihilated George Armstrong Custer and five companies of his Seventh Cavalry at the Little Bighorn.

Olive Pickering, born in 1853 in New Hampshire, became a teacher. "I was young and good looking and dressed well, and the school board probably knew that I needed a job, so they always gave me one," she explained to a friend. When an uncle named William Berry visited with tales of life in Montana Territory, where he had been a sheriff in Missoula, Olive begged her parents for permission to travel westward. In 1878, Olive and her eldest sister Mandana rode by transcontinental rail to Corrine, Utah, and then by stagecoach north to Missoula, where the twenty-year-old Olive began teaching in a one-room schoolhouse. Mandana, being less of an adventurer and complaining that Montana Territory "was not a fit place to raise children," returned to New Hampshire.

Olive Pickering, one of Missoula's first schoolteachers, welcomed the adventure. She was anxious for new developments in her life. She even became accustomed to the Indians who sat on the board fence surrounding the schoolhouse. Olive was intelligent and had a good sense of humor, but she was no socialite. She preferred visiting with people in her home and liked cooking and sewing more than politics. She later would be described as a self-isolated, shy woman who possessed strong opinions but rarely expressed them.[13] Jeannette would remember that her mother didn't have a leader's spirit but she had a will to make leaders. A friend described Olive as "kind, firm, and in a mild way domineering."

John Rankin and Olive Pickering married in August 1879. Jeannette was born the following June. Impressions each parent made on Jeannette were evident from the time she was a young girl. She learned about life in the East from her mother, who tried to steer Jeannette away from the influences of Civil War veterans who ranched and farmed near Missoula. Wide-eyed, Jeannette listened as old Confederates gathered with her father in the ranch parlor, spitting out tales of the war and life in the Deep South along with streams of tobacco. They were rough and frank in their talk. Jeannette loved it, much to her mother's displeasure.

From the start Jeannette was taught to do what all young Montana girls did in those days. She cooked and baked and learned from her mother how to make clothes and welcome friends who came calling. A seamstress came to the house every spring and fall to make the children's clothes but Jeannette, by her teenage years, began designing her sisters' dresses. Yet Olive Rankin later would describe her daughter as a daydreaming, unresponsive "problem child" who preferred political thought over education, religion and social life. Jeannette was restless and resentful of woman's work when it interfered with her political discussions or adoring attention from her father.

John Rankin treated Jeannette like a son, forcing Olive to turn her favors to Wellington, whom she dotingly called "The Boy" his entire life. Wellington's nickname, to Jeannette, implied their mother's blanket approval of everything he did or said. Jeannette and her brother would compete for family leadership throughout their lives. Edna, the youngest child, witnessed loud arguments over politics at the dinner table involving Jeannette, Wellington, and their father. Jeannette, even as a child, held strong opinions on politics, social issues and economics. She sometimes condemned bankers because, in her mind, they didn't create anything but instead betted against people. She made enemies as a child because of her convictions. By comparison, Jeannette rarely discussed politics or philosophy with her mother in those early years. Besides Philena's death, Olive had endured several miscarriages and sublimated her grief in cooking.[14]

The peculiar conflict between sister and brother invited profound influences on Jeannette's life. Wellington's sisters, when he was a child, loved and appreciated him — an adoration that sometimes stretched to the limits of tolerance — but in those early years Jeannette was the leader of the family and assumed in many ways the care of her brother and sisters. Edna was afraid of Jeannette and regarded her as a mother figure. Edna would dwell in Jeannette's shadow all of her life, always feeling that Jeannette was more intellectual and much brighter. Edna wasn't alone in her fear of Jeannette; two other sisters, Grace and Mary, lived under Jeannette's rule for much of their childhood and became accustomed to obeying their older sister's commands. The day would come when a national magazine writer would describe Jeannette's role in her family as "assistant mother," an oddly fitting title.

Relatives often would recall that her mechanical knowledge astounded them. She quickly found the heart of a problem and solved it. Stories abound of Jeannette's take-charge determination. Whether fact or family lore, these stories built a firm foundation for what was to follow in her life. When Jeannette was still a small child, her father brought machinery from nearby Missoula to lift hay into the barn. He harnessed a team of horses but the pulley mechanism jammed. The ranch hands scratched their heads in frustration, the story goes, but Jeannette explained to her father how to unravel the mess. He turned on his hired men in anger. "You haven't enough sense to do it yourself, you have to let a little girl tell you what to do," he told them.

Another time John Rankin tried to rent a house he owned, but a prospective tenant wanted a boardwalk built in front of it. Rankin, being a hard-nosed business owner, refused to honor the ultimatum. Jeannette bought a load of lumber and built it herself to consummate the deal.

Other oft-repeated testimonials of Jeannette's decision making involved animals. A gelding on the Rankin ranch trotted into the corral, whining in pain. Flesh on his shoulder was torn and hanging from a bad gash. While the cowboys wrestled the horse to the ground, ten-year-old Jeannette raced to the house for hot water and a needle and thread. She then stitched the wound. Her family would recall that in another instance she amputated a ranch dog's foot, mangled in a steel trap. Then she crafted a leather boot for the dog, Shep, to wear over the stump.

Although bright and quick-witted, Jeannette hated school. The ritual of reading, writing and arithmetic bored her. Friends would remember that while many of her classmates regarded her firm demeanor with awe, her grades were simply average. Idle talk irritated her, she considered athletics brutal (although she played basketball), friends could be gossipy, and she hated memorization and recital in school. Jeannette's membership with a social club named the Buds ended when she complained that the activities didn't challenge her enough.

Even as a child, Jeannette's compassion for other people became apparent to her family. She complained that the men working on the Rankin ranch should earn better pay. She talked about the importance of people having opportunities for happy lives. "I remember her, as a little girl, reading Bible stories," Wellington would recall years later. "I can see her reading them and the tears streaming down her cheeks. Probably, the persecution of Joseph or the brothers selling him. I can remember that very well." Another dimension to young Jeannette involved her fierce protection of her siblings whenever she thought neighborhood kids might hurt them. Her early conviction in shielding others from harm would grow into a much more substantial activism in adulthood. "She wouldn't take anything. She was going to be out there fighting, but she was a rebel, more or less, always," Wellington reflected.[15]

Jeannette loved to organize parties and picnics and camping trips. She had a secret picnic place in the woods on the ranch where her sisters were allowed to visit only on special occasions. On her eighteenth birthday her father built a dance floor on the front yard at the ranch and strung Chinese lanterns to light the evening celebration. John Rankin loved to tap dance. He could jump and tap his feet together twice before touching the floor. Wellington had another sort of merriment in mind. He and his friends greased a pig and let it run among the dancers. Then they unharnessed horses from guests' surreys, most rented from livery stables in Missoula, and strapped them to new surreys. Jeannette was furious that Wellington had insulted her guests, but their sisters cheerfully defended The Boy's youthful antics. During another party she took boys to her father's sawmill to show them how to cut a log.

As Jeannette passed her teen years her enthusiasm for group social gatherings faded. She sensed a greater urgency in her life, and although she was a typical turn-of-the-century American woman in her appearance, her father's influence had made a lasting impression. She had no patience for charming the male ego. She neither obliged the social formalities of dating nor paid homage to the popular female role in society: marry, raise children, keep the home and leave the important affairs to the man of the house. Hers was a different destiny.

Legend has it that her father's attitude toward militarism molded her pacifist views early in life, although Jeannette and several of her acquaintances disputed that as a myth years later. John Rankin had participated in an attempted Army assault on Chief Joseph and his peaceful Nez Perce tribe as the Indians slipped past a cavalry unit through the rugged

Bitterroot Mountains. Fort Missoula soldiers and civilian recruits, including Rankin, confronted Joseph in a timbered valley and ordered him to surrender. Joseph returned to his chiefs, presumably for consultation, and in the black of night his people crept past the sleeping military encampment. The silent defeat was a major embarrassment to the army. John Rankin and other civilians went home. The military encampment became known as Fort Fizzle.

Shamed, Rankin told Jeannette the soldiers failed to outmaneuver the peaceful Joseph and couldn't understand his quest for freedom. Rankin complained to his family that the military was a joke and that the soldiers "were too stupid for words." Just how that memory influenced Jeannette remains in dispute. In later life, she condemned a military attack during what became known as the Nez Perce war in 1877. Soldiers killed ninety members of the tribe in a dawn surprise attack along the Big Hole River in southwest Montana. "As the Indians came out of their tents, the American soldiers shot them, shot the medicine man and anyone who came out. It was a disgraceful act, the most outrageous thing that could happen. What Calley did at My Lai was nothing compared to what they did, the American army."[16] She was referring to the US Army assault on unarmed civilians in South Vietnam in 1968, led by Second Lieutenant William Calley. As many as 504 villagers were herded into an irrigation ditch and shot with automatic weapons. Many were raped and mutilated. The slaughter, revealed in 1969, prompted international outrage.

John Rankin had a practical reason for disliking military action because he was blinded in one eye and deafened when a cannon wad flew backward during firing, striking his head.[17] His experiences made a lifelong impression on Jeannette, who would remark as an old woman, "I grew up knowing that the military was a crooked thing."[18]

Much of the family lore from Jeannette's early life flatters her, but she also was prone to depression and, as a young woman, came to discover she had no direction in life. She yearned for a greater challenge than being a married woman, which in those days meant a life of baking, cleaning and washing clothes. For twenty years, Jeannette had been her father's confidante, associate and protégé. She had learned the artistry of manhood as it was known in those days: leadership, dissent and independence. She knew men might consider her an attractive prospect for marriage and motherhood, despite her assertive personality, and even deeper than her desire for independence was her loyalty to family. It was a deep and troubling conflict, one that throughout her long life would both define her achievements and invite ridicule from her critics.

As Rankin matured and finished preparatory school, she was unsure what should come next. The feeling was uncomfortable because the ranch and the big house on Madison Street had been safe and comfortable places to live. She drifted into the first-ever class at the new state college in Missoula without recognizing she was a few short years away from plunging into a lifetime of public activism.

She struggled to complete her formal education because her family expected it of her. She admitted she loathed college life. She wrote her senior thesis on the subject of small snails because she liked her biology teacher. Her professors remembered her as being a diligent but undistinguished student. Sometimes Jeannette challenged her instructors' wisdom. She would reflect years later that she was assigned to read aloud Alfred Tennyson's "The Charge of the Light Brigade," to which she responded, "This is hideous. I can't read it."

She wrote in her diary after she graduated in 1902 with a bachelor of science degree in biology: "Go! Go! Go! It makes no difference where just so you go! go! go! Remember at the first opportunity go!" Her words echoed those of reformer Theodore Roosevelt, who suggested: "Get action, do things, be sane, don't fritter away your time; create, act, take a place wherever you are and be somebody; get action."[19]

This was the beginning of something. Rankin longed to become a fighter like her father, possessed with his sense of civic accountability. John Rankin hadn't demanded academic excellence from his children, often hustling them off to the ranch before the spring term had ended, but he was determined not to restrict them from the free exchange of ideas.

As the gaiety of childhood matured to the serious business of adulthood, Jeannette took stock of her discomfort toward the traditional role of women. It wasn't the place for her, but she didn't know where she belonged. Her sister Edna, eleven years younger, grew up with the impression that Jeannette was restless and unhappy, resentful that she was thrust into caring for her brother and sisters. Jeannette's fitful mood became more apparent to her family in 1904 when John Rankin caught Rocky Mountain Spotted Fever and died within a few days at age sixty-three. He left an estate of $150,000, equivalent to more than $3.6 million in 2016.

She was nearly twenty-five years old. Teacher jobs in a rural school near the Rankin ranch at Grant Creek and at Whitehall, Montana, a small town east of Butte, ended abruptly. Jeannette was not inclined to make the best of an atmosphere she had found tedious and uninspiring as a student. Her parting with Whitehall led to some rumors that she left behind a romantic scandal, never confirmed or explained and possibly more fiction than fact. Another explanation was that she failed the state certification exam, conceivably out of disinterest for her chosen profession, but that too was speculation. She returned to the comfort of her family west of the Continental Divide, where she helped her mother cook for the cowhands and filled her free time with reading and dreaming.

While Jeannette Rankin foundered in Montana — her life sparingly innocent of commitment — steel and oil ruled the new industrial order back east. The United States had become the world's largest steel producer. Andrew Carnegie became the most powerful steel boss of all time. John D. Rockefeller did for oil what Carnegie did for steel, founding the Standard Oil Company. Investors enjoyed a ballooning prosperity. By 1892 more than 4,000 millionaires controlled America's financial future while Ellis Island welcomed a river of European immigrants, all of them hoping for prosperity, into the United States. In the 1880s alone, more than five million immigrants arrived, twice the number of any other decade. Irish, Germans, Italians, Hungarians, Poles and Russians swarmed into New York, Boston, Chicago and other eastern cities, seeking opportunity. Many fell into poverty. In ensuing years, the cities became ripe for exploitation and corruption.

A new economic order implied the strong survived by swallowing the weak. Capitalists believed politicians who tried to govern economics would upset the balance of money. In a reversal of political thought, democracy was identified with capitalism, liberty with property, progress with economic gains and the accumulation of capital. Because the nation's goals were identified with wealth, many new injustices were condoned to give the rich and influential what they wanted. Rankin someday would protest that the nation's preoccupation with wealth ensured wars could be fought for the economic profit of a few powerful people.

The nation's Progressive Era, taking root in the tenements of New York and Chicago and in muckraking books and political ideals, would open doors for Jeannette Rankin. By tens of thousands, women went to work in factories but their work often was far from humanitarian. Bosses skimped on pay, ignored dangerous working conditions, and demanded excessive hours of labor. While problems faced by the labor wing of the women's rights movement worsened, other women boldly cried for reform. Eventually Rankin's pathway to understanding would lead her far from Montana. She would find a home in the reform movement. Reform would lead her to suffrage, and suffrage would lead her to Congress.

    The suffrage movement had begun before the Civil War when three hundred women met in 1848 in Seneca Falls, New York, at the first women's rights convention. Momentum toward suffrage would falter during the long and bloody Civil War. In 1866, Lucretia Mott brought suffragists and antislavery activists together in a national convention in what would emerge as the first clear expression of equal rights for all Americans. The harmony withered the next year because of disagreements over support for the Fifteenth Amendment to the US Constitution, which would give black men the right to vote. The amendment was ratified in 1870, although women who tested what appeared as gender-neutral language were turned away at the polls. Wyoming Territory gave women the vote, followed by Utah Territory, but suffrage would be long in coming for most American women.

    Other activist organizations of women appeared. In 1874, women took to the streets of Cincinnati and Pittsburgh to protest the liquor evil, giving birth to the Women's Christian Temperance Union. In 1889, when Rankin was nine years old, Jane Addams and Ellen Gates Starr opened their Hull House social settlement in a neighborhood of Chicago known for rampant crime, illiteracy and malnutrition. It was wholly unforeseeable, in Rankin's early years in Montana, that she would travel with Jane Addams to Switzerland only thirty years later as friends and sister pacifists. Jeannette's youth was invested in the Rocky Mountains, where deer and elk fed in quiet meadows and creeks flowed cold and clear. The nation already had become a complicated and combative place for women. Her contributions remained years away.

The Twentieth Century suffrage movement lost traction in a stormy political climate despite years of arduous work at every level of society. Industrial growth promised prosperity but under terrible working conditions. Corporations merged into larger conglomerates that left common Americans empty-handed. In Montana, there was no better example than Standard Oil, which exploited lucrative copper mines in Butte by smothering opposition. In Butte and everywhere else, the time was ripe for change. Reform became more than just an ideal. Women rose to the task.

Jeannette Rankin — isolated, obscure, perplexed and impatient — traveled to Boston late in 1904 when news came that Wellington had fallen dangerously ill. A law student at Harvard University, he had left school after their father's death, returning to Missoula for several months to resolve John Rankin's business affairs. Wellington had been back in Boston only a short time when his roommate, Ellis Sedman, found him sitting dazed and unresponsive at his desk. As a child, Wellington had suffered a serious brain injury when he was struck in the head with a chunk of cordwood thrown from a wagon. Whether that incident contributed to his sudden illness wasn't clear, but the family suspected he had suffered a nervous breakdown because of his father's death.[20]

Jeannette packed a suitcase and departed on her first Eastern trip with a friend, Jimmie Rittenour, from Missoula. They stayed in Boston for six months. Socially, the visit was a wonderful experience. After Wellington recovered, the young women dated some Harvard men and even considered enrolling at the Massachusetts Institute of Technology. With complimentary tickets from Montana Senator Joseph Dixon, they rode the train to Washington to attend the inaugural ball of President Theodore Roosevelt.

The gaiety of upper-crust living held less interest for Jeannette than the filth and poverty of Boston's tenement slums. Here was squalor of the worst sort, so unlike the resplendent peace and beauty in the Rocky Mountains. She had been taught that hard work earned material success. In Boston many people lived in misery. Were they lazy, incompetent, apathetic? Rankin returned to Montana with impressions of two worlds. In one, she had tasted the sumptuous lifestyle of the rich. In the other, she had seen the decaying neighborhoods that weren't supposed to exist in a country founded on freedom and independence. Rankin already had concluded from the demise of the American Indian that aggression determined the distribution of human rights. Wealth and material possessions had cut a line of class struggle through American society. Boston dramatically showed this human conflict and Rankin knew it, even if she didn't take the immediate action she promised herself when she graduated from college.

Rankin spent the next two years toying with halfhearted pursuits. She tried working as an apprentice seamstress and then experimented with a correspondence course in furniture design. She read more than ever, absorbing opinions and ideas about economics, politics and philosophy. She seldom sat down without a book or magazine to explore causes, ideas, news, politics and current affairs. Her feelings of futility about what to do with the world fueled much of this intensity.

She chose to take action, as she had vowed in her diary several years earlier. Planning to visit an uncle, she boarded a train for San Francisco in the winter of 1908, unsuspecting of a new direction in life awaiting her.

3 ~ Awakening to national reform

'Nothing horrid about studying social problems'

Jeannette Rankin slept in a crowded passenger coach as the train chugged through moonlit, snowy mountains. Sporadically the engineer tugged the whistle rope, startling her awake. Her sudden bouts of inflammatory rheumatism, worse when she sat too long, sometimes caused unbearable pain in her arms and legs. Despite the welcome warmth of the coach, she dozed fitfully. The journey had failed to brighten her dusky mood. She felt a sinking confidence that she would make anything of herself. When she stepped off the train in San Francisco she hoped a few weeks near the sea would ease her pain and clear her mind.

Just what Rankin intended to accomplish in San Francisco remains lost in time. What is known is that her discovery of the Telegraph Hill settlement house, apparently by accident while she was out walking, set her on a course she would follow her entire life. Rankin climbed the steps of this strange new social invention, curious about the world within its walls, and found her future. Women and children, many of them immigrant Italian and poor, were learning how to survive and conform in their new country. Elizabeth Ashe, a nurse who managed the settlement with her close friend Alice Griffith, told Rankin she was witnessing a neighborhood inflicted with hardships.

Seeing the predicament of women and children, many of them destitute, touched the hardy Montana ranch girl's heart. Struggling to overcome their triple handicap of being immigrant, female and poor, the mothers invested countless hours of English and government lessons at the settlement. Telegraph Hill, packed with families from Italy, Ireland, Germany and Latin America, was in many ways a replica of Chicago neighborhoods where Jane Addams had founded Hull House a year earlier. Settlement houses opened in response to overcrowded apartments, serious health and sanitation shortcomings, and rampant joblessness. Eventually four hundred of them would open nationwide.

As precursors to modern-day community centers, they provided education, gathering spaces and medical and dental care. Ashe and Griffith had founded the settlement house in 1890 while teaching Sunday school at nearby Grace Cathedral. Ashe was the sole heir of an unmarried aunt, Camilla Loyall, who had inherited a substantial fortune from her sister, Virginia Farragut, widow of David Farragut, the US Navy's first admiral. Ashe, Griffith and eight other women started Willing Circle, which soon became City Front Association and then Telegraph Hill Neighborhood Association. Typical of social activism of the day, when socialite-type women would wade into impoverished neighborhoods in pursuit of reform, Ashe and Griffith opened a house on Vallejo Street that included a teaching kitchen, garden, a sewing school and visiting nurses.

The settlement house became a relief agency after the 1906 earthquake and devastating fires that followed. The next year, Ashe and Griffith moved the settlement house to Stockton Street, one of the poorest and worst-crowded portions of San Francisco. This was the house where Jeannette Rankin appeared in 1908. Streets teemed with residents from several countries. Many of them worked in the sprawling produce district to the South and canneries to the North. Italians had overcome their initial distrust of Ashe and Griffith and delivered fruit and vegetables to the house every day.

Although Rankin's time at Telegraph Hill would be brief, and she would say little of it later, the experience became a doorway to causes and reforms that would dominate her life. Rankin, curious, came to the door to find out what was inside. Ashe, known to workers as Betty, asked Rankin to volunteer a few days to help with childcare. Rankin agreed and stayed four months.

In a matter of weeks, Rankin became a serious student of the reform movement, forgetting the futility she had experienced in Montana. Here were people who shared her fledgling ideas about political justice, who readily accepted her empathy for their cause. She attended hearings on factory working conditions, wage legislation and child labor laws. Ashe and Griffith were driven women, versed in settlement house philosophy that federal and state governments had failed to enact laws to protect workers and families. Connections between the settlement house model and Rankin's developing beliefs about reform were stark.

She began to read the flood of reform commentary in magazines such as *McClure's*, *Colliers*, and *Harper's Weekly*, and from the pens of journalistic "muckrakers" such as Jack London, Ira Tarbell, Frank Norris, John Spargo and Jacob Riis. The woman who had been toiling at Hull House in Chicago for nearly two decades, Jane Addams, influenced Rankin with her belief that women should become active in social problems as a means of reform. Everything she saw and heard and read echoed her experiences in Boston a few years earlier.

Rankin left Telegraph Hill addicted to reform. As a child, when she considered training to become a nurse, she had lived in the nationwide shadow of humanitarian causes. Those causes had not surfaced, however, in free and independent Montana. Except for growing labor troubles in the clamoring industrial cities of Butte, Anaconda and Great Falls, most Montanans hadn't seen the class struggle found in older, more populated states.

Rankin hurried to seek practical training. Spending money her father had set aside for her education, she enrolled in the New York School of Philanthropy in the autumn of 1908. The school was considered the first social work school of its kind, devoted to teaching the field of charity. The school was only four years old and had fewer than one hundred students. Her brother, Wellington, was completing his final year of law school. Encouraged by Ellis Sedman, he had begun attending receptions of the Christian Science Society of Harvard. Jeannette became acquainted with Ellis. Wellington once thought their acquaintance would lead to a romantic relationship but Jeannette showed little interest. Eventually their sister Hattie would marry Sedman's brother, who would die during the Spanish flu pandemic in 1918.

Often adversaries, but nevertheless Rankins, Jeannette and Wellington never strayed far from their close emotional arena. Even in their early years they relied on each other for advice. In New York, Jeannette was a short train ride away from her brother in Boston. While he labored with torts, she began her education in the college of retorts. Jeannette and Wellington rarely agreed on matters of great importance but always consulted with each other nevertheless. This pattern of trust, however intense the conflicts between them, would sustain throughout their lifetimes.

Jeannette found the school structured on a belief that direct action to improve conditions hurtful to women and children was preferable to the older approach of attempting to change people to fit miserable conditions. This hallmark philosophy of the Progressive movement, known as "environmentalism," would evolve into a demand for more government protection of vulnerable citizens and control over dangerous and exploitative practices, such as child labor. When Rankin entered the school, charity was the only line of defense. What she learned in that single year would leave deep impressions on her and shape her thinking in politics throughout her life. The neighborhood was a laboratory for much of the curriculum. Only blocks away were the slums of New York City's Lower East Side where immigrants packed into tenement houses in microcosms of their native countries. It was here in the crowded cavernous streets of Little Germany, populated with denizens from Italy and Poland and other European countries, that Rankin's belief in government as a tool of reform took root. Tenements were crowded and often filthy. Immigrants who had come to America on promises of opportunity prowled the streets in search of work. Many turned to crime and underground economies. They shared no common language but somehow managed to buy and sell food from street carts. This was the real world, a place of passion and pathos far from the quiet mountains of Montana. Here in these streets bustled a mess and a mass of humanity. In the school, she found brilliant teachers bent on steering their students toward social change.

One of them was Louis D. Brandeis, one of America's leading lawyers and economic intellectuals, a scholar destined for the US Supreme Court. The faculty included Florence Kelley, founder of the National Consumers League that represented women in industry, and Booker T. Washington, the black leader and educator. Edward T. Devine, the editor of *Survey* magazine, was guest lecturer that academic year.

The concept of environmentalism, in Devine's definition, meant "the normal man, who is now crushed, will under favorable circumstances, rise unaided."[21] This is what he called a "new view of charity." Rankin was taught that Progressivism meant powers of the Constitution would be fully exercised to protect Americans from harm in ways charity couldn't. Carl Kelsey, a medical doctor, expressed the popular viewpoint in a lecture he gave while Rankin was at the school: "Heredity determines what each individual child may become; environment determines what he does become. The difference between children at birth is far less than we have been accustomed to think."[22]

While the average middle-class American woman was discouraged from reading anything more suggestive than the *Sears and Roebuck* catalogue, Rankin's teachers primed her with lectures about the history of human misery and the economics of civilization. The school rejected Herbert Spencer's view of social Darwinism, contending that his notion of survival of the fittest was a philosophy promoted by the rich to preserve wealth. In this spirit Rankin contemplated Simon N. Patten's *New Basis of Civilization*, which argued that misery and poverty could be eliminated by a more efficient society in which the consumption of goods and services was increased dramatically to distribute wealth. Patten concluded that economics manipulated American society in its ideas and sociopolitical beliefs, a view that would take root in her criticism of war profiteering three decades later. In a letter to her sister Mary, who was skeptical about such apparently socialistic ideologies, Rankin wrote: "There is nothing horrid about studying social problems. One dear man in a lecture spoke of Saint Simon N. Patten, and this is the way all of the school feel(s) toward him. The reason political economy has been so useless is that so many writers have taken the theories of old writers such as Adam Smith, Mill and Malthus and tried to fit them to present conditions or to fit conditions to false theories."[23]

The curriculum was blunt and intense, making the school an undesirable place for a faint-hearted optimist. Among Rankin's lectures was "Misery and its Causes," and despite being a Montanan who had enjoyed a rather resplendent upbringing, she satisfied the course requirements. Rankin studied labor disputes, criminal sociology, social reform, racial progress and the theory and practice of charity organization. Although she confided to her sister Mary that she expected to fail because she was competing with "such well trained college girls," she had earned two As and eight Bs by the end of the academic year.

Mornings were devoted to lectures, afternoons to "a sort of scientific slumming"[24] that was field work where students learned to apply their skills. Rankin spent two months studying general charity, two months studying the needs of deaf children, and two months working with the criminally accused in the night police courts under the supervision of Maude Miner, the chief probation officer of New York City's Magistrate Court. The work was dangerous for an unescorted woman. Rankin concealed a sap in a velvet party bag with drawstrings. Her lasting impression of human misery, however, didn't come from her professors' bleak economic outlooks or the morbidity of inner city crime, but from tragic living conditions she witnessed while studying deaf children in the Jewish-Italian district in New York City.

"I took the dearest ... sweetest little boy to an orphan society," she wrote her mother. "He was about three years old and the mother had two younger. The father is missing. If I had been near home I'm sure I would have wanted to keep him. He was so full of joy and life. The mother didn't mind losing him. She just waved her hand and said, 'By-by.'"

In her months of fieldwork, Rankin saw the strata of society from desperately poor to very rich. Impoverished women were working twelve-hour days at sewing machines in sweatshops and production lines in factories. Families lived in cramped tenements with ailing, hungry children and no fire protection. To the other extreme, a million middle-class and affluent women made popular the Woman's Club, which purportedly lobbied for juvenile law and child labor reform.

Only a daring minority ventured into public life in the first decade of the new century. The average American woman was expected to raise children, oblige her husband, and indulge in no behavior likely to embarrass her family. Popular magazines of the period depicted women as being engrossed with romance and family life. Completing an education that would equal today's master's degree, Rankin waited impatiently to intervene in the agony of a nation crying for reform. Hundreds of women dedicated their lives to the thankless missionary chores of the Salvation Army. Rankin, having no impressionable religious instruction, sought a different role. Thousands of women rallied to shut the saloons by outlawing liquor; Rankin, being a social drinker but having no hate for men who drank, showed no interest in joining their ranks. Millions of American women labored for the rewards of home and family; Rankin, being of independent spirit, felt the desire to crusade.

After she graduated as a qualified social worker in the summer of 1909, she yearned to put her knowledge to use, saddened by what she had seen and experienced but more determined to fight the causes that had bred it. With the words of her professors spurring her to action, she returned to Montana thrilled with the lure of reform. Initial attempts at shaping public policy fell short. Rankin confronted the sheriff in Missoula with a campaign to segregate women from men in the county jail. She found little support for another plan to establish a public bath house for loggers, tramps and other people who had no place to get clean.

Frustrated with her first defeat, she took a job with the Children's Home Society of Spokane, Washington, as a home finder, or more familiarly, a "baby placer." Finding decent homes for orphans was nearly impossible. One prominent publication of the day referred to such children as "hapless waifs" and wrote that Rankin's work with destitute women and starving children led her to the suffrage cause.[25] To her, children were traded like cattle. She placed an orphan with a family who soon decided they didn't want him. They returned the boy to the orphanage where he wept in Rankin's office. Finding the work intolerable, she transferred to an orphanage in Seattle, which did little to relieve her frustration with rules that governed adoptions. Much of her dislike of institutional work, she admitted, was in being a detached observer of unloved children.

Finally, she gave up after just a few weeks on the job. That little act of defeat led to the dawning of something bigger that would sweep her into national politics. Reform would not be accomplished from within institutions, but by influencing laws that governed them.

4 ~ Suffrage, one vote at a time

'One lone woman, who has not been able to ensnare a man'

The year was 1910. Progressivism was shining a light on the nation's problems, sweeping Jeannette Rankin along in its passion. The movement was hungry for willing, determined young workers who would sow the seeds of enlightenment and awaken Americans to the dark side of industry. As the first hint of a human rights movement in the new century, Progressivism was led by a coalition of intellectuals, farmers, laborers, suffragists and political activists, all of whom thought the federal government had abandoned the working class in favor of big money.

The Progressives, with roots in the earlier Populist movement, stood for a participatory democracy that included measures such as the initiative, referendum and recall. Rankin enrolled at the University of Washington in Seattle, intending to prepare for the arduous work of pushing social legislation. That the American woman who ventured into politics was seen as a freak or a fanatic by more conventional observers was of no consequence to her. Rankin's father had neglected to teach her that petticoats should not be mixed with politics. In her mind the time had arrived for women to explore the business of lawmaking. The national stage awaited Jeannette Rankin. At first she played a minor part among multitudes, but her day was coming.

One evening she found an advertisement in the university newspaper asking for volunteers to hang posters promoting woman suffrage. Her curiosity could not let the advertisement go unanswered. Soon she had collected a bundle of posters to distribute in the neighborhood. In bold letters, they exclaimed: "Roosevelt when Governor of New York in a message to the New York legislature urged woman suffrage." The significance of this message did not escape Rankin, who by that time had become aware that voting women could influence miserable social conditions she witnessed on both coasts.

She tacked the posters on every store façade and empty wall or board fence she could find. She scored a major victory for female assertiveness when she managed to place one in the window of the neighborhood barbershop. The American barbershop was a sacred male domain where a man retreated to the comfort of a leather reclining chair to read the *Police Gazette* amid frothy shaving mugs and the aroma of cigars and bay rum. While most women wondered what their husbands did when they went to the barbershop, they were afraid to ask and refused to stray near such a place. Rankin walked inside with a poster and told the startled proprietor she was going to hang it in his window.

Her work impressed a Washington suffrage leader who asked Rankin to join the state's campaign. Spring quarter at the university was nearly finished. Rankin went home for the summer, but she returned in the fall of 1910 and went to work in the small logging town of Ballard under the tutoring of Emma Smith DeVoe of the Washington Equal Suffrage Association. Rankin asked the town newspaper and a few ministers for names of women who might talk with her. She found one at home who was "perfectly lovely" and they talked into the afternoon. When Rankin went there a second time, the woman wouldn't open her door. Her husband had come home and, hearing what had been discussed, forbid his wife from further conversations with the new troublemaker in town. Rankin then arranged a meeting in a tiny room in City Hall to hear a speaker from Seattle. Seven women attended. Rankin was sent traveling across Washington seeking suffragists to organize into small groups. She thought she was being punished. Instead, she learned later, she was being groomed for bigger challenges.

Washington became the fifth state to enfranchise women after men voted, by a substantial margin, to give them that right. Rankin's role in the campaign was minor but for the first time she had witnessed an effort to sway statewide opinion. She had become a disciple of the belief that everything that was wrong with the United States was related to big money and inefficient government. Backing suffrage in Washington taught her that women could influence government. She had found a pathway to reform that was more productive than working among the specific social problems found in state institutions. The campaign organization she witnessed could be put to use in other states. Furthermore, suffrage meant genuine leadership because its success depended on the extent of hard work and initiative being committed to it. Rankin had disliked working in the orphanages, being impatient with policies and procedures. She also found it heartbreaking. To her, women were the force in social reform, using the vote to improve conditions for women and children everywhere.

Years later, Rankin would recall how "nothing in the world was as funny, at that time, as the women who wanted to vote." She told of walking past children one day who were waving a flag and carrying placards. "They were playing 'woman suffrage' because that was a funny thing to do," Rankin said.[26]

Rankin wasn't another Carry Nation, neither assimilating alcohol and religion with the suffrage issue nor battering the morals of her opponents with a proverbial axe. Her growing conviction was that women had to live with laws they had no voice in making and only they could change that. She was certain women embraced a special regard for the welfare of children that men didn't. It became her firm lifelong belief, grounded in a circle of female friends she met in New York's Greenwich Village. Rankin hadn't experienced childbirth but to her that made no difference in her ideas about the welfare of children. She knew plenty from her years as a surrogate mother to her younger sisters. In 1910, Rankin was no more of a visionary enthusiast than other Progressives who protested economic slavery and were unaware that world war would shove their movement aside. She was only a student of social change and unsuspecting of her forthcoming rise to fame.

With the celebration of the Washington suffrage victory foremost in her mind, Rankin rode a train home to Montana for Christmas. She prowled Missoula department stores for gifts and strung popcorn on the tree. It was a gay holiday, full of family charm, until she read in a newspaper that a lawmaker wanted to introduce a suffrage bill at the Montana Legislature in Helena. She recruited several men in Missoula to help her champion the legislation. They formed under the name "Equal Franchise Society" to avoid the all-too-familiar scorn evident in some states toward woman suffrage. Professor Joseph Underwood of the university was elected chairman. Washington Jay McCormick became vice chairman and Rankin, the group's secretary. At her request, the group dispatched her to Helena to lobby for the suffrage effort at the Capitol. She soon discovered a legislator had introduced the bill as a joke, but suffragists laughed right along, encouraging the good humor because they knew it would keep tongues wagging about their cause.[27]

Rankin met with many of Helena's most prominent women, all strong supporters of suffrage, to plot a strategy. She also persuaded the legislator who joked about the bill to champion it. Unexpectedly, Rankin went home to Missoula with a toothache. Before members heard of her absence they decided to send the bill straight to the House floor for a hearing. This was a rare procedure in a busy Legislature, but some men on the committee thought it would be amusing for a woman to argue for suffrage. Rankin hesitated at the prospect of addressing an all-male Legislature but soon announced she would accept the task. She hurried back to Helena. Her brother, by then an established attorney on legendary Last Chance Gulch, helped her write a speech. She practiced reading it to Wellington, a gifted orator, who made amendments and told her to try again.

Wellington had started his law career in the prestigious Helena firm of Cornelius Nolan and Thomas J. Walsh. Both men were strong figures in Montana politics and law. Nolan, an Irish immigrant, was a legislator. Walsh was an aggressive attorney with political aspirations and he, too, had Irish roots. Wellington was a strapping young man with a full head of groomed brown hair and a jutting jaw that suggested an uncompromising determination. He was a good match for his older colleagues.

Being stubborn, determined and a bit naïve, Jeannette promised hopeful suffrage supporters that she would silence the joking and sarcasm. While Montana men felt little animosity toward their women, previous attempts to give them the vote had failed. Rankin rode to the Capitol from her Helena hotel, flinching at every jolt in the road because of her uneasiness at what she was about to do. What could she say to keep the legislators from laughing, even with Wellington's careful coaching?

It was February 1911. The Capitol bustled with people

excited at hearing a woman speak from the legislative podium. Wearied by a long winter of writing stories about snowfalls and political slapstick, reporters came to life at this curious twist to the news. A churning sea of faces flooded the rustic chambers of the House of Representatives. Already, an hour before she would appear, men jostled for places to stand. The hubbub echoed in the hallways that cradled the huge room. The day outside was briskly winter but the galleries were crowded and hot. Bright gowns and feathered hats worn by women seated among the legislators splashed color over a House chamber accustomed to black suits.

Bouquets of flowers embellished the room, contrasting with the snow outside. Many legislators had contributed fifty cents each for violets ordered from San Francisco, a gesture some of them intended as a patronizing ploy. Others had considered the flowers a tribute to the woman they were about to hear. "The room was filled with blossoms," Rankin would recall, probably speaking as much of prospective votes as of flowers.

Men shuffled impatiently. Smoking was banned. Spittoons had been removed. Swearing was forbidden. Senators refused to attend as a formal body but adjourned business and most of them came anyway. Many of Helena's most prominent women sat in a row at the front of the chamber. The atmosphere felt like a circus. Suffragists were worried. This was a giant step for women in Montana. If Rankin's speech fell flat, suffrage would stall until the passing of time forced a more accepting attitude among the men who governed Montana.

At 2:30 that afternoon, Rankin walked into the House chamber. Five of Montana's leading suffragists escorted her. She waited nervously through two flattering introductions before approaching the rostrum. A surge of whispering feathered the room. Men expected to see a mannish old woman. Instead they saw a slender figure with frank, dark hazel eyes and sumptuous brown hair. Rankin, wearing a green velvet dress, appeared younger than her thirty years.

Although she had become accustomed to addressing unsympathetic audiences in the Washington campaign, she detected no hostility as she stared back at the people who were the blood of Mother Montana. They were her people. She saw all extremes of life: ruddy faces of loggers and miners, pale faces of men accustomed to office work, faces of affluence and despair, of trust and suspicion, of power and benevolence. Montana remained much of a frontier in the years before World War I. In some ways, Montana in 1911 was a microcosm of New York City, populated with immigrants who had landed at Ellis Island and traveled west. Many were Irish, others Scandinavian, some German, Welsh, British and Scottish, and the Legislature represented them all. These were her people. She looked back at them from the rostrum, knowing that they waited for nobody other than her. Rankin had memorized her speech but she faltered for a moment, unsure of what to say.

"Will they believe me?" she would relate later. "Do they know who I am?" The hushed audience watched her intently. Rankin swallowed hard. In the loudest voice she could muster, she began by merely stating that she was a native-born Montanan. The room exploded in applause. Could the speech be this easy, she asked herself? Further justifications for her presence followed. She was a taxpayer. She was inclined to complain about laws that fell short in protecting Americans:

"It is not for myself that I making this appeal, but for the million women who are suffering for better conditions, women who should be working amid more sanitary conditions, under better moral conditions, at equal wages with men for equal work performed. For those women and their children, I ask that you support this measure."

Rankin explained that Montana women had no desire to step down from the high pedestal on which Montana's men had placed them. They would prove themselves worthy of a role in lawmaking and government to end a national embarrassment, evidenced by national statistics, showing 300,000 women had been victims of white slave trafficking. She reminded her audience that women were asking for the same freedom for which men fought in the Revolutionary War. Every American knew taxation without representation was tyranny. She demanded to know why a mother should be expected to nurse her children through typhoid fever without the benefit of a vote to discourage conditions that gave her child the disease.

Notable in the speech was Rankin's deep suspicion of government without female representation. Having seen the pathetic lifestyles of New York City's poor, the decadence of the Boston slums, the language problems of San Francisco's Italian immigrants, clashes between men and women in Washington State, and having read the literature of muckraking journalists, Rankin concluded what many Montanans didn't: aside from tradition and ignorance, a concerted effort existed to prevent women and children, blacks, immigrants, the impoverished, the ignorant and the illiterate from participating in democracy.

Even in those pre-World War I years, Jeannette and Wellington knew that Montana government was capable of ignoring human rights issues — and subsequently preventing social reform legislation — because it was manipulated and coerced by the powerful Amalgamated Copper Company, which within a year would be renamed the Anaconda Copper Company. The Rankins were deeply suspicious of the company, which owned mines, smelters, timber companies and even newspapers under its heavy copper thumb. Editors were silent about labor reform and the women's rights movement. The *Anaconda Standard*, staffed generously with top journalists to rival the country's best metropolitan newspapers, boasted correspondents in Paris, London and New York City. Yet Marcus Daly, an original Copper King, ordered his newsmen to print nary a word about worker unrest in Anaconda and nearby Butte.

To Rankin, suffrage wasn't an issue that lawmakers should decide. Instead, it should be put before the people they represented. As she concluded her twenty-minute speech, she asked the representatives to submit the suffrage question to Montana voters at the next election. When Rankin left the podium, several House members followed with speeches of their own. One of them fretted that voting would encourage women to abandon duties in their homes. One suffrage supporter asked why the issue should be subjected to wit and humor. Some opponents countered with oaths of prejudice, ignorance and sensationalism. Rankin was labeled "one lone woman, who, unluckily, has not been able to ensnare a man."

At the end of the frivolity the respected Cornelius Nolan, a former Montana attorney general, stood to talk about what his mother had done for his family in Ireland. He talked about hardships and sorrows of pioneer women in Montana. When he encouraged support for suffrage, attitudes changed in the House. Most members voted in favor of the bill, and although it lacked the necessary two-thirds plurality for passage, the prospect of women someday voting in Montana emerged into statewide public debate in a single afternoon.

Rankin's speech at the Montana Capitol had ensnared something more valuable than a single man. She had gained an army of women. Montana women lost a skirmish but they acquired a leader. The copper press, usually quiet about such matters, unpredictably vaulted Rankin into the forefront of Montana's suffrage arena with fawning remarks about her earnestness and sincerity. Women across Montana wrote Rankin to complain that she hadn't asked them to join her at the Legislature. She saw that they represented a potential statewide organization and saved their names for later use.

While Montana women and other American suffragists fought their battles, a disaster in New York City pointed to the need for renewed vigor in the reform movement. On March 24, 1911, the lives of 146 Italian and Russian immigrants were snuffed in a fire at the Triangle Shirtwaist Company in downtown Manhattan. The factory had operated for years in blatant violation of city fire codes. Women leaped to their deaths from eight, nine and ten stories above the street after finding fire exits jammed shut or obstructed with piles of rags. Victims trampled in the panic or clawing at stuck doors were incinerated. Others fell to their death onto concrete. Some impaled on iron fences when they jumped.

New York had possibly the most sophisticated suffrage machinery in the nation when the disaster occurred, but the industry lobby was strong, supported by the pool hall antics of the city bosses. Suffragists wondered whether the disaster could have been avoided if New York women had gained the vote earlier. Reform was considered a logical extension of the ballot. Most of the workers in New York City's "sweatshops" were women.

The summer after the fire, Jeannette Rankin found herself working in the very borough where the disaster occurred. Harriet Laidlaw, leader of the Manhattan Borough of the New York Woman's Suffrage Party, was searching for a worker who could meet the challenges the district presented. Minnie J. Reynolds, another suffrage leader who had worked in the Colorado and Washington campaigns and would become one of Rankin's close friends, suggested that Rankin's "singularly sweet personality" found no suffrage work too commonplace, difficult or disagreeable. She was the woman for the job.

Rankin found New York suffrage politics quite different from the rural barnstorming in the West. Carrie Chapman Catt of the National American Woman Suffrage Association, learning how effective the assembly and election districts had been for Tammany Hall, developed an organization that reached to the precinct levels of the nation's largest city. Soon Rankin walked the crowded streets a few miles from Ellis Island where immigrants seeking opportunity filed through the nation's doors into a strange new land. She canvassed the chaotic tenement districts where the new horizons for many of the immigrants darkened, but where Rankin, offering hope for reform through suffrage, hustled support. Most of her work was done on the street where she often spoke from atop a wooden box. Because she had no one to introduce her, she hailed a passerby to listen, and then another, until a curious audience gathered. Although a difficult way to build a movement, this approach brought her face to face with people, taught her the rewards of building a street movement, and eased her fear of speaking to strangers.

Rankin's commitment to the cause found favor with her superiors. Laidlaw paid her three hundred dollars for six months' work, but the reward for Laidlaw and her colleagues was much greater: they had discovered the value of having Jeannette Rankin work for suffrage. At thirty-one years old, Rankin was on the cusp of emerging onto the national suffrage stage. Much of the lore surrounding her life had its roots in those early suffrage years when she circumvented clunky organizational procedures preferred by many suffrage leaders and took the message to the streets. Showing much of the cavalier independence that her brother and sisters knew from their childhood years, Rankin charged ahead. She was fearless in knocking on doors that might be slammed in her face. She survived bullies hired by the liquor lobby and street toughs who lashed her with obscenities and ridicule. The chore of preaching suffrage embarrassed some women trained as girls to submit to men. Rankin laughed at that. She had no time for such foolishness, as her brother Wellington could attest.

This cautious belief of subservience, embraced by timid women who found suffrage outrageous, was taught by Edward Clarke, a Harvard medical school professor. In his essay "Sex in Education," he documented his theory of "female weaknesses," that girls were born with smaller brains, and that their education "often leaves insufficient margin for growth." In Victorian reasoning typical of the times, he advised that girls whose brains were taxed too strenuously in the classroom would lose energy to develop their reproductive organs, and some would go mad. "When the school makes the same steady demand for force from girls who are approaching puberty, ignoring Nature's periodical demands, that it does from boys, who are not called upon for an equal effort, there must be failure somewhere. Generally, either the reproductive system or the nervous system suffers," he wrote.[28]

Many women opposed suffrage on grounds that it interfered with the serious business of the nation. Notable among the opponents was a bombastic New Yorker, Mrs. Arthur M. Dodge, who made sure her husband's name appeared on her public comments. She was president of the National Association Opposed to Woman Suffrage. In a letter to the *New York Times* she wrote in part: "The woman in politics and the woman trying to get into politics have contributed nothing to politics but increased election costs, more expensive and spectacular stunts, more bitter partisanship, and bigger bluffs than the men have made. The dignity, power and status of women in public life have not been elevated. Politics has not been purified." The *Times* opinion pages offered a far-reaching pulpit for Dodge and others who shared her beliefs.

Rankin's home state of Montana harbored anti-suffrage forces but they weren't organized or even in agreement for their cause. Many women who wanted to outlaw liquor saw how a right to vote could help their cause. Never once, Rankin said, did suffragists in Montana argue that they wanted to vote because they were better than men or wanted to "purify" politics. Instead, they wanted women to use their minds, make up their minds and express opinions.[29]

To think men would grant voting rights to women without enormous political pressure was silly, Rankin came to believe, making light of suggestions that women should wait their turn. Moreover, she deviated from the positions of stalwart suffragists such as Anna Howard Shaw and Susan B. Anthony, who openly and deliberately drove a wedge of disunity into the women's movement by chastising the immigrant community. They were angry that foreign-born men had constitutional priority over native daughters such as themselves. In their condemning speeches they alienated voters who had strong nationalistic ties.

Rankin understood their bitterness toward the immigrant vote but she found it appalling that they were willing to disenfranchise a third major political bloc (the liquor lobby and conservative anti-suffragists were the other two) by complaining publicly of the influence of immigrants instead of working for compromise. Old-guard suffragists like Elizabeth Cady Stanton and Lucretia Mott smoldered in their anger that large numbers of black men and immigrant men were illiterate but could vote, while educated and articulate native-born women were considered second-class citizens.

It was in 1911 in New York City when another encounter occurred that would shape Rankin's political and personal life. Fellow suffragist Cornelia Swinnerton invited her to a dinner club on a short street named Patchin Place. The mews in a Bohemian neighborhood in Greenwich Village was radically different from the life Rankin had known in Montana or seen on Telegraph Hill. Writers and artists clustered in brick row houses. Gas lamps illuminated the narrow street. Intellectuals gathered over wine and food in frenzied discussions about arts, politics, and news of the day. It was here, at Patchin Place, where Rankin fell into the Heterodoxy Club, the creation of a fierce suffragist named Marie Jenny Howe, a Unitarian minister.[30]

Dozens of women invited into the informal club were of Rankin's ilk, being of independent mind and social activism just like her, and most were considered radical feminists in the early definition of the term. Many were lesbian, openly talking of free love, but unconventional sexuality was only one of many topics examined over food. The women debated economics, psychology, education reform, labor tactics, disarmament, birth control, socialism, women's rights and pacifism. They did so with abandon. Heterodoxy was one of perhaps dozens of feminist debating groups of the era, but educated unorthodox women in its membership made it one of the more influential. They were social workers, lawyers, doctors, teachers, actors, playwrights, socialists, radicals, artists, and others. Like Rankin, many were active in the suffrage movement. Among them were political activist Crystal Eastman and labor investigator Elizabeth Watson, both of whom would emerge later in Rankin's political life.

Many of the women were destined to become Rankin's lifelong friends, although few as enduringly as Katharine Anthony and her lover, Elisabeth Irwin. Although Rankin's initial exposure to Heterodoxy was brief, friendships she made there would define her suffrage years and propel her into theories and ideas new to her. Her close personal relationships with Anthony, Irwin, Watson and a few other women in the club would supply persistent insinuations about her own sexual orientation, although without conclusive proof. Her closest friendships began in Heterodoxy, during spirited conversations about politics, law, pacifism and feminism. The Heterodoxy Club was the boldest adventure Rankin had undertaken. Many of her friends openly embraced lesbianism in an era when Americans never spoke the word. Most certainly it was different from her upbringing in western Montana.

Later in the summer of 1911 the California Equal Suffrage Association appealed to the national organization for a vigorous worker to join its central committee. In a demonstration of sharing that showed the sacrifices New York was willing to make for California, Laidlaw temporarily relieved Rankin from duties in the less hopeful Empire State campaign to help fight for a victory in the West. Progressives in California concentrated their work in rural areas, anticipating a smashing anti-suffrage vote by pro-liquor forces in the cities. Rankin scooted between mining districts without sleeping in the same bed twice. She was riding a stagecoach to Weaverville when it stopped for dinner in a camp named French Gulch where men drank in her dusty appearance from benches in front of saloons.

Sensing opportunity to win a few votes for suffrage, she went looking for men who would agree to announce that a woman would speak about suffrage from the steps of the hotel in a matter of minutes. Finding no volunteers for that duty, she persuaded a young boy who said he would "tip youse off to de bums." A few men arrived to hear Rankin's speech while a girls' band played for the event. While riding the stagecoach Rankin had met French Gulch's school superintendent, who told her the school had such a band. "I tried the men for years and they quit on me but the women have proved faithful," the bandmaster told her. During Rankin's speech, a woman yelled encouragement from across the street, which led to another speech to the camp's women in the hotel parlor the next day.[31] Rankin and other skilled suffragists dispatched to California campaigned furiously through September, doing all they could to organize women who would spread the word. Ballot corruption in San Francisco and other cities hampered the efforts of the suffragists, but their work in rural California proved enough to win. In October, suffrage won in California by a scant 3,500 votes out of 247,000 cast. Among the winning towns was French Gulch.

The picture was not as promising elsewhere. Rankin returned to New York after six weeks in California to help secure an amendment to the State Constitution in the 1912 Legislature. It was a daunting battle because opponents had killed previous bills before they reached floor debate. Rankin and dozens of other suffrage leaders stormed New York to build support for the amendment. Rankin was hired to lead the legislative lobby at the statehouse in Albany, where she came across young Franklin D. Roosevelt, a senator. She told him that women in some western states had the right to vote and were working for suffrage in states that didn't. Roosevelt said suffrage might work better in some states than others. Such a place where labor was more important that the vote, he said, was a New England cannery where women and children worked whenever fishing boats brought their catches off the Atlantic Ocean. Sometimes they were required to work at night after working all day, Roosevelt told Rankin, because otherwise "the fish might spoil." For years after that conversation, Rankin often cracked that perhaps New York didn't want suffrage because "the children might spoil, and they were just as important as fish."[32]

Suffrage didn't pass the New York Legislature in 1912, although suffragists and lawmakers alike gave Rankin credit for so changing public opinion that the amended bill passed both houses the following year. When the Albany program ended in March, Rankin returned briefly to Montana, intending to start a suffrage campaign in her home state. Laidlaw instead sent her to Ohio, where strong anti-suffrage forces and an inefficient, top-heavy state suffrage organization dulled the quest for a statewide vote. For eight weeks Rankin campaigned for suffrage, often standing alone at factory gates and street meetings, until she lost her voice. She complained she wasn't fairly paid and didn't know what was expected of her.

From the start, Rankin viewed several of her national suffrage sisters with suspicion. Modesty was not a virtue among suffrage workers, particularly because the woman who listened could not do much talking. Suffrage campaigning was the art of persuasion. Rankin's only reward for working long past exhaustion was the personal gratification of a winning vote and hasty thanks from her superiors before going to the next battle. She thrived on her mission despite tedious lecturing and traveling. Mostly working alone, she moved from city to city helping women organize, making speeches, building confidence and establishing money funds for future campaigns. Rankin suffered times of depression when things went poorly. She complained to her siblings and friends in letters that she was underpaid and her enthusiasm was being exploited. Despondent and overcome with exhaustion, she left for Montana in July 1912.[33]

While she worked elsewhere she had tried to keep the suffrage campaign alive in her home state. In Rankin's absence, Ida Averbach, the association secretary, wrote letters to promote the cause. It wasn't enough. Soon after her arrival in Montana, Rankin became the leader of a state central committee she hoped would lead a drive to win Montana women the right to vote. They had no constitution, bylaws or membership lists, relying on the sisterhood of their cause to bind them together. Rankin and her workers canvassed Montana, establishing suffrage clubs and appointing a representative in each of the fifty counties to pressure local politicians to respond to their constituencies.

Rankin taught tactics of persuasion to suffrage workers to get everyone talking about this new and important issue, the right to vote. They learned to force questions about equal voting rights on aspiring politicians, and when the candidates spoke positively, to applaud loudly and wildly. Suffrage became more popular. After the precincts had been organized, Rankin visited every delegate of the Republican, Democratic, Progressive and Socialist parties and asked for their support. Feeling the pressure from the precincts, they acquiesced.

When, in the fall of 1912, party conventions were held to nominate candidates for the next Legislature, suffragists asked Republicans, Democrats and Progressives to pass resolutions favoring removal of the word "male" from Section 8 of the Montana Constitution. Employing tactics used in national suffrage efforts, Rankin and other suffrage leaders persuaded Republicans and Democrats to drop the word, observing that some of the delegates viewed the resolutions as a joke. Once the parties had adopted their platforms, suffragists met with candidates to point out the change. Follow your party's wishes, each candidate was told, because the conventions have decided in favor of this important matter.

Candidates were asked to pledge that they would support suffrage bills. That winter, Rankin drove to Lewistown in central Montana on icy roads to ask newspaper publisher Tom Stout, a Democrat in the State Senate, to introduce a suffrage bill. She requested that Joseph Pope, a Progressive from Yellowstone County, do the same thing in the House.

Rankin and other suffrage leaders also started a letter-writing campaign to Governor Sam V. Stewart, urging him to recommend passage of the suffrage bill in his message to the Thirteenth Legislature in January 1913.[34]

Although Rankin's role in Montana suffrage had started with her speech to legislators in 1911, other Montana women had attempted to win the vote since before the 1890s. Suffrage campaigning had been a desultory effort, however, with only occasional attempts to convince lawmakers that women should have the right to vote. Political equality clubs lived and died as predictably as green leaves change color in autumn. Montanans weren't opposed to suffrage so much as they were unfamiliar with it. Women had been scarce in the large empty land until the turn of the century. State government was young. Debate over permitting women at the polls was fresh. What Montana needed was a leader who could stir up enough discontent to brand suffrage into the minds of every voting Montanan. Jeannette Rankin became that leader. The challenge was stiff, if an opinion by a Carrie Chapman Catt organizer meant anything. Helen M. Reynolds, who had sent a flood of pro-suffrage letters to Montana in 1896 with poor response, wondered sarcastically whether Montana women were an inferior race to take such little interest in their own freedom.

The Montana central committee gathered in the gallery on the day the Thirteenth Legislature heard opening remarks from Governor Stewart. With no joking or discussion, the lawmakers passed the suffrage resolution by a vote of one hundred to four. Rankin and other suffragists cheered at the final vote but work remained. Under a curious provision in the state constitution, which granted voters an election year to contemplate the resolution before it was placed on the ballot, they would have to wait nearly two years to relish a final victory. Stewart signed the bill on January 25, and suffragists proclaimed February 1 as Woman's Day in Montana. Their accomplishment was one for statewide celebration.

On the national front, meanwhile, the National American Woman Suffrage Association had appointed Alice Paul to lead its effort for passage of a federal amendment in Congress. She asked her close friend Rankin to help as a field secretary. Rankin traveled to North Dakota, where she spoke to eager crowds and helped engineer an overwhelming victory for suffrage in that state.

More than ever, Rankin found suffrage a fitting natural ally to the Progressive movement. Progressives were reformists who wanted antitrust laws to stop industrial consolidation, break the power of railroads and bust monopolies. To achieve these laws, they wanted more democracy by popular vote to gain more political influence from the middle class. Suffragists promised Progressives that a vote for women would double the movement's influence at the polls.[35] That was a specific belief Rankin would share all of her life. Her strong views of election reform and the role of women in democracy had roots in the elements of Progressivism. It was a powerful motivation for her as suffrage gathered steam. Soon it was clear that suffrage no longer was a joke or a whim. To many men, it was a threat. Trouble was in the wind. It came during a March 1913 rally in Washington, DC, while Rankin was busy organizing precincts in Michigan.

The march was scheduled for the day before Woodrow Wilson's inauguration to the presidency. Alice Paul thought a grandiose demonstration for suffrage would impress Wilson, the first Democratic president since Benjamin Harrison left office in 1893. The parade was heralded as the most elaborate protest ever made by American suffragists, although the committee had been allotted a pitiful yearly budget of ten dollars. Paul and her assistants figured women wouldn't win suffrage by federal amendment until suffrage first was won in a majority of states.

Five thousand marchers representing most states queued on Pennsylvania Avenue in sections of men, black women, immigrants and state delegates. The parade was rowdy and colorful to represent the heritage that spanned the nation's young history. Several women dressed like Indians. When the girl who was supposed to portray Sacajawea of Lewis and Clark expedition fame didn't show, Jeannette's sister Edna dressed in white buckskin to play the role.

The parade started in an orderly fashion at the Capitol and would proceed past the White House to Constitutional Hall. Minutes later, trouble began. Police seriously underestimated the number of officers needed for crowd control. (Later they were accused of doing it deliberately.) The marchers struggled through crowds from the start and took more than an hour to cover the first ten blocks. Half a million spectators poured from the sidewalks into the street, forcing marchers to squeeze through a gauntlet of disapproving men. Women were insulted, spat on, pelted with cigar stubs and even thrown to the street. The rowdiness of the march pointed to a new fervor sweeping the country. Suffrage had succeeded in engulfing all Americans in a growing cause. The plea for suffrage was heard, if not fully appreciated.

While Alice Paul kept Congress and President Wilson on notice with her relentless lobbying in the nation's capital, Rankin barnstormed across Michigan organizing local campaigns. After suffrage fell to defeat in that state, liquor interests came under suspicion of falsifying vote tabulations. Rankin's next stop would be Florida, her fourth state campaign since Christmas. The Equal Franchise League of Jacksonville applauded Rankin as "one of the best schooled and most enthusiastic suffragettes to be found in America," but opposition from conservative women's groups was strong. Rankin was portrayed as a "paid lobbyist" sent by Yankee women to threaten Southern modesty.[36]

The Florida campaign raised the explosive question of race. The political consequences of black women casting votes proved unthinkable to Southern white politicians. Attitudes toward race that had lingered since the Civil War and opposition from the omnipresent liquor industry defeated suffrage in the 1913 session of the Florida Legislature.

That June, Rankin returned to Montana to lead a meeting of the state committee in Livingston. As she had done in other states, Rankin helped women organize suffrage leaders in every county and workers in every precinct. She also gathered petitions for a mass demonstration in Washington, DC, on July 31, stopping thirty-three times in her drive from Montana. In a second Alice Paul initiative, pilgrimages of suffragists from every state would descend on the US Capitol to lobby for the federal amendment. Rankin left Montana by car after Independence Day. She made speeches in St. Paul, Chicago and Indianapolis, collecting more petitions as she traveled. On the day of the demonstration, suffragists drove to the Capitol from Hyattsville, Maryland, in a convoy of seventy-two cars. Rankin, wearing a broad hat tied with a green ribbon, held the Montana banner along the way. At the Capitol, two suffragists from each state called their senators and representatives to the Marble Room to present their petitions. Accompanying Rankin was Mary Land of Whitehall. After the women put every Member of Congress on notice, they adjourned to the Brighton Hotel for dinner.[37]

Rankin stayed two weeks in Washington, lobbying Congress by day with other members of Paul's congressional committee, and taking to the streets at night for open-air persuasions among people within hearing distance on the sidewalks. She returned to Montana in August 1913 to further organize districts and precincts, lending influence to the effort as both state leader and a national field secretary. After a short visit that included another state meeting, held in Butte, she went back to Washington to report on her activities as a field secretary to the National American Woman Suffrage Association. She helped lead a "Suffrage School" to train workers, but denied a request that she continue as field secretary. Instead, in 1914, she would take charge of the suffrage campaign in Montana and drive it toward a final vote. In doing so her political stock would rise beyond her wildest imagination.

5 ~ Barnstorming Montana for suffrage

'Ask your fathers why they won't let your mothers vote'

While Jeannette Rankin went stumping nationwide, Montanans remembered her arguments for suffrage. Nearly two years after she delivered her speech at the State Capitol, Governor Stewart persuaded legislators to support the suffrage amendment as part of the Democratic Party's reform package. With only two dissenting votes in each house, Montana's men were handed a referendum to decide whether their women should have the right to vote.

Rankin resurrected the card file of names she started three years earlier and began commanding the campaign. To win, suffragists needed to organize thousands of women across a sparsely populated state, five hundred fifty miles wide and three hundred twenty miles from south to north. Together they would work to persuade men to let them vote. Many people doubted the suffragists could blanket the far-reaching farms and rural towns and overcome opposition from the liquor industry, anti-suffragists and pro-Anaconda newspapers. Pessimists said no suffragist alive could accomplish such a feat in a short ten months. Banking that her earlier organizing work would pay off, Rankin set out to elevate the standing of Montana women from serf to citizen. Her campaign strategy was hardly revolutionary but mimicked efforts elsewhere. Stakes were high. Rankin didn't want to fail in her home state. Suffragists cast her as Montana's "girl next door," a political debutante with a homegrown charisma. It was implied Rankin was a firebrand, her torch burning bright from the nation's suffrage wars. Pro-vote women swept that heat and passion across Montana like a mid-summer prairie wind. "Why not Montana?" Rankin asked in a circular urging men to give women the ballot. Montana bordered two suffrage states, Wyoming and Idaho. Women in nine Western states and Alaska could vote, and nationwide, four million women could vote for president. "Women in our organization are from all walks of life, every political party and every religion and faith," her circular said. "We unite on one point: We all want to vote."

Rankin's disciples described her as electrifying. Critics painted her as a woman who needed a man's strong hand, or even a man's strong backhand. Much of the reaction, good and bad, grew from the public's preoccupation with this barnstorming woman who had built a national reputation for relentless campaigning. Using curious tactics that she extended even to children, Rankin perpetuated unrest about the standing of women. "Ask your fathers," she told children, "why they won't let your mothers vote."

Friends were convinced she could charm even the most stubborn suffrage opponents. In the words of Mary O'Neill, press secretary of the Montana Equal Suffrage Association, Rankin was a whirlwind worker, a young woman with the temperament of those who suffer and conquer, who inspired trust with her sincerity and unselfish work. Rankin did not wheedle or cajole as a fawning hussy as some anti-suffragists claimed, O'Neill would say. Instead, Rankin campaigned as an intelligent frontier woman who just wanted to vote in a nation boasting rhetorically of freedom and justice.

Wrote one reporter: "Let her get started, and she is as

ardent as Sylvia Pankhurst (a militant British suffragist). You would put her down as a determined 'men-you-just-have-to-do-it' and 'we-won't-take-no-for-an-answer' suffragist." Rankin, however, rejected the militant image. "We do not need militancy over here," she avowed. "We are getting the vote without resorting to violence."

Imbued with the reform spirit, Rankin saw herself as a champion of common people. Any fear of public speaking had evaporated somewhere along the endless roads traveled and among her hundreds of speeches, organized and impromptu, delivered to strangers. She lectured outside pool halls and saloons, chatted amiably at teas and drove to the most distant homesteads if she suspected she would gain even one vote. As she campaigned across Montana — preferring personal contact with average folk more than the forums of press and city lecture hall — her broad smile and slender frame became a familiar sight. She had little faith in petitions, thinking anyone would sign them for any reason. Yet suffrage leaders wanted petitions. She related years later: "I'd go into a saloon or anyplace and I'd say to the men, 'Did you vote for Delaney?' They'd say yes. I'd say, 'Well, I have a petition here for Delaney to do such and such. Would you sign it?' I came home with pages of signatures. The men who signed didn't know anything about what was in the petition. They knew Delaney; if they saw Delaney they'd say, 'I signed a petition for you the other day.' Delaney knew that if they signed that petition, they didn't know what it meant."[38]

Before the campaign ended, Rankin traveled 9,000 miles across Montana's broad empty reaches, making twenty-five speeches in twenty-five days. She even interrupted romping picnickers to ask for their votes. She never rode a horse to campaign, as some fanciful scribes had imagined, but her touring of the vast state was no less adventurous. Her automobile bogged to the axles in the mud of unpaved roads.

She rode in drafty trains that climbed steep mountains filled with spring snow. If she wanted to read at night, she sat on stiff furniture in hotel parlors lit by flickering smelly oil lamps. She often was isolated from family and friends and relied on benevolent farmers and ranchers to provide her supper.

Whenever possible, Rankin pushed the campaign to the precincts, recruiting inexperienced suffragists who would carry the message. They wanted to follow her and sprung to help. In a few years Rankin had risen from the doldrums of social work to a relentless passion so characteristic of people working for a cause. From mine gates and automobiles and flag-draped fair booths, Rankin and her army of workers informed women of the dangers of living under laws they had no power to influence. She appeared at courthouses and opera houses, dance halls and union halls, and spoke from stages in moving picture theaters. She aimed her speeches at women, addressing child illnesses and other perils of caring for a family without the protection of political representation. This angered some homemakers who complained suffrage would unseat them from the pedestals on which Montana's men had placed them. Wrote Mary O'Neill, in encouraging Rankin to hold nothing back when speaking to a convention of the state federation of woman's clubs in Livingston:

"You will know what I mean, but do give them all the dope you can about the influence of the women in behalf of the CHILDREN and appeal to the higher standard of MOTHERHOOD and truer home life as you did at Livingston, but even more so. That's the gush that gets to a public and the public is what we must reach and convince. That speech of yours at Livingston will do more to make suffragists than all the purely intellectual guff we might give them in a whole hundred years."[39]

Rankin told women they would not lose their place in the

family by mixing in politics, but she was careful not to offend men by suggesting women wanted power over their husbands. She argued the right to vote would allow women to help the home, not harm it. "It isn't right that we should be denied an expression of opinion in our own laws," she told anyone who would listen.

In echoing Progressive thought, Rankin envisioned a menu of social reforms that suffrage would bring. Among them were better working conditions for women. Women could lobby for government food and safety inspectors. Child and maternal welfare programs would offset high mortality rates. Typical of the reformist beliefs of the times, she held the Industrial Revolution accountable for enabling women to take factory jobs and other industrial work without the benefit of government social programs to help with their families. She asked why no protection was given to children who worked long hours under dangerous conditions.

By 1914, Rankin had become convinced that voting women could persuade Congress to enact health, welfare and workplace laws to mandate shorter working days, outlaw child labor laws and require inspections of dairy products. She suggested women could force the Montana Legislature to clear up the state orphan asylum to make it a model of womanly influence and a laboratory for the study of social problems. The asylum, Rankin told women, was a microcosm of all the social ills found in industrial society. The syphilitic child represented prostitution. The fatherless child introduced the problems of occupational disease and disaster, enforced idleness and desertion. Children raised by incompetent mothers meant neglect, industrial indoctrination and abandonment. Unmarried mothers and feeble-minded children resulted from failures in social rehabilitation.

Such a comprehensive examination of social problems was not widely supported or even commonly discussed in

Montana, despite the mining city of Butte being rife with vice of every sort and suffering from astounding safety and pollution problems. Rankin envisioned extensive political influence as a natural development of woman suffrage. Although her observations might have been premature, her solutions proved practical and were blueprints for social change decades later.

Less enthusiastic than Rankin were millions of American women who preferred to wait until changes became culturally acceptable before they partook of the freedom the changes presumably offered them. While thousands of woman worked for suffrage, better working conditions and prohibition of intoxicating drinks, many more resisted social reform to preserve their traditional niche in society. Nationwide, it was clear that change was afoot. The eventual emancipation of the so-called "weaker sex" was evident even in Shredded Wheat Company advertisements proclaiming that consumers who bought its products exemplified the liberated woman.

Rankin confided in letters to friends that Montana was ripe for woman suffrage. Repeated attempts at taking a suffrage referendum to the ballot, the influence of the Progressive and Socialist parties, a relatively minimal interference of the industrial and liquor lobbies, and the swing from agrarian society to urban industrialization helped push suffrage to the forefront of Montana politics. Naysayers aside, women were an independent breed in a new state and accustomed to sharing in the work of the West.

Being the state's leading female activist had its spoils. Rankin received plenty of proposals for marriage — her talent for baking pies supposedly was as renowned as her talent for getting votes — but she preferred the love of the cause over the love of adoring young men. Whether she was admired or hated, her supporters made sure her name was familiar to tens of thousands of Montanans. It didn't escape the notice of political leaders that Rankin had become a voice for women but a warrior among men. She had enemies, for sure, but she often earned praise for making sense when she spoke. Observed Tom Stout, elected to the US House of Representatives in 1913, the first year Montana had two seats: "Jeannette Rankin is one of the most successful campaigners that I ever knew ... by the charm of her manner and the force of her arguments."

Rankin's savvy on the campaign trail was her strongest quality. Some Montanans regarded her as disruptive and vain for daring to seek the vote. Others saw her as a folk heroine, sacrificing her money and time without a second thought. So tenacious was she at propelling the campaign at full speed that her close friend and tutor, Mary O'Neill, wrote from suffrage headquarters demanding she delegate more of her duties. Rankin collapsed into bed each night from exhaustion. She lost weight. Her face showed the strain. O'Neill cautioned her to avoid trying to accomplish six months' work in thirty days, but Rankin pushed on relentlessly, her eyes fixed on the distant goal of suffrage in Montana. The breaking point came in Butte, where Rankin threw a tantrum at suffrage headquarters, screaming and throwing things.[40] "Never mind if you do not convert the multitude," the motherly O'Neill consoled "Lively maiden" in a letter afterwards. "Others will follow after you who can complete the job. Try and not be selfish in the work, leave a twig or two of laurel for someone else who must come after. Discouragement and irritability will rob you of your priceless winsomeness and beauty, so forget you ever have a chance for either." O'Neill warned Rankin against "extreme fatigue" and sent her admonishments "with the sweetest love in my heart for you," but the letter was far from whimsical. "Here in Butte we are all ready to kowtow before you — that is everyone but me —

for once in a while I want to spank you good and hard. Now, will you be good?"[41]

Rankin, however, had no intention of leaving work undone. Alice Roosevelt with her flappers, cigarettes and social delinquency characterized one perspective of the "new woman," causing her father to cry in despair: "I can do one of two things. I can be President of the United States, or I can control Alice. I cannot possibly do both."

Rankin, fully armed with her petitions, banners and Progressivism, demonstrated the other perspective. She was addicted to social reform, and as many other reformers of her age, she rejected clothing fashions, smoking and bizarre social behavior as silly cultural fads. She was stoic about the lure of sex and apathetic toward business, the theater and sports. The social liberated woman exhibited the desires of romance and passion, which the politically liberated woman sublimated in an intense love affair with suffrage. Rankin already was past the popular marrying age when it occurred to her that she had missed her cue. Her commitment to social reform was a subtle statement of her personal loneliness. Rankin spoke little of her private life, prompting suffrage sisters to eventually forget she had one, and in the thrill of the fight for the ballot she buried speculation about her motives for such ardent public dedication.

Accolades meant little to her, but achievement meant victory and honor for all Montana women. The smell of victory tied Rankin to her campaign. This attitude caught the attention of the big New York newspapers, which remembered her work on the streets of Manhattan. She capitalized on her distinction and persuaded people of national reputation to join her. Among them were James and Harriet Laidlaw, who came to Montana to campaign.

James Laidlaw was president of the New York Men's League for Equal Suffrage. Harriet had been Rankin's supervisor in the Manhattan Borough of the New York Woman Suffrage Party. These affluent dissenters were Rankin's secret benefactors. The Laidlaws poured cash into the Montana suffrage treasury. Rankin was indebted. When the Laidlaws came to Montana she toured with them. Local suffragists preferred to fund their campaign through gimmicks such as "self-denial" week, when all worldly luxuries were exchanged for a contribution, but Eastern financial support was necessary to help Rankin and other full-time campaigners win in Montana.

Accompanied by a political reporter from the *New York Evening Post*, the Laidlaws arrived in Billings in late February 1914 for a six-day whistle-stop tour. Rankin rode on the train with them to Helena, Butte and Missoula. In those few days, the *Post* reporter bragged of her quick wit and clever tongue, disarming him of his desire to write a tough, unglamorous profile of Montana's leading suffragist. "Everywhere there have been very pretty exhibitions of affection toward this 'native daughter' whose Montana traditions and pioneer parentage are well known," he observed in a full-page article. "The adage about being a prophet without honor in his own country was not exemplified." At Rankin's request, other famous suffrage leaders from the East came to Montana as well: New York educator and activist Katherine Devereux Blake, "General" Rosalie Jones, "Colonel" Ida Craft, and Margaret Hinchey, the bare-knuckled Irish laundry worker from New York City. Standing on the rear seats of a touring car, Rankin and Hinchey spoke in Great Falls to a gathering of two hundred men who listened for two hours.[42] Wellington, always fearful that hecklers might hurt his sister, went along for the ride. "Well, how was she?" Jeannette asked Wellington after Hinchey finished speaking. "She was eloquent," he replied.[43]

Jeannette wasn't often confronted with threats and assaults

as suffragists in other states had experienced, although a political boss splashed a glass of cold water in her face. Her eyes were frosty as she promised the politician that Montana women would vote him from office. She shared her brother's temper. Wellington had big hands and enjoyed fighting and would have pummeled the man. Jeannette promised to destroy him with the votes of women.

She deliberately tarnished anti-suffragists and the liquor industry. The "antis" were composed of unorganized conservative women and the organized National Anti-Suffrage Association. Both groups worked from the premise that suffrage would disrupt home life and force women and children into the street as political operatives. Employing many of the arguments later used against the Equal Rights Amendment, the "antis" dragged moral and religious themes into their objections.

They clashed with Rankin in Helena when she debated Mrs. J.D. Oliphant, an anti-suffragist from New Jersey. Noisy liquor lobbyists packed the meeting. Oliphant spoke first and was given a deafening ovation. Rankin's friends begged her not to step onto the stage. When she brushed past them and began to speak, a chorus of boos smothered her words. Suffragists found opposition everywhere. Fearing the clout of the Women's Christian Temperance Union if women got suffrage, the liquor interests actively opposed the vote, appealing to Eastern associates for money to help their fight. The liquor interests were organized into the Montana Protective Association, which published the *National Forum*, the mouthpiece for its cause. When Clara Markeson, an anti-suffrage worker, met in Butte in early 1914 with the publisher of the *Forum*, Rankin found an opportunity to use the opposition to her advantage. She suggested in the *Montana Progressive* that the anti-suffragists were in collaboration with the liquor industry. Markeson was appalled that she was named in the company of such men. Her embarrassment and the subsequent decline of the "antis" benefited Montana's suffrage campaign.

A third group, sensing the popularity of woman suffrage and working to compromise it, was monolithic Anaconda Copper, one of the largest corporate trusts of the new century. The company controlled or influenced most of Montana's newspapers and many seats in the Legislature. Afraid that suffrage would lead to industrial reform, it waged a quiet campaign, resigned for once that public opinion had weakened its propaganda machine. Rankin ignored the company. The company eventually reciprocated.

Germany's declaration of war against Russia in August 1914 caught Rankin by surprise despite a summer of hostilities in Eastern Europe that began with the assassination of Archduke Francis Ferdinand. She blamed her ignorance on a poor education. Butte, the mining city, was a melting pot of immigrants from the feuding countries, and Rankin commented publicly while she was visiting: "If they are going to have war, they ought to take the old men and leave the young men to propagate the race." Newspapers in Butte said such a comment was inappropriate coming from an unmarried woman.[44]

The conflict in Europe, even if not widely understood as a cancer that eventually would spread to the United States, aroused concern in the suffrage campaign. Women saw war as a threat to their cause, as discussions in a national publication, *The Woman's Journal and Suffrage News*, soon documented. Rankin was hardly set apart in her opposition to war. She wasn't yet a declared pacifist. Her deep distrust of decisions made only by men, elected by men, was growing. She, like many suffragists, increasingly saw war as a demon that stole money from domestic needs. Jane Addams and Alice Paul, critical influences in Rankin's young life, led the pacifist wings of the suffrage movement. Minnie Reynolds, who mentored Rankin in suffrage, already believed that pacifism was a companion issue. Minnie J., as Reynolds was known, was a former news reporter in Colorado who had shifted her journalism career to New York where she also wrote novels. She was credited with urging Rankin to intertwine suffrage with pacifism. Other influences came from fellow members of New York's Heterodoxy Club, Rankin's outspoken reform education, and her own strong-minded beliefs.

Rankin and others thought that voting women would stop war and turn the nation's attention toward the needs of families. She was to reflect years later: "In talking to women, urging suffrage, we said over and over again that war was stupid and futile and couldn't be used successfully in adjusting human relationships. It was women's work which was destroyed by war. Their work was raising human beings, and war destroyed humans to protect profits and property."[45]

Jeannette Rankin and other suffragists planned a campaign that would culminate with the State Fair, held then in Helena, to seize the attention of every political candidate in Montana. Among those suffragists was the indefatigable Frieda Fligelman, Belle's sister, who helped keep the suffrage cause alive in Montana. Because so many people gathered on the fairgrounds, politicians came to the fair looking for votes before they began campaigning in earnest in their districts before the November election. Rankin would recall: "There were political speeches all the time, and the politicians had to go from place to place to make their speeches, since we had no other communication means. The roads were very poor. There were very few cars and very few telephones. It was hard for politicians even to get from place to place."[46]

Women across Montana who volunteered to work for suffrage showed tireless devotion for little recognition other than making candidates think they knew what would elect them. One woman drove thirty miles on a gravel road to attend a meeting. "Eventually we had most of the candidates talking about suffrage because they found it was the popular thing to do," Rankin would remember.[47]

The Montana campaign climaxed in September 1914 with a parade led by Rankin and Anna Howard Shaw, a medical doctor Rankin regarded as one of great female orators of her time. Behind them came female buglers, suffragists wearing yellow jackets, and small boys whose hatbands read, "I want my mother to vote." Banners streamed and onlookers yelled support from hotel windows as the procession of people, horses and automobiles wound its way to an auditorium for a rally in Helena's famous Last Chance Gulch district.

The rally was noisy and contagious, with new National American Woman Suffrage Association president Shaw reiterating Rankin's frequent observation that women should have the right to vote to determine whether men go to war. The rally otherwise was uneventful, suggesting a fading opposition. Perhaps Montana was ready to accept women as voters. As the election neared, suffragists flooded Montana with literature asking women to stand a block away from schools to hand out sashes of bright orange paper to children to wear on their hats or shirts. "I want my Mother to vote," the sashes read. Suffragists noticed with satisfaction that many of the children wore their sashes home after school.

The final strategy involved organizing women to watch polling places to discourage corruption. Many of them were recruited by telephone calls and letters. Others in far-flung corners of Montana received telegrams. Rankin had learned from suffrage campaigns in New York and other states how women lost heart because of voting fraud in the precincts. One suffragist in Montana shot back in a telegram: "We don't need to watch the polls. We have honest men."

Montanans went to the polls on November 3, 1914, a Tuesday. Rankin traveled to Butte to await election returns. The boisterous mining city, full of saloons, prostitutes, gambling houses, corruption and hard-boiled union workers, always proved a suitable measurement of Montana politics. Rankin felt at home in Butte anyway. Being a friend of labor, she distrusted Anaconda Copper. More than a Progressive by name, she resented big companies for their intrusions on human welfare. Butte was such a place. The city's labor class, plentifully stocked with Irish, Italian and Scandinavian immigrants, looked as familiar to her as the people she had met on the streets of New York. Driving a borrowed Ford, Rankin visited one precinct after another in Butte to find out if women were watching for voting violations. At several locations she found no women at all. Men advised her: "Yes, but we told them they didn't need to bother, that we would let them know what the vote was."[48] Rankin spent the day recruiting women to return to the polls.

In those days, election judges wrote duplicate sets of records after counting votes. One report was sealed with the ballots. The other served as the official record. In nearby Anaconda, home of Copper King Marcus Daly and his pro-company newspaper, *The Anaconda Standard*, judges told suffragists they couldn't make the votes public because they accidentally had sealed both sets of returns with the ballots. Rankin recognized the "counting out" as a political ploy common in other states. Politicians with something to gain would hide the count until they knew how many votes were needed to influence an election.

Rankin fired off a telegram to New York suffragists to advise them of the tactic. They in turn gave the story to the New York newspapers. The resulting publicity embarrassed the Anaconda machine politicians enough that they suddenly produced the results, although opposition to suffrage in the city of Anaconda and surrounding Deer Lodge County was suspiciously three times larger than that of any other county in Montana.

Not until Saturday, four days after the election, did newspapers disclose that Montana had become the first state to approve suffrage on the first referendum. The papers reported that 41,302 men had voted in favor of the amendment and 37,588 had voted to defeat it. Montana became the tenth state to grant suffrage. Montana's victory gave the West a solid bloc of enfranchised states to pressure Congress for a federal suffrage amendment. Although many Montanans had worked together to win woman suffrage, Jeannette Rankin's leadership was apparent from the start. Her knowledge of national suffrage strategies, and her personal connections with national suffrage leaders, led to a more organized and professional campaign that overcame traditional objections. Years later, Anna Howard Shaw commended Rankin's leadership for winning Montana.

Rankin never saw Montana suffrage as a goal unto itself. To her, it was a step toward an improved human condition. Early in 1915, Rankin convened a meeting of suffragists in Helena. The Good Government clubs who burned so much shoe leather in neighborhoods and precincts to win suffrage now swung into action to persuade politicians to act on reform measures. The clubs were hugely successful. By 1917, several laws would be enacted in Montana that protected families and workers — two of Rankin's principal concerns. Among them were an eight-hour work day for women; the Mother's Pension Law, boasted the best in the nation when it was drafted; the Lazy Husband Act, which made neglecting a wife or child a misdemeanor; an early Abandonment Law, which made abandoning a child a felony, and a worker's compensation act. A new Pool Room Law prohibited boys younger than eighteen from frequenting such establishments without written permission from their parents. Establishment of a state child welfare department was intended to protect defenseless children. A statewide survey would determine the condition of feeble-minded, deaf and dumb residents. Men no longer could will away their unborn children.[49]

Rankin had foreseen such changes and persevered with the preliminary work, hoping women would take their cue. Laws such as financial aid for dependent orphans, and a retirement fund for public school teachers, were enacted on the strength of female voters and enjoyed by everyone. It was a new era, where women who had worked beside men in frontier Montana now could work beside them in governing their new state.

While many Montana women who had campaigned for suffrage faded quietly from the streets to their kitchens as mothers and wives, Jeannette Rankin was feeling inclined to campaign for political office. She remained immersed in suffrage, traveling to Nashville to partake of the national convention and assisting as a congressional lobbyist in Washington, DC. She campaigned briefly in Pennsylvania where a man castigated suffragists as homosexuals. Rankin, offended, expressed her displeasure to her friend Antoinette Funk at the National American Woman Suffrage Association. "I know the work is hard and seems to be unsatisfactory, but you are a very important spoke in wheel, my dear, and we need all our spokes," Funk wrote back.[50] Finally, in June 1915, Rankin acknowledged her exhaustion and boarded a ship at Seattle for New Zealand, the first country in the world where women could vote. It was her first overseas trip in a lifetime of compulsive travel to escape stresses of American politics.

Rankin would tell friends and relatives that she abandoned her restful vacation soon after she arrived in New Zealand. In Auckland only a few days, she became curious how New Zealand women used their ballot. She contracted her skills as a dressmaker to pay for rent and food. Ignoring the standard wage of six shillings a day, she hired out for twelve shillings and got all the work she could handle. She boarded at a "Girl's Friendly," a cooperative home, where she encouraged other women to lobby for higher pay.[51] "I had very little money," she wrote to Harriet Laidlaw, "and when I found what a delightful, restful country it is, I wanted to stay, so I went out sewing by the day. It was such a splendid way to learn of the living conditions of the people."

Reportedly, the Montana suffragist entered New Zealand homes a seamstress and came out a crusader. She would tell people throughout her lifetime that everywhere she worked, she talked of the power of the vote and inquired about wages and the influence of labor unions. Rankin returned to America in the spring of 1916. As the ship sliced through the Pacific Ocean, her thoughts turned to the political helter-skelter atmosphere of a nation grappling with social change. She remembered the day, campaigning for suffrage in a small Montana town, when she heard war had erupted in Europe. She thought she was the only person who hadn't realized war was imminent.

President Woodrow Wilson, fearing the worst in Europe, built a bigger military even as he publicly decried war. Congress, with Wilson's approval, doubled the regular army in May 1916 and gave the War Department more authority. Another bill was signed to accelerate the building of a stronger navy. Wilson warned Germany to discontinue unrestricted submarine warfare. Meanwhile the Battle of Verdun, eventually to claim one million casualties, plodded into the history books.

To Jeannette Rankin, war was a frightening prospect. She would remember Civil War stories she had heard in Montana as a girl about bomb-torn bodies, homes burned and land laid barren. How could Rankin know — how could anyone —

that the terrible struggle in Europe would beckon a wider world war? Rankin would have something to say about this epic clash of men and guns. Across America, people would hear her words.

6 ~ Campaigning for U.S. House, 1916

'Shocked at the prejudice against a woman going to Congress.'

The power of the vote made Montana women a new and vital political force by the summer of 1916, when Jeannette Rankin considered a run for Congress. She remained their visible leader, reminding them that with citizenship came the duty to investigate political, industrial and social conditions, and to become educated voters. She had led women in achieving independence. Now she was telling them what they should do with it.

After Rankin left Montana for her national suffrage commitments, victorious suffragists put their Good Government clubs to work challenging copper politics in Montana. By this time, Rankin understood how to turn political machinery to other uses, to support other causes and possibly elect a woman to Congress. She saw a pathway when Democrat Tom Stout, after two terms in the House, announced he would retire from Congress. In her Progressivist mind, a congressional seat seemed logical for a woman seeking a federal suffrage amendment and the social reforms that would follow when women cast ballots. Montana was an at-large state, having no designated congressional districts where candidates could keep a tight grip on smaller electorates. Rankin thought she could nudge into the field on the strength of her reputation, experience and organization from the precincts.

Friends told her that a suffrage victory in Montana was no reason to think she could be elected to Congress. Some women insisted that until the United States adopted a federal suffrage amendment, no woman could win a national election. Representatives of some Good Government clubs encouraged her to try for a lesser office in the Montana Legislature. They feared she would fail miserably in her quest for Congress, humiliating women and hindering their reform work. Their lack of faith angered Rankin, who turned to her brother Wellington for advice. Although four years younger, he already had tasted statewide politics in a dismal run for the US House in 1914. Wellington, running on the Progressive Party ticket, ran last in a field of seven candidates. His future would look brighter. He was building a thriving criminal law practice in Helena and in 1919 would become Montana's attorney general. In 1916, he wanted a victory as much for himself as for Jeannette.

Wellington suggested that she invite thirty women from various areas of Montana to meet at the family home in Missoula to seek their advice. He told her he would drive from Helena, a distance of about 120 miles, to join in the conversation. By the time he arrived in Missoula the women, gathered in the parlor of the big house, had convinced Jeannette she shouldn't run. Angered, he told Jeannette: "Well, now, you're going to run for Congress and I'm not very much interested in whether these women go along with you or not. You're going to be elected." He left the room knowing he had made an impression. Sure enough, Wellington would recall years later, the women changed their minds and began planning a statewide campaign. Wellington considered himself a strong Republican but more from a family perspective than party loyalty. Jeannette thought she owed allegiance to her brother. "I'm not a Republican, but I'm running on the Republican ticket on account of Wellington," she told Belle Fligelman.[52]

Representative Joseph Dixon tried to stop Wellington in his tracks. Nobody would take Jeannette seriously as a candidate for national office, Dixon said. She would become a laughing stock in Montana. Dixon, later to become Montana's governor, doubted the time was right for a woman to run for Congress. Voters would consider her candidacy a freakish idea. Her support would be nominal. Dixon failed to persuade Wellington, who would come to regard his sister as "one of the best single-handed campaigners I have ever seen." Dixon also was out of touch with campaigns in several other suffrage states that were exploring the idea of electing a woman to Congress.

Young Wellington Rankin, for all of his personal and political faults, already was an influential politician in Montana. He was making headlines for his accomplishments in criminal law beginning with his winning defense of an accused killer, Mike Rodoman, in 1911. That triumph after a fight between two immigrants led him to start his own law firm. Rankin's reputation as a fearless trial attorney grew, especially after he punched a witness in the face during a wrongful death trial. "You cannot beat Rankin," it was said. When he threw his public image behind his sister's campaign, she gained the full weight of his influence.[53]

Jeannette announced her candidacy in a Butte restaurant on July 13, 1916. "The possibility of my being nominated," she told a friend a week later, "seems very good." She built her platform with planks for a national eight-hour working day for women, support for prohibition, revision of international tariffs, more laws to provide for child welfare, more efficient publicity concerning the business of congressmen and how they stand on issues, and most important to her, suffrage by federal amendment. She also campaigned for "preparedness that will make for peace," a vague nod to national defense that left her position open to wide interpretation.

She was the only woman in a field of eight candidates. She thought that because Montana would elect two at-large members of Congress, everyone could vote for one man — and her — without losing face. Perhaps a woman could win the second-highest number of votes. "Although it is a case of seven men against one woman, still I am entering the political fight unafraid," Rankin said. "The primal motive for my seeking a seat in the national congress is to further the suffrage work and to aid in every possible way the movement for nationwide suffrage, which will not cease until it is won."[54]

Banking on her brother's advice, Rankin stuck to her promise and filed on the Republican ticket, an odd move considering her strong Progressive leanings. She was firmly opposed to war and echoed the peace rhetoric of Woodrow Wilson. Yet she ran as a Republican knowing her attempt to challenge Democratic incumbent John B. Evans, trying for his third term, would prompt an immediate and bitter battle between an upstart female social reformer and a traditional old guard of politics.

Most of her Republican competitors had limited campaign experience. It was nothing more than a party of convenience for Rankin, a pathway to promise. Predictably her platform was nonpartisan. That provoked jokes among newspaper editors that she desired the Democrats to forget she was a Republican.

Once Rankin announced her candidacy, the uncertainty among Montana's suffragists diminished. Most had been skeptical except for an inner circle of friends in Missoula. The war in Europe had distracted from the fruits of Montana's suffrage campaign. Many women believed momentum had been lost but they united behind Rankin anyway. Wellington was unsettled. He saw suffrage as a moral obligation. Feeble-minded men could vote, he said, and thirty years had passed since black men gained the right to vote. "I am shocked," he wrote Jeannette, "at the prejudice that exists against a woman going to Congress."

With less than two months before the primary election, her campaign came alive under the slogan "Let the People Know." Belle Fligelman, known as "Generalissimo" because of her fiery passion for suffrage, quit her job as editor of the *Montana Progressive*, opened campaign headquarters in Wellington's law office in Helena, and began redirecting the organization that had won suffrage for Montana. Said the *Montana Record-Herald* of Fligelman: "80 pounds is really more than she weighs without overshoes, and she's a hair over five feet tall, in high-heeled shoes."

Fligelman had met Rankin in the summer of 1914 when, as a young news reporter, she was sent to cover the annual convention of the Federation of State Women's Clubs in the central Montana city of Lewistown. "I was quite terrified when he told me this because I had never been sent out of town to report anything before, and I wasn't quite sure how it was done," she would recall. "And he said, 'Jeannette Rankin's going to be there, you'll be interested in that.'" The club was packed with women who opposed suffrage. Many were homemakers who never had time for attending college. As Fligelman traveled seven hours on the train, she tried to figure out how she would send dispatches to Helena via telegraph. The next day, Rankin swept onto the stage. "She came out dressed in this beautiful tiger-colored, gold velvet suit and a big velvet hat the same color," Fligelman remembered. "She just held them spellbound. The minute she got out on the stage you could feel the electricity in the air."[55]

Fligelman recalled that Rankin mentioned every argument

against suffrage and refuted them all. Voting places weren't fit for women? True, because most votes were cast in saloons, but move them to a public building. No restrooms for women? Build some. Voting will force women to take jobs? Nonsense, voting would give women power to determine laws. "The government comes into our homes and tells us what to do, but we have nothing to say about it," Rankin told the women as she described how they could demand food inspections through the vote. The vote would make the home better for women and children.

"Men's ideas were different in politics," Rankin said, and while men were interested in public projects such as bridges and railroads, women needed to take command of community welfare. Only through the power of the vote, she said, could they achieve that. The editor of the local paper, keeping with the wildcat theme, had witnessed Rankin's off-the-cuff speech and described her "like a young panther ready to spring."[56] Fligelman, ever the suffragist at heart, joined Rankin's drive for the vote soon after the Lewistown appearance. They both spoke at a three-county picnic in the country town of Absarokee. The diminutive Fligelman, wanting people to see her, stood on the back seat of an open car. Rankin, much taller at five-foot-five, stood beside her to launch her voice over the crowd.

Wellington Rankin, meanwhile, had seen firsthand how his sister could stir emotions and win votes. He presided over the Helena Men's League for Woman Suffrage. He drew her campaign plans. He thought Jeannette could win extra votes in the eastern half of Montana if she took strong positions in favor of prohibition and a wool tariff to protect against unfair competition. He proposed that a Jeannette Rankin for Congress club be established immediately. Candidates for other offices should be encouraged to endorse her openly. Courting the suffrage lobby, Jeannette incorporated the entire program of the Good Government clubs into her campaign strategy.

By early August, only three weeks after Rankin had announced her candidacy, her campaign roared ahead. "Her nomination would advertise Montana from coast to coast ...," the *Montana Progressive* declared. Rankin's candidacy, the *Progressive* commented, was significant because she could become the first woman to sit in Congress. Her candidacy implied a new idea of democracy. The newspaper, clearly in the Rankin camp, said she was receiving letters of support from across the country. Nathan Godfrey, Republican candidate for railroad commissioner, told the *Helena Daily Independent* that he had been in New York when Rankin lobbied for suffrage at the State Legislature there, and "I was told that her work in the legislature was very efficient and that had gained confidence of the legislators and those with whom she worked, to a remarkable degree."[57]

At Fort Benton, where her father had bought oxen and set off to build a new life in Montana Territory forty-seven years earlier, a brass band announced her arrival in town. In another instance, a farm couple told Rankin they had traveled twenty miles in an oxen-hitched lumber wagon to hear her speak.

Harriett Laidlaw and a fellow New Yorker, Rosalie Jones, often were quoted in newspapers. "We are watching your political fight with great interest and your New York friends believe that a better congressman could not be found and a victory for you will mean a victory for suffrage throughout the country," wrote the enterprising Jones, a flamboyant demonstrator who later walked from New York to Washington, DC, to promote woman suffrage.

Rankin hit the streets, rarely diverting from the campaign blueprint of the suffrage wars. She and her supporters gave speeches on street corners as they had done in their quest for the vote. It was easier in Montana, Rankin would recall later, than working the streets in New York City for suffrage when finding a corner without a bar sometimes meant walking for miles. In Montana, she replicated all the tactics she had learned so well under more difficult circumstances elsewhere. She told stories of how veteran suffrage workers persuaded "new converts" to pass out literature to people assembled around street speakers. The literature contained provocative statements such as, "more girls graduated from high school than boys," and therefore girls deserved the vote. Offensive reactions often made the new suffrage workers more earnest. Rankin in her later years described how one man leaving the crowd muttered, "The speaker ought to be home rocking the baby." The son of the woman speaking heard him and replied: "I'm her baby and I don't want to be rocked."[58]

In many ways Rankin's unprecedented campaign for Congress mimicked what she knew best. The surprising Montana suffrage victory was still hot on the minds of residents. Unfazed by the rough talk of men, Rankin courted smelter workers at East Helena, Great Falls and Anaconda. She prowled the railroad yards at Deer Lodge, Havre and Livingston. In Wellington's view, Jeannette's informality disarmed people. "Her finesse in rough-and-ready places was as expert as in any Washington drawing room," commented a political reporter.

Wellington pored over the detailed election map on his office wall. Belle Fligelman flooded tips to the press. As in the suffrage days, Jeannette mingled with the voters, stressing the practical benefits of electing a woman to Congress and calling for laws governing mining, agriculture and labor. She proposed amendments to the Farm Loan Act to simplify it, and also to the Federal Grain and Inspecting Law, "so as to take this important matter entirely out of the hands of state political influences and make federal control absolutely conclusive."[59] By late August, Montana women who had worked for suffrage had thrown their election machinery into full throttle, declaring a statewide "Jeannette Rankin Day" to brand her name in voters' minds. Women mailed penny postcards by the thousands and conducted a telephone campaign on Election Day with the greeting: "Good morning! Have you voted for Jeannette Rankin?"

The strategy worked. Rankin swept the field of Republican candidates in the primary, defeating her nearest competitor, George W. Farr, by more than seven thousand votes. Rankin dismissed the bewildered men as afraid to meet voters. "My opponents had too much dignity," she said. Women had blanketed towns and cities across Montana with the message: "Vote for your local candidate and for Jeannette Rankin." On the Democratic side of the ballot, incumbent Evans had a greater margin of victory, but everyone was talking about how an upstart woman had trounced a field of men.

The battle was set for Montana's two at-large seats. Evans and another Democrat, Harry Mitchell, would square off against Rankin and Farr. The ballot also included two Socialists. Evans, being an incumbent of some repute, was considered unbeatable. Mitchell had support from one of Montana's most influential newspapers, the *Great Falls Tribune*. Farr complained bitterly to Wellington that Jeannette, although Republican in name, was running for office as an independent. Her strong emergence on the political scene worried Farr, who thought she wasn't playing by the rules of the game. Farr complained that the Rankins should campaign for him because he was the legitimate Republican candidate. Wellington scoffed at that. He paid no attention to Farr's campaign or the Republican hierarchy. Instead he financed Jeannette's campaign out of his own pocket.

She prepared for the general election in November. She started her campaign with a speech outside Larabie Brothers

Bank in downtown Deer Lodge. Anticipating her victory in the general election, other Republican candidates pounced on her coattails. "For the proper recognition of women in politics, every woman in Montana should support Miss Rankin for Congress," said Godfrey, the candidate for railroad commissioner.

They did. Rankin won the support of prohibitionists who, concerned with their own cause, had not contributed to the suffrage campaign in 1914. Also backing her in the race to the finish were many of the anti-suffragists who came to see her as a leader of women. Campaign cards handed out on street corners and community meetings described Rankin as "a keen thinker, an able speaker, and a tremendous worker." The cards noted she had lobbied two sessions of Congress for suffrage, and also legislatures in New York, New Hampshire, Delaware, Florida, North Dakota and, of course, Montana. "Has studied industrial and social conditions in almost every state in the union," read another card.[60]

Jeannette and Wellington forged a campaign of exposure. They would continue to build on the public attention she had received when she spoke about suffrage in the Montana Legislature. Her speeches resembled much of what she had said on behalf of suffrage, her platform of issues strikingly similar to that cause. "We wanted better protection for children, better protection for mothers. When I said it the second time they had heard it before and it wasn't a new issue," she observed years later.[61] Wellington was convinced that the more she was seen and heard, the more voters would accept her as a competent and qualified candidate for Congress. The context of history would show she was extraordinarily qualified for national office, even while lacking experience in elective positions traditionally available to men, such as the Montana Legislature and city and county elective offices. Rankin was far greater educated than the typical American woman, by virtue of the classroom and through her exposure to institutions such as orphanages and settlement houses. She was trained in political campaigning, she had stretched geographical boundaries to campaign for suffrage, and her leadership for the right to vote in Montana hastened the pace of her exposure to government. Rankin was an aberration of her times but hardly unqualified to represent Montanans in government. Her challenge was convincing voters of that.

It was becoming apparent to Wellington that Montana women, regardless of their party affiliations, were unifying behind his sister. Sensing that women would make the difference, Wellington organized a telephone campaign from Helena to push them into action in dozens of counties. Jeannette was on the move day and night making speeches and knocking on doors. When he could get a serviceable connection, Wellington tracked her down on the phone every evening to plan the next day's strategy. "They soon pictured her a winner before the campaign had gone very far," he would recall of potential voters.[62]

She ran strong in Butte where support from labor unions defied silence in the copper press. Because Anaconda Copper owned most of Montana's newspapers — big and small — and simply figured her bid for Congress was a wild woman's dream, company newspapers mostly ignored her campaign. Seizing opportunity, Rankin visited labor unions in Great Falls, Billings, and Missoula and met smelter workers in East Helena and Anaconda. The company fretted that if she were elected she would introduce pro-labor legislation hurtful to company politics in Montana. The company already had Wellington pegged as an anti-corporate attorney in alliance with other attorneys who shared the same view. Rankin's critics implied she only was joining a trend that blossomed female candidacies for Congress in Washington, Colorado and California. They underestimated her nose for drama.

She accused Congress of failing to protect the rights of children by appropriating $300,000 to study fodder for hogs while setting aside only one-tenth that sum to study the needs of children. "If the hogs of this nation are ten times more important than the children, it is high time that women should make their influence felt in Congress," Rankin admonished. "We have several hundred men in Washington to care for the nation's tariff and the irrigation and the hogs but there is not a single woman to take care of the interests of the children."[63]

Also helpful to her campaign was the potent influence of her family. Years and miles had pushed the Rankins apart, all intent on their own ventures, but letters and love had kept them a family. One of Jeannette's sisters had been married just two months, but she kissed her husband goodbye and hit the streets with a bundle of campaign pamphlets tucked under her arm. Another had a child only two years old but she traded diapers for doorsteps. Sister Edna, attending law school, abandoned the lecture hall for the political stump because she knew Jeannette and Wellington expected that of her. This swift onrush of ideas bewildered the matronly Olive Rankin, but the family would attest that she supported her daughter's candidacy.

Jeannette delivered her final speech of the campaign on November 6, 1916, in a Missoula theater. The Republican politician pretending to introduce her spoke for ninety minutes until the angry crowd chanted, "Rankin! Rankin! Rankin!" and drove him from the podium. Only hours before the polls opened, she observed: "I need only every other vote and then one to make a majority." She knew, too, that she needed men. Some would vote for her because they believed in equality. Others, intrigued by the sensation that would follow a woman elected to Congress, supported her as a joke.

Less commonly understood in Montana was the depth of her support nationally. Former President Theodore Roosevelt endorsed her, as did Charles Fairbanks, his vice president. Many prominent congressional leaders, familiar with Rankin from her suffrage work, wrote letters of support.

Even as Rankin barnstormed Montana, the shadow of war hung over Europe. England and France fought with Germany. Austria-Hungary declared war on Russia. In the United States, loyalties were divided among immigrants from those countries. Many German families had settled in the great farming belt that stretched from Minnesota west through North Dakota into eastern Montana. Still, the war seemed far away, rooted in the Old Country. Americans felt detached from that strife. The political mood was isolationist.

On Election Day, Rankin went to the polls in Missoula to cast her first vote. How surreal it seemed. One vote cast, for herself, wouldn't win an election. She was quite sure Wellington had voted for her in Helena, as had Belle Fligelman. She was assured of three votes but worried whether her campaigning stirred sufficient interest at the polls. As Election Day lapsed into darkness, Rankin began to worry she had lost. She reached for the black telephone in her house and asked "central" for the local newspaper. Cold gusts of November wind slapped the windows of the city room of the *Daily Missoulian* in downtown Missoula where an irritated editor answered her call. Curious voters had pestered him all evening. He was worried that the time would come for the presses to roll before his reporters had written their stories. Ballot counting was slow and results were sketchy.

"How did [Woodrow] Wilson come out?" Rankin asked, too nervous to reveal her identity. She inquired about a few other candidates before asking whether Jeannette Rankin had been elected to Congress. With a deadline bearing down and the confusion of incomplete voting returns littering his desk, the newsman was brief: "Oh, she lost." Dejected, Rankin went to bed and slept fitfully. The newsman had no idea of the outcome but she took him at his word. The newsman went back to his headlines and deadlines, unknowing that he just had rebuffed the first congresswoman in the history of the United States.

The nation was slow in recognizing Rankin's landmark victory. The morning headlines of November 8 reported that her Republican opponent, George Farr, had won the race. Waiting for election returns was tedious and agonizing for hopeful candidates. Radio broadcasting was years away. Television was unknown. Ballots were counted by hand. Everybody presumed votes were being manipulated in precincts where copper interests controlled the vote. Tabulation was show. As results dribbled into newspaper city rooms, Rankin prepared to concede her loss.

Wellington telephoned from Helena later that morning with heartening news. For five months, he had surveyed county-by-county historical voting patterns, and in looking over partial returns he saw that much of the Farr plurality came from the more urban western half of Montana. Even then Jeannette had eclipsed Farr in some mountain counties. Tabulation of votes in the far-flung prairies of eastern Montana had been slower. Wellington predicted those votes would elect his sister to Congress.

Later that day, the New York newspapers sent her telegrams asking if she had won. She replied that, yes, she had. Still, the Montana papers reported Thursday that she had lost, and again on Friday. The New York papers, doubtful by then, again sent telegrams asking how Rankin had fared. Finally, by Saturday, the Montana papers acknowledged her election to Congress. Wellington and Jeannette, sensing a conspiracy, surmised the bigger

Anaconda Copper papers had known the truth from the start.

Thanks to a coalition of suffragists, laborers and farmers, Jeannette Rankin became, overnight, the most talked-about woman in America. She received 76,932 votes, second only to John Evans at 84,499.[64] Both of them would represent Montana in Congress. Her campaign had cost seven hundred dollars, equivalent to more than $15,000 today, but long before candidates made costly investments in broadcast advertising. She had won election on a Republican ticket when Woodrow Wilson, a Democratic president, carried Montana by 30,000 votes and Democrats held the majority at the Montana Legislature. "I feel that the strenuous fight for suffrage two years ago was well worth the discouragements and dark days we went through, if the new voters appreciate their franchise enough to be willing to push further their fight for representation in their government," Rankin wrote her Montana campaign workers a week later.[65]

In the midst of troubling foreign war news, the nation went head-over-heels with delight at her pioneering election. War loomed on the foreign front and the issue of military preparedness threatened to choke the congressional calendar, but for a few raucous, carefree days, the nation turned its curious eyes to the Lady from Montana.

7 ~ Mr. Speaker, the Lady from Montana

'I am deeply conscious of the responsibility resting upon me'

Although panting from its coverage of the expenditure of flesh and money in Europe, the press gaily recorded Jeannette Rankin's election to Congress. Reporters and photographers from national publications thronged to the Rankin house in Missoula. Sacks of letters and telegrams, many adorned with colorful foreign stamps, burdened the weary mail carrier. Suffragists bridged their ideological rifts and beamed their approval. Montana had elected a woman to Congress while most states still denied women the right to vote. "Breathes there a man with heart so brave that he would want to become one of a deliberate body made up of 434 women and himself?" observed the *Courier-Journal* in Louisville, Kentucky.

Much of the initial reaction dwelled on the Montana upstart's appearance and domestic abilities. The *New York Times*, in a lengthy article five days after the election, quoted an unnamed female news reporter who claimed insight into the new celebrity's supposed preoccupation with homemaking: "She dances well and makes her own hats, and sews, and has won genuine fame among her friends with the wonderful lemon meringue pie that she makes when she hasn't enough other things to do to keep her busy." The *Times* story characterized Rankin as timid, concluded she was unknown in New York (contrary to the suffrage work she had done there), and debated whether her hair was brown or red.[66] The abundance of it was never questioned because Rankin, like most women of the day, kept loose hair in a box on her night table to braid into her pompadour for a fuller look.

Some publications embraced the cultural expectations of the day, reporting that she kept herself busy in the kitchen preparing meals and then adjourning to the sitting room for her needlework. The *Boston Globe*, taking the high road, published a political cartoon showing Rankin climbing the steps to Congress under the headline, "Hats off, Gentleman — Why, Certainly." Various Americans came forth to debate her constitutional right to hold office. John Allison of Nashville, Tennessee, argued that women weren't eligible to serve in Congress because the US Constitution said "he" instead of "she" or "the person."[67]

After 140 years, women and children now had an elected representative. Rankin had proven to Americans that women could make themselves heard. Many more battles would be fought, but women rejoiced at her election. They finally had a voice in Congress.

"Why — Jeannette Rankin — you have given Suffrage the biggest push forward that could have possibly been given unless we could have elected a Woman President," wrote Rosalie Jones from her apartment in New York City. "We really all ran with you, here in the East except perhaps a few old Suffrage mossbacks who thought 'that perhaps it was too soon etc.' You know the stupid old story."[68]

In a prepared statement to the press, Rankin promised to represent all American women and children. She would introduce legislation seeking an eight-hour workday for women, equal wages for equal work, and a federal suffrage amendment. Of interest to Montanans, she promised support for settlers' patents, reclamation projects and land laws. She also considered herself elected on a strong antiwar platform. Evidence of that was anecdotal at best, although a reasonable assumption given the nation's isolationist mood in late 1916. For her part, Rankin was more of a pacifist than voters might have suspected. She and Wellington had built her victory on coalitions, causes and ideas. Her campaign wasn't a single-minded grab for antiwar votes.

Rankin attributed her election to the spirit of the pioneer days, when men thought of women as kindly as they thought of themselves. This feeling of equality was undiscovered in many other states, making her a unique candidate in a unique era, elected on a wave of fresh awareness in politics. The new member of Congress had prepared for Washington's sacrosanct male political world with years of practiced talking points about women, children and social reform. Her opponents balked at this apparent ruination of respectable government. Entrepreneurs tried to benefit from her election.

Charles Easton, a jeweler in Bellingham, Washington, wrote to assure Rankin that her election to Congress was the biggest news in national politics since Abraham Lincoln. "The impression that some have that woman is not fit for public service in all lines of work, if true, is explained by the fact that men are failures as a rule in domestics," he wrote. "My wife is my equal, and, I love to consider her my superior in mental capacity, and I would consider myself a failure if I could not claim to be her equal in domestic science and the common duties of life."[69] Letters contained proposals of marriage and requests for a portrait. An automobile business offered a free car if her ownership could be advertised. A toothpaste firm wanted a bite of the action with a promise of five thousand dollars for a photograph of her teeth. Comic Christopher Morley wrote in the *New York Times Magazine*, in part:

I wonder is she old and stout

Or is she young and pretty?
How long the members will stay out
Who are on her committee....
We'll hear no more of shabbiness
Among our legislators.
She'll make them formal in their dress;
They'll wear boiled shirts and gaiters.[70]

Such publicity troubled Rankin. She was the champion of social and political ideas, not money gimmicks and patronizing poems. Overzealous reporters reached for adjectives to describe the new Member of Congress. Many of them ignored facts. Only when America rose to her feet to gander at the Lady from Montana did Rankin realize her election had won more than a vote for women. Publicity rained on her. The swift, crazy public attention was hard for her to comprehend. Suddenly it mattered what she said or didn't say, what she wore, how she walked, whether she ate eggs for breakfast, fought Indians or wore chaps. She was labeled "The Maid of Missoula," portrayed with her hands in her pockets and a cigar clenched in her teeth. Many newspapers gushed with tales of her fashion sense. The first wave of public inspection of this creature from the frontier scared her a little. She found it disturbing that a woman, particularly one voted to Congress, would be treated with so little dignity. Yet publicity of any nature kept woman suffrage in the headlines. Telegrams arrived from all over the country and even from Europe. A telegram of congratulations came from British novelist Marie Corelli, who had written three dozen books to huge popular acclaim.

Overwhelmed with the attention, Rankin refused to leave her house until the "moving picture men" and news photographers who waited on the street had left. She watched them from the parlor, where an oil painting of the family ranch decorated one wall and framed photographs of national suffrage leaders graced another. To Wellington, her sudden and uncharacteristically shy behavior hurt her politically, at least for a short while. Jeannette gave it no further thought. The Montana Republican Party, still stinging over Jeannette's race for Congress, took responsibility for the news blackout, fearing excessive publicity might portray her as a freak and taint the party's image.

Thoughtful and provocative articles filtered through the screen of yellow journalism. In one instance, she was lauded for her "great oratorical power" because of her demonstrated influence on audiences. Louis Levine, professor of economics at the University of Montana, wrote in the *New York Times*:

"It would be premature to expect Miss Rankin to give a definite answer to the many concrete questions which the acutely curious or the insensitively studious like to ask," Levine wrote. "She will have plenty of time between now and her first appearance in Congress to think many things over and to form opinions on a number of vital issues." Levine was, like Rankin, an outspoken dissenter who thrived on social causes and scholarly investigation into change. He was a renowned teacher with doctoral degrees in economics and sociology and, despite being suspended for conduct prejudicial to the university's welfare, he maintained a reputation as a man of integrity. Levine's unerring studies of civilization were as reliable as his candid observations about people. With emotion and reverence, he wrote of Rankin:

"There is great surprise in store for the members of the new Congress when they convene in Washington next year and meet their first woman colleague, 'The Lady from Montana.' They will have to throw overboard a lot of mental baggage which they may have valued very highly for many years. They will find in their midst not that impulsive irrational, sentimental capriciously thinking and obstinately feeling being which many imagine woman to be, but a strong and well-balanced personality, scientifically trained, accustomed to strict reasoning, well versed in the art of politics, inspired by high social ideals, tempered by wide experience."[71]

Rankin had a less lofty opinion of herself, evident in her first public statement the day after she ignored deflated newsmen outside her house. "I am deeply conscious of the responsibility resting upon me. I earnestly hope that I may be of some substantial service, however slight, to the men and women of Montana, my native state, and of the nation." She repeated the same sentiments in a speech at the University of Montana, her alma mater. Most of the university's 600 students crowded into an auditorium to witness this curiosity of history. Among them stood a "movie man" who had struck a deal with the dean of women to show university buildings in exchange for filming the first woman elected to Congress.[72]

Rankin stepped into the national spotlight with great care. So many people were watching. She was an instant celebrity, revered by many, hated by some. Her earlier work had been as a volunteer, not as an elected representative. Showing an awe of Congress that afflicted many freshman members, she hoped to ease into her new role with dignity and a sense of duty. No longer Jeannette Rankin of Missoula but the first American congresswoman, she had to act deliberately, presenting her progressive ideas in an orderly manner. "Miss Rankin rose to meet me," a Chicago news reporter wrote of meeting her. "Instead of a Junoesque type of woman, I saw a slender creature with a wealth of soft, curly hair, a pair of wistful dark eyes, and an expression that radiated the joy of living. The hand she extended in greeting was small and slender."[73] Few people doubted that her election to Congress was an outstanding feat in the young century. Her voice no longer was that of a starry-eyed suffragist but one representing all American women. Even so, practical challenges awaited her. Rankin read a new book, *Your Congress*, that explained rules and procedures for new members.[74]

Seizing on her instant fame, Wellington contracted with the Lee Keedick Agency of New York City for Jeannette to present a series of speeches at $500 each, "a lot of money for a young girl from the country," he would say later.[75] He either overlooked or ignored a clause stating the contract would be canceled if war were declared in Congress and Jeannette voted against it.

She inspired curiosity and awe even on trains as she rode eastward to New York City in February 1917 to begin her lecture tour for Keedick, advertised as "Manager of the World's Most Celebrated Lecturers." A Western Union messenger, escorted to her Pullman car as the train crept through snowstorms in Pennsylvania, marveled at the "striking appearance" of the Honorable Jeannette Rankin when she handed him a message to send by telegram.

Rankin's speeches in New York would be the first since her appearance at the University of Montana after her election. New York reporters came knocking at Harriet Laidlaw's house at 6 East Sixty-Sixth Street, where Rankin was staying, and wouldn't be shooed away. Giving interviews in the parlor, Rankin revealed that she went to moving picture houses to watch silent films for relaxation. One newsman felt compelled to report that she was dressed in "pretty French heels" and her "chestnut hair was not barbered but coiffed — Pompadour." It was further observed that contrary to public opinion she wasn't dressed in "spats, spectacles and stiff shirts" but rather in a soft and clingy gown that showed off her "pleasantly rounded" neck.[76] It wasn't disclosed whether he would call on her again.

A day earlier, President Woodrow Wilson had announced Congress would meet in special session. Everyone suspected what he intended. Rankin was cautious in her remarks to reporters. She admitted only to her support for a constitutional amendment permitting woman's suffrage and for a creating a federal children's bureau. Rankin "would not state whether she was a pacifist," the *Washington Post* reported on February 27.

With Wellington by her side, Jeannette went to Carnegie Hall the evening of March 2 to address three thousand people who had come to see the curious Lady from Montana. Theodore Roosevelt sent his regrets that he couldn't attend the lecture. "I most earnestly hope that you, and those like you, will make and keep the Republican Party loyal to the spirit of Abraham Lincoln,"[77] he wrote Jeannette. Newsmen covering the event spared no restraint in their flowery descriptions. One of them was Peter Clark MacFarlane, who wrote the following opening paragraph in an article for *Collier's Weekly* magazine:

"Charm would be the first word in describing her. She wore a simple frock of flesh-colored georgette crepe with a wide band of fur at the bottom; her hair was coiled loosely and dressed rather low at the front as if to conceal the fact that her brow is high; her face was always smiling, and her voice, at the beginning of the address, seemed always about to break into the laughter of irrepressible youth. Judging by appearance from the tenth row in the orchestra, the speaker might have been nineteen or twenty-three; yet, judged by the sapiency of her words, she must have been much older. Her manner was altogether unassuming; it lacked either pose or staginess and kept reminding one of an awfully nice girl talking to a Sunday-school class. Yet, young and parlor-bred as she appeared, the speaker was the Hon. Jeannette Rankin of Montana, the first woman member of the House of Representatives."[78]

Carrie Chapman Catt introduced Rankin as one of seven

"independents" elected to Congress, somehow ignoring her election on the Republican ticket. Suffragists dominated the audience. The great hall darkened, leaving a patch of light on the main stage. When Rankin approached the podium in her white evening dress, the people applauded enthusiastically. The nation's first woman in Congress smiled in appreciation. The audience gawked at this petite spellbinder, this crusader for social causes, this irrepressible suffragist.

Rankin spoke on the subject of "Democracy and Government," condemning corporate greed and outlining a theme that Americans should become more fully in charge of their government. She opened by informing her urban audience of free land still being given away in Montana, of the state's vast wheat fields producing enough flour to provide eighteen loaves of bread for every American. It was a speech Wellington had drafted, full of Rankin ideology and lacking any insight into what she intended to accomplish in the House, but in every respect, the speech detailed an agenda for her entire life. The *New York Times* said Rankin "spoke easily, without notes, and discussed the present day political machinery with the ease of an old-time politician." She spoke of wanting to elect presidents by popular vote, granting proportional representations in legislative assemblies, and giving women a voice at the ballot box to decide whether their sons should go to war. Portending her lifelong distaste of industrial economies, she condemned companies that profited from many for the pleasure of a few. "The life of the laborer is not considered of much value," she said. "Injury and violent death are very frequent. We are beginning to have occupational diseases. So now we have real labor problems. ... Industry, like government, exists only by the cooperation of all, and, like government, it must guarantee equal protection to all. ... Each day we feel the question asked why, with our improved means of production resulting in such splendid material products, have we failed to increase the products of human happiness? Is it necessary to have so much poverty, misery and crime? With these questions the demands of the people for a controlling voice in their destiny will be imperious. This means we must have democracy in government, in industry, in social life if we are to have social growth."

Possibly clarifying Catt's introduction, Rankin told the crowd that an "old-fashioned Republican" in Montana had complained during her campaign for the US House of Representatives that she had never voted the Republican ticket. "When I did vote for the Republican ticket I was accused of voting for myself, but in political life one is accused of so many things it is hardly worthwhile to deny them," she said.[79] After finishing her speech, Rankin attended a ball at Hotel Marseilles, sponsored by the Seventeenth Assembly District of the Woman Suffrage Party. It was presumed she danced, but with whom wasn't reported. Tickets to the "popular priced ball" were two for one dollar.

By the end of March, Rankin delivered a dozen more speeches in New York, Rhode Island and Connecticut. Each time she related how voting women might help the United States stay a course for peace. War was close, forcing news editors to give the encroaching conflict more space and greater "play" each week. Quietly at first, and then more noisily, the hostile situation among belligerent nations in Europe played on America's conscience. President Wilson tried vainly to demonstrate his Princeton-style moralist and progressive principles in diplomatic talks with the Germans, who thought they were too powerful to bow to cloaked threats of war. On February 25, 1917, Wilson learned that Germany was plotting against the United States.

British intelligence agents had intercepted secret orders sent from German foreign minister Arthur Zimmerman to the

German ambassador in Mexico, telling him that if the United States declared war, an invitation should be extended to Mexico and Japan to join the Central Powers. The British leaked the order to Wilson, who found himself questioning whether his 1916 campaign slogan, "He kept us out of war," had been premature.

On March 1, the president released the message to the press and, despite an isolationist national temperament, the revelation shocked Americans. Wilson wanted to reinforce his proposal to Congress to arm merchant vessels against German submarines. He thought public opinion would strengthen his hand. He was right, but a "little group of willful men" in the House of Representatives and the Senate talked his bills to death. The president, fearing attacks, armed the vessels anyway. His efforts were in vain. German U-boats sank three ships only two weeks after Wilson's second inauguration. The Lady from Montana, meanwhile, tried to maintain her posture as an elected representative of women and children. She was, above all, expected to lead the charge for a constitutional woman suffrage amendment.

Wilson's release of the Zimmerman communication worried suffragists, who besieged Rankin with inquiries about how she would vote on a war declaration in Congress. Her mission underwent a new trial. She had been speaking generally of United States defense policy, advocating only a coastal defense to discourage invasion, but her principles had gone untested. Suddenly everyone was talking about war. Rankin viewed the national sentiment and Wilson's moralist predicament with sarcasm. She ridiculed his campaign slogan as a superficiality that didn't commit him to anything.

Theodore Roosevelt, in a move Wellington thought was an attempt to influence Jeannette's thinking before she went to Congress, invited the Rankins to dine at his Sagamore Hill home in Oyster Bay, New York. It was the most important political engagement in Wellington's life. He had been a fan of the former president since the heyday of Roosevelt's Bull Moose Party. Wellington had campaigned as a Bull Moose for the US House of Representatives in Montana in 1912 but fell to a thumping defeat. His position was decidedly "anti-copper," placing him at odds with the influential Amalgamated Copper Company from the start. Now that political risk paid off. He would share an intimate conversation about national politics with his hero, a man whose reputation remained larger than life. Wellington couldn't wait. A chauffeur came for Wellington and Jeannette in mid-afternoon because Wellington was worried they would be late. After more than an hour in the car, Wellington realized the driver couldn't find Roosevelt's house. "I loved Theodore Roosevelt and admired him," Wellington recalled years later. "I was so beside myself that I debated seriously just beating the hell out of this fellow. I just had the most terrible time controlling myself. I was just crazed. We couldn't phone Roosevelt and tell him that we were late because he had a private phone. All we could do was keep going."[80]

They finally arrived at Roosevelt's home at eight o'clock. They stood there, trying to find the bell at the front door. Jeannette laughed. The harder she laughed, the more Wellington fumed. Finally, he laughed too. Roosevelt wasn't at all bothered at the late hour. They talked until midnight in front of a massive fireplace as big as a single room. Roosevelt pulled several worn volumes about Abraham Lincoln from a bookcase, handing Wellington a book with notations written in every margin. Roosevelt, revering Lincoln's leadership, said he never let a day pass without reading from that book.

Although his hardline positions on American military policy had turned many people against him, Roosevelt was more adept in his politicking than most people understood.

Surely his invitation to the Rankins was no casual affair. Throughout dinner he talked about his fear that President Wilson would lead the nation into war. "We were going to go to war and it was a crime, a shame," Wellington recalled years later. Roosevelt brought several photographs to the dinner table. They showed him with the Kaiser in Germany. Roosevelt flipped them over to show comments the Kaiser had etched on the back of each photo. They were good friends, Roosevelt said, telling Wellington and Jeannette the Kaiser could have been talked out of war.[81]

Unexpectedly, the opinionated ex-president didn't ask Jeannette how she would vote if Wilson asked Congress to approve a war declaration. Sitting in the company of the famous man didn't seem outrageous because Roosevelt was a friend of the West. The robust outdoorsman cheered on national parks in Montana and North Dakota and understood why people preferred solitude. She reflected later: "He realized that I was a symbol of democracy and he didn't want that symbol destroyed. He was friend of my brother's."

After the initial agitation of the Zimmerman note, pressure escalated from friends, suffrage colleagues and especially Wellington to support an upcoming war vote. Jeannette's official duties as a member of Congress began at noon on March 4, 1917, although the 65th Congress wasn't scheduled to assemble until December 3, more than a year after Jeannette's election. Already her secretaries had opened her office at the Capitol. On March 20, Anna Howard Shaw sent a letter to Rankin to apologize for her belated congratulations. "You remember I did not think your candidacy wise," Shaw wrote from Florida. "I thought it was too soon for a woman to go to Congress and I was too fond of you personally to see you ridiculed, persecuted and misrepresented as I feared you would be.... I was mistaken ... the great change which is sweeping over the country in its attitude toward suffrage ...

has done away with all of the ground for fear."[82]

On March 27, Rankin traveled to Chattanooga, Tennessee, where a women's club would "tender" a luncheon in her honor at Hotel Patten. Rankin arrived on the train at dawn. She rested a few hours, dined with several dozen women at tables adorned with suffrage themes, and then lectured that evening at Pilgrim Congregational Church. An "overflowing house" was predicted for the lecture, attended heartily by members of the Chattanooga Equal Suffrage Association. All of them were listed in the *Chattanooga News* by their husbands' names, as societal norms dictated in those days.

"As you no doubt know, the recent election was the first in which the women of Montana participated as voters, and they surely shattered some traditions brought some radical changes," Rankin was quoted in the newspaper. "One of these latter was to elect me, who had never before held a political office of any kind, as a representative to Washington. Another was voting 'dry' the state, which for many years had been known as the 'wettest' in the Union."[83]

Rankin's official appearance as the country's strange new wonder would come much earlier than she expected. President Wilson called an emergency session of Congress for April 2. She interrupted her speaking tour and hurried to Washington.

Early that morning, a reporter from the *Washington Times* appeared at Rankin's apartment at 2230 California Street to interview her. He asked what significance she intended to bestow on her term in public office. Flustered at being called to Washington unexpectedly, she explained: "You know, I am in a pretty predicament. I had no idea Congress was going to open so soon. At least, I didn't realize it and I made engagements to speak which kept me from getting here until today.... I have so much to learn that I don't know what to say and what not to say. So I have just decided not to say anything at all, for the present at least."

Rankin fretted over the reaction of Capitol Hill's cigar-chomping, desk-pounding veterans. She knew that in the fragile climate of suffrage, a show of ignorance about the transaction of business in Congress could play into the hands of her critics. Because she was the first woman to take a seat, even if it was a whopping 131 years after the nation's founding, she would become an easy target for critics who were intent on upholding the stereotype of female obedience.

For this, Rankin had good reason to exercise care. In some circles, she had been cast as a misplaced housewife who would lend comic relief to the intensity of America's serious political matters. "Not long ago she tramped through deep snow potting bears and wolves, just for pastime," wrote one breathless reporter, dutifully assuring readers that Rankin "refused to forsake the old household arts — cooking and needlework."[84] Another account called her "a slip of a girl" while other salacious stories portrayed her as an Annie Oakley suffragist right out of cattle country who packed a .44-caliber six-shooter and trimmed her skirts with fur. Her physical appearance was given such prominence that Americans might have known her as a painted cowgirl hussy of the Calamity Jane variety.

Luckily for Rankin, more accurate comments from responsible people balanced the picture. Zoe Beckley satirized in the *New York Evening Mail* that she was "glad, glad, glad even to Pollyannaism that Jeannette is not 'freakish' or 'mannish' or 'stand offish' or 'shrewish' or of any type likely to antagonize the company of gentlemen whose realm had hitherto been invaded by the petticoats."[85] Said a Montana rancher in an interview with the *Chicago Sunday Herald*: "Jeannette will make 'em sit up and take notice. She comes from fighting stock and carries a kick in her arguments." Said Wellington of his sister: "Her life is devoted to the cause of mankind and government, first, last and always."

Despite all the ballyhoo, Rankin remained typically feminine from the mass of brown hair streaked with gray to the tops of her less fashionable, but more practical "ground grippers." She wore her hair *a la Pompadour*, emphasizing its abundance and presumably to draw attention away from her nose, which she thought was too large. She dressed in well-fitted and expensive New York-made garments. In contrast to many plump women of the day, she had an air of Montana hardiness about her.

Writer Donald Wilhelm recounted in an article in *The Independent* how he had anticipated interviewing Rankin as "something of a social event" but found himself stammering in her presence. He said to her: "I hardly know whether to address you as 'Congressman' or 'Miss Congressman' or 'Congresswoman' or as 'Miss Congresswoman' or as 'Miss Rankin.'" Looking him over, Rankin coolly replied: "It makes no difference at all."[86]

Lita Barnett, one of Jeannette's teachers, described the Rankin family as "the most forward-looking, democratic family I have ever known. Perhaps their mother instilled into them the desire for reform work; they all have it. Their home was a tranquil, peace-loving place for constructive thinking." Jeannette, Barnett said, was a self-effacing person caught in a swirl of fame. "If Jeannette Rankin were to come up to us now, if I were to greet her and beg her to tell me all the election story, she would say with a twinkle, 'Oh come now. Let's go out and buy a hat.' She is a womanly woman."[87]

In a symbolic thank you for her election to Congress, national suffragists representing all factions arranged an honor breakfast for Rankin at the Shoreham Hotel in Washington, DC, before her introduction to fellow Members of Congress on April 2. Many of the women were the old mothers of suffrage, much older than Rankin. Some had worked since the days of Reconstruction after the Civil War when suffrage became entwined with slavery abolition. "The day of our deliverance is at hand," suffrage legend Carrie Chapman Catt told 150 women gathered in the room. "And I know, as we all know, that this deliverance is to be at the hand of a woman." Said Julia Lathrop, a national children's advocate: "Now that we have a pull in Congress, there is no telling what we will accomplish." Harriet Laidlaw rose to "shout hurrah for Jeannette Rankin."

It had been a good winter for suffrage. In February the legislatures of Ohio and Indiana had given women the right to vote. In March, the governor of Arkansas had signed a bill granting women the right to vote in primary elections. It was the first break for suffrage in the entire South. Soon after came Nebraska, Michigan and Rhode Island. The latter, the first state for suffrage on the Atlantic seaboard, gave women the right to vote for presidential electors. In fewer than eight months, state legislative action had raised the number of electoral votes, dependent in part on women, from ninety-one to 172.

That day in Washington invited true hope of a suffrage victory. Food went uneaten as women diverse in opinion as National Woman's Party leader Alice Paul, suffrage lobbyist Maud Wood Park and writer Katharine Anthony spoke of the "sterling worth of the feminine legislator," their hearts light with rare joy after years of hard work and frustration.

When the suffragists finished their testimonials, Rankin rose to speak. The women pushed back their chairs and stood for an ovation. Rankin, wearing a black sailor hat and a dark chiffon gown over white silk, stood in embarrassment beside a bank of red and yellow spring flowers. She waited for the clapping to stop, eyes sparkling from tears, before she began her prepared text. In a low-pitched voice, easily heard in the dead silence of the room, she spoke. "There will be many times when I will make mistakes," she said. "I need your encouragement and support. I know I will get it. I promise...."[88] Some reports claimed she sank into her chair, biting her lip.

The breakfast had been a forum for strong, confident words from many mouths, but with a theme: Jeannette Rankin. Only thirty years earlier she had been racing through the range grass surrounding her family's ranch house. Now she was the hope of millions of women and intended to represent them the best she could. All western states and some Midwestern states had given women full voting rights before Rankin's election, but others had approved only partial rights and most of the eastern and southern states had refused suffrage. Only a federal amendment would erase decades of frustration. Rankin's constituents in those states sensed she would listen to their needs and demands. They tugged at Rankin mercilessly to represent them.

Her suffrage sisters expected a right to vote by federal amendment. Farmers in eastern Montana who had voted her into Congress wanted tariff protection from agents who bought grain at second-grade prices and sold it at a premium. She had campaigned on that very point, expressing concern that once war ended in Europe, needy countries would flood the United States with goods.[89] She promised farmers that she would work to simplify the Farm Loan Act and seek amendments to the Federal Grain Grading and Inspection Law "as to take this important matter entirely out of the hands of state political influences .... Only by so doing [sic] can the existing evils of state political control be done away with."[90]

Miners back home wanted protection from the copper corporation that employed them. Julia Lathrop depended on Rankin to secure legislation to help the US Children's Bureau. Alice Paul wanted her to represent pacifists. Carrie Chapman

Catt discouraged a pacifist stand, envisioning it would imply an image of hysterical women ill-suited for congressional duty. Wellington, her brother, implored her to avoid controversial issues — especially a conspicuous vote against war — to preserve her reelection chances in Montana.

The many faces at breakfast that morning reminded Rankin of the immense task awaiting her. White armbands in the room signaled hostilities between pacifist Paul and militarist Chapman Catt. A truce had been called to celebrate Rankin's election. Paul sat on Rankin's left; Catt, to her right. Each foresaw an opposite role the new member of Congress must play to make women a powerful force in government.

If a war declaration came to a vote in Congress, Rankin would face the uneasy task of deciding which suffrage faction she should represent. Considering that her immediate intention was to unite all American women, this was a tragic turn. All the national political parties had adopted resolutions calling for suffrage by federal amendment. The Socialist Party had been the first in 1912. The Republican, Democratic, Progressive and Prohibition parties had followed in the summer of 1916.[91] The United States already was more than a century old and women still couldn't vote. Suddenly the nation had changed in a few short weeks. Jeannette Rankin was about to taste the power of war.

8 ~ A symbol for women, then comes war

'Why should violence be more patriotic than reason?'

From the Shoreham Hotel, the nation's first woman in Congress rode to Suffrage House, the national headquarters at 1626 Rhode Island Avenue, where she spoke briefly from the balcony to a crowd on the street. Then the big moment came to make her debut in Congress. She climbed into the back seat of an open touring car, smiling at onlookers while the gloved, capped chauffeur eased the automobile into a parade that included suffragists from nearly all forty-eight states.

The flag-draped automobiles swept down Pennsylvania Avenue. Crowds of people hurrying toward the Capitol cheered as they witnessed the Lady from Montana making history. Rankin, hardly comfortable with the fanfare, waved back. When the procession stopped near the South entrance to the Capitol, photographers rushed to her car, pushing and shoving for a clear portrait.

Already that morning the Capitol was swarming with hundreds of peacekeepers, known as "antis," who had come from New York to protest potential United States involvement in Europe's fighting. They wore white badges that read, "Keep Us Out of War," and carried white tulips. As the day wore on, hundreds more protesters arrived from western states. Squads of police kept them at bay in the broad plaza in front of the Capitol. Delegations of "Patriotic Pilgrims" and other militarist groups jeered and hooted from the sidelines.[92]

Rankin stood on the Capitol steps beneath the Dome while dozens of cameras clicked away. Then she hurried to the Cannon House Office Building where she rode Elevator No. 7 to the third floor. She walked down a white corridor with high ceilings to room No. 332, across the hall from Moses Kincaid, a Republican from Nebraska. A Democrat from Maryland, Jesse Price, occupied an office to one side of her. To the other was Representative William Carter, a Republican from Massachusetts. Florence Leech, Rankin's secretary from Valier, Montana, had arrived early to open the office and prepare Rankin's calendar for the sensation that would follow. Spring flowers of every accent and hue decorated sills and shelves.

Before Rankin could remove her gloves, delegations of clamoring school girls, pacifists, anti-pacifists and others surrounded her, eager to shake her hand. Admirers shoved autograph books at her. Some asked to carry part of her bouquet when she took her oath of office. She would earn $7,500 a year as a Member of Congress, equal to the buying power of more than $137,000 a century later. To Rankin the election wasn't about money but at last, a voice for women and children. She rarely mentioned her salary.

She walked to the Capitol from her office just before 11:30 that morning. Throngs of suffragists had come to see her step into history. Pages and doorkeepers ushered visitors to the galleries. Many people in the crowd speculated aloud about how the woman who had caused so much national excitement would look and act in a sea of men. It was a bellwether day in Congress, until then an exclusive place for male lawmakers in the nation's entire history. Half an hour before noon, every seat in the galleries was filled. People crowded into the aisles. A buzz of conversation rippled over the crowd as members of the House assembled in the august chamber below. They drifted to their seats as the hands of the big clock turned under the press gallery, where news reporters watched with pencils poised. A door near the front of the chamber opened.

Clutching her bouquet of purple and yellow flowers, her hat hung in the cloakroom as decorum dictated, Jeannette Rankin entered the House of Representatives at five minutes to noon. She gripped the arm of her Montana colleague, John Evans. She wore a dark blue dress, trimmed with lighter blue and white chiffon, tailored by a New York dressmaker who had exchanged his services for legal consultation with Wellington. This was a concession for her because she enjoyed making her clothes. The silky gown "made you wish you had bet with the man who had predicted she would come dressed as a cowgirl from the ranch," cheeky Belle Fligelman would muse years later.[93] Eventually Jeannette lamented that her many fine dresses, including three evening dresses she wore in Congress, had been packed into trunks at one of Wellington's ranches and eventually stolen. "I haven't got anything to show for them, except some pictures," she told her friend Hannah Josephson.[94]

Hundreds of her colleagues waited in the chambers. They rose and applauded as Rankin entered. Ellen Maury Slayden, a gossip of the Washington social set and wife of a Member of Congress from Texas, observed in a published journal of memories: "And here she was coming in, escorted by an elderly colleague, looking like a mature bride rather than a strong-minded female.... It would have been sickening if she had smirked or giggled or been coquettish; worse still if she had been masculine and hail-fellowish. She was just a sensible young woman going about her business.... She was not pretty, but had an intellectual face and a nice manner."[95]

Rankin stopped at a seat on the center aisle of the Republican side in the second row from the back. Wellington and their mother Olive Rankin watched from the crowded gallery. When Jeannette's name was bellowed during roll call, opening the Sixty-fifth Congress, the tide of men around her stood and cheered. Handkerchiefs waved from the galleries. The ovation continued until Rankin rose and bowed first to the Republican side, then to the Democratic side. Speaker James "Champ" Clark pounded for order.[96] Before the new Representative Rankin could sit, men jostled to shake her hand. They stood in line behind Evans, all of them waiting for an introduction to this female creature voted to sit among them. She returned the courtesies with a frank smile. The informal reception went on for hours.[97]

The House was evenly divided, with 215 Republicans, 215 Democrats and five independents. First came the reelection of Clark, a Democrat from Missouri, followed by a swearing-in of new members. When Rankin went forward to take her oath, Evans walked with her. Although a Democrat, he sat with her on the Republican side most of the day. Also visiting was Montana's Thomas J. Walsh, who came from the Senate to partake of this historic moment.

When the long business of organizing the House started, Rankin introduced her first legislation. She joined five representatives and five senators in a joint resolution calling for suffrage by federal amendment. It was a landmark moment, however subdued by war news. Rankin did her duty as the nation's most influential suffragist. Congress had defeated the legislation previously because of opposition to woman suffrage altogether in some states, mostly in the South, and because of a related belief that states should decide their individual suffrage laws instead of making it a federal issue. Political parties in 1916 had called for suffrage through state action, not federal amendment, but suffragists weren't discouraged. Strong suffrage machines had been built in northern states. Women in six states voted in the 1916 presidential election. The first woman was voted into Congress. Jeannette Rankin, iconic in every way, took her elected seat as suffragists neared ever closer to their destiny.

A procession of details about standing committees, conferences and agendas continued until 7:47 when the House adjourned. It would reconvene in less than an hour, at 8:40, to hear President Wilson's speech about the war in Europe. Rankin, all the buzz, had yet to make her own speech on the House floor. The *New York Sun* cast a curious premonition of her symbolism when it predicted that the first time she arose to make a speech she would create a greater stir than the day Buck Kilgore of Texas kicked down the Speaker's door in the House of Representatives in a partisan row over federal election bills. The strapping Texan left quite an impression, smashing the nose of a fellow member who was standing behind the door. Comparing Kilgore's wreckage to Rankin's first words was an odd reach but the imagery was clear. He was remembered. So would she.

Seating the first woman in Congress was a comforting distraction to the president's forthcoming war message, which he would deliver to a joint session of House and Senate. By late afternoon, the plaza outside the Capitol teemed with sightseers, police, pacifists, suffragists and news reporters. A troop of cavalry arrived to guard the president.

The United States had already broken off diplomatic relations with Germany. Still, some members of Congress believed Wilson would not ask for a war declaration. They thought of Wilson as an isolationist, if not a pacifist, but headlines screamed something different. In February 1917, German U-boats sunk 785,500 tons of American shipping, including two United States ships that had received warnings only minutes before torpedoes struck, allowing crews to escape. More attacks followed in March. Wilson was worried.

The president quaked at what he was about to ask of the 65th Congress. He understood he would be asking for license to expend American lives. Ten minutes before he spoke, Rankin and other House members returned to their seats. Spectators packed the public galleries. Foreign ambassadors and their wives filled the Diplomatic Gallery. Extra chairs were placed in front of the chamber for senators, cabinet members, Supreme Court justices and experts on international law. Brittle silence gripped the hall.

At mid-evening on April 2, Wilson departed for the United States Capitol in his black Pierce-Arrow limousine. The nation awaited his speech. Crowds lining Pennsylvania Avenue clapped as the president swept past them. He was an uncomfortable leader, worried his call to arms would be a stunning contradiction to his campaign promise, "He kept us out of war," that he delivered with such passion five months earlier. Everyone knew what Wilson was about to do. In recent weeks, German submarines had torpedoed and sunk four American ships. The war in Europe riled many members of Congress, most of them Republicans, who called for American intervention. Wilson already had met with his cabinet. Secretary of State Robert Lansing and nine other members encouraged him to place the war question before the nation's lawmakers.

The city shook with war news. Wilson entered the joint session at 8:37 p.m. to a prolonged welcome. When the applause died, he rose to the podium and spoke of "the spirit of ruthless brutality" that war would bring. He recalled that he had, in his message to Congress on February 26, favored a foreign policy of "armed neutrality." That was no longer practical, he said, because the German government now regarded American merchant ships as pirates. Wilson had decided that Germany's reckless aggression would continue unless the United States raised a military to help the Allies. "We have no quarrel with the German people," he said, "but only with their aggressive rulers." The Prussian autocracy had filled the United States with spies, Wilson said, who had tried to persuade Mexico to turn against her northern neighbor. The United States would fight a war not only for itself but for the German people and all nations big and small. His speech, recorded as "House Document Number One" in the new Congress, argued that aggressive actions by the German government amounted to war against the United States. "We must make the world safe for democracy!" he implored to thundering ovation. Wilson warned of "many months of fiery trial and sacrifice ahead of us."

Having imparted a request for war, the president left the Capitol at 9:11 p.m. for the White House. There, in the Cabinet Room, he sat "silent and pale" with his secretary, J.P. Tumulty, for a long time. Finally, Wilson said: "Think what it was they were applauding. My message today was a message of death for our young men. How strange it seems to applaud that."

The Senate began debate on Wilson's request the next morning, voting in favor on April 4. Only six senators opposed the resolution. One of them was George Norris, a Republican from Nebraska, who said passing it meant "we will have joined Europe in the great catastrophe and taken America into entanglements that will not end with this war, but will live and bring their evil influences upon many generations yet unborn."[98] At midmorning the next day, the House Committee on Foreign Affairs moved to the floor a resolution declaring war on Germany. A prayer opened what would become a fifteen-hour debate: "Great Jehovah, if it be Thy will to bring peace and liberty to the world, give speedy triumph to our armies."

Jeannette Rankin had never cast a vote in Congress. She

had come to the House of Representatives from Montana amid great pageantry and curiosity before celebrations over the first woman elected to Congress suddenly withered in the presence of war. Rankin told her secretaries, Belle Fligelman and Florence Leech, that everyone assumed the debate would end early that evening and the House would vote to embrace war. Arguments wore on, seemingly unlimited in their length, as members of the House rose in turn to offer fiery endorsements of a call to arms, or eloquent appeals to reconsider. Many members wept as they spoke. "It takes neither moral nor physical courage to declare a war for others to fight," said Representative Claude Kitchin of North Carolina, who led Democrats in the House. "Half the civilized world is now a slaughterhouse for human beings. This nation is the last hope of peace on earth, good will toward men. I am unwilling for my country, by statutory command, to pull up the last anchor of peace in the world and extinguish during the long night of a worldwide war the only remaining star of hope for Christendom."[99]

Representative Fred Britten of Illinois threatened an amendment to the war resolution calling for an act of Congress before American troops were sent to fight on land in Europe, Asia or Africa. "I do not believe the great masses of our people are in favor of such a resolution [meaning a complete declaration of war], and I am certain they are opposed to the use of our military in the bloody trench warfare which has already annihilated the flower of the youth of the most civilized countries on earth," he argued. The amendment failed.

By the morning of April 6, it was reported, 100 speeches had been made in the House for or against the war resolution. Jeannette Rankin, an accomplished orator, remained silent. The crowd never left the galleries. Everyone wanted to witness impassioned arguments and tearful pleas. Lobbyists poured into the Capitol representing every known "patriotic militarist" and "idealistic pacifist" organization in the country, all of them arguing for their cause. Belle Fligelman later recalled that it was an easier time for Members of Congress who supported war "or who had the capacity to confuse war with patriotism."[100]

In the hours and days after Wilson's address, anxious friends and adversaries crammed into Rankin's new office to convince the Lady from Montana how she should vote on the war resolution. This wasn't just any vote. It was the first national vote by a woman. Rankin's vote would define women for the ages. A few earnest men and women came to urge her to stand firm with her pledge to vote against war. Far more attempted to persuade her that failing to vote in favor of a war resolution would delay suffrage a quarter of a century. They said it would show women as unpatriotic, weak and sentimental, and hurt the states that had passed suffrage referendums.

Scores of women who urged Rankin to change her mind were renowned suffragists. Many of them had contributed generously to her campaign for Congress and to the dogged campaign for a constitutional amendment that would assure them a place at the ballot box. Rankin owed gratitude to these women. Only a few days earlier, their political views were identical to hers. Now her friends were telling her she would pay a heavy price to honor her personal convictions. Some of them, Fligelman would recall, accused the Lady from Montana of exposing American womanhood to the world's scorn by refusing to face this international emergency. To this, Rankin replied: "Why should violence be more patriotic than reason?"[101]

By the age of thirty-six, Jeannette Rankin was a passionate reformer. She took the position that government could and must provide relief for Americans. Her election to Congress made her the headline of a decades-long, evolving story. Every woman in America who wanted the right to vote knew about Jeannette Rankin. She had arrived in Washington as a novelty to men but a beacon for women. The suffragists who supported her expected she would win them an amendment to the US Constitution to cast ballots and determine their political destinies. That's what they wanted from her. Lesser known was her distaste for war, which she saw as an illogical response to international disputes. It was deeply imbedded in her, even intractable. That's what her brother Wellington knew. He pleaded with her. Don't vote no.

After President Wilson's plea for war, in which he reasoned that German aggression endangered American democracy, arguments raged in Rankin's office for hours. She had been absent from the House chambers for most of the debate that followed Wilson's address, held captive by the many people who crowded into the room.

One of them was old guard suffrage leader Carrie Chapman Catt, who had returned to New York and hurried back to Washington on a late-night train. She pleaded with Rankin that voting against the war resolution would destroy any hope of a federal suffrage amendment, which Catt saw as Rankin's principal purpose in Congress. Harriet Laidlaw, whose money had largely sustained Rankin since the early days of suffrage and helped fund her congressional campaign, also urged a vote for war. Don't cast a vote that impresses on a nation of men, she told Rankin, that women are too weak and incompetent to hold office during a crisis.

The horde began the emotional tug-of-war early on the morning of April 5, a Thursday, and carried it into the night. It was well past midnight, on Good Friday, when the assemblage in her office thinned. Finally, her pleading friends had worn her down. She was beginning to doubt herself, thinking that maybe she owed them a vote for war. As people drifted away, Wellington Rankin pulled out his fob watch to check the time. The fateful vote would come soon.

At thirty-two years old, he already was one of Montana's best-known criminal trial lawyers. A marvel in the courtroom, ambitious for his Republican Party, for himself, and most generously for his sister, he leaned forward as she sat tormented behind her desk. Laidlaw and her husband James, one of New York's great bankers, remained there too. On this night, these three confidants feared Jeannette would wreck the cause of suffrage. They argued anew with her.

Deep into the chilly night, when word of an impending vote still hadn't come, Wellington dispatched Belle Fligelman across the lawn to the Capitol to measure the progress of the war debate. "Why don't you go over to Congress and see what's going on over there?" he told her in a tone of voice that left no room for dispute. Secretly he wanted to remove the diminutive but fiery little suffragist from the argument.

Belle shared Jeannette's beliefs to the core because they had fought together in Montana's suffrage campaigns. She was loyal to Rankin, unfailingly so, sharing her convictions, doubting nothing. Fligelman, her tiny feet churning her down the dark sidewalk outside the Capitol, watched white doves sweeping into the light that shone on the magnificent dome high above her. She saw them as an omen of peace. She, like Rankin, abided by the belief that war was a creation of men. All those doves in flight reminded Fligelman of the woman she had come to admire. To her they were very much alike, those doves and the Lady from Montana, symbolic to the end. In Fligelman's mind the soaring doves stood for something that was good and free.

Inside the Capitol it was different. Men in black suits rushed about shouting orders. Momentum was building toward a war vote. When she returned to Wellington with the news, he tried once more to dissuade Jeannette from committing what he recognized as political suicide. Vote a man's vote, he told her. Vote for war.[102] Jeannette's pacifist idealism worried Wellington. He knew she acted from conscience. To him, politics was first about survival, not philosophy. In the first few moments of his sister's congressional career, he feared that she was about to ruin her political future. To him, politics came down to details and strategies and often brutal, impersonal decisions.

Wellington had pledged to join the Army Tank Corps to demonstrate his support for the war. The *Montana Progressive* newspaper had described him as "young, vulnerable, controversial, aggressive, vigorous," and to Jeannette he was all of those things. He had been a godsend as her campaign manager. Without his political intuition and party connections she would have lost. He was proving a nuisance with his prediction that if she voted for peace, she would destroy her political support back home. She had campaigned for Congress on the promise that she never would vote to send Montana boys to war. Despite suggestions to the contrary, constituents had implored her to avoid war, but months before the torpedo attacks in the Atlantic Ocean.

Wellington argued that she could go on record against war by speaking on the House floor of its futility. He wanted her to avoid accusations that women "were all alike and opposed to war for sex reasons."[103] She resisted his pleas. Both the Rankins knew Jeannette could avoid controversy by passing on her vote, hardly an unusual occurrence for a freshman in Congress. Both knew that would never happen. After acknowledging that his sister would prefer to go to prison or burn at the stake than vote for war, Wellington conceded. Vote your conscience, he told her.

9 ~ First woman in Congress, first vote

'I want to stand by my country, but I cannot vote for war.'

The bell had rung at last, signaling a call to vote. Jeannette and Wellington Rankin walked out of the House Office Building, joining a parade of troubled faces. Fligelman, exhausted, returned to the apartment she shared with Jeannette and went to bed. Decades later she would remember her distinct hope that Jeannette would notice the doves soaring at the Capitol, easing her pain. Belle hoped that night that Jeannette, the Lady from Montana, might be the most compelling symbol of all. When Rankin entered the House, she found haggard men slumped in their seats. Voices drifted from the galleries above her, where behind fluttering handkerchiefs and crumpled evening editions of the *Times* waited the spellbound faces of men and women who wondered how the first woman in Congress would vote on the war resolution. Messengers and soldiers rushed around in all directions. Hard-boiled representatives listened solemnly to eager lobbyists. Several lawmakers, shouting from the benches, declared their desire to vote for war. Others wept.

Britten of Illinois, a proponent of the resolution, asked the House to return the declaration to the Committee on Foreign Affairs for an amendment stating no American would be sent to Europe, Africa or Asia without the consent of Congress.

Members killed the motion, believing soldiers would not be sent overseas anyway. Representative Murray Hulbert, a Democrat from New York, arose and moved for adjournment until Monday. He was Catholic and didn't want war declared on a holy day. His motion failed. His attempt to move the war resolution back to committee for further discussion failed as well. Arguments for a war declaration dominated. Some members thought the Huns would turn and run at a threat of American intervention.

Rankin took her seat toward the back of the great hall in the House of Representatives. The debate wore on. One member after another arose to argue in favor of war. The Lady from Montana, barely acquainted with House rules, remained silent. She glanced now and then at the big clock above the ranks of witnesses to this historic event.

Peace never seemed so lonely, unpopular and untried. Exhausted, Rankin fought the impulse to cry. The debate was nearly finished and soon she would be required to cast her vote. Just two days earlier, the Senate had voted eighty-two to six for a war declaration. The Senate had voted with only eight abstentions, and a similar determination for a war declaration was evident in the House. Tonight, a nation stirred by President Wilson's call for intervention in a European war pressed Rankin and her colleagues for action.

Across the nation, pro-war speakers preached the virtues of patriotism. Newspaper accounts detailed how the country was arming itself. Woodrow Wilson, in his haste to equip a huge American army, commissioned the military to buy miles of cloth for uniforms and bandages even before Congress decided the war resolution. Bids went out for leggings, shoes, hats, buttons, badges, tents and neckties. The War Department determined how many safety pins a volunteer army of two million men required. Manufacturers produced tent poles, rifles, batteries, butcher knives, saddles, horse brushes and telescopes.

"The vast expenditures of the Allies in this country have perfected American manufacturers in producing shrapnel and explosive shells," the *San Francisco Examiner* had reported on April 1, 1917. "Rifle manufacturing is by far the most difficult of all munitions business, there being over 2,000 operations in the manufacturing of a single rifle."

Secretary of the Navy Joseph Daniels and Secretary of War Newton D. Baker appealed to the nation's young men to join the military. The American mood rapidly accommodated their pleas. Telegrams poured into the Oval Office, beseeching President Wilson to clothe his notions of mercy and humanity in a doughboy's uniform to intimidate warring nations and bring quick relief to misguided and suffering people. Americans were dizzy with war fever.

It was three hours past midnight on Good Friday. In minutes, the resolution would come to the House floor. From their lair in the press gallery, reporters watched America's first woman in Congress alternately bow her head and raise her eyes as if in search of advice from a higher power. How would she vote?

They saw a distraught thirty-six-year-old woman. She was, some of them wrote, a pleasant contrast to the stark background of pressed black suits and starched white collars. She lifted her anguished face to look at the high ceiling. Strands of her hair, tied in a knot at the top of her head, hung somewhat loose and tousled. In public appearances Rankin wore a hat, believing it detracted attention from her nose and a scar on her neck. *The Nation* wrote in a seemingly autopsy-like fashion that her nose was her most distinguishable feature, "which is large, straight in outline, and fairly dominates the face, particularly in profile. The chin stands out well, but is round, and reduced in conspicuousness by a fulness [sic] of the cheeks which extends down to the line of the jaw." *The Nation* also commended her for "unmasculine makeup" and for prompt and regular attendance in the House chambers. Tonight she wore no hat. She clasped her hands to her throat, more out of distress than trying to hide her scar.[104]

In those final moments before the roll call, she thought of the many arguments of the past three days. Everyone except the pacifists urged her to vote for war. She couldn't ignore the pleas of her many suffrage sisters who had begged her not to jeopardize the chances of a federal suffrage amendment with an unpopular vote. Rankin would say later that to her, war seemed futile, absurd and criminal. It slaughtered young men and ignored, she would argue, the welfare of women and children. She had no doubt that Congress was being asked to vote for a commercial war — that none of the idealistic hopes that Wilson expounded would be realized. As early as 1914, Rankin signaled her belief that greed caused wars. She wrote to New York legislator Stephen J. Stillwell that "there can be no solution of such problems as international war and our brutal treatment of each other as long as we have a great economic war going on."[105]

She found the rhetoric of the militarists easy to dispute, but to oppose Wellington and her well-meaning friends and supporters pained her. She promised to listen to anybody who favored war. She would not vote until the final moment. During the suffrage campaigns, when she had come to the House as a visitor, she had watched indecisive members sometimes delaying their votes until the second roll call. That's what she would do on this night.

She suspected Civil War veterans in the House would vote against the resolution because they knew war was neither a noble principle nor a path to glory but a killing field. She saw hesitation all around her. The business of deciding war wouldn't come after cool heads reviewed facts. Declarations of war came from anger, from emotion, and passion swirled around Rankin like an eddy. Speech after speech, person after person, accusation after accusation, declared that a vote against war was unpatriotic. It would mean opening the United States to enemies who would invade and destroy.

Finally, at nearly three in the morning, the reading clerk began the roll call. "It was so quiet in the gallery and on the floor it seemed you could hear the workings of a man's conscience," Fligelman would remember.

"Rankin?" called the clerk. She didn't answer. A great silence settled on the room.

"Rankin?" he asked again. Still she failed to respond. She stared again at the ceiling, her face drawn with despair. As the clerk resumed his roll call, the galleries hummed. Was the Lady from Montana going to wait for the second roll call to cast her vote? That procedure was reserved for members of Congress not seated for the first roll call. Rankin's fellow lawmakers turned in their chairs and stared at her, mystified. Perhaps she was too new to understand all the rules.

Representative "Uncle Joe" Cannon of Illinois entered the chamber after the first roll call and, after being told that Rankin hadn't voted, went to her. She lifted her expectant eyes. "Little woman," he reportedly told her, "you cannot afford not to vote. You represent the womanhood of the country in the American Congress. I shall not advise you how to vote, but you should vote one way or the other, as your conscience dictates."

Nothing was more frightening to Rankin than the prospect of stalling suffrage for American women. Worse yet, the idea that she would be sending American sons to war made her blood run cold. She felt gentle pressure on her shoulder and looked into the eyes of her friend and comrade in the struggle for suffrage, the incomparable Quaker pacifist Alice Paul. "Who wants the vote at this price?" Paul asked softly.[106]

"We'll keep on working, Jeannette. Vote your conscience." Rankin squeezed her friend's hand and turned her attention back to the podium.

Reading clerk Patrick J. Haltigan began the second roll call, this time getting to "Rankin" much faster. She hesitated. Then she rose from her chair to speak the thirteen words for which she would be most remembered: "I want to stand by my country, but I cannot vote for war." Simple words, spoken quietly enough that many people in the chamber didn't hear her, but fodder nonetheless for a storm of national criticism from everyone convinced that women were unfit to hold public office. For a moment she remained standing to cries of "Vote! Vote!" Then she sank back in her chair with the words, "I vote no." They were inaudible to almost everyone.

A few people in the gallery applauded. Then a hush settled over the great hall. Rankin had violated a precedent, as old as the nation, that forbade House comments during roll call. That was a privilege reserved for senators. The reading clerk, too shocked to hear her vote over the noise, came to her on the floor to verify her vote. He then went to House Speaker Champ Clark for instructions. "Continue the call," Clark told him, and the clerk recorded Rankin as having cast a no vote.[107]

She bowed her head until the roll call was finished. Forty-nine of her colleagues voted with her but the outcome was clear. In precisely twelve minutes the US House of Representatives had voted to declare war on Germany. Thus, thirty-two Republicans, sixteen Democrats, one Prohibitionist and one Socialist had voted no. Rankin hurried out of the House. For the first time in the nation's history, a woman had participated in a referendum on war. She consoled herself that the first vote cast by a woman in the US Congress was a vote for peace. Little did she know how that single vote, in good ways and in bad, would define her life. So many people would know her as a champion for peace and justice. Others would remember her as a historical oddity and condemn her for treason. Yet, something new and different had happened. Congress had heard the first words ever spoken by a woman from the floor in either chamber. Like the breaking of dawn that was soon to come in Washington, it was a new day for American women.

Fiorello LaGuardia would recall that moment in his autobiography years later: "The clerk read the names slowly. Every Member was in his seat. 'Yes,' Aye' and an occasional 'No' resounded solemnly in the tense chamber. The clerk reached the 'Rs' and Jeannette Rankin's name was called. It was a firm and unbroken rule of the House that no comment could be made during a roll call. It was either 'Yes' or 'No.' Then Jeannette Rankin broke a precedent of 140 years.... There was a hush. The reading clerk turned to the Speaker. Tally clerks awaited instructions. 'Continue the call,' said Champ Clark, and Miss Rankin was reported in the negative."[108]

Some minutes later the House adjourned. It was 3:14 in the morning. The final vote: 373 for war, 50 against, nine not voting. So in the coldest, darkest hour of Good Friday morning, the "People's House" had approved President Wilson's request to start war with Germany. Possibly more significant than Rankin's iconic election to Congress was that the first woman in American history had cast a vote against an international conflict.

Jeannette joined a scowling Wellington in the hallway. Together they left the Capitol and walked in the cool night air. The sun would rise in a few hours. Wellington found his sister subdued. "You know you're not going to be reelected," he admonished her. It pained him to talk to her this way. In his mind he was her closest friend. He knew the pressure he had put on her hurt her more than anything else. Again, he expressed his worry about her political future.

"Wellington, you know I'm not interested in that. All I'm interested in is what they will say fifty years from now."

Wellington, although angry at the outcome, had known deep in his heart how his sister would vote on a war declaration. She didn't see any hypocrisy in voting the way she did even when his money had helped finance her campaign. It was the Rankin way. Nevertheless, he was crushed that she actually did it. Asleep in the apartment she shared with the first woman ever elected to Congress, Belle Fligelman awoke suddenly to Wellington's persistent voice. "Think what you've done!" she heard him say. Belle squinted at the alarm clock in the weak light from the parlor. The hands showed nearly four hours past midnight on Good Friday, April 6, 1917.

Again Wellington spoke, his temper rising. "Think what you've done!" Jeannette had succeeded in her promise to take a stand against war. She saw her vote as a humanitarian gesture, not the work of a politician fretting over reelection. She had no idea what would come next. Wellington's reaction was only the first ripple in a tidal wave of anger. Much of the discontent came from suffragists who applauded Rankin's honesty but found her careless to the cause, deaf to the drumbeat for an inevitable war.

10 ~ A pacifist is born

'Gripped by a desire to express a woman's horror of war'

When the Senate convened that morning, Vice President Thomas R. Marshall signed the House resolution. A bicycle messenger raced the single sheet of parchment down Pennsylvania Avenue to the White House, where the president dined with his wife Edith. At thirteen minutes after one o'clock, observing the occasion in a short ceremony, Wilson signed the war declaration. At the stroke of a pen, the United States entered what would become the First World War. Within eighteen months more than 322,000 American troops would die or suffer wounds.

An instant after Wilson signed for war, White House usher I.H. Hoover hurried into an outer office where Lieutenant Commander Byron McCandless awaited word of the signing. He stepped outside where he waved signal flags to alert the Navy Department. Wireless operators flashed the news to the Atlantic fleet while whistles blew in Washington. Minutes later, the president signed a proclamation forbidding alien enemies to possess guns or wireless apparatus. Another order called for taking possession of seized German ships. Plans were made to arrest "scores of spies" and to dismiss government employees suspected of pro-German activities.

The nation's first woman in Congress avoided the Cannon House Office Building that day. She stayed at home, unwilling to face friends she had disappointed. Many suffrage leaders — except for Alice Paul, who was jubilant — reacted sadly to Rankin's vote and spoke in the past tense about the prospect of a federal suffrage amendment they had chased so long. It was fair to note that a nation at war wouldn't have time for much else. Still, Rankin became a target for many Americans incredulous that she could be elected to Congress when many states didn't even allow women to vote. Mountains of mail, toted to Rankin's office in blue and white canvas bags, told of the nation's temperament. Although she was one of fifty-six members of Congress voting against the war resolution, she had provided ammunition her male critics needed to discredit the ability of a woman to hold high public office. "You should have a picture of yourself as people really see you," advised Edwin J. Heath of Washington, DC. "You are just a cheap little actress, putting on a sob act to land publicity to help sell tickets for your lecture bureau...."

Much of the reaction, fierce and immediate, came from people shocked that this new creature in Congress — the American woman — should do something that attracted so much attention. "It is possible that no more dramatic scene has been staged in the House of Representatives than when Miss Rankin, casting her initial vote in the lower body, interrupted the roll call to say, in thirteen words, that she could not vote for war," reported the *New York Times*.

For months after her vote, theorists and academicians struggled with interpretations. Somber editorial writers, thumbing through reference books in their newspaper offices, debated the implications of her statement. Did Rankin mean to say that she could not stand by her country if its will was to vote for war? Or did she mean to say that, "I want to stand by my country, therefore, I cannot vote for war?"

That mattered little to people who interpreted the role of

the American woman as a fainting hysteric with a weak will for bare-knuckled male politics. Much criticism focused on Rankin's gentle weeping which, like her tiny handbag, was pinned on her as the emblem of her gender. The daily press, including her hometown newspaper in Missoula, Montana, reported in bold headlines that she had sobbed when she voted. Reporters who had not seen the drama were writing stories about it. Journalist Ernestine Evans, watching Rankin from the balcony, said she saw nothing of the kind.

Ellen Maury Slayden noted, "Miss Rankin's weeping and hysterics when she cast her vote are almost entirely apocryphal." Maud Wood Park, a Capitol Hill suffrage lobbyist who had been sitting in the gallery, remembered Rankin as being composed. Representative Fiorello LaGuardia was asked whether he had seen her weep. "I do not know, for I could not see because of the tears in my own eyes," he said. LaGuardia, who would become one of Rankin's closest friends, later wrote in his autobiography that most members who voted for war "did so in the firm belief that no United States soldier would be sent overseas."

However elusive the facts, the suggestion that a pioneer woman wept in Congress sold newspapers in 1917. In this inference, dozens if not hundreds of papers convinced the American people that Rankin was a blubbering, incompetent fool. An incident of a few second's duration was transformed into a major news event. Among the more objective students of Rankin's vote was a rabbi who questioned why critics had seized on a weeping argument to deny women the ballot. "I have more respect for a woman who cries before she votes upon whether or not we shall have war than for the man who goes to a saloon and takes three highballs in a similar situation," he said.

Wrote Vachel Lindsay to Jane Addams at Hull House: "I hate a hyphenated American. If I had been in Congress I would have voted with Miss Rankin and would have considered it a sufficient reason to say, 'I will not vote for war till she does.'" To the contrary, some women like Kate Hegeman of New York ventured the opinion that Rankin's vote put her crosswise with the majority of Americans and interfered with a war that would bring "permanent peace" to the world.[109]

In surveying the public mood, "Tattler," a columnist for *The Nation* magazine, wrote: "Whether she was visibly and audibly overcome by her emotions — a question on which much stress is laid in certain quarters — we may leave the historians to decide among themselves. Male lawmakers have occasionally exhibited emotional weakness under equally trying conditions, without provoking invidious comments on the capacity of their sex as a whole. Miss Rankin, having happened to be the first and only woman in Congress when the war crisis arose, it is far too soon to draw sweeping conclusions on the wisdom of our latest suffrage experiment." The Tattler speculated that Rankin had killed her chances for political prestige and predicted her attitude toward war never would be expunged from the public record, however earnestly she might devote her energies elsewhere. Of course, this was the same argument Wellington had made to dissuade his sister from casting a vote against war.[110]

Many suffragists believed Rankin's vote had cost them everything in the darkening climate of war. Within a few days they celebrated and dismissed the significance of her election. Some suffragists decided Rankin had become too radical to represent their cause. The hawkish Carrie Chapman Catt remarked bitterly to a friend that Rankin was a "sure enough joker" who hurt the suffrage movement for failing to support war. The Secretary of War appointed Catt to the Women's Committee of the Council of National Defense, of which Anna Howard Shaw chaired, which within six months would implicate thousands of women in wartime activities.[111] Publicly, Catt was benign. "Miss Rankin has done nothing to be ashamed of, far from it, and she can be counted upon to do nothing that she need be ashamed of," she said. "She did her duty as her duty appeared to her. ... I predicted two weeks ago that no matter how Miss Rankin voted she would be criticized. If she voted for war, she would offend the pacifists. If she voted against it, she would offend the militarists."[112]

Harriet Laidlaw had watched the war vote from the House gallery before she returned to New York City. To her, Rankin became a tragic figure in an iconoclastic moment in history. Describing Rankin's personal agony as "one of the most terrible mental struggles any woman ever had," she told the *New York Times*: "It is not true that Miss Rankin wept, fainted, or had to be carried from her seat. She was perfectly composed. She had been asked by so many of her friends to vote for the resolution; at the same time, she was gripped by a desire to express a woman's horror of war and her principles against it. When she finally voted, she voted with intense sincerity, knowing that she was not doing the popular thing, but refusing to allow herself to be governed by motives of expediency. She just couldn't vote for war."[113]

Always the practical woman, Rankin considered the weeping stories the only weapon the militarists could use against her. They did it effectively, and the hyperbole soon cast her as a tragic misled woman who had exceeded her capabilities. Failing to deliver a public explanation after her statement, "I want to stand by my country, but I cannot vote for war," led to more criticism. Given no more substantial basis to judge her character, her silence made her the target of ridicule and scorn. "The statement she made on the floor of Congress is equal to saying, 'I know what my duty is, but being a woman, I can't do it,'" concluded Guy Norman, a Rhode Island state senator.

Some critics were unable to accept the innovation of a woman voting on serious political matters in Congress. Robert Watson, a Scotch-Presbyterian minister, complained to his congregation that if Jeannette Rankin was not willing to stand by her country in a "terrible and trying" hour, she should resign at once: "We need women who have the spirit of Mary of Bethany to strengthen us for the hard but necessary sacrifices that confront us." Typical of contrary points of view, Annie S. Peck of New York wrote: "No women can represent all women any more than one man represents all men. Let us, either men or women, not be too savage or unkindly critical of a young woman who in a difficult, untried position acts conscientiously."[114]

In Montana, Rankin's predominately rural constituency relied on her to introduce legislation that would improve their farming and mining interests, but they did not expect her to take a controversial position that would distract attention from their agendas. Her hometown *Missoulian* newspaper, under the ownership of Joseph M. Dixon, had supported Rankin during her congressional campaign. When he sold it in April 1917 it became an Anaconda Copper mouthpiece and its editorial mood became ugly after her war vote. A front-page political cartoon showed a beautiful, busty girl in a white robe presenting Uncle Sam with a lengthy scroll of war pledges. The caption, blossoming from Uncle Sam's mouth, said: "Any gift from the city that gave us Congressman Rankin will be doubled accepted." Imojean Earl Younger, an apparent Montana native, saluted Rankin's patriotism for standing against war but wrote: "What has possessed the entire state of Montana? They seem to have gone war crazy. I was surprised in the recent papers I've seen at the fighting spirit manifested."[115]

The unanswered question, however, was why Rankin should receive more negative attention for her vote than all the men who joined her in protest, or the men who abstained to avoid trouble with their constituencies. Courtesy and justice, her sympathizers argued, demanded she should receive no more critical attention for her actions and votes from editors and correspondents than any other new member of Congress. The symbolism of her presence took a new twist. How could one woman represent womanhood more than one man could represent manhood?

As the first woman in Congress, Rankin could not avoid the landslide of public scrutiny. "I feel it is a source of satisfaction that you, representing in a way all the women of the country, took the stand you did," wrote an office secretary for the Woman's Peace Party, who thanked Rankin for her "splendid" defiance of war. The "practical men" of the House believed she missed an opportunity to assist the advancement of women in federal government circles, although they generally regarded her vote as one dictated by women's distaste for war.

If anything saved Rankin from the wave of criticism, it was the empathy of her more endearing colleagues in the House who attended to her as a big family of boys fawning over a little sister. She accepted their companionship with dignity. While fellow members of Congress overwhelmed her with attention, the press continued to rant about her unsuitability for office. A reporter who cornered her to ask if she had found any new boyfriends among fellow members was told abruptly: "I expect to put in my time here learning the ropes."

She had a greater worry, too. She suspected an international plot to lead the United States into war — if not by research, by instinct — and was suspicious of the Lusitania incident, when the Germans torpedoed and sank a British ocean liner with 128 Americans among the passengers. Rumors that the passenger ship was loaded with explosives as a decoy to entice the Germans into battle — and subsequently, the Americans into war — abounded freely after the powerful ship perished in fire. If Rankin sensed a conspiracy she didn't mention it on the House floor in the days after she cast her vote.

Rankin's many critics, in their haste to pin a badge of treason on the "Lady from Montana," failed to understand that she saw in their enthusiasm for a European war a corresponding disinterest in American women and children. Naive or not, Rankin simply thought her vote against war with Germany stood as a greater act of patriotism than sending young men into combat for an uncertain purpose. She was fond of relating how fellow House member James Mann had said to her after the vote: "If I had known you were going to vote against it, I might have had the courage."[116] Rankin was convinced that a secret vote would have defeated the resolution. She was bewildered at the impetuous cry for blood. While pro-war lobbyists peddled their influence on Capitol Hill, Rankin was driven home. A week that had begun in glory ended in sorrow.

America's intervention in a European war changed Rankin's world overnight. No longer a darling of curiosity, she suddenly was impugned in a wave of military bravado. Many other members of Congress spoke blissfully of sacrificing lives for democracy and freedom. Soon, young men would crowd into recruitment offices. Troop trains brimming with human cargo would chug east to waiting ships. Spanking new flags would be unfurled. Newspapers would tar "Huns" and pacifists as German sympathizers. Lessons from the Civil War and the Spanish-American War were cast aside. At first it was a time of swagger and merriment as the nation bent its shoulder into war.

In Rankin's view, forgotten were the sea merchants who grew rich from the protection of a wartime American military. Forgotten was the steel industry, which built artillery and ammunition and pocketed millions of dollars in profits. Forgotten were the swelling ranks of blanket manufacturers, horse trainers and clothing designers. Forgotten were thousands of destitute young men who rushed to military recruiting depots to sign on for food, clothing and shelter.

Rankin, in letters to her family, foresaw the grief and despair war would bring. Could the United States practically, logically or morally wage war in pursuit of peace? To use violence as a club without being clubbed? Rankin's term in Congress had just begun. The elusive suffrage amendment awaited her. Now she would begin navigating through a storm of war legislation to fulfill her destiny.

11 ~ Social legislation in a War Congress

'It was a woman's job to get rid of war'

Only a few weeks had passed since Jeannette Rankin took her seat in Congress. Already, her conscience had become her political Achilles heel. Critics had given her a stiff strapping for her perceived indiscretions. The influential *New York Times* printed the names of the fifty members of the House of Representatives who had voted no in a prominent list at the top of the front page, as if to persecute them for their stand. Of the fifty, only Rankin evidently merited attention in the accompanying story and the *Times* spared no restraint from stereotypes. She was described as overwrought, "overcome by her ordeal," and recovering at home from the strain. The *Times* account attempted to squeeze every ounce of drama from Rankin's vote, real or imagined. "Practically every member in the House turned toward the seat where the 'lady from Montana' sat. Those in the galleries leaned forward. Miss Rankin was evidently under great mental duress. Her appearance was that of a woman on the verge of a breakdown. She clutched at her throat repeatedly. Now and then she brushed back her hair, looked upward at the stained-glass ceiling, and rubbed her eyes and cheeks nervously. She clasped and unclasped her hands as one does under the stress of unusual emotion."

For Rankin and her colleagues, the war quickly marched

forward. The United States had a problem. Congress declared war without having sufficient forces to do the job. The federal army numbered barely more than 120,000 troops. President Wilson soon called for one million fighting men. Six weeks after the declaration, only 73,000 had volunteered. Secretary of War Newton D. Baker persuaded Wilson to institute a draft, known as conscription, commencing a debate in Congress. "We got a desk full of telegrams from Montana supporting the president's bill," secretary Belle Fligelman would remember. Letters came from the Helena Hardware Company, Yellowstone Mercantile Company in Sidney, and the Rotary Club of Butte, among hundreds of others. All the letters sounded much the same, as if dictated by a central office. Rankin was furious. People kept talking about something they didn't understand, she told Fligelman. "She was never one to be patient at people who didn't catch on to things quickly," Fligelman would recall.

Rankin's impatience with perceived stupidity was a flaming corner of her character. She had no regard for men who argued off point, such as questioning her intellect because she was a woman, or for women who framed their thoughts on what their husbands permitted. "She could make you feel like a crawling ant but she wouldn't come at a person directly," reflected Rankin's niece, Dorothy "Mackey" Brown, years later. "There was a trail of smoke about her."[117] In the midst of a tirade Rankin was having one day over the conscription legislation, an *Associated Press* reporter making his daily rounds stopped to talk with her for a story about the bill. Rankin was fuming at her desk behind a partition. When Fligelman told her why the reporter wanted to see her, Rankin replied loud enough for him to hear, "Tell him to go to hell!" The newsman wheeled and strode from the room, never to return. For better or worse, her newspaper publicity suffered a brief decline.[118]

Rankin finally voted in favor of the conscription bill, aware of intense support for it back home in Montana. She sometimes lost confidence, thinking her symbolism had shattered, and afraid her mission in Congress was in shambles. She fought on. The nation's sudden interest in war took on a life of its own. A letter came from Howard H. Gross, president of the Universal Military Training League in Chicago. Unwittingly, he told Rankin that mandatory training of American boys before they reached the age of twenty "will do more to regenerate American manhood than anything else." He also commended her for an outstanding session of Congress, although his statement, "if it is his pleasure that I may do so," showed his carelessness in addressing the nation's first female member of Congress. "It must be relief sometimes to get a bouquet instead of a brick," he wrote her.

Fourteen days after Rankin's first-ever vote in Congress, she made her first parliamentary speech at a hearing as the Senate Committee on Woman Suffrage considered a federal amendment. Rankin sat in the front row with Carrie Chapman Catt, who brought a circular stand holding silk flags representing twenty-two nations that had given their women the right to vote. Also arguing in favor of the legislation was Senator Walsh of Montana. Rankin spoke of a need for federal action because many states required excessive voting majorities to approve suffrage. Among them, she said, was New Mexico, which required a three-fourths majority in each state house, a three-fourths majority of all votes cast in the election, and a two-thirds majority of votes cast in each county, "so that a very small majority working actively in one county could defeat the measure."

In her testimony, Rankin condemned the argument for state-by-state action as a jumble of rules, laws and irregularities. Voter fraud was rampant. Seeking suffrage through state legislatures was costly and redundant, she told the committee. After a week's recess, Rankin spoke again to the committee, as did several members of the National Woman's Party. This time, she took a different tact, using mobilization for the new world war as an argument. Without enfranchisement of women, she said at the hearing, national labor standards would deteriorate during the war: "The standards which we seek to protect and develop will rise in proportion to the amount of democracy we have in our institutions, in proportion to the amount of individual responsibility that is felt by the workers themselves."[119]

Woman suffrage would move ahead in the Senate by September 1917 when the committee delivered a favorable report on the resolution. The issue faced a tougher challenge in the House, where it had been assigned to the Judiciary Committee. Rankin and other supporters of an amendment pressed for a separate woman suffrage committee. War legislation delayed the matter several weeks until House members approved the proposed committee. Meanwhile, suffrage activism escalated across the country.

Rankin's determination on behalf of suffrage had its rewards. A legend had been born. Visitors to the House of Representatives asked tour guides to point out the Lady from Montana before seeking luminaries such as Speaker Champ Clark or Joe Cannon. If the tourists expected an Amazon freak, as some magazines popularly portrayed Rankin, the woman they saw in flesh and blood surprised them. She was neither beautiful nor statuesque in the classic Gibson Girl sense, yet people who saw her said they detected a persuasive personality in the way she carried herself. Businesses recognized that the name Jeannette Rankin meant gold if they somehow could attach it to their products. Executives from Semmes Motor Company, hoping to profit from her image, nevertheless promised they wouldn't use her name for sales purposes even if she bought a "Dodge car" from them.

A month after her critical war vote, a Republican opponent in the Montana primary election that Rankin won killed himself, allegedly despondent because of her victory and possibly of her fame. Jacob Crull of Roundup, Montana, who had served one term in the Montana Legislature, swallowed muriatic acid on the steps of a funeral parlor in Elkhart, Indiana. "I'm heartbroken," he said before he died.[120]

Rankin wasn't the hard-boiled suffragist exploited in political cartoons, at least as Belle Fligelman observed her. Rarely was Rankin without companionship of a colleague when she was on the House floor, falling into whispered discussions about proposed amendments and jotting down suggested changes with pad and pencil. To the careful observer, she was rather conservative, preferring to study the affairs and procedures of the House.

Her more hawkish constituents in Montana hesitated to appreciate these cautious attributes of their unique representative. The war hysteria spread rapidly throughout Montana, with the vitriolic Will Campbell, an Anaconda Copper newspaper editor, fanning the flames. Campbell and his cronies continued to thunder about Rankin's vote against war with Germany. They argued against her presence in Congress, intertwining innuendos about her integrity as a citizen with tales of German outposts hidden in the vast prairies of north-central Montana. Rankin undertook the sale of Liberty Bonds, partly to ease misgivings among people back home, but in hopes she would expedite a war she couldn't support. The four issues of Liberty Bonds would raise billions of dollars for war, promising Americans that for each $18.75 they spent they would earn $25 when the bonds matured after ten years. Eventually the war would cost an estimated $22.6 billion, much of it plucked from pockets of ordinary hard-working Americans and paid to contractors who would exploit patriotic fervor to fleece the government.

Rankin told her secretary, Fligelman, that if the country was intending to have a war she wouldn't work against it. "We should do everything to make it easier for the boys," Rankin said. The new woman in Congress, Fligelman would recall, tended to other business in her office with full concentration but the cloud of war didn't dissipate. Rankin traveled to Montana where she intended to speak on behalf of the bonds in Deer Lodge, but the town greeted her with locked doors. In another town, Montanans were so bitter about her vote against a war declaration that she spoke to a handful of people in a park during a blizzard, where she held onto a fence so she wouldn't be blown to the ground.

That Rankin struggled to sell Liberty Bonds in Montana while movie idol Douglas Fairbanks had the attention of a crowd at the New York Public Library with his plan to deck the Kaiser showed how hard she worked to help her constituents forget her vote. She feared losing their support for social legislation, particularly a suffrage amendment. As the war gained momentum, appeals to help Montanans hit with hardship and prejudice arrived at her office in growing numbers. She exchanged a series of letters with Fred Futter of Great Falls, who at age thirty-two wanted to become a clerk in the Army. He was a United States citizen but born to naturalized parents from Hanover, Germany, and he was partially blind. Rankin peppered the War Department with inquiries but to no avail, in part because of the family's German heritage. "Regretting exceedingly that we can find no way for you to be of service in the manner you prefer," she finally wrote Futter. Other letters from constituents included a nurse who wanted help securing Red Cross work on the front lines of battle, a farmer recovering from hernia surgery who suddenly was drafted for duty, and various military transfers and assignments that seemed in violation of law.[121]

Rankin confided to friends that she felt deep satisfaction in knowing she had made her debut in national politics and survived. Just what she meant by that was unclear, because in her brother's opinion her defeat for a second term in Congress was all but certain. "Miss Rankin has a hard job," observed writer Gilson Gardner. "If she pleases half the suffragists she will be pretty sure to offend the other half. If she pleases one political party she will offend the other. And every girl in her state and district who wants a job and can't get it will be quite sure that woman suffrage is a failure."

Constituents and friends inquired whether her vote meant she had lost all respect in Congress. Rankin, in private letters, replied that in her campaign she had judged the mood of Montana as overwhelmingly against war. She had detected a shift in national public sentiment immediately before the resolution, yet letters and telegrams from Montana had been sixteen to one against war. "I tried to let Montana people know that whenever a question arose of which I had received no definite instructions from them I would vote in accordance with my highest ideals," she wrote. This highest ideal — daring to raise a voice for women in an atmosphere of war — set in motion Rankin's lifelong commitment to pacifism.

During the suffrage campaigns, a New York school principal named Katherine Devereux Blake led 15,000 teachers in a strike demanding the right to vote. Apparently impressing on Rankin that peace was a natural extension of suffrage, Blake gathered 355,000 signatures of schoolchildren protesting possible United States involvement in the European conflict. To Rankin, that action meant war was a learned habit rather than an instinct. "One of the first things we had talked about in woman suffrage [was] that it was a woman's job to get rid of war," she said.

As the onset of World War I brought the Progressive Era to a crashing halt, Rankin understood more clearly the relationship between war and social legislation. War, to her, was a method of destroying civilization. Social legislation was a means of offering the best to humankind. At first, she remained more of a reformer who saw war as a detour from a higher social order than a pacifist who would object to war for moral and spiritual reasons. Rarely did her religious beliefs surface, although she plainly thought organized religion had contributed to war and social disease. In her mind, the many priests and ministers who condemned her vote reinforced that thought.

Rankin's subsequent associations with the teachings of Indian pacifist Mohandas K. Gandhi and the writings of philosopher Henry David Thoreau and British sociologist Benjamin Kidd, made her, anachronistically, a pacifist. From the moment she cast her vote for peace in the shadow of World War I, she also was an enduring feminist, deciding war was a theatrical display of force serving no useful purpose for American women. At the instant she defied the warnings and pleadings of friends and relatives to stand in the House and vote a conspicuous "no" against war, she made a statement that peace was woman's work. Not yet a full-fledged pacifist, she worked less for the inner contentment of peace than for the greater good of women.

"The feeling aroused in Congress over the war was something of an achievement," the *Des Moines Register* in Iowa said of Rankin's vote, "and will go much further to fortify women in politics than any goals she could have made with friends of the war measure."

In May 1917, less than two months after the war declaration, Rankin delivered a speech on behalf of the Lever Bill, which authorized the Secretary of Agriculture to take control of the production and conservation of food in wartime. Her testimony on the Lever Bill would become her first legislative success. She proposed an amendment calling for the employment of women in the food industry. "Our higher educational institutions have been turning out a large body of women who are trained to deal with fundamentals from a scientific standpoint," Rankin said. "It would be to the advantage of the government to utilize the services of trained women in the place where they would count the most for the country during the present crisis and in the future." Rankin's amendment passed and the Lever Bill, enacted into law, established a Food Administration and later prevented price-fixing in the food industry.[122]

In July 1917 she attempted to help impoverished military families struggling when their men were sent to the war. Her bill requesting $5 million for dependent families of soldiers and sailors went to committee and never came to a vote.

Incidents such as the Federal Bureau of Printing and Engraving scandal fed Rankin's opinion that war steered government away from needs at home. To her, if the scandal proved anything, it proved honesty was absent in times of international conflict. The magnitude of world war attracted extraordinary numbers of women to factory jobs made available when men departed for war and new orders flooded production lines.

Rankin was at work in the House Office Building one day in the summer of 1917 when a constituent from eastern Montana made an alarming allegation that Printing and Engraving was being run like a New York factory sweat shop. The woman's sister worked in the bureau, which in the prosperity of war was printing currency and Liberty Bonds faster than ever. The woman told Rankin that employees had complained for years to their representatives in Congress but nobody would help. Now, in wartime, it was worse.

"But here I am," the woman told Rankin. "I am your constituent and I'm telling you the girls down at the Bureau are desperate and you're the only person they can turn to."

"Why are they desperate? What's the trouble?" Rankin

reportedly asked her constituent.

"Lots of trouble. There's an eight-hour rule for all government bureaus but Printing and Engraving is running on a twelve-hour day. Girls are fainting at their presses and going to the hospital with injuries from falling on their machines. They get so tired they don't know what they're doing." Some of the workers, the Rankin constituent said, were forced to work as long as fourteen hours for as little as twenty cents an hour.[123] Women who complained were threatened with sexual assault. Director Joseph Ralph denied requests to transfer to other agencies.

Before confronting Ralph with the allegations, Rankin decided to visit the bureau as a sleuth to observe the complaints personally. Identifying herself as another congressman's constituent, she toured the plant. Many of the 4,000 workers, most of them women, were required to stand into the night at counting machines to inspect bills and bonds for errors. The women said they would lose their jobs if they didn't comply with demands for overtime. Rankin could see that bureau managers ignored the eight-hour workday common in federal offices. She returned to her office and wired her friend Elizabeth Watson, a New York private investigator who once disguised herself as a convict at Auburn Prison to gather information for the New York Prison Commission. Watson assumed a job on Rankin's secretarial staff, disguising herself under a fake name, and gathered affidavits from employees and doctors that documented the bureau's poor working conditions.

A few days later, Rankin met Director Ralph in his office and showed him the evidence. Ralph yawned and said he would talk with Treasury Secretary William McAdoo about her investigation. He said his workers preferred longer days for fatter paychecks and argued he was short of laborers to meet the demands for more currency during wartime. Rankin reminded him that the Civil Service list bore the names of 500 people seeking employment. She alleged that forced labor had been a habit in the bureau for years.

Ralph had begun his career at the bureau as a plate cleaner in 1895. He became director in 1908. His job history included time as superintendent of construction at Ellis Island. Rankin, friendly to labor, saw him as a longtime bureaucrat and felt certain he would ignore her complaint. Earlier protests by the National Consumers League, the National American Woman Suffrage Association, and the National Women's Trade Union League had left him unimpressed.

Rankin decided to gather more evidence. Secretly, she invited dozens of female workers to meet at her apartment on California Street on a Sunday morning. "She hopes you can come and bring as many girls as care to come also," Rankin's secretaries wrote in a letter to Mary Riordan, a worker in the Wetting Division. When women, many of them mere girls, crowded into Rankin's apartment, she recorded their complaints in a card index. It was a tactic she had learned in the suffrage movement. She then visited Secretary McAdoo, threatening a congressional investigation if he failed to act. The meeting came right before the July 4 holiday but Rankin, with her secretary Belle Fligelman in tow, was in no mood to celebrate. When Rankin said that she would make a statement in the House about irregularities in the bureau, McAdoo's assistant paled. "You can't do that!" he exclaimed. "That isn't the way things are done in Congress. After the holiday you can come back and we will talk this over sensibly." Rankin again declared that an investigation would occur. McAdoo must have sensed her determination. By the time she returned to her House office he had scheduled a hearing on bureau conditions. Rankin and Fligelman were startled, suddenly worried that the girls who had talked freely with them might be hesitant to testify over fear of losing their jobs.

Rankin sent a telegram to her brother, informing him she was shocked at bureau conditions. "I found them unspeakable. ... Several men need pasting. Wouldn't you like to attend to them?" she wrote. She also had allies in her investigation, including Representative W.F. Stevenson of South Carolina, who wrote on July 6: "I am with you for all I am worth." That day, Secretary McAdoo wrote Rankin: "The Bureau of Printing and Engraving has been called upon to do a tremendous amount of work, due to America's entrance into the war, and undoubtedly the pressure has been great, but no one would regret more than I if any hardship has been imposed upon the woman employee."[124]

The pressure was getting to Rankin, causing sudden severe attacks of pain and burning in her face, lips and jaw. She suffered from a nerve condition known as *trigeminal neuralgia*. Desperately she sought more medication for her illness. She wrote to a "Dr. Sample, Sr.," in Saginaw, Michigan, to thank him for the "little black pills" he gave her when she was sick in the Fordney Hotel while working for suffrage a few years earlier. "I hesitated about writing because I was afraid you would advise me to stop using them. I did not want to receive such advice because I have been taking them so long now that I do not wish to get along without them." She subsequently received a receipt for "2.00 cash" for 300 pills, of an undescribed nature, from Weeks Drug Store in Jackson, Michigan. "You may of course get what amount you wish of these pills at any time," pharmacist E.W. Goff advised her.[125]

On July 9, 1917, the Treasury Department conducted a one-day hearing. Two hundred women arrived to testify. In six hours, forty-six of them told the investigating committee that overtime was compulsory. Sick leave, rest periods and vacations had been denied on the excuse that a nation at war must maintain production.

McAdoo's committee reported that the printing of Liberty

Bonds and bank notes had imposed a great burden on the agency but "all pressing orders are now well in hand." McAdoo ordered eight-hour days, six days a week, at Engraving and Printing. Rankin wasn't satisfied. Neither were hundreds of workers who held a mass meeting the next night in the bureau's dining hall. Reduced hours created another problem because they were unable to earn a living wage working for pennies for hour earned in regular time. The same amount, twenty to twenty-eight cents an hour, had been paid in overtime. Rankin declared her intent to introduce legislation that would match suitable compensation to the eight-hour day for all workers at federal agencies. McAdoo, meanwhile, ordered that any employee wanting a transfer to another government job could apply.

Racial overtones and allegations of mismanagement also plagued the bureau. Some workers protested Ralph's hiring of "Negro help" during the rush to wartime production. "The negroes have been swarming in here like bees," one of them complained to Rankin in an unsigned letter. Another worker, Dorothy Reiter, informed Rankin that the bureau director was trying to make thirty male employees eligible for conscription into military service. "If he can spare 30 men now, what was the necessity for working them and the women helpers to the verge of nervous prostration before you championed their cause?" Ellis Sedman, married to Rankin's sister Harriet, wrote her for confirmation of a rumor that the bureau had printed wedding invitations for a relative of Secretary McAdoo.

Pressure on the Printing and Engraving director grew. The internal hospital was fitted with "ambulance tables or cars" that were wheeled into workrooms to carry away workers who fell ill at their machines, the union newspaper *The Masses* alleged in its September 1917 edition. Girls helping printers make bank notes and Liberty Bonds on power presses lifted their arms as many as 6,000 times in eight hours. Four of five girls and women employed in the bureau worked twelve or more hours a day, seven days a week, the newspaper said.

On the evening of October 4, the *Washington Post* printed an Extra edition with the news Ralph had resigned to become president of United States Intaglio Surety Company, a banknote company. Later he would become assistant to the president of US Steel Corporation. Joseph Medill McCormick, owner of the *Chicago Daily Tribune* and like Rankin a freshman in the House, reportedly told her: "I've never had any use for muckrakers, but I certainly appreciate what you did."[126]

The Carpenters' District Council and other unions commended Rankin for her effort to "remidy [sic] the evils" in the bureau, and eight workers there wrote to thank her. "You have been to us a Florence Nightingale...," wrote Agnes C. Jones, Eva A. Alsop, Ethel Brady and others. An anonymous letter written in August thanked Rankin for her detective work and her vote against war with Germany. "You have more friends than you know. Perhaps you will never know most of them."

In exposing the bureau scandal, Rankin brought her strong and idealistic support for labor into public view. The Federal Employees Union had never been able to organize workers in the printing bureau to any great extent. Rankin helped Gertrude McNally, the union secretary, launch a campaign under the new director, James Wilmeth. Through pickets and other tactics, the workers organized the largest federal union yet. Rankin's intervention wasn't surprising, considering her early love affair with reform. The scandal was a clear case of the government abusing the people it represented and, to Rankin, overlooking it was hypocritical and immoral.

Publicity over Rankin's investigation attracted new requests for similar detective work at department stores and various government agencies, including the Auditor Department of the US Post Office, where alleged persecutions of workers had resulted in suicides. Among those requests was a plea to look into the foundry operation at the Washington Naval Yard, where men worked long hours at crucibles bubbling with as much as 700 pounds of hot metal at 3,000 degrees or more.

Rankin thought if industry could control people through labor, it also could control people through government. She was naturally inclined to hate corporate electioneering. She had seen plenty of proof in Montana of how some candidates would perform like puppets for selected financial interests. She was less concerned about the workers' affiliations as much as injustices against them. In typical Rankin fashion, she saw the woods beyond the trees.[127]

Keeping with this theme, the Lady from Montana sided with striking miners in Butte, Montana, in the summer of 1917. Their fight with Anaconda Copper in the city known as "The Richest Hill on Earth" came after the worst mining disaster in American history. On June 8, 1917, a fire roared through the deep shafts and stopes of the Granite and Speculator mines, killing 163 men. Many of the dead men were found piled against illegal concrete barriers that blocked their escape into adjoining shafts. Three days later, workers formed the Metal Mine Workers Union and demanded that the mammoth Anaconda, which owned more than a quarter of the world's copper production, recognize the union and make much-needed labor reform. Butte resident Mrs. H.N. Kennedy wanted Rankin to initiate a federal investigation into the fire and the company's "rustling card" practice that required workers to carry a card stating they had been loyal to company policies. The rustling card, a condition for employment, was intended to quiet miners' complaints over unsafe practices. "Our men are conducting themselves in such a dignified manner that they command the respect of all," Kennedy wrote Rankin. "More charred bodies are brought to the surface every day and buried without any possibility of identification."[128]

The new union, seeking the company's acceptance as the bargaining agent for all miners, condemned the use of rustling cards. Demands included compliance with state mining laws, a wage increase, and recognition of miners' rights to free speech and assemblage. By July 29, about 15,000 workers in Butte, Anaconda and Great Falls were striking.

Rankin couldn't ignore the fuming confrontation in Butte, a city that had produced a labor vote for her in 1916. Her intervention in Butte's problems would cement her image among some people as a proponent of radical labor. However volatile that theory, Rankin did represent Butte in the House. She also had strong ties to suffragists there including her longtime mentor Mary O'Neill. Her opposition to the Anaconda Copper politics was undeniable, evident long before her Carnegie Hall speech where she said, "Our natural resources ... our mines, our water power, our timber ... are concentrated in the hands of the few."[129] The omniscient industrial powers in Butte, never lacking a will to attack, brought on a fight. Rankin was happy to oblige.

The company unleashed its newspapers, like rabid dogs, to ravage the strike as unpatriotic and funded by "disloyal elements." Only the *Butte Bulletin*, a pro-labor newspaper, printed a conflicting point of view.[130] The company refused to recognize the miners' demands, assailing them without mercy in copper-instructed editorials. The company had clear control of the mines. It wanted the miners to remember that. Production came to a standstill.

Rankin, ever the reformer, never disguised her pro-labor sympathies. In the context of world war, she seized on causes of workers whose safety and welfare fell by the wayside in a rush to arms. "The misguided patriots who urge the breaking down of all our standards at this time apparently understand the laws of psychology as little as they understand the laws of human conservation," she said in one interview.[131] In Montana, Rankin's exasperation with the company in 1917 unleashed a summer of labor intervention that, much as suffrage, would define her first year in Congress.

The Butte strike took on greater significance because the company blamed miner unrest on insurrection of a radical labor organization known as the Industrial Workers of the World, or "Wobblies," which was overstated but not untrue. After the mine fire, the Wobblies saw an opportunity to recruit Montana workers. Frank Bacorn, who represented the Great Butte Copper Company, wrote Rankin in August 1917: "You must know that while the working men here are of superior intelligence and while the great majority of them are decent citizens, yet the population of this city includes many hundreds, perhaps several thousands, of the worst characters in the world. Not only does it seem that the IWW includes a larger percentage of this class than does any other organization, but it is true that its tenets include the confiscation of property and sabotage, and its practices include violence from assault and battery to murder — the so-called 'direct action.' Its threats here include dynamiting and the setting on fire of the mines. It is universally believed here that only the presence of soldiers and the feat of martial law prevents a reign of terror."

These activist Socialist laborers were encouraging miners to grab control of company property, and when Rankin was asked by the Metal Mine Workers to find a federal investigator to visit Butte, she began making inquiries. "Am doing all in my power to secure federal aid in maintaining order in Butte," Rankin notified labor organizer Joe Kennedy by telegram in Butte.[132]

Perhaps men in power did not take her seriously because she was new to Washington politics and a woman. Their hesitation in investigating the strike led to the lynching of Wobblies organizer Frank Little, who was wrestled violently from his room in an uptown Butte rooming house by six masked men and dragged screaming behind an automobile as his kneecaps scraped off. The kidnappers, roundly suspected as company thugs, finally relieved Little of his misery when they hanged him from a railroad trestle near Centennial Brewery. Pinned to Little's torn clothes was a note bearing the numbers 3-7-77, the well-known warning resembling dimensions of a grave that came from Montana's territorial vigilantes. News of Little's demise flew through Butte's crowded mining districts and even to Great Falls, several hours' drive north, where the Metal Trades Council condemned the crime as a gesture of company brutality.

Rankin's pipeline of information from Butte was her suffrage ally, Mary O'Neill, who stood fast to her belief that danger in the mines was the true cause of labor strife in Butte, not outside agitators as the company had claimed. "You know this IWW howl is only a poisonous cloud sent out to discolor clear-sightedness into real conditions," she wrote Rankin.

Rankin's concern for workers and her belief that government should regulate industry caused her to consider intervening in the Butte strike personally. O'Neill thought Rankin's visit would be a political masterstroke. Wellington suggested she hint to Cornelius Kelly, vice president of Anaconda Copper's operations in Butte, that miners had invited her to act as a mediator in the strike.

In August, Jeannette sent a telegram to John D. Ryan, the company's chief executive, to notify him of her intention to discuss the Butte strike in the House of Representatives later that week. "I do not wish to do you any injustice so desire a conference with you before that time that we may better understand each other," she wrote.[133] Ryan didn't respond. Wellington, meanwhile, advised his sister against taking sides when she addressed the House. "Present facts that will warrant investigation but do not prejudge," his telegram read. "No doubt that the IWW are in some instances endeavoring to harass the government and should be stopped." Then, in a nod to the union, he also wrote: "The capitalist should also pay wages."[134]

Jeannette ignored Wellington's advice. Applauded from the galleries as she assailed the "Copper Trust," she asked Congress to empower President Wilson to seize and operate copper mines essential to the war effort. Her comments infuriated the company because Rankin's bill would allow federal troops to control mines in Montana and Arizona if an unresolved dispute led to violence, lowered production, or interfered with the national defense. Rankin argued on the House floor:

"In a crisis of this kind, coming as it does in time of war, when all our national attention should be centered upon the enemy and not on local difficulties, there should be some effective means by which the government would be able to protect itself against a decrease in necessary productiveness, and by which the people of each state would be guaranteed the protection provided by the Constitution of the United States." She blamed labor troubles in Montana on the rustling card practice. Intimidation of workers, she said, had reduced copper production from 30 million pounds a month in Butte to 12 million pounds.

Rankin's speech sounded like a warning of concern for the war effort but it wasn't that at all. Instead, it was a thinly veiled attempt to compromise the company's influence in Montana. Cornelius Kelly fired a response to her: "The unwarranted attack made by you without an investigation upon the Anaconda Company and its officials precludes your being accepted as mediator or my conferring with you relative to existing labor troubles." Rankin, refusing to disguise her misgivings about the company's browbeating of miners, decided to travel to Butte anyway. O'Neill appealed for her immediate presence: "Every moment precious now officials determined to force own terms before can reach here miners and unions depend on your personal presence to get better terms." She also wired Rankin: "You cannot be too cautious. This is the hour to prove your courage."[135]

From labor's point of view, Rankin was a champion. Company newspapers in Montana fought back. The *Helena Independent* painted her as an IWW sympathizer in Montana who was deaf to complaints of violence in other states. The *Great Falls Daily Tribune*, very much a mouthpiece for copper fathers in the Hennessy Block in uptown Butte, penned facetiously that perhaps other members of Montana's congressional delegation could help relieve Rankin's emotional burden. The editorial echoed the days and weeks after her vote against war with Germany, seizing on her gender as a biological weakness. "We would willingly and gallantly do anything we could to calm Jeannette's frazzled nerves," the *Daily Tribune* tittered. "It might ease her heavy load of responsibility if she would allow them to share the burden of protecting Montana, which presses all too heavy on her frail shoulders. ... She has found out who is responsible for the murder of Little, the IWW leader in Butte. It was not a gang of six masked men as the papers have stated. It was one masked man, and his name is John D. Ryan. Miss Rankin with a woman's superior intuition has peered under the mask and discovered the murderer."[136] Letter writers to some Montana newspapers contested the company's complaints of IWW unrest as exaggerated. The real causes of labor protests, they wrote, were unsafe conditions and rustling cards.

On the eve of Rankin's arrival in Butte, fellow suffragist Mary Stewart attended "a protest meeting of the radical magazine editors" at Madison Square Garden in New York. "Max Eastman was among the 'talkers.' He praised Jeannette lavishly and all the people cheered," Stewart wrote to Belle Fligelman.[137]

Thousands of cheering miners greeted Rankin when she stepped onto the train platform in Butte. Wellington, who accompanied Jeannette, stared at the sea of people with astonishment.[138] Leslie Sulgrove wired Belle Fligelman: "More than ten thousand representative men and women met Jeannette at the train probably the biggest and most enthusiastic demonstration ever held in Butte try to get in Eastern papers." The police department, fearing her presence would incite more violence, dispatched six officers to whisk her to the safety of a hotel. Being told that the acting mayor had canceled a parade in her honor to prevent a disturbance, Rankin stood on the seat of the car and shouted to the crowd: "Good Americans must obey the law. There will be no demonstration tonight."[139]

Only a few days earlier, she had crucified the company in an interview with the *Washington Times*. She knew the company would react with malice to the comments she made in Congress and told a reporter: "They'll try to do to me just what they have done to everyone who ever tried to oppose them. ... They own the state. They own the government. They own the press. ... First I'll be roasted from one end of the state to the other. ... Years ago they used to do desperate things to people who fought them. Their methods are gradually becoming more refined. Now they use political ruin, social ostracism, financial ruin. Every newspaper will print my shortcomings, real or fancied, in the largest type. They'll do everything to discredit me, both in Washington and in my own state. They probably won't assassinate me, because they use more subtle methods now.... If the Anaconda Company prevents my ever returning to Congress, I'll at least have the satisfaction of having done what I could for my constituency while I was here."[140]

In her first few days in Butte, Rankin conferred with union representatives and local officials. Kelly remained on the sixth floor of the Hennessy Block, refusing to talk with her. While she was away from Congress the work accumulated. A telegram from Belle Fligelman showed the difficulty of keeping current with congressional business by limited means of communication: "Revenue bill expected to return from Senate in about ten days Kitchins office announced no active business from House until then when do you expect to return sent story to Butte but two bunches of letters to be signed were sent to Missoula yesterday shall we keep on sending them Mrs. G impatient for message from you Bureau Engraving still quiet. Belle."[141]

On August 18, Rankin spoke to 15,000 miners and their families who packed the Columbia Gardens ballpark to the outfield fence. She told them that misguided patriotism allowed the government to ignore industrial conditions during war. She sympathized with their demands, and although she didn't endorse violence by Wobblies, she condemned Frank Little's murder. She also promised to work for better conditions in the mines and a peaceful end to the strike. "It doesn't matter from the government's point of view what party these miners belong to, or whether they're in the union or not in the union," she told them. "What we need are laws that will protect anybody that's working."[142]

After her speech, applause reportedly lasted fifteen minutes. "Meeting a tremendous success biggest meeting ever held in Butte...," Rankin wired her mother in Washington, DC. The strike, and Rankin's clamorous speech, came while federal troops occupied Butte to protect wartime copper production. The chain of events showed the value of Butte to the nation's military and why the company succeeded in branding the union as unpatriotic for daring to strike.

In a curious gesture a day after Rankin spoke in Butte, the acid-tongued editor of the *Helena Independent* wrote to offer an olive branch of sorts. "I have been a better friend of yours than you think I have and to show you I am human, I am writing you this tonight as tired as I am of criticising [sic] you and seeing you criticised," wrote Will Campbell, stating flatly that Rankin was wrong about labor unrest. "If you were my sister I should ask you to gracefully admit your mistake when you return to Washington. Perhaps I should plead with you to do so, because you have made a very grave mistake.... Personally I admire you very much, your personal character, your nerve, your womanhood, your individuality and your good luck — but I cannot agree with your course for the good of the country and the peace of Montana."[143]

Rankin returned to Washington where she worked hard to take the Butte labor issue to President Wilson. "Go to it kid we are for you more power to your elbow, The New York Bunch," read a telegram from fellow Heterodoxy member Elizabeth Watson, still marveling at Rankin's investigation into the Bureau of Engraving and Printing.[144] Rankin met first with Bernard Baruch, the new boss of the War Industries Board. She told him of her sympathies for the Butte miners and asked Baruch what could be done. He told her to make an appointment with President Wilson, which she did through his secretary, J.P. Tumulty. At mid-afternoon on October 1, Rankin found herself at the White House in the presence of Woodrow Wilson. "He said very seriously to this young congresswoman who was scared to death, 'The thing you should do is see Mr. Baruch.' I said, 'I did and he told me to see you.' The president threw his head back and laughed because he knew then that I was just being given the runaround."[145] Rankin tried to use the war to her advantage, telling Wilson that the spirit of patriotism fails when workers feel nonproductive. After leaving his office she was embarrassed to learn that the strike had been settled secretly a few days before her final appeal to the president.

Despite condemnations from copper hacks and men in high places who pulled their strings, letters of support for Rankin's pro-labor efforts flooded into her office. "You are the first representative to my knowledge that has every tryed [sic] to defend those workmen that have to work underground for existence," wrote Fred Schottelkorb of Livingston, Montana. From Butte, Pastor Lawrence A. Wilson of the Silver Bow Ministerial Association wrote: "You have succeeded in forcing upon the ears of the public the cause of the miners, in a way no one in Butte could have done. And from now on we will find it easier to resist the tyranny of a corporation which had all but silenced criticism and fair discussion." Samuel Rice of the Industrial Protective Association of Miles City, Montana, conveyed to Rankin "heartfelt thanks" and condemned Anaconda Copper's "reptile press" for its predictable refusal to investigate labor matters. She received a petition of support from dozens of farmers in Winifred, Montana, and encouragement to run for reelection from James L. Wallace, a Missoula attorney: "You have lost some of your 'Parlor Friends' of last year but the loss is more than compensated in the vote of the farmer and the worker."[146]

In September 1917, a month after her confrontation with labor management in Butte, Rankin secured a life insurance policy from O.P.H. Shelley, a general agent for California State Life Insurance Company. After she signed the policy in Helena and returned to Washington, her brother Wellington persuaded Shelley to add a double indemnity clause without

Jeannette's consent. Whether the timing of these decisions resulted from some fear of harm from the company was only speculative. The Rankins were powerful political names by then in Montana but they knew well Anaconda Copper's intolerance for dissent and its influential reach. That very month, Mary O'Neill wrote to Jeannette that government agents raided the new Metal Mine Workers union headquarters but discovered nothing of a seditious nature, nor evidence of IWW influence. She also wrote that rumors of a mine strike settlement were "all bunk" and that Montana Senator Thomas Walsh had suddenly appeared in Butte to investigate the strike. "My but the Senator looks badly, just all broken up over the death of his wife," O'Neill wrote from her office at the Wall and Jackman Co. in the Hirbour Block. "But he really seems more human than formerly."[147]

Even as Rankin was branded a labor radical, legislation associated with World War I continued to dominate the national agenda. History would show that within three months of the declaration of war on Germany in April 1917, the first American infantry troops arrived in France. Witnessing the rush to arms from the moment of President Wilson's impassioned speech, Rankin became obsessed with the idea that women should use the power of the ballot to stop war. It was an anachronism of those emotional, desperate times that she voted in December 1917 in favor of a declaration of war against Austria-Hungary. President Wilson reprised his April call to action, summoning a joint session of Congress to ask for a broadening role for the United States in the hostilities. Some members of the House of Representatives expected another antiwar statement from Rankin when debate began on the declaration, but she surprised them with a much different response. Toward the end of the debate she spoke:

"I still believe war is a stupid and futile way of attempting to settle international difficulties. I believe war can be avoided and will be avoided when the people, the men and women in the United States, as well as in Germany, have the controlling voice in their government. Today special interests are controlling the world. When we declared war on Germany we virtually declared war on Germany's allies. The vote we are to cast is not a vote on a declaration of war. This is a vote on a mere technicality in the prosecution of a war already declared. I shall vote for this, as I voted for money and men."[148] She could have avoided a vote, as thirty-nine of her colleagues did. Or, she could have opposed the declaration, as only Meyer London, a Socialist from New York did. An editorial writer at the *New York Times* immediately recognized the conflict between this vote and her opposition to war with Germany, smirking, "It is better to be right part of the time than wrong all the time."

In voting for a declaration of war against Austria-Hungary, whatever her reasoning, she missed a generous opportunity as the first woman in Congress to cast another shadow of doubt over the American role in World War I. It was increasingly evident that her first vote had wounded, if not killed, her chances of securing a second term in Congress. The new war declaration would significantly broaden the war and enable the military to transport more men to the battlefield.

Rankin defended her vote on grounds that because war was declared, only an increased expenditure of money would expedite the inevitable killing and hurry the warring nations to the conference table. She supported the Wilson Administration in its subsequent war politics, except for the Espionage Act of 1917. If history judged that single inconsistency in Rankin's determined opposition to war, her vote for the Austria-Hungary declaration was nothing more than a hollow gesture to save herself from a society mad with the fever of war. She commented sarcastically: "Small use will it be to save democracy for the race if we cannot at the same time save the race for democracy."

Rankin plunged into the war activity, trying hard either to hasten an end to the conflict or help constituents forget her controversial vote against war with Germany. She saw herself as a guardian of Montana boys heading to combat in Europe and to American women and children who became victims of the madcap domestic confusion. Her correspondence from that period showed genuine attempts to help Montana residents who found their lives upended by military duty. Rankin's inquiries to the War Department typically received polite but disinterested responses.

In a yearlong contract Wellington arranged with the *Chicago Sunday Herald*, stories began appearing under Rankin's byline discussing topics such as wage problems of women working in defense plants, the protection of women in the crisis of war, and toil-worn child workers on the farm. "Women must not only prepare themselves ... for thrifty administration in their kitchen, but also for professional and paid work," one such essay advised. Belle Fligelman ghostwrote the $100 weekly columns with hasty editing from Rankin, who had little time for the chore and possibly little interest. Before the war debate began in April 1917, Fligelman spent every weekend for several months at the Rankin home in Missoula, gathering anecdotes and tales for her stories from Olive Rankin, by then a plump woman with a tiny high-pitched voice. Jeannette approved most of the final drafts before they were sent to Chicago.[149]

In Washington, DC, Jeannette and her mother lived together in the St. Nicholas Apartments on California Street. So did Fligelman and Florence Leech at the start of Rankin's term in the House. Later, Jeannette's sister Harriet and her two young daughters came to Washington after her husband's death from Spanish influenza. Harriet, known to her siblings as Hattie, needed a distraction from her grief. With the apartment so crowded, Leech moved elsewhere and Fligelman found a furnished room near the Capitol.[150] Montana visitors frequently stayed overnight at the apartment as well. Olive Rankin kept the apartment in good order, as she was accustomed to doing so well with a large family in Missoula, and Fligelman would recall how Jeannette and her mother got along well.[151] The old woman, relentlessly cooking and cleaning even with a hired girl's help, tottered about the apartment on a pair of high heels until Jeannette bought her a pair of flat shoes.

Jeannette hosted dinners at her Washington apartment for Montana boys who sat stiffly in woolen khaki and asked questions about life in Washington and reports of fighting in Europe. Fligelman remembered that Rankin had a magnetic personality because "she had so much life in her," but to her, Rankin's nature never left a feeling of awe. She just swept people into conversation. For some boys, the prospect of returning for another of Rankin's Montana-style meals would end in the muddy trenches of Belleau Wood and the Battle of Argonne Forest.

For friends and colleagues, Rankin held Sunday evening salons in her apartment to feature notable people such as Richard Child, an international news correspondent. After World War I he became editor of *Collier's Weekly* and in the 1930s, a promoter of Italian fascism. At the time of Rankin's invitation to her salon, however, he was founder of the Short Ballot Organization, which sought to simplify government by reducing the number of electors on ballots. That was a popular belief among Progressives, attracted support from Woodrow Wilson, and fit well with Rankin's conviction that government needed a closer companionship with the American people.

People paraded to Rankin's office to witness the historic

person featured in all the newspapers and to shake her hand. Distinguished visitors would include Mary Walker, a medical surgeon during the Civil War who was awarded the Congressional Medal of Honor for her duty. She was so frail that two days after she visited Rankin she was blown off the steps of the House Office Building in a strong wind and killed. Also listed in the visitors' book were Dr. David Starr Jordan, peace advocate and lecturer; Benny Leonard, lightweight-champion boxer; writer and close friend Katharine Anthony; attorney Ellen Spencer Mussey of Washington, DC, and Helen Louise Johnson, head of the economics department of the General Federation of Women's Clubs. So colorful were the comings and goings by many people eager to see the nation's first female Member of Congress that novelist Booth Tarkington's wife, Susannah, came to Rankin's office one day with a handsome big diary. Fill it up, the beaming woman said, because Americans will value your words. Rankin, loathe to document her life, never did.[152] Children of House members flocked to her, wanting to sit on her lap during formal meetings. Some clung to her skirt when she stood, unwilling to part with her.

Rankin's work on behalf of suffrage attracted constituents convinced she had the courage to circumvent bureaucracy and provide answers to their long-sought questions. Three hundred letters were carried to her office each day. While most members of Congress employed only one secretary, she needed three. Louise Puffer joined Belle Fligelman and Florence Leech, who had helped Rankin in the Montana suffrage campaign. Miss Puffer, as she addressed, was an officious conservative political operative from Boston who knew where the government skeletons were buried. She once said to Fligelman, a true-hearted Progressive: "How it is that you, from Helena, Montana, have these wild ideas?"

Every letter got a reply. They contained proposals of

marriage, included requests for research on legislation, and asked Rankin to seek pardons for friends in penitentiaries. They demanded action on homestead entries. They complained about her vote for peace — and applauded it. She received dozens of letters informing her that new baby girls were being named after her. One letter, from Miss Jeannette Rankin Smith, included a photograph of the girl. Rankin pinned the photos to a wall in her apartment. The brisk pace of business in the Rankin office left little time for Fligelman and Leech to marvel at the history unfolding around them. "We learned a lot about the mechanics and the shenanigans of government," Fligelman would recall years later. "Florence and I agreed that we had much more respect for the Montana Legislature after we had seen Congress in action."[153] Although war measures dominated the bill calendar in the House, Rankin made headway with work of her own. The House was beginning its debate, in earnest, on the suffrage bill. Finally, Rankin would move to center stage on important lawmaking.

Many of the more elegant photographic portraits of Rankin, by the famed Matzene Studio in Chicago, were taken in the year after her election. She was very much aware of the public's interest in her. In early January 1918, she wrote a tailor in New York City requesting a "pretty brown silk dress" to wear on the House floor. She wanted a "simple but handsome frock," ready to wear in six days.[154] The Lady from Montana wanted to look her best when one woman and dozens of men plotted the voting future of American women.

12 ~ Overcoming objections to national suffrage

'Would anything shock women as much as blind children?'

Throughout the summer and fall of 1917, momentum built for woman suffrage. Hardly an organized effort, but effective nonetheless, the drive for a federal amendment gained power on the strength of several successful state campaigns and a White House picket campaign by the militant Alice Paul, the doe-eyed Quaker, and her Congressional Union colleagues. Picketing had begun in the spring, soon after Congress declared war on Germany, beseeching President Wilson to announce his public support for suffrage by federal amendment. "Mr. President, How Long Must Women Wait for Liberty?" read one banner typically displayed by suffragists standing silent vigil outside the White House gates.

Police ignored the protests until suffragists, in October, accused Wilson of lying to Russia that the United States practiced democracy. Violence greeted the new banners. Spectators assaulted many of the women, including Paul, punching them and throwing them to the sidewalk. Through the fall, several of the women were jailed at the Occoquan Workhouse in Virginia, where they eventually went on a hunger strike and some were forcibly fed. Jeannette Rankin, not yet a disciple of civil disobedience, didn't agree with their militant tactics but privately encouraged them, thinking that any attention drawn to suffrage was better than none at all. She visited the prison one day with Belle Fligelman and Republican US Senator George McLean of Connecticut, who had been clerk of that state's Board of Pardons for seventeen years. They found suffragists dressed in gray flannel gowns and wearing braided hair. As publicity for their cause mounted, President Wilson pardoned the women before Congress reconvened in December.[155]

Support for woman suffrage moved ahead sharply in 1917. Women won the vote in North Dakota, Ohio, Indiana, Rhode Island, Nebraska, Michigan and Arkansas. In autumn, all eyes turned to New York, where a crucial referendum would determine the strength of congressional hearings for a federal amendment. Members of the New York Woman Suffrage Party, worried that Rankin's vote against war with Germany would hurt their cause, voted against inviting her to campaign for suffrage. Anti-suffrage forces, in a gesture of desperation, had resorted to linking German insurrection with women's right to vote. The reasoning was flawed, but it was handy for them to imply that Rankin had anti-American sympathies. Rankin went to New York anyway, in October, to help paste the signatures of one million women who wanted the vote onto boards for a suffrage parade.[156] Nonplussed at the negative attention, suffragist and nursing reformer Lillian D. Wald, founder of the Henry Street Settlement in Manhattan, featured Rankin at a dinner party to meet "some of our public-spirit minded people."

Before Christmas in 1917, Rankin introduced legislation that would allow women to retain their American citizenship when they married foreign men. She wrote the Rankin-Sheppard bill after a plea from Crystal Eastman, one of her close friends from the Heterodoxy Club in New York. Crystal was a sister of Max Eastman, editor of the Socialist weekly, *The Masses*. Miss Eastman wanted to marry a British man and was about to move to England with him, but did not want to lose her citizenship in exchange for an act of love. "We must not forget that the self-respect of the American woman will not be redeemed until she is regarded as a distinct social entity, unhampered by the political status of her husband or father, but with a status peculiarly her own and accruing to her as an American citizen," Rankin said. Her bill failed but later passed under other sponsorship.

Not long before Christmas, the US House Woman Suffrage Committee began work with ten members, including Rankin, in favor of extending the right to vote. Three others opposed any change in the law. Although Rankin's opposition to world war had commanded the headlines and branded her infamously in the minds of many Americans, suffrage remained her significant work. More than an icon for years of failed state and federal suffrage votes, Rankin was the first flesh-and-blood female presence in Congress.

Her election was no accident. She was a legitimate, elected public official, sent to Washington by a progressive western state. Suffragists of all stripes, regardless of their political affiliations and personal disagreements, depended on her to carry suffrage legislation to victory. Public curiosity over a woman in Congress would please Rankin, and bring her substantial fame for the times, but politicking for woman suffrage on the House floor was a tall order. The quest for a federal amendment had begun in 1878, introduced by the old mothers of suffrage, Elizabeth Cady Stanton and Susan B. Anthony. The House had rejected similar legislation for an amendment in 1915. The Senate had done the same in 1914.

Now, in late 1917, the House was poised to make history. Rankin's temerity from the state suffrage campaigns would be sorely tested. A bloc of Southern states, where a Jim Crow poll tax remained commonplace to discourage black men from voting, stood deeply opposed to suffrage. Some members of Congress viewed women as being ignorant in the serious affairs of a nation at war. No man in Congress was accustomed to negotiating with any woman in everyday politics, much less debating a momentous decision to amend the US Constitution.

Some members remained fierce in their opposition to women casting ballots. Rankin had been warned not to tangle with a Massachusetts Republican, Joseph Walsh, considered furiously anti-suffrage. When he heard she had an upcoming speaking engagement in his district, he warned her against tampering with his constituents. That night, Rankin told the audience they had a good representative in Congress named Joe Walsh. "He performs a great service for the people all over the country because he sits on the [House] floor and objects when certain bills come up that shouldn't be passed unanimously. He is the only one to object, and by objecting to these unanimous consents he helps the whole country. But, there's one thing wrong with him and that's your fault, not his. You women haven't convinced him that he should vote for woman suffrage."[157]

When Rankin returned to Congress after the speech, she attended a meeting of the Committee on Woman Suffrage. Democrats held a slim majority in the House because of the party's coalition with four Progressive, Prohibition and Socialist members. The coalition therefore owned all the committee chairmanships. Some of the Republicans had hoped that Democrats would vote for Rankin to lead the suffrage committee. Rankin told the committee that she didn't want the chairmanship because she saw the appointment as controversial and didn't want to encourage votes against suffrage. She said she preferred that the ranking Democrat, John E. Raker of California, continue his work. "Joe Walsh got up and tried to be consistent but he couldn't. He wanted a Republican chairman, but he didn't want me and I didn't want it, and he didn't want to be on my side. He was awfully mixed up in his opening speech."[158] The committee decided as Rankin asked, on grounds that it meant more votes for suffrage. It was with a stroke of fierce irony that Rankin wouldn't lead the charge for suffrage. As the most probable member of Congress to argue for a suffrage amendment, she had pushed for creation of the committee and was appointed to it. The *New York Times* mused: "It was estimated that enough Democrats would concede the place as one upon which their feminine colleague had a particular claim."[159]

Busy as she was working on suffrage legislation, Rankin found time to shop for holiday gifts she sent to several women. One recipient was Wellington's secretary, Helena Stellway, who wrote from Montana to thank Jeannette for her gift of "dainty pink undergarments," which she described as "adorable," as well as for "the cute little 'garterettes' or whatever their name may be, with the cunning French bows."

The Committee on Woman Suffrage opened five days of hearings on the matter on January 3, 1918. It was the fortieth time suffrage supporters introduced legislation in the House. Old-guard suffragists such as Anna Howard Shaw, Carrie Chapman Catt and Maude Wood Park shuffled forward to testify in favor of an amendment. They knew the political arena well. Opponents included Lucien Howe, a medical doctor who tried to make a case that if women voted their children would go blind for lack of attention. He cited a malady he called "purulent diseases of the eye" that led to blindness, inferring gonorrhea but refusing to utter the word. "How do you expect women to know this disease when you do not feel it proper to call it by its correct name?" Rankin asked him. Pointing out that some states outlawed women from talking about venereal diseases, she told Howe: "Do you think anything would shock women as much as blind children? Do you not think they ought to be hardened enough to stand the name of a disease when they can stand the fact that the children are blind?"[160]

In another instance, Rankin challenged a so-called statistician's testimony that socialist, pacifist and pro-German voters had pushed woman suffrage to victory in New York just months earlier. Determining that he had alleged to know the breakdown of voters by gender in Montana's suffrage victory, she asked him: "How could you tell a Democratic woman's vote from a Republican woman's vote?" He replied, after a moment of hesitation: "Well, that part of it was just estimation."

On January 9, President Wilson announced his support for a federal amendment. The committee sent a favorable resolution to the House floor. Representative Walsh, meanwhile, came again to sit beside Rankin in the House chamber. He apologized for opposing her leadership on the suffrage committee. His friends had written him letters advising that she spoke well of him in his district. She had a new friend and ally. When woman suffrage was coming to a vote in the House, she went to his office. "Now, I'm not asking you to vote for woman suffrage if you don't believe in it, but I am asking you not to make a speech against it," she told him. Walsh: "But if they say —." Rankin: "Just leave the room." Walsh: "Well, I'm having a hard time to vote against it."

On Walsh's recommendation, Rankin opened the House suffrage debate on January 10, two days after President Wilson delivered his idealistic "Fourteen Points" speech in which he justified United States involvement in World War I as a moral undertaking that would ensure postwar peace in Europe. Rankin's address would attack war as the foundation of social problems but it also had a greater significance. At last a woman's voice in Congress spoke on behalf of her own gender. Her speech came at a time when Prohibition would be enforced as a national measure. Child welfare had become a national issue. Nearly a year had passed since Rankin's landmark vote to oppose United States involvement in the Great War, as it was known. Passage of the Selective Service Act in May 1917 led to the drafting of 2.8 million American men.

By the time the suffrage debate began, thousands of fresh troops were being dispatched to France every day. Armies had tromped all over Europe, pounding magnificent old cities into rubble. Hundreds of thousands of American troops had endured mustard gas, cholera, trench foot, rat bites and other horrors of trench warfare. The boys who kept journals wrote of being buried alive in bomb blasts and fearing the dreaded whistle calls when troops were ordered to charge into cratered fields to face hails of lead.

Speaking on behalf of House Joint Resolution 200, to propose a constitutional amendment extending to women the right to vote, Rankin launched into an impassioned speech portraying war as an ogre that stomped on the human condition. It was only a few weeks after Woodrow Wilson signed the Prohibition amendment into law. Like many suffragists, Rankin had lost patience with continuing indifference toward woman suffrage. Political pressure from high places was mounting, however, as Theodore Roosevelt and other American leaders announced their support for a federal amendment.

In her speech, lasting nearly thirty minutes and ending in prolonged applause, Rankin invoked many arguments from her state suffrage campaigns about how government had ignored women and children. With the abundance of coal, and with great stretches of idle, fertile land, Rankin pointed out, babies continued to die from hunger and cold. Soldiers died from lack of a woolen shirt. Might not women provide the resources of human needs? She asked of her colleagues:

"Might it not be that the men who have spent their lives thinking in terms of commercial profit find it hard to adjust themselves to thinking in terms of human needs? Might it not be that a great force that has always been thinking in terms of human needs, and that always will think in terms of human needs, has not been mobilized? Is it not possible that the women of the country have something of value to give the nation at this time? ... For seventy years the women leaders of this country have been asking the government to recognize this possibility. ... The boys on the front know something of the democracy for which they are fighting. These courageous lads who are paying with their lives testified to the sincerity of their fight when they sent home their ballots in the New York election and voted two to one in favor of woman suffrage and democracy at home. ... Can we afford to allow these men and women to doubt for a single instant the sincerity of our protestations of democracy? How shall we answer their challenge, gentlemen; how shall we explain to them the meaning of democracy if the same Congress that voted for war to make the world safe for democracy refuses to give this small measure of democracy to the women of our country?"[161]

Rankin also challenged lawmakers from Southern states to break away from their fear of granting black women the right to vote. African American men, many of them former slaves, won the right to vote in the Fifteenth Amendment in 1870, but states quickly countered that constitutional right by enacting poll taxes and literacy tests. Outside the law, white racist groups such as the Ku Klux Klan, Red Shirts, and White League intimidated black voters from casting ballots.

The movement for woman suffrage wasn't without its demons. Some women still seethed with resentment over what abolitionist Frederick Douglass famously coined "the Negro's hour" after Congress approved the new federal amendment. In that era of Reconstruction after the Civil War, lawmakers made extravagant arguments for why black men should vote and women shouldn't. The orator Douglass lost favor with suffrage leaders when he argued that the country needed black men voting while women at least had vicarious influence at the polls through marriage.

Rankin and other suffragists found "the Negro question" unsettling. Prejudice against Americans of color was rampant. Arguing for a federal amendment became a hopscotch through a twisted history. Opponents of woman suffrage found a handy parallel in their opposition to civil rights. Women, like Negroes, had smaller brains. Women, like Negroes, would think emotionally in trying times. Women, like Negroes, would drag inconsequential matters into the serious business of lawmaking. In her later years, Rankin would recall a brisk exchange in Congress with Senator John Sharpe Williams of Mississippi. "If we passed your amendment, then Negro women could vote," he told her crossly. Rankin, never short on wit, retorted: "But couldn't you keep them from voting the same way you keep the Negro man from voting?"[162]

The conflict represented the color barrier still very much accepted in large portions of the United States in 1918. Rankin said to fellow House members: "Are you gentlemen representing the South, you who have struggled with your Negro problem for half a century, going to retaliate after fifty years for the injustice you believe was done you so long ago? Have you not learned in your struggle for adjustment in the South to be broad and fair and open-minded in dealing with another franchise problem that concerns the whole nation? ... There are more white women of voting age in the South today than there are Negro men and women together."[163]

Representative Raker followed with a speech of his own, confronting arguments that blacks deserved the right to vote before women. Many Southerners argued that suffrage would double the ignorant electorate. In response, Raker argued that white women in the South outnumbered colored women by two times. It was time for opponents of woman suffrage to quit hiding behind the "camouflage" of the Negro question. "Woman suffrage is no longer a controversial question, it an established fact in nearly half the territory of our country," he said on the House floor. "No one denies that the coming of woman suffrage over the entire country is inevitable."[164] When one witness at the committee hearing alleged that suffragists were trying to change state constitutions that were "adopted by the people," Rankin shot back: "May I ask who are the people?"

Representative Richard W. Austin, a fellow Republican from Tennessee, took to the House floor to commend Rankin as the "real leader and invincible champion" of the suffrage cause. "In all fairness, she well deserves the chief credit for the victory which I hope will be achieved here today for human rights, for equal justice, for the blessings of liberty, for the freedom and enfranchisement of one-half of 100 million Americans," he said. No greater ovation was heard in the House, Austin said of his nine years as a member, than when Rankin opened the suffrage debate that morning. "It was not so much an endorsement of the subject she championed, as it was a just tribute to an able, popular and successful woman," he said.[165]

James R. Mann of Illinois, the House Minority Leader, said to Rankin one day: "You and I will put through this woman suffrage. We don't care what anyone else says, we'll do it." Before the vote on January 10, he became quite ill and was sent to the hospital. At the last minute, after seven hours of speeches had been made for and against the suffrage bill, Mann came through the door "looking like death," as Rankin would remember the moment. House members rose in a body to applaud Mann for his determination. Mann suspected the vote would be close and it was. Suffrage carried a two-thirds majority by one vote, 274-136. Of all the Southern delegations, only Tennessee and Arkansas voted in favor. Rankin's one-time nemesis from Massachusetts, Representative Walsh, voted yes. The will for woman suffrage had survived the House, and Rankin would receive much of the credit for victory, but it died in the Senate by a narrow margin. Numerous attempts to revive legislation during the 65th Congress would fail, but suffragists celebrated even defeat, sensing their time was coming soon.

Rankin, meanwhile, launched into other legislation intended to improve the fortunes of women and children. In October 1918 she joined with Julia Lathrop of the federal Children's Bureau to introduce first-ever legislation to encourage instruction in female hygiene, maternity and infant care. Known as the Rankin-Robinson Bill, (later Sheppard-Towner) the measure was designed to educate women about venereal disease and birth control, and curb infant mortality. It would appropriate $480,000 a year, divided equally among the forty-eight states, if they made similar appropriations. An additional sum of $1 million would be shared on the same terms, and eventually $2 million. The legislation regulated midwifery, provided for education of maternity and infant care in rural America, and overall aimed at improving public health in places lacking it.

The bill was dear to Rankin's heart, full of passion for people in need, but it fell to immediate criticism that it duplicated existing programs and amounted to socialistic health care. When a House Labor Committee hearing was held, Rankin felt certain the bill would pass to the House floor. Opposition came from the American Public Health Association and the Bureau of Child Hygiene in New York City. Those organizations called for amendments that would prevent overlapping efforts. In response, Rankin pressed for immediate passage with amendments to come in the following Congress. The bill passed the Senate but failed in the House.[166]

Rankin blamed the war for the bill's defeat under her sponsorship. She viewed social legislation as something that aspired to a "higher good," a humane responsibility that required government to feed, clothe and protect vulnerable people. Fighting a war was to her far more than a social impracticality; it was a moral crime, requiring lying, stealing, killing and hate to survive. Many Americans supported the measure but Congress gave it little attention. The Children's Bureau and the American Public Health Association had pushed such legislation for years. Rankin's representation was the only hope they had in an otherwise hostile climate.

In another instance, in 1918, she fought for farmers. Rankin spoke on the House floor about inequities in government loans. She asked for an amendment allowing farmers to grow wheat through advances and loans. It would cut costs of production and transportation and support tariffs on foreign farm products. Summarily she urged the passage of legislation to cut Montana farmers free from the strings of state political control, a slap aimed at the copper interests. That legislation, too, made no headway in a war Congress.

Rankin next attempted a resolution seeking American recognition of Ireland's independence, but conservatives interpreted it as a tool of the Sinn Feiners, an anti-British, Irish nationalist group. Irish-Americans in Montana, congregated mostly in the labor cities of Butte and Anaconda, wrote to express their delight with her actions. Pro-war newspapers grabbed the opportunity to continue their lectures on Rankin's unsuitability for office. "Her action will give rise in some quarters to the suspicion that her vote against war was not prompted by feminine repugnance to violence of all kinds, but by a disloyal dislike of violence employed against the enemies of her country," observed the *Toronto Mail and Empire*. The *Adrian Telegram* of Michigan labeled Rankin as "the female LaFollette," and the *Helena Independent* of Montana spoke of "our busy war obstructionist," whose bill "has for its purpose the stirring of trouble in the United States and thus complicates the work of the nation in fighting Germany."

Meanwhile, Montana's political obstructionists were busy stirring up trouble of their own. Anaconda Copper lobbyists in the Legislature succeeded in dividing the congressman-at-large state into eastern and western districts with the slogan, "Do you want to keep a woman in Congress?" Rankin was gerrymandered to the West, isolating her from farmers on the eastern plains who had voted for her in 1916.

She had barely any support from Montana newspapers, and furthermore, the war fervor was at its height. As early as February 1918, she realized that as Wellington had predicted, she had no chance for reelection. "She just got furious when you mentioned she would never be elected again," Wellington would recall. "She wouldn't talk to me on the phone. She wouldn't answer the phone. I could never get her on the phone. A woman of terrific conviction. I never knew of a woman in the United States with stronger convictions than she had and a greater adherence to what she thinks is right. She didn't give a damn. She'd make mistakes; she would starve. She would do anything [to avoid war]."[167]

Jeannette complained bitterly to family and friends in private correspondence that the consuming business of war left her no hope for constructive social legislation. She wavered on whether to make another run for Congress and finally telegrammed Wellington halfheartedly: "I do not want my family and friends to make the necessary sacrifices unless they feel that there is a chance for success." She received a weak reply of support and, acknowledging that she wouldn't win reelection to her House seat, chose a bolder alternative. On July 16, 1918, she announced plans to campaign for the Senate. Her slogan: "Win the War First." If nominated and elected she promised to urge President Wilson to bring war to a victorious conclusion and to vote for every measure he recommended to more efficiently prosecute the war. She received strong backing from the Nonpartisan League, a North Dakota farm organization that moved into Montana in 1918 and seized on Rankin's popularity in rural districts as evidence of her political promise.[168] She had cracked the House. Now she would try the Senate, full to the last seat with men.

13 ~ Weathering an assault on civil liberties

'You have a hard fight with Jeannette Rankin in the field.'

Jeannette Rankin launched a campaign for the US Senate in the midst of the worst witch hunt of civil liberties in Montana history. Even before the State Legislature created an extralegal Montana Council for Defense and gave it extraordinary powers, Rankin's iconic vote against war with Germany in 1917 supplied emotion for a sweeping condemnation of her candidacy. Public protest over that single action, however contrived and inflated by war zealots, wouldn't be sufficient to derail her political future.

Montanans, despite organized efforts to create an illusion of a state mad for war, had among their ranks large numbers of pacifists who would vote for Rankin. Immigrant families from Europe, including Germans and Irish, had no appetite for destruction in their homeland. It's true that Montana sent a larger percentage of its men to fight than any other state. What wasn't disclosed in this alleged fervor for war was that enlistments came adorned with a large asterisk. When war was declared with Germany, 12,500 Montanans volunteered to fight. The federal government, overestimating Montana's population, drafted an additional 28,000. Representing fully 10 percent of Montana's population, those 40,500 men were glorified inaccurately, and unfairly, as evidence of the state's insatiable appetite for World War I.

The Montana Council of Defense was a vile civilian organization, born in the winter of 1918 with power to harass and humiliate citizens who dared to practice their First Amendment liberties. It resulted from President Wilson's encouragement to states to promote mobilization for war. Quickly it became a tool to chase down imagined sedition, espionage and disloyalty. Tactics to intimidate Montanans included keening theories of German infiltration. Purported as evidence of that was anyone who spoke German, possessed a book about Germany, seemed to have too much money, failed to spend liberally for liberty war bonds, or refused to kiss an American flag. One sheriff prohibited foreign-born citizens from discussing current affairs in public. The reign of suspicion perpetuated by newspaper editor Will Campbell, of the Montana Loyalty League, and ten other council members would turn neighbor against neighbor and result in beatings, prison terms, rampant prohibitions of free speech and a mighty book burning in Lewistown as residents purged the town of anything German. Flames illuminated the night sky for miles.

Inevitably, the Montana Council of Defense found comfort in the tentacles of Anaconda Copper and held firm. Most of its members had strong company connections anyway. Now they had been given power, nearly without limitation, to impose the will of the company in an era laden with labor unrest. "The voluminous correspondence of the council, as well as the thick volumes of verbatim testimony, indicated that again and again in matters ranging from the appointment of County Council members to sabotage and spies, the council sought the advice of the Anaconda Company — and followed it," wrote historian K. Ross Toole.[169]

Because of the war, Montana in 1918 was far different from the adventuring state that elected Jeannette Rankin to Congress two years earlier. The powerful inquisition of the defense council, and its brotherhood with the unforgiving copper conglomerate, would be demonstrated in its attacks on US District Attorney Burton K. Wheeler and striking miners in Butte. This political machine — more than a lobby because it owned Montana politics and drove citizens into fearful submission — opposed any citizen who supported Rankin, including socialist farmers in eastern Montana.

Rankin had other challenges, too. She received no support from some national suffrage leaders, in particular the back-biting Carrie Chapman Catt, who viewed her as too controversial. "Whatever she had done or will do is wrong to somebody, and every time she answers the roll call she loses us a million votes," Catt said.[170] Rankin's late entry into the Montana Senate race led to a scramble for money, ideas and volunteer labor. Her sister Hattie, who lived in Washington, DC, took control of the campaign almost from the start because the intended campaign manager, Mary Stewart, quit suddenly when her father died. Hattie wrote letters and sent telegrams to Jeannette's suffrage allies and to friends from her Heterodoxy Club days in New York. She asked Harriet Laidlaw, Jeannette's longtime suffrage ally, for permission to use her endorsement on campaign letters sent to Montanans.

Hattie filled her correspondence with appeals for cash and quick action. She explained that the law allowed Jeannette to spend only $1,100 in her primary campaign but that money raised elsewhere would finance 75,000 postcards mailed to Montana voters. "It is obvious that eleven hundred dollars in a state the size of Montana is inadequate," Hattie wrote one supporter. Meanwhile, two dozen "bureau girls" from the federal Bureau of Printing and Engraving began working afternoons and evenings in Rankin's congressional office to address postcards. In Montana, Mary M. Dean of Helena became campaign treasurer. Hattie also assembled a reelection committee that included Laidlaw, Minnie Fisher

Cunningham of Texas, Margaret Driver Robins of Chicago, Martha Bruere of Washington state, and Rosalie Whitney of New York. By this time, Rankin's secretary and suffrage sister, Belle Fligelman, had married Norman Winestine and moved to New York City and Hattie became her sister's office manager. Ever the activist, Belle jumped into the campaign with such exuberance that Hattie wrote her a letter of thanks, signing it, "With loads of love to you and your Sweet Lover."

With the primary election fast approaching on August 27, 1918, and only $258 raised, volunteers flocked to Rankin's campaign. "I just couldn't bear that Jeannette wouldn't be returned [to Congress]," wrote Laidlaw, a committee volunteer for the New York Federal Food Board. Hattie disclosed in a letter to Whitney of Brooklyn, New York, her optimism that "even the papers that are against her are admitting that she's apt to win." It was late July and Rankin was campaigning in Montana. "She will have a chance to speak to five or six times as many people as she had the opportunity to speak to during the last campaign," Hattie wrote.[171]

Some constituents questioned her intentions. Wrote Annabel Rooney to one of the Democratic contenders: "It is hard to know her personally and not feel a very small affection for her, but since she has entered politics, we feel that she had been the narrowest of politicians and as a Congressman a colossal failure."[172]

Rankin's opponent was Oscar M. Lanstrum, a Helena physician and publisher of the *Montana Record-Herald*, one of only a few papers that reported news of her campaign. The Spanish flu pandemic, already on its way to killing 5,000 Montanans, afforded him a high profile as he went from house to house carrying his medical bag and making speeches in towns and cities about how to prevent the disease. The flu so worried people that they didn't want to congregate in meeting halls. Rankin often found entire towns shuttered when she went to campaign. One trip involved riding the train from Helena to Lewistown, a central Montana farming and ranching city where she intended to campaign. When she arrived that evening she found nobody on the streets.[173] She lost the Republican primary to Lanstrum by less than five percent of the votes: 18,805 to 17,091. Harry H. Parsons, a Missoula attorney, trailed with 5,878 votes and Edmund Nichols had 3,443. The showing was remarkable for a candidate pounded in the copper press by powerful pro-war interests such as Campbell and his Council for Defense cronies. Rankin thought that losing by a mere 1,714 votes was hardly a defeat at all considering the circumstances.

Jeannette told Wellington she wanted to enter the general election on a third party ticket. He agreed she should try. Her Democratic opponent was Thomas J. Walsh, an incumbent senator and, like Wellington, a Helena attorney and Wellington's former boss. Walsh was a flamboyant, cold-eyed political leader, held in high esteem, and after Rankin's defeat in the primary he was confident he would be reelected. He had a good record in the Senate and wore the appearance of impeccable integrity despite his Anaconda Copper connections. Carrie Chapman Catt cheered for a Walsh victory and seemed oddly detached from Rankin's work for a federal suffrage amendment. "We have never had a better friend, more willing to fight for us on all occasions, than Senator Walsh.... Now Miss Rankin has announced that she proposes to run independently.... For her sake as well as ours it is most advisable that she should quit at this stage."[174]

By September 1918, Walsh heard rumors that Rankin was going to campaign on the National Party ticket. The rumor proved true, for Rankin was a certified candidate. The National Party had been founded by socialist John Spargo, author of *The Bitter Cry of the Children*, an expose of laboring children and their dangerous working conditions. Although the party was a coalition of pro-war Socialists, anti-war Progressives, prohibitionists and farmers, many of whom embraced in some fashion Rankin's ideologies, she recognized it more as a vehicle for her candidacy than an expression of her political beliefs. The party did, however, endorse a suffrage amendment and the Progressive principles of initiative, referendum and recall. The National Party also called for public ownership of major industries including railroads, oil wells, timber lands and metal mines.

Rankin received an endorsement from the Nonpartisan League, an amalgam of mostly sheep and wheat ranchers in northeastern Montana impressed with her voting record on farm legislation. Many of them, like Rankin, opposed the war. Backing also came from Montana's Irish, happy with her congressional resolution to support Ireland's right to political independence. With the twin pillars of Butte miners and rural farmers behind her, Rankin began to think she had a strong chance of winning the election. So did Walsh.

"There are a great many farmers who have strong radical ideas and who are very much opposed to the war, a good many having the idea that Wall Street and the munitions manufacturers of the east have done a great deal to bring it on," an associate wrote Walsh.

Walsh worried that Rankin would steal his political base, which included Butte's strong unions. "Every influence possible should be brought on Wellington not to have her run," wrote attorney Cornelius Nolan to Walsh. Wellington was asked to convince Jeannette that Walsh could get her an overseas appointment, the purpose of which would be to retire her from politics gracefully. Wellington and Jeannette heard rumors that people thought she had been bribed. They agreed she should continue her campaign to prove she hadn't accepted money or political favors.

Walsh tried another tactic. R.R. Purcell, the mayor of Helena, had urged him "to arrange with John D. Ryan [president of Anaconda Copper] to have the company quietly get in line because you have a hard fight on your hands with Jeannette Rankin in the field." Walsh sought support of Anaconda Copper by withdrawing his nomination of Burton K. Wheeler for reappointment as US District Attorney. Wheeler, an enemy of the company, was accused of sympathies toward the Germans and the Wobblies, a radical labor organization. Wheeler resigned, enabling conservative voters to support Walsh. The company flooded his campaign with cash.

Meanwhile, the copper press had a field day trotting out twisted but vivid condemnations of Rankin's failures. The tirade-tongued Will Campbell led the pack. He envisioned German planes flying over Montana, commended Frank Little's savage hanging as a blood-quickening act of vigilante justice, and spared no ink in his barrage of Representative Rankin. Branding her as "consciously or unconsciously a member of the Hun army in the United States," Campbell put his pen to work in the shrillest portrayals he could muster. "Jeannette Rankin is a socialist announcing her candidacy on the republican ticket that she may secure a higher seed in American affairs to carry out her economic program which it so happens is the military program of Germany as testified to a thousand times in a thousand courts where agents less valuable to the Beast of Berlin have been convicted," he wrote.[175] A borrowed editorial from a Toronto newspaper mocked her antiwar vote and portrayed her as a friend of radical labor: "Miss Rankin's tears were not for her own countrywomen who perished on the Lusitania, nor for the victims of German lust and cruelty in Belgium, but probably for the able-bodied loafers, members of the IWW, who form a considerable element in her own state and who, in her mind's eye, she probably saw in uniform, either the khaki of the United States army or the less attractive garb worn extensively in federal penitentiaries."

In Montana in 1918, only 140,000 votes were required for a majority in a congressional election. Belle Fligelman, now living in New York City, surmised that Rankin could collect half those votes from farmers, several thousand more from Socialists, and the balance from "public-spirited citizens" inclined to look beyond copper-fueled cynicism. Fligelman wrote that newspapers controlled by the mining companies had "ventured so far from discretion as to declare that she voted against conscription, in spite of the fact that the *Congressional Record* clearly reports her vote in favor of this measure." Some newspapers had deliberated confused two conscriptions bills, Fligelman said. Rankin, like most House members, had opposed the president's conscription bill. She voted in favor of a bill drafted in the House Committee of Military Affairs, as did most House members.[176]

The copper press ignored Rankin's third-party candidacy, instead embracing Walsh and Lanstrum as the only realistic contenders. Exceptions were the Wellington-owned *Havre Daily Promoter* and the labor-controlled *Butte Daily Bulletin*, which said of Rankin in an editorial: "With a steadfast courage ... she has spoken for the lowly and the oppressed with no possibility of reward.... She is stronger than the servile Lanstrum ... and brave enough to risk her political fortunes for what she believes is right."[177]

Carrie Chapman Catt, continuing to badger Rankin for failing to comply with her wish to vote for war with Germany, endorsed Walsh for his "continued and invaluable aid for federal suffrage," while Rankin got the support of Frances Willard, national president of the Women's Christian Temperance Union. Some Rankin opponents, worried over her alliance with labor, accused her of Bolshevik influence in the classic Russian sense. It was a blatant, and unfounded, attempt to insinuate she was communist.

The election took place less than a week before the armistice would be signed in Compiegne, France, on November 11, 1918. Voters went to the polls in the midst of the Spanish flu pandemic, which already had killed waves of American soldiers outfitted for combat in Europe. The flu also greatly diminished the number of Montana voters, as did a sudden snowstorm that hit northern Montana. Rankin ran a distant third in the general election with 26,013 votes to Walsh's 46,160 and Lanstrum's 40,229. She came close to winning in Mineral County, in the western portion of Montana, but she carried only three northeastern counties where the Nonpartisan League had strong membership.

Rankin had not expected to win the election, thinking it hopeless from the start. Privately she lamented how an expression of peace — her vote against a declaration of war — had ruined her in Congress. Wellington, although by that time ashamed he had tried to persuade her to vote in favor, had been accurate in his prediction that she wouldn't be reelected. Americans' attitudes toward war in 1918, however, were worlds apart from 1916. Everyone had heard of the horrors of trench warfare. As American casualties mounted, the war's purpose remained unclear.

It was implausible that a majority of Montana voters would oppose Rankin because of her war vote, especially given that many of her constituents opposed war just as she did in 1916. It's more likely that she lost because she and Lanstrum split the Republican vote.[178] In context, her vote totals were remarkable given the chain of events, intended or otherwise, that defeated her. A Rankin election to the US Senate would have made history, again. The first woman in Congress was out of work. Carl W. Riddick, a rancher and county assessor, replaced Rankin in the House.

The Sixty-Fifth Congress closed for business in March 1919. Not until that summer did lawmakers approve the Nineteenth Amendment that gave women the right to vote. Montana was one of the first states to ratify the amendment. Tennessee, in August 1920, cast the final vote needed to place the amendment in the Constitution. The victory came forty-one years after Susan B. Anthony and Elizabeth Cady Stanton drafted their original amendment. Women had initiated nineteen campaigns to pass a federal amendment and even more campaigns in states from New York to Oregon. They had pushed changes in state legislatures 480 times and lobbied state constitutional conventions forty-seven times.[179] It was with no small irony that suffrage came after the first woman in Congress had lost her seat. Did the long-awaited amendment arrive because of Rankin's presence in the House and her corresponding effort for suffrage? Had the issue evolved to its natural conclusion? Although it was difficult to measure judgments of such historic proportions, Rankin's unfailing devotion to the suffrage cause was unmistakable, her auspicious presence in Congress a blessing for American women. Seating a woman in Congress also was a probable prerequisite for a federal amendment. Rankin's election, however controversial in some quarters, left many anti-suffrage arguments sounding silly and outdated. One of the arguments that had endured so long — that each state should decide whether women vote and for what — began to lose appeal as pressure grew on Congress to decide the issue. Rankin, quick to find self-serving duplicity in anti-suffrage arguments, noted it was Congress and not individual states that made the decision to enter World War I. "That same action should be used for women who are struggling for democracy," she said.

After World War I ended, the 1920s offered a golden age for peacemakers. Looking back on the war, in which 117,000

Americans died, proponents of peace began to explore alternatives to such human wreckage. One of them was Jeannette Rankin, embittered that war had been an affront to the welfare of women and children and on a personal front, to her ambitions to promote a national agenda on their behalf. She found herself suddenly unemployed, like all members of Congress who lose their seats. On a little plot of land in Georgia, she set out to prove to the world peace was much more than a fleeting notion embraced by the nation's first congresswoman.

14 ~ Turning to Georgia for world peace

'People interested in humanity more than in cold dollars.'

A blue Japanese lantern cast soft light on Jeannette Rankin's graying hair and her light summer dress as little barefoot boys knelt around her. Some of the faces were white, others black. The boys listened in rapture to her tales, so transfixed by visions of Gandhi and the Congress that the watermelons hanging to cool in the well were forgotten. In words and gestures, Rankin sketched pictures of intrigue in the humid Georgia air, while a chorus of crickets hummed to her voice. The little boys spent many steamy nights at Rankin's house, drawn to her stories. They had unkempt mops of hair and ragged trousers but they always wore clean shirts when they came to visit. They listened in the soft light as she spoke of faraway places.

In Rankin's stories, life in Georgia was simpler than elsewhere in the world. This was rural America, comfortably detached from bustling urban centers. A bucket was made do for a sink. Pecan and fruit trees provided the shade for the house and larder for the pantry. Breathing old Southern tunes on a juice harp was the heart of family entertainment. In the morning, when the bright sun burned the dew off the ground and sticky perspiration drove boys to the swimming hole, life in Georgia would return to its familiar routine. In the encroaching darkness of summer evenings, the boys didn't ask why this enigmatic woman had come to Georgia. Yet the story affecting Rankin the most is a story she did not tell them. The temperament of the changing times had derailed her public life and left her adrift, estranged from even many of her suffrage sisters. Suddenly the crowds were gone. The cheering was muffled. Even critics who couldn't seem to let go of her antiwar vote had lost interest. Rankin's political future had become yet another casualty of the Great War. Facing the postwar years was a greater challenge for her than campaigning for Congress. Now she stood alone.

In Georgia, Rankin was a humbled woman. She had no platform, no constituency, no title. She thought she had bled her final political fortunes from Montana. Her time in the US House, however brief, would inspire other women to take seats in Congress. First among them after Rankin's departure was Alice Mary Robertson, a Republican from Oklahoma, in 1921. Robertson opposed legislation in favor of women, immigrants and veterans, said politics was too immoral for women, and was voted out after one term. Then came a succession of women who rode their husbands' elective coattails. Rebecca Latimer Felton, a Democrat from Georgia, was given a ceremonial appointment to the US Senate. Her tenure when the chamber was in session lasted just twenty-four hours. A Republican from Illinois, Winnifred Sprague Mason Huck, served just fourteen weeks on an interim appointment. That year, in the 67th Congress, Republican Mae Ella Nolan of California became the first widow to succeed her husband. She finished her husband John's term in the House and was reelected to a second term, becoming the first woman to hold two consecutive terms in Congress.

Rankin, while in Congress, had become enchanted with the South. She had determined from talking with Southern members of Congress that: "The attitude of the South is toward peace, for another war would not necessarily mean more production, higher prices, and more grain. It is easier to talk to people who are interested in humanity more than in cold dollars." She wanted a place where her ideas could prosper, a place where she could build a movement that would grow and influence peace campaigns in other states. She found in the South a fertile field of politics, pregnant with possibilities for a peace movement, because in her estimation southern congressmen had led opposition to declaring war on Germany and starting a world war.

Among the notables were Claude Kitchin of North Carolina, who had struck the poignant scene in the House of Representatives condemning the atrocities of war, and editor Clark Howell of Georgia's *Atlanta Constitution*, who promised, "tears will someday move all the women of the world to be consulted before the 'War Lords' tear their sons from their bosoms." Rankin, although remembering how many southerners vigorously opposed suffrage, nonetheless praised them for questioning the morality of war. The issue of war and peace was close to the maternal heart of southern motherhood, and for that, Rankin was fortunate. "What could I say to my son if war comes, if I take a stand against war?" a Southern mother asked.

"Surely," Rankin replied, "you don't want to say to him, 'I haven't turned my hand to stop this war.'"

It never occurred to Rankin, ever the ideologue, that Georgia had a rumbling undercurrent of military adoration that contradicted her beliefs. Even arguments with her brother over her vote against a war declaration would pale compared with a clash brewing in Georgia. She chose to move to Georgia on the advice of friends, who suggested she settle near Athens where she could have the benefit of country living not far from the state university. During the Christmas season of 1923 she paid $500 for a sixty-four-acre farm near Bogart, ten miles west of Athens. The farm lacked structures except for a small "cotton house," but Rankin envisioned the land as her eventual depository of memorabilia and a base for peace operations lasting into the mid-1930s.[180]

Rankin also had practical reasons for choosing Georgia. She wanted to own a house in a balmy climate. She wanted to know people with black skin because her association with them had been limited.[181] Rankin assumed, to a degree wrongly, that Georgia would embrace sentiments for peace because of suffering from the Civil War. She would discover the contradiction soon enough. The farm was an unlikely home for an emerging pacifist, miles away from the whirl of politics in Washington, DC, and the Heterodoxy Club in New York. The grounds were a paradise of tangled honeysuckle and grapevines and wild plums and wild cherry, beckoning Rankin to drop her load of worry and enter into its Garden of Eden. The fragrance of flowers, the lyric-voiced birds and the vivid reds and yellows and greens made the farm a deceptive place. It was a lulling world where war did not exist.

Rankin decided to maintain a simple existence in Georgia when she needed a rest from her national politicking, but hidden in this simplicity was a purpose of extravagant proportions. Replete with a penniless lifestyle and a wealthy personal philosophy, she intended to convince the world that peace could succeed with a woman's coaxing. Georgia would become her laboratory for an experiment, a "center of infection" from where a peace epidemic could spread.

"Aspasia is a pioneer," Katharine Anthony would write of Rankin, assigning her a pen name for a series of stories appearing in *Women's Home Companion* magazine. Anthony thought her good friend resembled in vision and intellect the Greek goddess of that name, who had led the women of Athens to revolt. "She would never buy a farm which others had cultivated. She likes to blaze trails for others to follow and plough new lands for others to cultivate. The edge of cultivation has no terrors for Aspasia. She would always go beyond the edge and set her plow in virgin soil."

Anthony was one of Rankin's dearest friends, a sister in spirit. They had met two decades earlier at the School of Philanthropy in New York. Anthony, once a college instructor, was educated in history and psychology and began writing biographies with national success. Her book *Catherine the Great* and her subsequent *Queen Elizabeth* eventually would sell more than 100,000 copies apiece. That was a staggering readership for its time. Soon after, Anthony spent a month with Rankin at her Georgia farm to write for the magazine. It was there that Rankin's nickname was born.

At age forty-four, Rankin had found a fourth base of activism. The first was the will of the West to give women the vote. The second was the status quo eastern establishment. The third was the political heartbeat on Capitol Hill. In Georgia, her new and quiet scheme to start a peace movement started innocently enough. The farm had acres of neglected land. With no running water, no electricity and no toilet, the homestead was lost in the rural South. Predictably, Rankin bought it for these reasons. Her first mission was to rebuild the farm into a prototype of self-sufficiency. With the help of two sharecroppers who did the sawing and nailing, Rankin designed and constructed a functional one-room house. Life in Georgia in the 1920s was mostly provincial, with poor sharecroppers struggling to rise out of the farm depression that had gripped them since the Civil War.

She hadn't lost her childhood will to remain resourceful and frugal. Drawing seventy-five dollars a month from her father's estate, she found no difficulty in adjusting to poverty around her. To Rankin, it was indecent to display wealth. She knew Wellington would make sure she never went hungry. She earned money from her speaking honorariums. She remained enough of a curiosity to draw gatherings at schools, civic clubs and churches. She had acquired a reputation as a compelling speaker, known for her ability to make people laugh even as she drove home her more serious points. As the speaking engagements dwindled, so did her income.

The house exuded Rankin's newfound ideology. Having no kitchen facilities in the main building, she extended a plank of wood to the rustic cotton crib. It became her cookhouse. She had no sink but instead drained water through a gasoline funnel sunk into the counter to the ground outside. Reports varied on her cooking ability. Earlier publicity lauding her extraordinary skills in the kitchen might have been fabricated or at least exaggerated. She apparently cooked well only when she wanted to do so, which wasn't often. To some family members, her cooking was awful and she didn't care what she ate. She loved buttermilk more than coffee or tea. Often she drank a raw egg.[182]

Although most homes in rural American had outhouses several dozen feet from the house, Rankin built her toilet inside a small closet in the cookhouse. The convenience of having the toilet handy to the house was contrary to the bother of having to empty the apple box commode, which she pulled through a small trapdoor on the side of the cookhouse. Frequently she found herself taking a quick jaunt down the lane with commode in hand, watching for unexpected guests. Rankin drew her water from a well with a rope and a bucket. Light came from lanterns and candles. Steam from a car radiator, which Rankin had improvised along one wall, supplied heat on cooler days. Water pipes ran from the radiator to the fireplace where the water was heated.[183]

The plain, whitewashed house, which ceremoniously she named the *White House*, hardly was fitting for a former member of Congress, especially the first woman elected to a seat there. Much like a modern-day hippie gone back to the land, Rankin enjoyed the trivialities that made her a rebel among her contemporaries. She slept in the screened porch until the water froze in her glass on the nightstand. Reluctantly, as if disturbed by autumn's calling, she moved her bed inside the house as the weather cooled. Although this Spartan existence seemingly conflicted with Rankin's opinion that women should have the power to improve conditions in the home, she was at ease. By the time she moved to Georgia she had dispensed with social convention. She had been booed, ostracized, insulted and spat upon. It was of no consequence to her that her enemies condemned her for stirred up trouble in politics instead of being home with a husband, caring for children.

Rankin didn't exhibit frills and false impressions. Her stubborn resistance to the conventions of society invited frustrations. At middle age she found herself single and often lonely, married only to the cause of reform. Even as a girl, Rankin behaved as a serious young woman ignored by adolescence. She wouldn't be giddy, self-obsessed or frivolous. Her younger sister Hattie was carefree and lively with the boys, who came merrily to the Rankin home to charm her. More than once Jeannette had watched with some jealousy. Family and friends thought she wanted to have boyfriends, but she lacked the patience for what she saw as the silly social details and formalities that accompanied such relationships.

As a grown woman, she looked back on a few romantic interests, but none of the men she had known inspired her to marriage. She told friends that she avoided intimacy because it threatened her independence. She was fond of joking about marriage, partly from the pleasure of seeing men subdued by women, partly from the fear of being subdued herself. When asked by a Boston woman about the possibility of a woman being elected president, Rankin replied: "Why, certainly. It is inevitable, and more important, even desirable. That time is

not very distant. Probably fifty years, possibly sooner."
"Will the men want a woman president?" she was asked.
"They'll be delighted," she said. "A man inherently likes to be governed by a woman. Matrimony proves that."[184]

Marriage in the pre-World War II years demanded that women discard their opinions and assume those of the family leader — invariably the husband — with convention and grace. Rankin, conversely, refused to become chattel for a man. "My family always have been alarmed at the inclination I have to select unpopular causes, but at the present time I see no more urgent cause for women to back than ... outlawing war," she told a Cleveland, Ohio, audience soon after moving to Georgia.

Florence Kelley, general secretary of the National Consumers League, hired Rankin as a field secretary in November 1920. Issues on the organization's national agenda closely aligned with causes Rankin had pursued in the suffrage campaigns and in Congress. Among them were child labor laws, an eight-hour workday and federal protection of women and children.

Rankin's first assignment was to push for passage of the Sheppard-Towner Maternity and Infancy Act, the social welfare legislation she had introduced in the 65th Congress as the Rankin-Robinson Bill. Kelley, exasperated that two years and seven months had passed since Rankin introduced the measure, complained that 625,000 babies had died from preventable causes in that time. "Our standing among the nations measured by maternal mortality has fallen so that we now rank number seventeen," she wrote. More states, including "conservative Delaware," had enacted birth registration laws but South Dakota, Nevada, Arizona and others remained glaringly void of protections. President Harding, she wrote, wanted federal legislation passed to resolve the problem.[185] In its original form, the legislation called for annual federal appropriations to states to improve the health of expectant mothers and their babies in rural districts. Rankin had testified for the legislation before the House Labor Committee in January 1919 but the bill died before she left office. The new bill, similar to hers, overwhelmingly passed both chambers in Congress in 1921 and Harding signed it into law. It created thousands of child and maternal health clinics, many in rural areas.

For the next four years, Rankin lobbied for state and federal legislation affecting women and children, struggling to make "live issues" out of reform legislation. For a woman shy and indecisive as a college student, she was persuasive before college audiences. She spoke at universities in Iowa, Nebraska, Illinois, Kentucky, Ohio and Missouri. Apart from her salaried job with the National Consumers League, she remained active in the League for Peace and Freedom, addressing its Fourth Congress in Washington, DC, with the words: "The human spirit ... must be won by a positive vision of a world at peace, a world in which life and not death is honored, humanity and not wealth is not valued, love and not hate is practiced. A nation must see that war is a crime before there can be a spiritual awakening ... to find another way out."[186]

Rankin's vision of women and pacifism as a conclusive alliance surfaced often in her speeches and personal comments. "The peace problem is a woman's problem," she said in support of the Washington Conference on Limitation of Armament in the early 1920s. "Disarmament will not be won without their aid. So long as they shirk ... something will be radically wanting in the peace activities of the public and the state." Despite predictable scorn from men toward women's pacifism, she said, "I am aware that men are disposed to look down on the temperamental pacifism of women (which in spite of all the exceptions is a psychological fact) as something which the manly man would scorn to imitate. However, there is no other way that I can see in which peace can be realized except through forbearance from fighting on the part of men as well as women.... Therefore, peace is a woman's job."[187] In the same speech, Rankin also acknowledged that because of "the loss of social approval," pacifism would become a more difficult struggle than suffrage.

Rankin took a leave of absence from the Consumers League in the spring of 1924 to return to Montana to help Wellington in his campaign for the US Senate. In a curious turnabout of opponents, he was facing Frank Bird Linderman, an author of Indian tales and a Republican who lost to Jeannette in her election to the US House. The winner would stand against Thomas J. Walsh, the Democrat who defeated Jeannette in her bid for the US Senate in 1918. In the end, Wellington lost the primary by a narrow margin. Jeannette, tired of politics for the moment, quit the National Consumers League to begin her Georgia experiment.

Few people who knew her well believed she had put speeches and lobbying behind her. Georgia was a distraction, yes, but her mind always was active, even when she tilled the rich black soil in her garden. Behind every innocent appearance was a purpose. "I remember the outhouse in Bogart," said Dorothy McKinnon Brown, a niece. "I felt very sorry for myself, since we had *The Nation* and *The New Republic* for toilet paper, and very rough paper it was, while all our neighbors wiped on catalogues with slick paper."

Rankin's exile in Georgia meant she had the freedom to enjoy the contrast of blue-collar labor and white-collar intellectualism. As the hot sun burned her skin a reddish brown, she struck the pose of a struggling dirt farmer, an earthy woman gone back to the land. She could tease her supper from the garden one week and testify before the staid faces of a congressional committee the next. Much to her mother's dismay, Jeannette wore ragged clothes when she was at the farm. Olive Rankin, in her early years of marriage, had bathed every afternoon and donned a fresh dress before her husband returned home for work. When Olive visited Jeannette's farm she scolded her daughter for wearing her bathrobe, sometimes days at a time.

Mother Rankin, known as Ollie to her children, demanded to know how Jeannette could be serious about this business of lobbying for peace while being so sloppy with her appearance. Jeannette's opinion of clothes was simple. Why throw out a new pair of stockings if one had a flaw? Certainly one run did not make a stocking colder. She was not interested in wasting valuable time changing clothes when she could read a book or write a letter. Her family thought she sometimes adorned herself like a Christmas tree with costume jewelry. Rankin wouldn't spend money for real jewelry and didn't wear makeup. On more formal occasions she made a plain dress look good with imaginative maneuvers of needle and thread. She liked to look dignified in public but didn't really care what anyone thought about her appearance in the privacy of her farm.

In the spring of 1925, Rankin left her farmhouse to become field secretary of the American Section of the Women's International League for Peace and Freedom. It was a familiar association. Six years earlier, after she finished in Congress, she had gone to Switzerland as one of six American delegates to the Women's International Conference for Permanent Peace. At age thirty-nine she was the youngest member of the delegation, which included luminaries Jane Addams and Dr. Alice Hamilton, known for bringing the study of industrial diseases into the realm of medical science. The conference, involving thirteen countries, formulated changes to the Versailles treaty that President Wilson later rejected as profoundly impractical. In a final act, women renamed their conference the Women's International League of Peace and Freedom. In January 1920, the League sent Rankin to the US State Department to seek the early release of all prisoners of war and to propose that all political offenders be set free. It was a futile effort but typical of her willingness to confront men in power.

Rankin's new commitment to the organization in 1925 would require constant travel. The task of organizing districts and making speeches felt very much like what she had done for woman suffrage a decade earlier. "The work of educating the world to peace is the woman's job, because men have a natural fear of being classed as cowards if they oppose war," she told an audience in Cleveland, Ohio.[188] She described war as a "mad dog that should be locked up" and admitted her family's concern at her headlong devotion to unpopular causes. In dozens of public appearances, she spoke of her belief that women must work to outlaw war, and she urged them to form councils that would promote peace.

Rankin attacked her new job with predictable gusto. "Do take care of yourself, and don't get too overtired, and know that anything I can do to save, or help you, will only make me too happy," wrote Dorothy Detzer, the organization's executive secretary.[189] Despite appearances of concern, the office scheduled a blinding chain of appointments that pushed Rankin relentlessly across the countryside. Whether a result of her fame or a desire to exploit it, the demanding schedule in a single month illustrated her impending fatigue. In March 1925 she spoke at a college in Toronto, Canada, and then two days later, at a YMCA luncheon in Dayton, Ohio. She also addressed audiences in Boston, New York, Philadelphia, Cleveland, Chicago, Milwaukee and St. Paul that month, taking overnight trains on her interstate journeys. One train trip in Delaware lasted only seven minutes; others, most of a day or night. At the Germantown Colored YMCA, fifteen "industrial girls" heard her speak. A mass meeting at the William Penn High School for Girls drew one thousand students. Appearances included teas, chapels and buffet suppers.[190] "Peace is certainly more popular than it was six months ago. In Detroit they had reserved 134 places for the luncheon and 235 came," Rankin wrote Marion Holmes in Boston. The dean of the English department at the State Normal School in West Chester, Pennsylvania, welcomed Rankin back with a promise of a full day's schedule. Her appearance so influenced students, he wrote, that he supplied them all with copies of the book *The Abolition of War*. "The attitude of the student body toward an out and out and absolute pacifist is gratifying," wrote Robert T. Kerlin, who concluded his letter by condemning the "capitalistic causes of war."[191]

From Washington, an admirer named Flora Belle Surles wrote to commend Rankin on the "size of audiences" she was attracting. Surles, who was then a secretary at the Women's International League of Peace and Freedom office, had taken a liking to Rankin while she was in Congress. "Did you realize that you have reached 14,000 people, besides radio audiences?" Surles asked in one letter. A few weeks later, after an annual peace meeting, she wrote: "May I say, personally, I am very glad you have had this little connection with us, and I'm hoping very much that after the summer vacation you'll be with us again. It always seems a privilege to me to work with one like you, and I assure you it's a personal pleasure to do so."[192]

As Rankin raced from venue to venue, J.P. Nunnally, a justice of the peace and neighbor in Bogart, wrote her with a tale of woe about drought on her farm. Peach trees and vines had suffered, roses weren't growing and some pecan trees were dying from the tops down. A neighbor had a serious illness. She was in Washington, DC, at the time, far from Georgia's rural quiet, but the letter drew a hard distinction between slow life on the farm and fast politics in the nation's capital.[193] It wasn't quite enough to turn Rankin's heart back toward Georgia. By late spring of 1925, however, she began questioning the purpose of her assignment. "I have spoken to a good many people and traveled a good many miles," she wrote a friend, Josephine Wilkins, in Georgia. "There is a tremendous amount of sentiment but it is unorganized and inarticulate." She also complained to Dorothy Detzer in Washington, "time is wasted unless better arrangements are made." Seeking Rankin's commitment to continue the work, Detzer replied: "I'm sorry that the routings, and perhaps other things, are not done as efficiently as you would like." Detzer also scolded Rankin for threatening to abandon an arranged appearance: "Greatly disturbed by your telegram insist you be there for large luncheon as per agreement."[194] Finally, complaining that she saw no larger purpose in the Peace and Freedom organization, Rankin resigned her job, giving up a $250 monthly salary, and went home to Georgia.

She organized clubs for boys and girls in Bogart, much as she had learned to do at the School of Philanthropy in New York and the settlement house in San Francisco. The girls' Sunshine Club concentrated on sewing, cooking, reading and learning parliamentary law. Rankin made seven bathing suits from cloth obtained from a nearby cotton mill. The girls didn't like the suits, thinking they looked like winter underwear, until Rankin dyed them a bright rose.[195] Boys' activities were less structured. She read peace stories to the younger ones and helped the older ones build crystal radio sets. They came to her farm often barefooted and riding mules. They danced and sang to ragtime melodies.[196]

Rankin often invited people to stay at her White House for a few days. Eventually she built bedrooms to accommodate guests. Invariably, dinner conversations turned to talk of war and peace. Rankin became ecstatic, her eyes wandering among her guests to draw them into the debate. If anyone said, "Oh, but you can't stop war," she threw up her hands in dismay and exclaimed, "Why do you say that? They said you couldn't stop cholera and you couldn't stop small pox, and women could never vote. I hate these nevers."[197]

Her back-to-the-land existence, a spare manner of living, wasn't without subsidy. Her brother Wellington — a fervent believer of the patriotic implications of war — helped stock her cupboards and buy her gasoline as she waged her private peace campaign. The money came not as an endorsement of Jeannette's politics, but to help pay their mother's expenses when she lived there. In the 1920s, Jeannette helped raise her sister Edna's children, Dorothy and John, after Edna's divorce. John died at summer camp at age seven. Jeannette cherished her niece Dorothy like a daughter, raising her into adulthood.[198]

Wellington was generous in his financial support. Back in Montana, he had ascended to the top of Montana politics. After a spell as Montana's attorney general that included a law-and-order campaign against bootleggers, he resigned in 1924 when Governor Joseph Dixon appointed him to the Montana Supreme Court. He replaced Charles H. Cooper, father of Hollywood cowboy actor Gary Cooper. Wellington spent only a year on the high court. In late 1925, President Coolidge made him a US district attorney. Wellington's quick legal mind served him well in the courtroom. He was shrewd like his father and steadily built his bank account. Wellington sent money to Jeannette whenever he thought she needed it. He often disagreed with her ideas but brotherly love simply was stronger than his distaste for some of her causes.

In the seven years since she left Congress, Jeannette persisted with her passion for reform. While Americans were singing, "Yes, We Have No Bananas," Rankin stood firm in her belief that the peace movement could bear fruit. She had become a full-fledged pacifist. "Seven years after the war to end war we still find war a legal, honorable, patriotic, institution for attempting to settle international disputes," Rankin wrote. "The League of Nations recognizes it as the final arbiter. International law is the law of war. Wars of aggression are lawful. It is perfectly legal for a nation to go into another country, with or without cause, kill the inhabitants and take their possessions if they do it in the name of war."[199]

The 1920s became a turbulent time in America. President Warren G. Harding died of a stroke while in office. Tennessee schoolteacher John Scopes was arrested for teaching evolution in violation of new state law banning the teachings of Darwin. In the ensuing "Scopes Monkey Trial," defense attorney Clarence Darrow sparred with three-time presidential candidate William Jennings Bryan in a legendary debate of modernity versus fundamentalism. A jury found Scopes guilty. In another notorious courtroom drama that captivated the nation, Italian immigrant radicals and accused murderers Nicola Sacco and Bartolomeo Vanzetti were executed by electric chair after years of appeals.

In a show of power calculated to silence doubters of their strength, forty-thousand Ku Klux Klansmen marched to the US Capitol, their white robes billowing as they swept down Pennsylvania Avenue. It was a reminder that despite women having the right to vote, deep racial divisions remained and numerous devices and intimidations discouraged black women from voting.

Dark as the decade was, it also was an age of triumph and enlightenment. In 1927, aviator Charles Lindbergh completed the world's first solo transatlantic flight. He became a national hero after he guided the "Spirit of Saint Louis" in thirty-three hours from New York to Paris. Buster Keaton's comedy classic *The General*, considered by many people the greatest silent film ever made, hit the theaters. Then came Al Jolson's *The Jazz Singer*, the first talking motion picture, dropping a curtain on the silent film era. In books, F. Scott Fitzgerald published *The Great Gatsby* in 1925; Ernest Hemingway followed with his novel *The Sun Also Rises* in 1926. A baseball legend named Babe Ruth hit his 60th home run for the Yankees in the 1927 season, breaking his own record of 59. Ruth's record would stand for more than thirty years.

It was against this national backdrop in the postwar United States that Jeannette Rankin showered her ideas for peace on Georgians who lived near her farm. Soon she was talking with university intellectuals in Athens, closely similar to the Heterodoxy group in New York. By 1928 she had a circle of acquaintances with a common goal.

One evening thirty-five people met in the studio apartment of Lucy Stanton, a prominent Georgia painter, to form a foreign policy club that within weeks would become the Georgia Peace Society, a name revived from a group formed at the University of Georgia in 1872 to heal wounds from the Civil War. The new peace society continued its strong university affiliation. Inez Burnet, married to the university's library director, became president. E. Merton Coulter, a history professor and a faculty advisor to the university's International Relations Club, was named vice president. Rankin was elected secretary, but retained leadership with a clause stating she had the power to call the meetings. The group included locally prominent women and men whose purpose was to study American foreign policy to encourage the settlement of international disputes by arbitration. Rankin initiated most of the activities. The society usually convened only when she was in Athens.

Participants at that first meeting adopted and circulated a

"War and Human Nature" resolution that said war should be condemned as a legal crime. Its purpose was to encourage nations to resolve their disputes in international courts. "War is an outworn institution, as untrustworthy as the duel in the present enlightened stage of human nature," the resolution read in part.[200] Subsequent discussions centered on the Kellogg-Briand Pact, an agreement signed in the summer of 1928 by the United States and several European countries to outlaw war. It eventually would fail for lack of any enforcement language, and within twelve years all the signatories would be embroiled in a world war like no other. For that short time, the pact offered hope to pacifists like Rankin who saw it as the first of many steps to prevent another world war. She guided the Peace Society into a resolution supporting the treaty.

Soon after, the society joined with the Georgia League of Women Voters to sponsor a state conference for the Cause and Cure of War, the first of forty-eight such conferences nationally. It opened in May 1928 with delegates attending from ten sponsoring organizations. Rankin and Coulter participated in a roundtable discussion of international peace pacts, the League of Nations and various arbitration treaties. Conference attendees urged ratification of Kellogg-Briand, expressed appreciation to 1924 Republican and Democratic parties for favoring international arbitration, and called on Georgians to initiate public activism to protest war.[201]

"Legislation is an index of progress in education and is valuable in itself only when it measures intelligent public opinion. The ballot is the great educator of the masses," Rankin wrote that year. She took the position that war should be proclaimed as a crime. Speeches that Rankin wrote often drifted into suggestions of socialism, calling into question whether elective government could corral its impulses toward war. "Today the fomenters of war, the imperialists, militarists and profiteers, are on the side of the law when they work for war," she wrote in a 1928 speech. "The great masses of people, women, organized workers, and workers on the soil who know the devastation of war are working against law when they work for peace."[202]

The conference received favorable publicity in Georgia newspapers, including the *Macon Telegraph*. Editor W. L. Anderson wrote: "If world peace is to become a reality, it will become so because the great masses of men and women have been taught...to believe in at least the possibility of outlawing war. This is the task...which the Georgia Committee on the Cause and Cure of War has set for itself."[203] Two subsequent conferences in 1929 and 1930 drove the point home that the Georgia Peace Society had embarked on a mission to outlaw war. In July 1929, Rankin addressed the annual meeting of the National Education Association in Atlanta, entitling her lecture, "Teachers and World Peace." She was by then the new field representative for the Women's Peace Union. Adopting a constitutional amendment to make war illegal for any purpose was necessary "to build a structure and temper for peace."[204] Rankin took advantage of her presence in Atlanta to lobby for a constitutional amendment at the State Legislature. She spoke on behalf of a House resolution to make war legally impossible but Speaker Richard B. Russell, who later would become a US senator, led a successful effort to defeat it. The Women's Peace Union, disagreeing with her emphasis on street-level involvement, did not renew her contract.[205]

By the 1930s, American pacifists sensed fresh threats of war. Japan in 1931 had invaded and was occupying Manchuria in defiance of Kellogg-Briand. "Do you want to help China?" a militarist asked Rankin. "Of course I want to help China," she replied, "but I am not going to throw myself out of a 17th story window to help China."

American sentiment against war had cooled during the Flapper Era. Pacifists sensed a new urgency to their work. A wave of national regret over World War I would bring Rankin and other pacifists to the forefront of an unprecedented debate over war profiteering and the role of the United States in international affairs.

15 ~ One woman against war

'War is the slaughter of human beings, temporarily enemies'

Some of the most defining years of Jeannette Rankin's life came in the 1930s, when she embarked on a relentless campaign to expose profits from war. That era would be known first for a catastrophic Great Depression born of the stock market crash of 1929. International trade would fall by more than half, American crop prices by sixty percent. Unemployment in the United States would shoot to a staggering 25 percent. Persistent drought in the nation's heartland would lead to "Grapes of Wrath" scenarios of dusty worthless farms and entire families clunking westward in old trucks in search of jobs that would pay for food. Their congregations in shanty towns known as "Hoovervilles" would last until Franklin D. Roosevelt's "New Deal" legislation started the United States on the road to economic recovery.

The 1930s would be remembered for another unprecedented era in American history as well. It would be the golden age of pacifism, a time of frank national debate over the price of war, a time of regret over the losses of the First World War. Pacifism and its close cousin of that era, isolationism, grew strong in the 1930s because of persistent suspicion that Roosevelt and other leaders would start a war to resuscitate the nation's economy. At least that's how

Rankin and other pacifists saw it. By reputation of those words she uttered in Congress in 1917 — "I want to stand by my country but I cannot vote for war. I vote no" — Rankin was among the best known pacifists of that era and the only one driven by an insatiable urge to show she was more than a historical footnote. She would leave her fingerprints all over the frantic investigation into war profiteering.

In October 1929, the very month that the stock market plunged and a run on bank deposits began, Rankin applied for a job at the Quaker-founded National Council for Prevention of War (NCPW). She wrote Frederick Libby, executive secretary, who wanted her to manage a regional office in Atlanta. Libby was a teacher and a Congregational minister who became a Quaker. He had worked for the organization since it began in 1921 as the National Council for Limitation of Armaments. By the time Rankin joined the NCPW it represented more than two dozen national peace organizations. It stood strong against public spending for armaments and condemned war profiteering by private companies. Much of its work was accomplished through public education campaigns and mailings. In the early years of her employment, Rankin would find this approach to her liking, but eventually her enthusiasm would wither.

When Libby postponed the project — the first of many disappointments she would face with the NCPW — she appeared at his office, telling him angrily of her regret at not having a permanent job: "Nobody wants me. I hate day-to-day jobs and have had them all my life."[206] Finally he hired her as a field secretary, but because her paychecks were small and irregular, the job title was more honorary than enriching.

That was the price of peace, however, and Rankin was prepared to meet the commitment with her self-induced appearance of poverty. She sometimes talked as if she were desperately poor, feeling it morally wrong to look wealthy despite her late father's money-building ventures in Montana and her brother's occasional deposits in her banking account.[207] Some of her relatives would remember that when she wasn't making public appearances she often looked unkempt, wearing an old sack dress, her hair crying for a brush. On public occasions, she could be quite charming. When she wasn't living on her farm in Georgia, she kept an apartment in Washington, DC, for her work in that city. Willie Snow Ethridge, a Georgia writer who was an activist in the anti-lynching movement, described a dinner Rankin served one night at her apartment. Ethridge and her husband Mark were there. So was Representative Walter Lambeth of North Carolina, whom Willie described as "a handsome, pleasant-talking bachelor." Rankin prepared creamed chicken and rice, a salad of fresh vegetables, "thick, dark crackers like pumpernickel," and brought cheese, jam, ice cream and cake to the table.[208] Whatever her private preferences, she remained famous for what she had achieved. Across the country, even more girls were named after her. One of those instances came in 1931 when Wellington Rankin received a letter from his sister's namesake in Phoenix, Arizona. Wellington, by then Montana's attorney general, replied to Jeannette Rankin Fields on official stationery from his office in Helena. The young namesake had written Wellington in hopes of reaching Jeannette. "No doubt you were named for her. She would be glad to hear from you," Wellington wrote, sharing that Jeannette lived on a farm in Georgia. "You were named for a very courageous woman who has never sacrificed her conctious [sic] for the sake of policy."[209]

Soon after she began work for the NCPW, Rankin searched for a soapbox, as she had done all her life, to promote peace her own way. The Georgia Peace Society, and other Rankin ventures such as the Georgia Conference on the Cause and Cure of War, had succeeded in creating public awareness of the peace movement. Nevertheless, she felt her Georgia experiment had failed.

The National Council for Prevention of War kept her moving in a whistle-stop campaign for peace, scheduling her state-by-state appearances in such rapid sequence that often left her stranded on railway platforms and in dingy hotel rooms, waiting for money, reservations and orders. In an ordeal reminiscent of her days with the Women's International League for Peace and Freedom, she endured hasty schedules, sophomoric calculations by headquarters staff about the political makeup of her audiences, and tea parties hosted by banal, conformist matrons.

In the autumn and winter of 1933 she barnstormed across the country making a series of appearances on behalf of the NCPW. She spoke to a Rotary Club in Flagstaff, Arizona, and visited a NCPW chapter in Eugene, Oregon. She portrayed war as frivolous and kept her audiences interested with her humor and stark facts. "She made all preparations for war to seem to be so absolutely silly and nonsensical that one wonders why we keep it up at all," wrote Pastor Harry L. Allen of the Methodist Church in Pomeroy, Washington. "She held the large attendance in rapt attention for the major portion of an hour."[210] Her tour that fall included a speech to the Montana Legislature, delivered with emotion. "It was the finest speech on war prevention I have ever listened to ... I have heard dozens of world peace lectures, but never any so eloquent, so informative and so convincing as that given by Miss Rankin," declared Belle Fligelman Winestine, hardly an impartial observer. "The galleries were packed solidly, and buzzing conversation in the halls after the talk showed clearly that even the legislators, who are generally unmoved by anything except a mines tax or prohibition, were deeply impressed."[211]

Women and children added their support to Rankin's

efforts. Commented a West Coast member of the NCPW: "We can scarcely praise Miss Rankin too highly for her clear insight into the whole question of war and peace, her keen analysis of the problem, her practical plans for attacking it, and the enthusiasm she inspires by showing her audience how the ordinary citizen may actually accomplish much toward the establishment of permanent peace. With all of her public work and experience she remains delightfully feminine, and her sense of humor is a saving grace and a refreshing oasis in [a] desert of bitter problems."[212]

Selma M. Borchardt, a teacher at Roosevelt High School in Washington, DC, wrote Rankin in February 1933 to commend her for giving a peace talk to 1,600 students. One of the girls in an English class later wrote, "I think Miss Rankin is right. It would be better to think about whether we should fight, rather than how we should fight."[213] First Lady Eleanor Roosevelt, in a letter to Rankin, agreed that if the will for peace could grow in the hearts of women everywhere they might be able to calm the tense situation in Europe. "At present it is very difficult to deal with Germany normally or rationally, because while she is demanding that other nations disarm, she herself is arming in every way she can under cover. I think the only thing we can do at this time is to keep people as calm as possible — the women especially — in all countries," the First Lady wrote.[214]

A membership drive for the Georgia Peace Society in 1935 offered regular membership for twenty-five cents and cooperating membership for one dollar. "These small fees are asked to cover postage for announcements," the flyer said. A nucleus of supporters in Athens wanted to recruit members statewide to join in an upcoming state meeting.[215] Rankin found an opportunity to awaken the state's support when, under the auspices of the NCPW, she started a debate with Carl Vinson, a prominent war hawk from the Tenth

Congressional District in Georgia. In 1931, Rankin conducted a referendum poll in Georgia to oppose a $616 million naval building bill. Vinson, known as "the Admiral," had introduced the bill in Congress after he was named chairman of the House Naval Affairs Committee. Rankin viewed the bill as an insult to the taxpayer. Vinson's home newspaper, *The Macon Telegraph*, agreed. "It is absurd for a nation with a tremendous deficit to go spending money for a great many of its family," the newspaper said in an editorial.

To support her pro-peace stand, Rankin solicited 159 postcards from sixty-two towns protesting the bill. She presented them to Vinson during lunch one day. He accurately accused her of trying to build support to defeat the bill when it came to a vote in Congress.[216] Because of widening sentiment against the legislation and pressure from Rankin and her allies — the Georgia Peace Society and the Georgia Committee on Disarmament — the bill died in committee. Rankin's satisfaction didn't last long, however, because the Vinson bill resurfaced in 1933 and passed Congress the next year. Rankin wrote of the legislation, which authorized the expenditure of a billion dollars for naval armament: "Nothing since the war has been so ominous."[217] Contrary to her predictions, Vinson was reelected to Congress by a three-to-one margin over his opponent.

By 1934 Rankin had built a reputation in Georgia as a woman forever doing work that women weren't supposed to do, passions not in vogue with the times. True to the turbulence in her life, she remained out of step with history, but her work became fashionable as the era of antiwar specialty groups swept into full swing. Lobbies such as the NCPW and the Georgia Peace Society flourished because leaders like Jeannette Rankin made them go, but they were not the will of the people. Personalities built the antiwar groups of the 1930s. During the Depression, many Americans appeared less interested in threats of world war than being fed and clothed.

Rankin's work had few rewards. If she gave a speech and received promises in return, she knew she had done her job well. If she was given money, she had gained a convert. It she won a volunteer, she had lessened the forces of war by one. The psychology of dissent was not for timid souls. Rankin sustained a hectic daily routine that exhausted most enthusiasts. She struggled for nine years to build awareness in Georgia.

Sometimes she behaved as a woman driven by a fear of failure. She took vacations to Montana and projected moments of leisure to casual observers, yet she never let her mind break free from work. Securing international peace became her single chosen destiny. Alternately she would be forced to consider herself a failure. In 1933, complaining to Libby about an upcoming speaking tour, she revealed feelings of futility:

"I don't know how I could possibly spend three months traveling and survive. It is going to be very difficult for me to keep going for the three months of the Western trip. It is quite necessary for me to be at home to relax and secure courage to go out and face the cold, stupid world again.... To put it mildly, making people listen to me is part of the work that appeals to me very little."

But Rankin did it anyway, sensing the approach of war. She was in no danger of being aloof and misguided. *Public Opinion Quarterly* and other publications forecast the rumblings of war in Europe. She spoke of foreign powers as if they were little children. In a mood of futility and anger, she again wrote to Libby: "I am feeling very much let down, after making twenty-two speeches and driving the car over a thousand miles, getting more than sixty resolutions with every congressional district in Georgia represented, and spending one whole night catching a train, then to have England and France acting like stupid children.... [President] Roosevelt decides to build tanks and airplanes while the Disarmament Conference is still struggling."

As early as 1929, Rankin had pushed for constitutional amendments to outlaw war. One was proposed by the Women's Peace Union and introduced into the US Senate by Lynn J. Frazier of North Dakota. Rankin wrote: "There can be no compromise with war; it cannot be reformed or controlled; cannot be disciplined into decency or codified into common sense; for war is the slaughter of human beings, temporarily regarded as enemies, on as large a scale as possible."[218]

Rankin's foes often insinuated she hated men. To some people her persistent public portrayals of women as saviors of men seemed more inflammatory than she might have intended, or realized, but that single-minded notion became her mantra during the turbulent antiwar years of the 1930s. In an era that gave voice to fanatics such as the Fascist-leaning Father Coughlin and the dictatorial Huey Long, Rankin's peace message sounded mild by comparison. Nonetheless she gave her critics plenty of ammunition. Men fight, she wrote, because "they are afraid there won't be enough to go round. They have a deeply rooted belief that ultimately the only way to get something is to take it away from somebody else. They are temperamentally competitive. Probably this comes from the primitive masculine way of fighting the rival for the possession of the female."[219]

Rankin's organizational work in Georgia included advertisements for the Georgia Peace Society at county agricultural fairs. Two slogans in prominent display at the Athens Fair in 1934 aimed at biblical and lyrical fairgoers: "All they that taketh the sword shall perish by taxes," and "You can no more win a war than you can an earthquake." Large maps of Europe, paired with photos showing the horror of war, were meant to acquaint viewers with the futility of intervening in a foreign conflict. Volunteers distributed literature explaining the social costs of war munitions. Students gave peace talks. Rankin's approach was in line with her belief that Americans had been taught a "war method" that insightful education by peace activists would reverse. "When the people have been taught the sensible and civilized manner of settling disputes, they will vote against warfare and we shall have world peace," she said.[220]

Rankin made a case that munitions makers, shipbuilders and others were spending $2 million a day for propaganda to support war. In an appearance before the Senate Committee on Naval Affairs in 1934, she said profiteering should be apparent to anyone who had wanted to see the truth. To Rankin, construction of a new fleet of ships would serve two purposes only: security for merchant ships to expedite profiteering, or transportation of military forces overseas. "These ships are not being built with the idea of defending our shores. The only real purpose these ships can serve is to give shipbuilders contracts, and to give the munitions makers contracts. The purpose of this bill is to keep the shipbuilders and munition makes and profiteers in running order so that they can make more profits. There is no reason for a war scare today," she testified in a congressional hearing on proposed expansion of the Navy. "I represent the common people, the people on the farm and the people in the cities, and the women who feel that this is a total waste of money."[221]

Liberally quoting a popular national news article written by Wayne Francis Palmer, a former naval officer, Rankin described how a fleet of ships was obsolete in the days of bomber planes. She said ships could operate only if the enemy overlooked the potential of smoke screens and scrambled wire communications, which as Palmer had written, would make ships "deaf and dumb." Palmer's position was that large fleets of ships would fail as fighting units because they lacked sufficient communication devices to coordinate their power effectively. Susceptible to garbles and to jamming by enemies, ships' communication equipment often proved more of a hindrance than a help, Palmer wrote. "In the next great battle at sea it will be a toss-up as to whether the greatest danger will come from the enemy fleet, or each fleet will constitute the greatest danger to itself."[222]

One of the most prominent neutrality actions of the 1930s, known as the Ludlow Referendum, proposed to require by constitutional amendment that Americans vote on whether to enter a foreign war. The only exception to such a referendum, if a country first attacked the United States, meant that Representative Louis Ludlow and his supporters wanted a new national defense policy to head off American participation in another world war. Ludlow, a Democrat from Indiana, had revived a decades-old movement that began before World War I. Rankin, under the auspices of the National Council for Prevention of War, lobbied hard for the legislation. Its eventual defeat — and President Roosevelt's opposition to it — caused her to question "why he felt it necessary to threaten war, why he distrusts people, and what he intends to do to keep us out of war?"[223]

One of the darkest times in Rankin's life came when she was swept into a bitter feud with the American Legion. It exposed Rankin's distance from the prevailing national conservative mood depicted in Sinclair Lewis' *Main Street*, demonstrated the growing struggle between pacifists and militarists, and contradicted Rankin's mistaken assumption that Georgia would offer little resistance to her peace epidemic. The impending confrontation would cause her more distress than did the widespread national anger over her vote against war with Germany in 1917. If she had considered how her squabble with the Legion influenced public opinion — most Georgia newspapers actively endorsed her and her cause received immense publicity — she might have been grateful she had gained a measure of respect in exchange for encumbrances of a local controversy. Suddenly, the fighter for peace and a leader for human rights found herself retreating from military veterans for more than two years.

The controversy started with a commendation from the Georgia Peace Society. Rabbi Abraham Shusterman of the Athens Synagogue said of Rankin, on behalf of the Society: "She had induced us with the conviction that the individual effort is meaningful and efficacious.... She has brought us the enthusiasm to make ours a truly moral nation.... Finally, Miss Rankin has brought us a new vision of the meaning of democracy."

Rankin's reputation as a peacemaker earned her a contract to deliver four lectures at Brenau College, an all-women liberal arts school at Gainesville, sixty miles from Atlanta in the Blue Ridge Mountains. She arrived for the first lecture in October 1934. Vice President H.J. Pearce Jr., administering the college while his father was away, introduced Rankin to journalism and political science students as a likely candidate for a "Chair of Peace" that Brenau College trustees were thinking about establishing. An overzealous news reporter made notes and raced from the room. The next day, the *Atlanta Constitution* incorrectly reported that Brenau College had hired Rankin as the first "Professor of Peace."

The story stirred to action members of the American Legion's Atlanta Post No. 1, angry for years over Rankin's influence of "the young womanhood of the South" and her pointed criticism of American military expenditures. This was the first indication in Georgia of resistance to her peace campaign. The Legion wanted to drag her into a controversy to force her to stop teaching "communistic" principles.

Kenneth Murrell, commander of the Atlanta post, promised that the American Legion would resist any efforts by Brenau College to teach pacifism to its students. He talked of a spirit of unrest and uneasiness throughout the world, and warned that to create an interest in any "ism" other than Americanism among youth was "un-Americanism." In response, Pearce said that the Legion misunderstood the nature of the proposed chair. He suggested that making an inquiry before taking action would have prevented wild accusations.

The fight had begun. Rankin faded temporarily from the scene as the Legion aimed its initial assault on Brenau. The college and the American Legion traded jabs until Pearce, speaking for his father, Brenau President H.J. Pearce Sr., told an Atlanta newspaper he could not accept such righteous statements as the true sentiment of the American Legion. Cleverly, he suggested Murrell must have been misquoted, saying neither Washington, Jefferson, Lincoln, Woodrow Wilson, Jesus nor the Apostle Paul would be acceptable as Americans under the restrictions to which Murrell was credited.

The Legion then turned its attention to Rankin. She remained at her Georgia farm with the dispute fresh in her mind, thankful the Pearces had come to her defense, yet suspicious that much of their interest was inspired by the publicity being enjoyed by the college. "Atlanta Post No. 1 does not want the school of thought propagated by Miss Rankin to take root in the South or anywhere else," Murrell wrote in a letter to the Brenau vice president. "We will use our efforts to counteract the influence which Brenau will exert with Jeanette [sic] Rankin as a member of its faculty."

The Legionnaires received little sympathy in their plight to save Georgia from Jeannette Rankin. "Why is it that supposedly responsible Georgians are so fond of making themselves ludicrous?" asked the *Richmond News Leader* of

Virginia. "Is there something in the atmosphere down there which is conducive to such antics?" The *Memphis Commercial-Appeal* of Tennessee said the Legionnaires were being hypocritical in assailing a college and a woman dedicated to the understanding of war and peace. "It seems rather ridiculous, therefore, that there should be raised a great outcry against the appointment of Miss Jeanette [sic] Rankin," the newspaper said.

And from the *Gainesville Eagle* of Georgia: "As we see it, the Legionaires [sic] of Atlanta went off half-cocked, and most unwise in their choice of words, and are making accusations unfounded by the facts. The only way their act would be justifiable, as we see it, would be for Miss Rankin to be a rabid pacifist, unwilling to protect her nation's honor and integrity to any cost and preferring, instead, to turn the country to an invader rather than fight. Knowing Miss Rankin, we know this to be untrue."

Although the Great Depression threatened any chance of money for a Chair of Peace anyway, the arguments continued. As if begging for an opportunity to decide the right to agitate for peace, college professors, students, national news magazines and friends sided with Rankin. Observing "an outburst of fanaticism in Georgia right now," the Reverend D. P. McGeachy, a Presbyterian minister from Decatur, wrote to her: "I wish we had a thousand teachers like you in the South. ... I wonder when the American Legion will come to see that they have no monopoly on definitions or opinions in a country like ours. Sometimes I get a little hopeless about these dear fellows but surely the World War did not take away all the sense God gave them in the beginning."[224]

An editorial in the Brenau student newspaper saw it this way: "We say welcome to Miss Rankin. We feel that a Chair of Peace at Brenau may be the greatest step towards progress that has ever been made.... Welcome to all those whose desire it is to build of America a more wonderful nation. We are not Hottentots, not Communists, nor radically free thinkers. We are Americans interested in the affairs of our country."[225] Editorialized *The New Republic*, a national news opinion magazine: "If the American Legionaires [sic] thought they could turn Miss Rankin from her purposes, they were naïve. Having braved the ill wind of a whole nation, it is not likely she will be disturbed by empty flag waving and a few harsh words."[226]

But she was. In a two-page typed letter to the president of Brenau, Rankin felt compelled to defend herself. She described herself as having no political affiliations despite having run for Congress on the Republican ticket. She also wrote that she had "never subscribed to the doctrines of communism, nor am I connected directly or indirectly with any organization which is committed to such doctrines," and that voting against world war was her right as a patriot and a congresswoman. "I ask those who would condemn me for such a view whether subsequent events have not justified my vote. Would such critics favor another such war, and on the same terms? ... The sum of my reputed radicalism seems to be my opposition to war, to competitive armaments and to predatory interests," she wrote the elder Pearce. "I have no quarrel with the American Legion. I grant them the same American and constitutional freedom of conscience and freedom of speech which I claim for myself." Rankin mentioned Woodrow Wilson as a pacifist, a revealing concession given her strong feelings against the president during World War I. Wilson had mistakenly thought the war would end all wars, she wrote in an atypically understated tone devoid of any regret.[227]

In a late December letter to Haywood Pearce's wife, Rankin disclosed that the American Legion attack had disrupted her Christmas preparations. Once again she mentioned British author Benjamin Kidd's book *Science of Power* as giving "the most complete arguments for women taking their part in the world...."[228]

H.J. Pearce St. accused the Legion of throttling freedom of speech by attempting to dictate what subjects should be taught at the college. He invited Murrell and eleven Legionnaires to dine in the college dormitory one Sunday afternoon and listen to Rankin speak in the college auditorium that evening. Murrell refused. Pearce then met in his office with a committee of Legionnaires who agreed to speak on peace from their point of view. The first lecturer was Capt. A.L. Hensen, director of the Veteran Service Bureau in Atlanta, who argued that conscription was a peace measure. Meanwhile, the Brenau board of trustees collected money for the Chair of Peace. Fifty-thousand dollars would be devoted to the professor's salary and $100,000 would establish a Department of Peace, hardly a modest sum while many Americans occupied soup lines as the Great Depression wore on. Faculty members generally assumed the college president would recommend Rankin as the first occupant of the new chair.

Brenau hoped the disciplines of economics, politics, international law, diplomacy, international finance and history could expose the causes and costs of war. Despite the wide scope of the intended Chair of Peace, the Brenau faculty did not balk at the inadequacy of Rankin's formal education, which included few of the subjects they wished her to teach. Her decades of political achievement and self-study erased concern for any academic shortcomings but did not reduce evidence of her poor spelling and distaste for writing.

Because the Brenau controversy arrived at the heart of a nationwide economic catastrophe, the dream of a peace professorship died for lack of hard cash. Murrell, angry over a

Brenau newsletter than he thought had omitted the American Legion point of view, had the last word. He told Brenau that a "Chair of Citizenship" would serve as a more sensible endowment to show "appreciation for our time honored principles of government under the Constitution...good American institutions of national import have warned that there is a very pressing need for this." Among them, he wrote Pearce, were the United Spanish War Veterans, The Daughters of the American Revolution, the Boy Scouts of America and the Benevolent and Protective Order of the Elks. All of them, Murrell said, "expressed grave concern over the brand of citizenship" taught in the United States and wanted "Americanism" taught in schools.

Then his missive got uglier. Rankin, he wrote, was an officer of at least five communist organizations including the American Civil Liberties Union. He didn't name the others. ACLU literature "was being secretly circulated in Georgia by a negro under the assumed name of Angelo Herndon, (later attempting to incite insurrection in Georgia), and which literature urged the overthrow of Constitutional government by violence." On a third point, Murrell wrote that Rankin had advised ROTC students at Griffin High School in Georgia to become "slackers" and to refuse to wear Army uniforms. Evidence of these allegations, Murrell said, could be found in "communist literature in our files."[229]

Even after the American Legion controversy faded, resentment toward Rankin's presence continued elsewhere. Macon evolved to a hotbed of conservatism since the *Evening News* lauded Rankin's efforts with the Georgia Peace Society six years earlier. W.T. Anderson, who edited the *Evening News* and the *Macon Telegraph*, characterized Rankin in an editorial as a moral loser whose friends were pacifists, defeatists and communists. Evidently, in his mind, they ranked equally as worthy of scorn. He accused her of trying to undermine manhood and patriotism. Her vote against American entry into war in 1917, he complained, had helped give the Germans the impression that America would not fight, therefore prolonging the war. "All this pacifism just invites war, and the more encouragement given to the people of the Rankin type, the more certain is disaster," he wrote.[230]

The Macon critics quieted their attacks for several months, but when Rankin returned to the area in October 1935 to build public sentiment for the Kellogg-Briand Pact on behalf of the Georgia Peace Society, a newspaper columnist accused her of being "fired from the faculty of one of the South's finest schools." An innocuous Legionnaire named Bill Janes wrote in an *Evening News* column, "Up Pops the Devil," that Rankin was branded a rank communist in Atlanta district court and was accused of belonging to several communist organizations. Janes claimed Georgia newspapers had commended the American Legion for exposing her and said she was preaching doctrines that were un-American and not needed in Georgia.[231]

Rankin returned to her boarding house at Sandersville that evening to find a copy of the newspaper on the porch. The allegations shocked her. She showed the column to her landlady. "Look what they said in the paper," Rankin groaned, slapping the newspaper. The woman looked puzzled. "Isn't it true?" she asked.

To Rankin, the column and ensuing publicity threatened to destroy her peace work in Georgia. Privately, she appealed for support from Roger Baldwin of the American Civil Liberties Union, who had persuaded her in 1920 to join the union as one of seventy members of a national committee. She also sought help from Frederick Libby of the National Council for Prevention of War, and Fiorello LaGuardia, her friend from Congress who since had been elected mayor of New York City. "Their continuous stories that I am a communist are getting quite unbearable," she wrote LaGuardia, hoping he would assure her not to worry. "If I sue, I may need your deposition that I am not a Communist. It seems silly to worry about it, but they have some queer laws in Georgia and the people take them rather seriously."

Rankin asked the ACLU to provide evidence she was not a communist. Baldwin advised her to reconsider suing the *Evening News*, suggesting that newspapers band together when in trouble. Earlier, however, he had expressed his private concern for her predicament. "What a tough bunch you ran into," he wrote in a penciled scrawl at the bottom of an official letter to H.J. Pearce, the Brenau president. Baldwin told Pearce that the ACLU defended communists just as it would anyone else whose constitutional rights were attacked. "We might just as fairly be characterized as a Klan organization because we have defended the rights of members of the Ku Klux Klan," he wrote.[232]

After Rankin decided to sue Bill Janes and the *Evening News* for libel on her brother's legal advice, Libby responded to her plea for help. The executive board of the National Council for Prevention of War voted to give her $500 to help pay legal fees, stipulating somewhat condescendingly that she hire a competent lawyer. She employed Walter G. Cornett, an Athens attorney, who promptly filed a $50,000 libel suit on grounds that any of three wrong statements Janes had made were sufficient to win the case. Cornett wrote Harry F. Ward, chairman of the ACLU, that Rankin:

"Will stand or fall in this State by results of this case and, of course, if she is driven out of Georgia she will be followed elsewhere by the same forces. We Georgians have prejudices deep rooted in our back-ground."[233]

Rankin hoped the libel suit would vindicate her from the barrage of propaganda and would encourage more responsible newspaper reporting of the pacifist cause.

Experience had taught her that newspapers sometimes failed to correct misrepresentations. She believed that the only answer was to sue and establish the facts in court. H.J. Pearce Sr. supported Rankin, writing in a letter to the editor of the *Evening News* that he was in thorough sympathy with those people who were trying to establish Americanism, but greatly saddened by the rabid attacks on "good Americans" such as Rankin. Editor Anderson felt the pressure, but not until more than a year after the libel occurred did The Macon News Printing Company agree to settle out of court for $1,000 and a published retraction.[234]

Rankin accepted, but reluctantly. She felt tired after two years and wanted to forget the matter. She did so with regret. She had hope the publicity of a jury trial would have forced a fresh look at peace and exposed the people who had contrived such attacks. "They gave me $1,000 and said I was a nice lady," she said of the conclusion. Anderson printed a front-page retraction: "She is held in the highest esteem for the sincerity of her efforts. She has an international reputation as a pacifist. This newspaper disagreed with her only in the matter of disarmament." Only through "rush and oversight" had the paper printed the Janes column, Anderson said, and it "was not representative of the attitude or opinion of either of the Macon papers."[235]

Most of the ammunition used to make war on Georgia's leading peace advocate apparently had been lifted from a self-published book entitled *The Red Network*, which listed Rankin among 1,300 Americans accused of membership in communist, socialist, radical, anarchist and International Workers of the World organizations. Elizabeth Dilling, the author, was convinced she must expose "the truth about the Communist-Socialist world conspiracy." Dilling ambitiously listed the names of the suspected organizations and the people affiliated with them. The American Legion, believing the book Bible-like proof for its cause, bought copies and sold them in Georgia for one dollar each to sustain its allegations against Rankin.

The settled court case marked the end of one of the most difficult times in Rankin's life. Had she not experienced such image roasting before, the American Legion might have driven her from Georgia. Instead she turned on the militarists in defiance, although she cherished scarcely half a victory, and with fourteen volunteers at her command, campaigned intensely to defeat Carl Vinson for reelection. His district included Macon and Sandersville, where she found little support. Rankin spent about $3,400, a considerable sum at the time, distributing literature and putting on mass meetings and children's parades. Children dressed in costumes carried banners with slogans such as "Join the Navy and See the Next World War" and "The Perfect Soldier, Headless."[236] Rankin sent a letter to peace activists pleading for campaign money. She suggested pageants where children would carry banners that made fun of war with the slogan: "We Want More Captured Cannons." Other sections of children would carry signs stating their desire to become lawyers, doctors, nurses, parents and farmers. Yet another section would bear the message, "War Will Make Us—" with various ending words intended to display the tragedies of war.

Behind those signs, Rankin wrote, "have the crippled, the blind, the orphans, the widows, and so on, making it as gruesome as possible."[237] Nobody stepped forward to campaign against Vinson. Rankin ran short of money. He was reelected by such a large majority that she believed she had guaranteed his victory by her mere presence in his district. Instead of hurting him, Rankin and her fellow pacifists brought out his largest vote ever. "I am very tired," she confided to Libby after Vinson had been renominated. "If we would only make peace a hot issue."

Rankin's supposition that Georgia was an ideal antiwar state had been overshadowed by the Brenau incident and the Janes libel suit. Wouldn't the same state where the Ku Klux Klan found its revival in 1915 try to obstruct a woman dedicated to civil rights among nations? As one observer wrote in 1930, Georgia unquestionably was the stronghold of "militarism, professional patriots and rotten politicians." That woman, Mrs. C.A. VerNooy of Athens, belonged to the American Legion Auxiliary. She commended Rankin for having a "genius for organization" and said she was "a wonderful 'mixer' and people adore her."[238] Rankin's Georgia experiment was a personal failure in some regards. The United States had evolved into an era of big business where dollars for war dwarfed pennies for peace. Rankin's street-level stumping had proven effective during the fight for suffrage. The politics of war was an enormous and complex beast and she knew it. "We are walking in the direction of war and we can get a war anytime the munitions makers and profit makers demand it," she complained in frustration. Money, she argued, was the motive for war. She told a congressional committee:

"You should pay thirty dollars or whatever the soldier's wage is, to everyone, and let everyone have a tin cup and bread card and subsist on the same food that the soldier does, beginning with the president. For members of Congress who have voted for war, not only the thirty dollars a month but also the honor of carrying the flag in battle, so that they would feel that they are doing their bit."[239]

At the twentieth anniversary of US entry into World War I, Rankin emerged a leader again, using old suffrage ploys such as banner-carrying children — "War Will Make Us Lame, Blind, Orphans, Armless, and Humpbacked" — to demonstrate the casualties of armed conflict. Never would she abandon such stark images of war's dirty story. Sensing an approaching shadow of war once again, she intensified her crusade for peace.

16 ~ Lobbying Congress for peace

'It is perfectly possible to take the profit out of war.'

It was 1937, a full twenty years since Jeannette Rankin's milestone election to Congress. The nation had changed since the era of suffrage sisters and doughboys. Americans found distractions from the financial and social consequences of the Great Depression in the arrival of swing and the big band craze of Benny Goodman, Tommy Dorsey and Glenn Miller, sentimental movies such as *Every Day's a Holiday* starring Mae West, and radio variety shows that had a mood and taste for everyone. Even the ominous cold winds of the "Roosevelt recession" that blew into the United States that spring didn't shake the confidence of people wanting more from life than dread and discord. Unemployment remained high, but many Americans found money to enjoy movies, automobiles, books, magazines, theaters, phonograph records and, with the repeal of Prohibition, legal drinking. Jeannette Rankin, ever the political activist, shunned the jubilee of arts, music, sports, literature and drama. Instead, she foresaw trouble in Europe, again.

From the congressional office of the National Council for Prevention of War in downtown Washington, DC, she gazed across bustling Northwest 17th Street to the State Department, a symbol of authority on which she affixed a stare of apprehension and distrust. Two decades after the war to end all wars, the news from Germany wasn't good. The fascist Adolf Hitler was busy crushing opponents, consolidating power, defying treaties, issuing Nazi propaganda, rallying hate. In October 1936, Hitler and Benito Mussolini of Italy formed the Rome-Berlin Axis. The Nazis, in 1937, opened the Buchenwald concentration camp, the largest on German soil, to imprison political opponents. Already, their war on Jews was in full force. Nazis prevailed in their four-year-old boycott of Jewish businesses. They banned Jewish books. Jews were prohibited from holding government jobs and teaching positions at universities. Rankin's speeches and letters would show that she knew of Germany's aggression and dreaded it, sensing a monumental echo of the First World War. The twentieth anniversary of that war presented her with a fresh public platform at a time she needed it most. She used it to remind her fellow Americans that while government paid for war with their taxpayer dollars, men and women in military service paid for it with their lives.

"Be not satisfied with a reprint ... about profiteers in Europe, but insist upon having information regarding our own American patriots who are willing to give the life of your son for their profit," she wrote. In the midst of economic greed, she wondered what had happened to the "traditional responsibility from time immemorial to care for the children, to nurse the sick, to feed the hungry, and to protect the old."

She was a leader among pacifists, predicting the onslaught of war and trying to stop it. A majority of Americans believed the nation should have avoided involvement in World War I, opinion polls showed, and Rankin's ideas were popular again. She was telling Americans that unless the profit was taken out of war, the "flaming youth" of the 1920s would become quite literal again in explosions and gun battles. In the first six months of 1937 she would deliver ninety-three speeches to about 21,000 people in ten states and the District of Columbia. She also gave four radio addresses. From October 1937 through June 1938, she would speak 149 times to audiences estimated to number a total of 34,000 people. On the radio, she would speak fourteen more times.[240] Rankin told interview Sylvia Press on WINS radio in New York what it was like to enter Congress in 1917 as the only woman among 434 men: "I simply decided that I could always talk to one man alone, and that I would just forget all the rest. That was my psychological approach to the problem."[241]

Rankin then told Press she wanted to talk about the title of the fifteen-minute program, "Ballots or Bullets?" Rankin said she "never regretted" voting against war with Germany in 1917. Men who supported war, she told Press, did so out of habit. She and other members of Congress who opposed war thought of peace as a more noble pursuit and each side voted accordingly, she said. And then: "The only intelligent thing to do is to follow the dictates of your heart."[242]

Any reader of current affairs could learn of war profiteering. It was Rankin's belief that unless public opinion favored peace, munitions makers would force a war to deplete their stockpiles. The Senate's Special Munitions Investigating Committee — more commonly known as the Nye Committee — in 1935 had paraded before its benches tales of outrage about the corporate encouragement of war. Charging that arms manufacturers bribed government officials, disregarded national policies, sold weapons to enemy countries, lobbied for military appropriations and thrived on excessive profit, the committee accused the "Big Three" — Bethlehem Steel, Newport News and New York

Shipbuilding — of collusive bidding on naval expenditures in 1933 to drive up profits and minimize competition.

Assistant Secretary of the Navy Henry L. Roosevelt, and Rear Admirals Emory Land and Samuel Robinson were asked to explain why they had failed to defend the nation's pocketbook in their approval of a $288 million contract. They testified that they were ignorant of shipbuilding costs and didn't know that corporations had conspired to raise prices. Investigator Stephen Raushenbush was astonished. He asked why the Navy failed to question Bethlehem's $3,542,000 increase in bidding, within seven months, on identical ships. Senator Arthur Vandenburg expressed shock that the Navy, in its ignorance, was linked to the conspiracy.[243]

The hearings fed Rankin's disgust of war. They also confirmed her arguments in speeches and radio addresses. To her, the military was structured to encourage collusion with enterprising corporations. "Is the Navy for the defense of our shores? Or to protect American private property on other continents?" she wondered aloud many times. Even as early as 1933 she had argued before Congress that war was fought for economic profit. In testimony on the exporting of arms and munitions, she debated with Melvin Maas of the House Foreign Affairs Committee:

Maas: "Do you believe that traffic in munitions is in itself a cause of war?"

Rankin: "Yes, I believe that wars in the past have been started that way."

Maas: "It appears that the real causes of war are economic."

Rankin: "Yes ... under the economic system war eventually comes, but in the meantime we can get rid of this habit. If we develop the habit of peace and think in terms of peace, we could cease to operate under the militaristic system."

Maas: "I still contend that to solve the problems of war you have to solve economic problems and not militaristic problems. The militaristic follows as an incident of the economic...."

Rankin: "The militaristic system forces an economic problem upon us...."

During the Depression when luck was laid low, Americans were less interested when Rankin spoke of threats to their pocketbooks. After the America First organization began to find its public voice, more glaring facts of profit flaunting emerged that supported her allegations. John T. Flynn, a journalist who had helped found America First, wrote a newspaper column with startling disclosures: A $1,386,193 bonus had been awarded to Eugene Grace, president of Bethlehem Steel Corporation, for the production of ships and steel in 1917. A World War I profit for the United States Steel Corporation exceeded $1 billion, equal to the pay of two million American soldiers in the trenches and fields of France. A $32 million profit — a 200 percent increase — was enjoyed by the Utah Copper Company in 1917. The meat packers — Armour, Swift, Morris, Cudahy — had tripled their profits in 1917.[244] Rankin was fond of pointing out that flour mills, button makers and shirt tailors were given "educational orders" for huge increases in manufacturing in the event that war was declared.[245] All profited, and on it went.

Rankin told the House of Representatives Committee on Military Affairs that anti-profit legislation only blinded Americans into thinking war could be fought without profit. Conscription was forced during World War I, she argued, because otherwise the poor man was unwilling to fight a rich man's war. Rankin had kept a brochure from World War I promoting universal military training as a "moral asset" for impoverished Americans. "The slums in our great cities are filled with human derelicts; wrecks who might have been saved by the discipline and training which the military camp would give," the brochure read.[246]

One of the anti-profit bills she criticized as a sham was the McSwain Resolution, which sought to limit industrial profiteering. In Rankin's estimation, it didn't go far enough. By 1937, Rankin already had witnessed numerous bills presented to take the profit out of war, all of which seemed to elude the target: corporations that made money from the deaths of American soldiers, sailors, Marines and pilots. She testified: "It is perfectly possible to take the profit out of war. It is not possible by any of the schemes rich men suggest, and you haven't had any proposals for taking the profit out of war from the poor man."

She was asked: "So you think we made a mistake in going to war with Germany?"

"I made no mistake, I am sure of that. I am glad voted against it," she replied.

"Who won?" asked another committee member.

"We all lost," a colleague answered.

"Who won the San Francisco earthquake?" asked another.

Rankin repeated one of her favorite rejoinders: "You can no more win a war than you can win an earthquake."[247]

Twenty years after her vote against war with Germany, Rankin held fast to her belief that the war declaration prevailed only because at least 200 members of Congress had been cowed into supporting it on threats that only a foreign war would forestall Germany's invasion of the United States. "Now, the reason those men in the House voted for war, all but the forty-nine, was that they had war habits in their tradition, history and hearts," she testified at a US House hearing on declarations of war. In 1917, she said, "I voted against war because for seven long years I had been developing peace habits. ... I said it was woman's work to raise human beings and that human beings had been sacrificed in war for profit, and inasmuch as women had to take the responsibility of protecting their work so because I had answered every argument for war in my own mind and had acquired peace habits, I voted against war."[248] Had those members defended their principles, she argued, the United States would have saved billions of dollars in war expenses and prevented thousands of combat deaths. "The question is now, have the people of this country learned their lesson? ... Only the expressed desire of the people to go in the direction of peace and away from war will prevent the same few who got us in the last war from getting us into the next. ... When a government is controlled by a few special interests they are able to deceive the people into believing that the progress of the people is served by going to war. ... War destroys democracy. After twenty years we are just approaching the point where we are again thinking of democratic measures that were considered before the war."[249]

Rankin's distaste for battlefields and killing persisted. Long after World War I ended, she ridiculed President Wilson's slogan, "Make the World Safe for Democracy," which she described as "a task no war at any period of history ever could have done — a task beyond the power of war to accomplish." That war did nothing to calm tensions among European nations, she wrote, but led to militarization of American youth in their schools "and every other channel available." The war to end war, she wrote, was a "magnificent dud" that left the world in a moral crisis.[250] Rankin claimed from podium and panel that the greed of war producers was leading Americans into another world conflict. Who was responsible? Rankin blamed the munitions makers, who built the actual implements and materials of war — cannon, guns, ammunition, tanks, military aircraft and naval vessels — and the banking, industrial and commercial firms that profited by war. She fumed that the greatest threat to peace was the propaganda portraying war as honorable and patriotic.

Rankin thought that the issue of military preparedness, which justified the expenditure of billions of dollars for the sake of national defense, was a misnomer. She contended that the military was being armed not for defense of American shores, but to protect American financial investments in foreign countries. "The word 'preparedness,' according to its most frequent present use, comes under the title, 'deception as a fine art,'" Rankin quoted pioneer aviator Charles A. Lindbergh in one of her radio speeches. "It was seized on by the war-munitions lords as a substitute for 'armament,' because armament would suggest what was really meant."

In the twenty years since Rankin's dramatic vote against war with Germany, her hair had gone white. Her face was fuller. She had lost the youthful appearance raved over so vividly when she came to Congress in 1917. *United Press International* described her as "the original No-woman" for casting an antiwar vote. The anniversary pushed her to deciding that her fateful vote had invited persecution from hawkish Americans. She told the *New York Times*: "It was a military necessity to destroy me and the only way to do it was by ridicule.... I knew if I voted against war I probably never could come back, and I don't mean back to Congress. I knew it would take years for people to overcome the feeling they would have against me." Rankin said she never believed stories that Germany would invade the United States if Congress didn't approve a war declaration. "It never occurred to me that everybody wouldn't understand that, just as I did," she told the *Times*.

Twenty years after that vote, Rankin traveled to Germany with her nephew, John Kinney, who planned to study in Heidelberg. "The planes were flying over and you would think war was almost there," she would recall of her time in Germany. Her nephew, fearful of his aunt's outspoken nature and worried she might provoke trouble, found himself "hushing her up" on several occasions. Fear of war also was evident in France and England, where she saw citizens learning how to use gas masks and signs pointing to air raid shelters. After six weeks of travel she sailed home on the *Duchess of Richmond* passenger liner. She then would write: "The German people recognize from the results of the last war that even in victory there is nothing to be gained by bloodshed and destruction."[251]

That year, Rankin told an audience in Beaumont, Texas, that before she was elected to Congress she visited some Capitol Hill offices and sat there thinking how she would arrange her furniture when she had an office of her own. War stamped out such everyday thinking. She would recall "a terrific, crushing sense of responsibility" when silence fell across the House of Representatives when the time came to vote on whether to fight Germany. Twenty years later, she remembered Woodrow Wilson's measured words, "grave and ominous," as he asked Congress for a war declaration. In 1937 she drew parallels between Wilson's presidency and Franklin Roosevelt's. Both men had campaigned on the premise the United States would remain peaceful with its neighbors. Both leaders, in Rankin's opinion, bowed to arguments that only military "preparedness" would keep the country safe from invasion. Arsenals grew, heavier guns were manufactured, and "other horrors concocted by modern science for war on human beings," such as poison gases and deadly chemicals, were invented. "Are we never to be disillusioned?" she wrote. "Have we learned nothing from the two decades? Did the brave boys who went to war in 1917-18 and never came back actually die in vain? Must the whole ghastly story be repeated?"[252]

In articles, speeches and letters, Rankin in 1937 held fast to her belief that broad oceans and friendly relations with

Canada to the North and Mexico to the South would isolate the United States from world disputes. "What nation would attack us?" she wrote. "For what reasons would we be attacked?" Rankin's isolationist convictions were hardly radical for the times.[253] Throughout the 1930s, diverse groups of Americans embraced isolationism. Memories of World War I suffering and a preoccupation over the Great Depression at home dampened any enthusiasm for foreign conflict. Condemnations of war profiteering by Rankin and North Dakota Senator Gerald Nye and many others hit newspaper headlines. Peace organizations in several states linked the cost of armaments to everyday people. A flyer distributed by the Alabama Peace Society said the price of a single bomb (then valued at $1,300) would pay the salaries of two Alabama grade school teachers for a year, or buy work mules for fifty-two farmers. The nation's military outlay, the flyer calculated, exceeded the combined value of its cotton and wheat crops.[254]

By 1937 tensions in Europe and Asia grew far worse. Germany, Japan and Italy signed pacts to assist each other in acts of aggression. The Second Sino-Japanese War had begun. President Roosevelt, in favor of more international activism but constrained earlier that decade by an isolationist US Congress, delivered a speech in October that compared international aggression with a disease that lawful nations must "quarantine" to prevent further violence. Roosevelt, in Chicago, warned that American peace might be challenged by aggressor nations: "There is a solidarity and interdependence about the modern world both technically and morally, which makes it impossible for any nation to isolate itself from economic and political upheavals in the rest of the world, especially when such upheavals appear to be spreading and not declining."

Rankin's interpretation of this statement was that Roosevelt had abandoned neutrality and was eager to push the United States into war, a complaint she explored widely in those 149 speeches she made in the subsequent eight months. In Fulton, Missouri, she met with the congregation of a Methodist church and students at Westminster and William Woods colleges. "We have to outlaw war between nations," Rankin said of the Kellogg-Briand Pact. "If we keep that treaty this period will be written down in history as the time when the nations gave up war. If we don't keep that treaty, this will merely become a part of the Dark Ages in historical works."[255] She reasoned that the United States was the best-equipped nation in the world to repel invasion. Why did the military persist in training men and buying munitions? "Anyone with common sense knows that a lot of little boys lying on their stomachs shooting popguns is no defense in a period devoted to poison gas and bombing planes," she expostulated in one of her many fact sheets objecting to military training.

"Preparation for war leads to war," she repeated in stump speeches. "If we are to have peace, we must achieve peace by preparing for it. Some government must take the lead, but it can only be taken when there is an enlightened public opinion demanding intelligent action."[256] Rankin blamed propaganda for creating ignorance she labeled "the fear psychosis." She was quoted in *World Outlook*:

"We Americans must be aware of 'holy wars.' Ask the American people to give their lives in a foreign war for the expressed purpose of turning attention from the economic and social problems at home, or to solve unemployment by making munitions, or to protect their homes by fighting in a country thousands of miles away, to believe that we can profit in other people's wars without being drawn into them, and their scornful laughter would ring around the world. But ask them to fight for a lofty ideal or even to protect their homes without mentioning the attacking country which high-pressure propaganda can make appear reasonable, and that is quite a different story."[257]

Rankin remained steadfast in her commitment to staying neutral. She was foremost a pacifist. If anything, the twenty years since her vote against war with Germany had fortified her anger. War had derailed her campaign for suffrage in 1917. War stole money and resources from social needs. In Rankin's view, war reappeared in all its fury at intervals of history, bringing the same futile intentions and predictable sad defeats.

Jeannette Rankin was one woman against war. Her writings from the period showed she viewed international war as a scoundrel for human justice and an enemy of democracy. To her, the United States had a moral obligation to outlaw war as the international General Pact for the Renunciation of War had outlined. More money should be spent on diplomacy, less on preparing for war. The United States should work for disarmament and mutual trust. Her radio speeches denounced "war-mad rulers" and dictatorships that denied "common people" a voice in stopping war. Repeatedly she portrayed war as the antithesis of human progress. Spending for war, she argued, invited bankruptcy, heavy taxation, and human misery.

At a hearing before the House Committee of Foreign Affairs, the chairman chastised Rankin for trying to arrange a meeting of her own to persuade Members of Congress to oppose involvement in the European conflict. "You may sit down, if you desire," chairman Sam D. McReynolds told her. "I prefer to remain standing," she replied, explaining she was a lobbyist working for the National Council for Prevention of War. Her answers were short but Rankin did acknowledge that she had called a meeting because a Member of Congress, unnamed, had asked her to do it.

To that McReynolds replied: "The committee has always

tried to give everyone a hearing and tried to be fair, but we are somewhat amazed when an effort is made to organize another committee by a lobbyist. We do not appreciate it and I think I speak for the sentiments of this committee when I say that." He then gave Rankin a chance to speak on the proposed legislation, but she deferred to Florence Boeckel, the NCPW's associate secretary, who spent the next hour defending the position of "mandatory neutrality" that intended an abolition of war by Congress. The law would restrict the president's power to declare war and curtail the shipment of arms and munitions to belligerent countries. Boeckel warned the committee against supporting "discretionary neutrality," which she said would give the president broad power to take sides in conflicts and hand war-making power over to the executive branch of government.

"Are we in danger of attack from Japan?" Rankin wrote in the fall of 1937. "Here is 'an annual war scare' on the part of professional militarists. Which is just another way of saying that jingoists prefer to emphasize the possibilities of discord rather than the probabilities of peace. Japan needs our trade. Her navy couldn't leave her own waters."[258] In September of that year, after Rankin returned from a short vacation in Europe, she implored recipients of NCPW correspondence to write President Roosevelt to protest war. The Neutrality Act, passed by Congress, offered proof that Americans wanted peace, she wrote. "Those who fight or those who take sides are not helping human progress. They are simply adding to the devastation and confusion. If you want proof of this, go to Europe and see today the same problems that threatened in 1913 and 1914. Nothing was helped by war."[259]

Several times in the two decades preceding 1937 she visited Congress as a lobbyist, giving thousands of words of testimony to committees on disarmament, profiteering and military appropriations. Her seemingly fearless criticism of war propagandists earned her the reputation of an elder stateswoman among pacifists who shared her viewpoint. One inspired political observer concluded she was the best antiwar lobbyist ever.

Rankin's deliberate suspicion of government and the corporations that pushed lawmakers to the brink of war found admiration in the eyes of many people, including Gaylord Douglass, a faculty member of the Wellesley Institute in Boston. Like Rankin, he was an associate secretary of the NCPW. He wrote Frederick Libby concerning Rankin: "Politically and personally, she is incomparable." A friend to Douglass said: "She brings the most challenging message we have ever had. If there was a Jeannette Rankin in every State our country would never go to war."[260]

Libby, as Rankin, was a longtime peace agitator whose ideas again were in vogue. He seized on her leadership qualities. In a letter to Management Ernest Briggs Inc., a New York speaking bureau, he explained that Rankin: "Is one of the most attractive women speakers in the public eye today. Her vote against the World War when it mean political suicide was just like her. She has convictions for which she is willing to die any time but fortunately lives to give brilliant expression to them with a force and sincerity that carry conviction."[261]

Having worked for the NCPW for eight years, Rankin was tired and wanted to return to her Georgia farm for a rest. The congressional work had been unusually demanding. Libby pushed her for more results. He circulated a prospectus promoting the reputation of the NCPW through the public distinction of Jeannette Rankin. Libby's bold gesture in trying to cast the weight of its convictions on her slender shoulders didn't surprise her. She had been using the NCPW reputation for years to the same advantage. She didn't mind carrying the load but Libby's outfit barely paid her expenses. Soon, she asked Libby to fill his letters with cash instead of apologies.

The NCPW publicly promoted Rankin to lunch-counter Rotary Clubs and cautious school superintendents as a stirring, intellectual speaker. The NCPW saw her as a natural attraction for favorable news coverage. As war again darkened the globe, the organization prepared a strategy for exploiting her family's political history and her prominent reputation as the nation's first woman in Congress. "The most startling and truthful of statements uttered by John Doe is not news but a far less interesting statement from Jeanette [sic] Rankin ... is decidedly news," the prospectus said. It also contained an interesting anachronism, stating, "this is the 20th anniversary year of her first vote against war."[262]

Nationwide lobbying by peace advocates became so intense by 1937 that it culminated in a battle with pro-war advocates to win confidence of average Americans. *Public Opinion Quarterly* estimated the presence of fifty national "patriotic" organizations, twenty-seven national peace organizations, and forty-three national organizations working for international diplomacy. High school students assembled to hear a pacifist deliver a speech one day. On the next, they heard pro-war comments from the Veterans of Foreign Wars.

Among other organizations representing the militarists' point of view were the American Legion, the Daughters of the American Revolution, the United Spanish War Veterans, and the Navy League of the United States. Resisting militarists' arguments and generating propaganda of their own were the NCPW, the Fellowship of Reconciliation, the War Resisters League and the League for Industrial Democracy. The noncommittal American was caught in a swirl of public debate, the very essence of democracy. The tool of mass education succeeded in deluging school and home mailboxes with instructions explaining how to join any particular movement. Full-page advertisements graphically portraying the horror of war competed with full-page advertisements boasting the glory and honor of military preparedness.

One of Rankin's favorite tools for peace propaganda was George Gershwin's Broadway musical, *Strike Up the Band*, and she particularly found irony in one verse: "We're in a bigger, better war for your patriotic past-time. We don't know what we're fighting for, but we didn't know the last time." Hard-hitting books like Engelbrecht and Hanighen's *Merchants of Death*, Charles Beard's *The Devil Theory of War*, and Walter Millis' *The Road to War* contained documentation of corporate plans to supply belligerent nations such as Germany with food, clothing and munitions for their armies. The books were published at the zenith of the munitions debate in 1934 and offered considerable support to war critics that economic collusion in years preceding 1917 would happen again.

While the Nye Committee was uncovering economic motives for war, a lengthy article in *Fortune* magazine entitled "Arms and the Men" revealed how Germany was arming with the help of fearful European neighbors and American profiteers. The NCPW circulated 100,000 reprints.

Rankin used these revelations to her advantage. She argued repeatedly that American public opinion was being manipulated to promote war spending. She blamed financial pressure by controlling corporations for America's entry into World War I. Newspapers, she said, encouraged profiteering with editorials on the merits of patriotism and the publication of news dispatches from war zones. Rankin disliked the term "patriotism," invented in her estimation to imply that anyone failing to endorse war was a traitor. She pointed to the General Pact for the Renunciation of War, endorsed by the United States and signed by sixty-three nations. To her, the United States faced difficulty in conforming to the rules of the pact because propaganda coming from the profiteers was overwhelming. War always had been legal, honorable, justifiable and "patriotic" — history books were quick to find romance even in the tragic Civil War — and a paper agreement to stop war was an exercise in futility.

As one of the strongest critics of wasteful military spending, Rankin sought to link sloppy finances to government contracts with war profiteers. In her mind the profiteers were ghoulish companies that waited for bursts of emotion and then struck lucrative deals at taxpayer expense. In one position paper, in 1936, she repeated Army Major General Johnson Hagood's comments to the House Committee on Military Affairs that the National Defense Act "stands today like a great machine with many of its essential parts missing." He continued: "The War Department and the staff departments generally control the expenditure of millions in time of peace and billions in times of war, yet this organization is so complicated that no one can explain it, much less work it under stress of war.... The war department contains three groups of agencies all covering the same subject and each trying to outdo the others in the assumption of responsibility and in the exercise of authority."

Rankin cited some of the Army's "decorative features" that to her would never be missed. First would be the cavalry, "picturesque but too slow for modern war." Polo ponies for officers cost taxpayers almost a million dollars a year. Money was spent for a chemical warfare department, separate from an ordinance department. Pack trains were no match for modern armies. "Principally useful for practise [sic] in wrangling mules," Rankin wrote. "Contemplating all of this curious machinery, the civilian is not surprised to learn that the military intellect is as much baffled by it as is his own."[263]

Just as Rankin did, Frederick Libby portrayed the American military as a gluttonous budget giant with no table manners. The Army's preoccupation with cavalry horses, he wrote, prepared the nation for Civil War-era fighting.

Compulsory military training in colleges was money lost on all but the most enthusiastic students. Even in the opinion of military leaders, the volunteer Citizens' Military Training Camps served no military purpose. Money was spent on archaic institutions such as the National Board of Rifle Practice. Libby wrote: "The Army is overstocked with the older officers, which is killing the ambition of the young men. We have an officer to every eleven men, which is twice the normal figure."[264]

In her public addresses and personal letters, Rankin spoke of military stockpiling of hundreds of thousands of Jeep motors, kept in warehouses where they became obsolete before they were used. The Army was being trained to fight in foreign countries. The Navy was being trained to fight in foreign seas. Neither was being trained to defend American soil. Raking gunfire from enemy fighter planes would decimate the cavalry. Rankin never tired of putting these facts before the public. "It will take ... action on our part to sober the war-mad rulers," she told one audience. "It is the American people who decide whether or not they want to prevent war."

Rankin's blueprint for peace had three strategies. Employed together, she said, they would prevent war. The American military should protect domestic shores rather than to fight in foreign countries. A permanent neutrality law would stop war profiteering. Congress should have no power to declare wars. Her letters and speeches detailed how to put these points into action. Predictably, she aimed her message at American women in the hope they would put the power of their vote to good use. "Woman alone can stop war," Rankin said in a radio speech. To a friend in Los Angeles, she wrote: "You remember the struggles of those who opposed war during the wild intoxication nearly twenty years ago. It is a very difficult thing for anyone to be elected to Congress. At first glance it appears that money is a great essential, but the money is helpful only when it represents energy in disseminating ideas."[265]

Rankin also was full of homespun anecdotes about the nation's preparation for war. A country that arms itself seeks trouble to play with its new toy, Rankin believed: "When countries are armed they are like the little boy who received the gun and the diary for Christmas. The next day he wrote in his diary: 'Snowing, can't go hunting.' The third day he wrote: 'Snowing yet, can't go hunting.' The fourth day he wrote, 'Snowing still, shot grandma.'"

She recalled a story told by a Sunday school teacher, who asked a group of young boys to share, with their class, good deeds they had performed that week. As the bigger boys were reciting their good deeds, the eyes of the smallest boy sparkled as he made up his story. When his turn came he said: "I saw a big boy jumping on a little boy and I took an axe and cut his head open." To Rankin, always relating homespun anecdotes, that story demonstrated the difference between aggression and defense: the punishment inflicted was worse than the crime committed.

"Europe Doesn't Want War," Rankin titled an article she wrote for the North American Newspaper Alliance in September 1937. "Nobody wants war. And even powerful dictators cannot go farther than their people will carry them." She also predicted that Germany and Italy, "the most feared countries in Europe," wouldn't "rush into war in the immediate future." Much of the article, co-written with Rankin's early House secretary and suffrage friend, Belle Fligelman Winestine, made a case for why peace would prevail in England, Turkey, Scandinavia and Russia.[266] Rankin and Winestine drafted the article two years to the month before Germany's invasion of Poland. Declarations of war on Germany by the United Kingdom and France came two days after that attack.

Being a pacifist, Rankin found little wonder that the military was prepared to fight in foreign wars and had no intention of training for coastal defense. In private correspondence, she referred to President Roosevelt as "the dictator" and accused him of preparing people for war instead of defining American defense boundaries. She would cling to a lifelong hatred of Roosevelt. "I campaigned in Georgia and I had a Georgia Peace Society that went beautifully until Roosevelt came in and got strength and then he turned it over, when he started preparations for the Second World War," she said later in life.[267] The peace society endured through 1937 but with her decisive failure to stop Carl Vinson's reelection, and her preoccupation with the national antiwar movement, it nearly fell apart.

Four days after Christmas in 1937, Rankin entered the studio of the Inter-City Network radio station in New York City shortly after 8 o'clock in the evening, clutching her speech in one hand and nervously awaiting her turn at the microphone. She had spoken on a national radio network before — including the previous April on the day of her twentieth anniversary of her vote against war — but she struggled to find fresh arguments because everybody was spending money for propaganda. Rankin planned to tell her audience to disregard the war propaganda and work for peace. She knew she must leave a lasting impression.

At 8:45, she sat before the microphone. She thanked the station for the opportunity to talk on the air. "Nineteen thirty-seven is ending with everyone hearing a great deal about war," she told listeners. "There is propaganda everywhere, propaganda for war and propaganda against the war. You who are listening are in a tight place. It is hard for you to know how to weigh all sides and come to a sane conclusion."

Rankin told of an experience in Missouri, where she met a

man reprimanded by his wife for not believing stories about war atrocities. The man could neither read nor write, and his wife told him, "If you could read, you would know these stories are true." The man replied, "If you could not read, you would know they are not true."

People huddling around crackling radio sets in living rooms heard that the propaganda Rankin despised most was what she called "it can't be done" propaganda by people who said, "Well, we've always had war and always will." She asked her audience: "Where would we be today if the leaders of humanity had listened to 'It can't be done' — Columbus, Washington, Susan B. Anthony, Pasteur, Edison, the Wright brothers? What if we have had war in the past? The men and women living in homes, loving their children, don't want war. Why should they let it come?"[268]

Rankin thought she knew the answer. Decades of conflict suggested that war was essential to American values of freedom, liberty and the pursuit of happiness. In the public glorification of war, statues made heroes of soldiers, memorials enshrined the dead, movies dignified killing and hymns brimmed with emotion. Rankin wanted to break this habit, which she found ingrained in her own personality. Decades of imbalanced folk tales had taken their toll on her. She admitted during hearings on amending the Constitution to outlaw war: "We cannot get away from our tradition.... I still hate England, but I know I should not."

Not until one night at her Georgia farm did she understand her own fears and misconceptions about breaking the war habit: "When I first came to Georgia, I would lock the door, and then at night I would hear every pine cone that fell. One night I forgot to lock the door and I didn't hear the pine cones. Locking the door was what frightened me."

To Rankin, Americans were taught fear. Eliminating war propaganda, she wrote friends, would end the habit of jumping into war to settle international disputes. To do that, women needed their voice in government. The suffrage movement taught her that serious social problems arose when only half of the American population was represented in federal government. Repeatedly, she touched a common theme: "The only safe way of preventing war and waste and confusion will be through broadening the base of political control.... Peace is coming not through political leaders but through the voter. The great value of political action lies in its power to educate the masses."[269]

Educate, she did. She mailed letters on behalf of the Georgia Committee on the Disarmament Conference, coaching prospective activists on how to write letters to President Roosevelt and members of Congress. The letter to the president, she wrote, should include "a detailed description of some concrete case of suffering caused by the depression and then close your letter with some question asking him what can be done to hasten the reduction of armaments so that the money may be used to prevent suffering the world over."[270]

In her relentless campaigning for peace, Rankin filled the void resulting from the death of peace matriarch Jane Addams, who had labored to open America's eyes to the horrors of slum living, the cogent power of the "weaker" sex, and the brutality of war. Rankin had spent a few months at Hull House in Chicago after she left Congress in 1918 and had joined with Addams in 1932 in the NCPW's "To Chicago" plan as women, children and college students converged on Republican and Democratic party conventions with antiwar sentiment. They became friends bound by their identical approach to securing the change needed to establish and maintain peace.

Jeannette Rankin and Jane Addams agreed that peace should start with the teamster behind the plow, the preacher in the pulpit, the garment seamstress at the sewing machine, and the newspaper editor, the firefighter, the delicatessen proprietor, women with children crying for more food, and the black man looking for his first job in a white city. "Ask the Congressmen if they are willing to let the people have a direct vote before there is a declaration of war," Rankin said in a 1937 radio speech. "They let the farmers vote on whether or not they want to kill little pigs. Why shouldn't the mothers and fathers vote on whether they want their sons killed?"

The transformation of life in the slum world surrounding Hull House demonstrated what Jane Addams believed the poor and downtrodden could attain if they were given encouragement and conviction. Rankin took the position that people were fools to wait for their government to give them privileges they deserved under the US Constitution. Unlike Frederick Libby, whose pacifism came from his conversion to the Quaker religion, Rankin felt a compelling responsibility to improve what she believed were abuses of American civil rights. They differed fundamentally in how to sustain the peace movement. Rankin believed, as her Georgia peace experiment confirmed, that only spontaneous protest would slow the war machine. Libby wanted emphasis on top elected officials first with peace percolating to neighborhoods and farms. Rankin thought the plan was ridiculous. She couldn't come to terms with Libby over basic policy, particularly her anger that the council had become timid and reluctant to challenge Roosevelt. Finally, she left the organization, sensing she had fallen out of vogue.[271] Fewer people wanted to hear her speak. Many of them had tired of debating war and peace. The Great Depression had been a wearing time, filled with hunger and homelessness for many Americans.

Rankin lamented that convincing the nation's war lords to court peace was as futile as fighting a way to settle international disputes. "No one fears the results of the peace worker who made sentimental speeches at ladies' teas, but when pioneer work is done among responsible citizens, it is a different story," she wrote. Rankin said war was the greatest menace to society because it killed the finest men, had an aftermath of disease, caused a deterioration of the race and eventually would destroy it. She pointed to the catastrophic burden of the taxpayer who must pay for war debts, veterans, machinery and war "reconstruction." In a moral tone, she questioned why innocent people were subjected to bombing planes and chemical warfare, masterminded by people in safe places many miles away.

By the late 1930s, the Nye Committee had concluded in its investigation that thwarting munitions manufacturers would reduce or eliminate the incentive to become involved in foreign markets on the precipice of war. Charles Beard had pointed out in his book, *The Devil Theory of War*, that American businesses had invested $7 billion into World War I in just three years preceding the war declaration. Beard contended that President Wilson was forced to commit the United States to war to prevent a domestic banking crash.

His small book, filled with secret cables between Wilson and Robert Lansing, who in 1914 was chief lawyer for the State Department, documented financial investments in the war efforts of foreign countries. The resulting big prosperity became insecure by 1917, when American business, led by the J.P. Morgan Company of New York, feared financial collapse if the military did not move to protect American investments on foreign soil. Beard estimated that such greedy speculating cost the United States $100 billion, including outlays for pensions, bonuses and other war charges. It was an extraordinary sum in 1917. The death and suffering could not be measured. Beard theorized that the stock market crash of 1929 resulted from war profiteering.

By 1939, Rankin broke from the National Council for

Prevention of War. It had promoted her widely to American audiences but used her badly for ten years. Lack of money was an immediate problem. Her Georgia farm had caught fire and burned to the foundation in 1935. Unable to rebuild, for she had neither the time nor the money, she bought another farm near the small town of Watkinsville, about ten miles from her Bogart farm. It needed repairs and she found herself turning to Frederick Libby for help. "Am living in true Georgia fashion," she wrote him. "No money. The stores are furnishing me with food and gas. They say, 'It's been so long since we've had any money we done got used to it.' Please don't think I can get used to it."

Libby had sympathy for Rankin's impoverished lifestyle, but times were hard for the NCPW, too. He forwarded Rankin a pittance of her pay only infrequently, forcing her to write him in 1938: "I've no doubt money is slow in coming in, but if you can send me some or put me on a weekly payroll it will help a lot. It hurts my spirits so to be broke."[272] Because of Libby's Quaker allegiance to peace, he found purpose in poverty of his field workers. Rankin, having no such religious inclination, suspected Libby was exploiting her.

Other NCPW workers whispered among themselves that because Rankin's brother had a prosperous law practice, her paycheck could be spent elsewhere in the organization. This infuriated Rankin, and when Libby asked her to begin a peace society in rural Colorado, she flared at his insolence. "My day for doing the spade work as I did in Georgia is past," she quipped, thinking him insensitive to her needs.

Rankin's financial feud with Libby and the NCPW involved more than her paycheck, however. She hated that the NCPW had to compete with other peace organizations for a dwindling reservoir of peace funds. She was impatient with some of her colleagues, including Florence Boeckel, who wanted to put more emphasis on congressional work. Mostly,

Rankin was angry that her unveiled dislike for Libby's inability to feed his workers was leading her to ineffective door-to-door work with little reward or recognition from him.

As mild disagreements grew into a bothersome rift, Rankin resigned. It was uncharacteristic of her to remain that long with an organization. Since her early days in the suffrage campaigns, she had been a maverick, working loosely within the philosophies of established groups while following her intuitive moods. She hadn't changed. Even members of the Georgia Peace Society resented her independence, calling her a dictator in private, and accused her of using the name and letterhead of the organization to her own end.

Rankin had little patience for compromise. Even as she had testified as an expert witness on munitions control before the Nye Committee, she drifted from precise lobbying techniques of the NCPW, casually tossing her personal ideas to the congressmen on a whim. Libby had cautioned her to avoid direct attacks on President Roosevelt, fearing they would might discourage public support for the NCPW, but she did so anyway.

While the NCPW and many other pacifist groups were prepared to accept compromising anti-profit legislation as a better-than-nothing proposition, Rankin introduced her own plan to slash profits from war. Her solution was to have the Secretary of the Treasury withdraw all money and credit at the first hint of a national emergency, replacing it with fiat bills equal in face value. The "emergency currency" would be legal tender for the duration of the war. When peace was restored, each person would have his frozen prewar credit or peace dollars returned, at the value at which they had been exchanged. The fiat dollars then became worthless, allowing no one to profit from war.

The plan was not feasible to employ because of the immense task to exchange money or credit in the midst of an emergency, and because American investments started long before an outbreak of war. Rankin proved, however, that as a single citizen she had a plan to offer, although it was not well received by the Nye Committee. She complained miserably that her plan wasn't adopted because "you seldom meet those who want all the profits removed."

The Nye Committee never proposed a sensible plan to take the profits out of war, in Rankin's opinion, but continuing investigations led to the Neutrality Act, the first of four neutrality laws enacted in the 1930s. The new law put a mandatory embargo on arms and munitions to belligerents, forbade American ships to transport munitions to countries at war, and later restricted loans to warring countries. In 1939, a month after she resigned from the NCPW, Rankin testified against the latest neutrality legislation in Congress. President Roosevelt had tried to renew the "cash and carry" provision of the law, which would allow selling war supplies to belligerents in Europe as long as they paid in cash and arranged for transportation. Luther A. Johnson of Texas, a member of the House Foreign Affairs committee, oddly asked Rankin to confirm that she was the first woman elected to Congress. She did. Only one of the twenty-four committee members, she pointed out, had served with her in 1917. That was George H. Tinkham from Massachusetts. Faces had changed, a predictable result of representative government, but the isolationist years of the 1930s ensured Rankin a more sympathetic hearing in her arguments against world war.

Informing committee members that she represented nobody but herself — "I am not a paid lobbyist, and I do not represent any officially" — she stated her opposition to extending the "cash and carry" provision to appease Roosevelt. "The term 'cash and carry' is a slogan and very deceptive. It is merely words, unless it is clearly stated, 'cash and carry' what? Arms or foodstuffs? And 'cash and carry' where? To friends or enemies? And when? During war or an armistice? ... The cold fact is it provides for the sale of arms." Rankin ended her appeal that it was the job of Congress, not of the president, to represent American people. "I have met few Congressmen who do not subscribe to this view. That is why our democracy is worth fighting for. The first step toward fascism is to ignore or decrease congressional powers."[273] Rankin's view of a government that fully represented the American people was a thread that ran through her life from her reform education onward. In that instance, in 1939, it also harked to her distrust of Roosevelt.

Rankin's peace plan called for an International Court of Justice, a world peace court that would bend governments of the world to the power of opinion. The world court would be comparable in status and operation to the United States Supreme Court, which Rankin believed had functioned flawlessly with the tool of public opinion. She was a proponent of a world court because she thought the General Pact for the Renunciation of War — merely a condemnation — and Kellogg-Briand, which outlawed war, would succeed only until economic disputes between nations began.

She proved right. The arrival of a new world war over money and territorial boundaries meant killing millions of people. Rankin favored peace pacts as acknowledgements by nations that war failed to solve conflicts, but made new ones, but she wanted a stronger voice to protest war.

Rankin got her chance. Americans listened, but this time she had a mission better defined — and lonelier — than any she had experienced.

17 ~ The lonely dissenter

'The problems of 1916, unsolved by war, are here today.'

As Adolf Hitler's Third Reich rumbled through Europe and Americans bickered over the shipment of arms and munitions to belligerent countries, Jeannette Rankin thought about campaigning for Congress on a peace platform. Public opinion had been trapped in a monumental tug-of-war between pacifists and militarists, starting with a gentle pull in the early 1930s and culminating in frenzy in the early 1940s.

Rankin was among those pacifists who pulled the hardest. She delivered a radio address in Helena, Montana, to talk about the role of women in democracy. War between the United States and Canada had been outlawed for 100 years, she said. Norway and Sweden did the same, and so did Belgium and Holland. "If the war method can be abolished on one border, it can be abolished on all borders," she said, persisting in her belief that the geography of the United States made it safe from attack, a common isolationist position before the missile era.

"An army of 300,000 men is no force at all to come against the United States. It would take millions of men to make any impression on this country. They could not come, as we did [in World War I], 7,000 at a time, for our ports are fortified. They would have to bring their army all at one time, together with their food and all their military supplies. Fifty-thousand men at a time would take all the boats of Europe." She also embraced Charles Lindbergh's belief that European airplanes couldn't threaten because they were built for heavy loads and shorter distances. "There is an enormous amount of propaganda over the country that airplanes are a dangerous innovation," she wrote in one 1930s-era speech. "It is generally recognized that their military value in attacking a country has been greatly over-emphasized."[274] How much Rankin bought into Lindbergh's alleged sympathies toward Germany remains unknown. The America First cause that he championed in 1940 aligned with her ideas in many respects but she never belonged to that group. Instead she shared portions of America First philosophies that matched hers, particularly their disdain for FDR. "Today the only difference in our situation is in mechanical developments," Rankin said in her Helena radio address. "In 1916 I talked from the street corners; now it is over the radio. ... Governments still cling to the war system, and the problems of 1916, unsolved by war, are here today."[275]

Being a habitual wanderer, she returned to Montana in the spring of 1939 and drove through the state's western district to take a public opinion poll of her own. She was not pleased with what she heard, or at least what she heard that fed her convictions against war. President Roosevelt had created suspicion of pacifists with his warnings about the military buildup in Europe. Rankin's consensus was that peaceful Montanans who once deplored war now feared they could not survive without it. She fired off a letter to Frederick Libby: "Again we hear that the troubles of the world are caused by the 'damn pacifists.'"

Feeling sure that economic policies would drive Americans into another world war, she urged Montanans to lobby their elected representatives in Congress to avoid using violence to cool the war in Europe. Americans should have every means that money, ingenuity and science could devise to protect the United States from invasion, she said, but they should not intervene in century-old European problems based on changing and unknown facts.

For a few months, Rankin considered filing for Congress, uneasy that she would face a new generation of residents undecided and unprepared for war. The newspapers in Montana mostly dismissed her as a longtime resident of Georgia, a truth she found difficult to escape despite summers spent at the family's Avalanche Ranch east of Helena.

Rankin set out to prove them wrong. She spent all that spring and summer at the ranch. In the fall of 1939 she drove her car, alone, to fifty-two of the fifty-six high schools in the western congressional district to talk about peace. Whether all schools were quite happy to see and hear the first woman ever elected to Congress remained a matter of interpretation. She mailed letters to principals informing them when she would arrive at their schools. She omitted her return address so they couldn't object. At most schools, she found a welcoming acceptance. Some of the smaller ones even brought fifth graders into their auditoriums and gymnasiums to hear her speak. She encouraged students to talk with their parents about violence in Europe, which had accelerated that fall with ugly speed.

In September 1939 the Nazis invaded Poland. Then Britain, France, Australia and New Zealand declared war on Germany. Canada followed with a war declaration a week later. The United States declared its neutrality, but Rankin heard the drumbeats of American intervention again. She implored schoolchildren to write their representatives in Congress, and to President Roosevelt, asking how their country could avoid war. Rankin wanted the schoolchildren to know that to write a letter to the president wasn't a classroom exercise but a duty of democracy. "Now if your mother cares three cents for you, tell her to write a post card to the president," Rankin told them. She coached them on what to expect: the first reply would come as a form letter to which students should graciously respond that they appreciated hearing from their elected officials but they still needed answers to their questions. That letter would go to the secretary who sent the form letters. She then would feel compelled to show the second round of student letters to her boss. Students should continue writing letters in polite tones, but pressing for real answers. Sometimes, Rankin said, she suggested that they write, "I was talking to a group of people and they wanted to know this answer," to impress members of Congress of a wider interest. She would reflect, years later: "You can turn a congressman completely over if you have enough of that kind of letters going to him, because he realizes what is happening in the district, and what the people in the district are thinking. Eventually, he'll write you an honest letter."[276]

Rankin started her high school presentations with a story about how girls once weren't allowed to attend school: "And some man wanted to educate his daughter, and they found that women could learn. And so now we have the schools with boys and girls. We got the vote in Montana, and they sent me to Congress. And we should have more women, and so on. And then I said, 'When I was in high school and a member of Congress came and talked to us, they talked to the boys and told them what they could do. They could do all these things, and someday one of these boys may be President.' And then they'd see the girls, and they'd smile at the girls and say, 'And perhaps one of these young ladies will be the wife of a President.' And I'd put it all together logically, but now I've forgotten just how. I'd say, 'Now we know the girls can do many things. And someday we will have a woman President.' And they roared with laughter."[277]

That spring Rankin visited most of the precinct leaders in the western district counties. She asked them if it would be possible for her to win election to the US House of Representatives. The news wasn't good. Democrats ruled in the western district, numbering about 12,000 more than their Republican opponents. A new generation of Montanans knew little of the legendary Lady from Montana. Now her youth was long lost, her suffrage campaigns buried in the history books. Headed into her sixth decade, Rankin was already in the twilight of life expectancy for that era. In that context, any run she would make for Congress would be nearly as remarkable as what she did in 1916.

By June 1940, Germany had invaded most of Europe and Italy had declared war on Britain and France. The novelty of Rankin's sensational election in 1916 had faded. Now other women sat in Congress. The winds of war blowing across the Atlantic Ocean made peace a less popular belief. Her campaign would be much tougher this time, twenty-three years after her single term in the House of Representatives.

Rankin at least had maintained her legal voting residence at Avalanche Ranch. Again she turned to her brother for advice. Could she win in western Montana? Wellington was doubtful. The incumbent, Norwegian immigrant and retired Navy doctor Jacob Thorkelson, had embarrassed himself in Congress with pro-Nazi, anti-Semitic diatribes he had tried to insert into the *Congressional Record*. His unremarkable term in the House meant he was a vulnerable candidate, but good or bad, his name was a familiar one. To win, Jeannette would have to take western Montana by storm, shaking the dust off her political heels in a matter of weeks. On June 5, 1940, one day before the deadline, she filed for the House race in Montana's First District. The campaign was a deliberate attempt to avert United States participation in another world war. Six days later she celebrated her sixtieth birthday. For her, peace was a lifetime pursuit.

Her campaign platform, with the slogan, "Prepare to the limit for defense, keep our men out of Europe," was nailed solidly with pro-peace planks. Rankin rallied the cause of pacifism defiantly. She solicited criticism, knowing that if Montanans did not want peace, she did not want to represent them in Congress. She said in a campaign speech reported in the *Butte Daily Post*:

"We have a marvelous opportunity to build a race of human beings superior to anything we have produced because we have the traits, culture and experience of all the nations mingled in our blood. In the present crisis, the strength that is needed is the contribution of women in realizing that they must do something now if they are going to prevent this nation from becoming involved in the chaos of Europe. As women we will join together and say, 'We are going to protect our product, our young manhood.'"

Carefully she sampled the public mood. The St. Louis Button Company offered her 50,000 celluloid campaign buttons stating, "Jeannette Rankin for Congress," for $440. Somewhat timidly, she ordered only 10,000, waiting to see what support she would find among loggers and ranchers in western Montana. While women, pacifists and disgruntled Socialist farmers predictably backed her, support also came from prominent American men — leaders of liberal political thought — who long before 1940 had overcome concerns about the "weaker" sex and welcomed her into their ranks as a fighter and a dissenter.

Representative Harold Knutson of Minnesota wrote: "Jeannette Rankin is one of the great humanitarians of the age. Miss Rankin has labored ... for legislation that would help the lot of the underprivileged, the friendless and the toiler." Said Senator Robert M. La Follette of Wisconsin, whose father had been among the leaders in the fight against the war declaration of 1917: "America needs leaders in Congress like Jeannette Rankin."

Bruce Barton, for many years one of the most widely published writers in national periodicals, wired a dispatch to Montana asking Rankin if he could assist her campaign. Bennett Champ Clark, a Democratic US senator from Missouri and son of the famous Champ Clark of the First World War Congress, crossed party lines to endorse Rankin's candidacy. "I had the pleasure of knowing you and of observing your work in the very trying position of being the first woman member of ... a war congress," he wrote to her. "I admired your courage and ability."

Gerald P. Nye, the Congressman before whom Rankin had testified, noted that the primary purpose of every American should be to keep the country out of war. "Jeannette Rankin has won so profound a place in the peace cause and work that her presence in Congress in these times would serve a most salutary purpose," he said. "I only wish she was in the harness here now."[278] Among the best promotions came from her old friend Fiorello LaGuardia, who as mayor of New York City had won prominence fighting graft and corruption. He was a renowned voice for the oppressed and the poor.

Rankin had met the "Little Flower" when they had been freshman members of Congress in 1917, and although he was commissioned a lieutenant in the US Air Service later that year, they had fallen into a warm relationship that appeared just short of love. LaGuardia was short on height but Rankin saw him tall on intellect and honesty. In his egalitarian personality, she found a man who appreciated her without questioning her motives in politics.

The extent of their intimacy was unknown even by people closest to Rankin. A confirmed loner, she rarely talked of personal desires. Her reticence would bewilder skeptics who couldn't accept that a woman so famous didn't have a man — or at least a woman. Because of her close friendships with so many women over the years she would be rumored a lesbian, although perhaps more by researchers after her death than by people of her time. Various anecdotes of failed romances fueled rumors over the years but proof has been elusive.

Belle Fligelman Winestine, never a person to exaggerate, once overheard Wellington telling someone that the scar on Jeannette's neck was from an attempted suicide over a failed romance. That salacious story was never proven either. The scar, which Jeannette often hid with high collars, faded over time.[279] Winestine knew that Rankin wanted romance. The problem, Winestine would recall, was that men found Rankin's commitment to principle and her presence in Congress unladylike and disturbing. "She would have got married if she had found someone who was worthy, I'm perfectly sure," Winestine said.

Then there was Wellington. Jeannette's only brother, although sometimes boorish and downright rude to her, was her gold standard. Whenever he faced public criticism she instantly defended him. Jeannette adored Wellington. Family and friends generally believed Jeannette thought she couldn't find a man to measure up to Wellington. She never questioned how Wellington behaved and often was quite dependent on him.[280] In return he was declarative in his admiration for her. "I never saw a woman like her," he once told an interviewer.

LaGuardia wasn't intimidated at all by Jeannette but instead, her family members said, love-struck. He took Rankin to dinner that first year she was in Washington. In ensuing years, they would become frequent dinner companions and he telephoned her whenever they both were in Washington. Rankin deplored "kitchen gossip" and surrounded herself with men who matched her intellectually but often feared her. Even as she flirted outrageously she told family and close friends that she feared her life would change if she married anyone. In matters of the heart Jeannette felt inferior to her sister Hattie, one of the most popular girls in school, but in matters of the mind she was too preoccupied with causes and ideas to let a man court her for long. LaGuardia, who enjoyed her intellectual gifts, clearly was in favor with her.

Once he slid his arm around Jeannette and said to her youngest sister, Edna: "You don't know how hard I tried to get this gal to marry me." Rankin's supreme independence, however, had left no room for marriage. In 1929, LaGuardia married Marie Fisher, his Washington secretary. They adopted two children. He invited a scandal in the Rankin family when, during World War II, he asked Jeannette to have breakfast with him at the Mayflower Hotel. Jeannette told her mother, who was appalled at her daughter meeting a married man at a hotel, and Jeannette backed out.[281]

In his autobiography, *The Making of an Insurgent*, LaGuardia referred only to Rankin's presence in the War Congress of 1917, but after she filed for Congress in 1940, he jumped to her aid: "Jeannette Rankin has the training, experience and understanding to intelligently serve the people of Montana.... I know of no one who has kept in closer touch with economic, social and political conditions in this country. ... This woman has more courage and packs a harder punch that a regiment of regular line politicians."

Rankin printed most of the political promotions, including LaGuardia's endorsement, in her campaign pamphlet. Curiously absent was a letter from Norman Thomas, the Socialist candidate for president, who had told Rankin he would support her because she was unopposed by a Socialist candidate and because she strongly opposed totalitarianism, whether fascist or communist. Rankin had voted for Thomas each time he ran for the presidency.

With the primary election less than a month away, Rankin put to use many of the campaign tactics she had used since the Montana suffrage campaign of 1914. She unleashed a tide of women who organized in towns, cities and counties. In Beaverhead County in southwestern Montana, they bought advertisements in the Dillon newspaper. In other cities and towns women went to local radio stations, asking for air time, and spoke on Rankin's behalf to clubs and public gatherings. She took her arguments to the people, covering most of the district by car. The only difference was that in 1916 she was explaining why women should have the right to vote. Now, she told women to use their vote to prevent going to war. When she met women for private conversations, she admitted her regret that she couldn't do more as a lobbyist to avert war. She knew the United States would be swept into European violence. She just didn't know how soon. Rankin carried her message from the Bitterroot Valley in the First District's south end to the Flathead Valley farther north. Wellington worked the phone from his Helena law office until he was hoarse. He tracked every movement in her district, precinct by precinct, on a map pinned to the wall beside his desk.

In the midst of her congressional campaign Jeannette went to Headquarters, Idaho, to visit her sister Grace. Jeannette's luggage had been lost on the road. When she was asked to address the Legislature, she borrowed an ill-fitting suit of clothes. "Belle Winestine literally basted her into the skirt," a Rankin campaign worker, Frances Elge, remembered later.

Believing world war was inevitable, Rankin hoped she would be sent to Washington by people who believed in peace. She got her wish. On July 18, she emerged from the primary election with a victory over Thorkelson, her closest opponent, by a vote of 7,299 to 6,214. Convinced she had secured an antiwar mandate, Rankin wrote to Frederick Libby that her nomination "proved that the people in this district don't want to send men to Europe."[282] In her later years she would credit the women of western Montana for electing her. "I was the only symbol against war that they had an opportunity to vote for. I think that regardless of party and regardless of the position in life or anything else, when they got in the booth the women had the feeling that I would do everything I could to protect their young men."[283]

With Thorkelson vanquished, only Democrat Jerry J. O'Connell blocked Rankin from a new term in Congress. The Butte attorney, an alleged communist sympathizer, had served in the US House from 1937 to 1939. He had lost reelection to the House after that single term in a bitter fight with Thorkelson, seen as the copper candidate. Now he squared off against Rankin. The Anaconda Copper press, hating both candidates, said little about the race. O'Connell had blown the whistle on the company's attempt to evade an excise tax on imported copper. Rankin remained a friend of labor. McConnell tried his best to stain Rankin with the American Legion's allegations of communism in Georgia years earlier, but he had his own problems. Just before the campaign he alienated Catholics by divorcing and remarrying.

A stronger candidate would have made more of Rankin maintaining a residency in Montana for political purposes despite a two-decade existence in Georgia. Although national sentiment was shifting to the right of the political spectrum, Rankin found herself elected as a peace candidate to the 77th Congress in an election year that returned Franklin D. Roosevelt to the White House on promises the nation wouldn't enter foreign wars. Contrary to Rankin's Republican victory, the Democratic Party won huge pluralities nationwide. She defeated O'Connell by a vote of 56,616 to 47,352 in the November 1940 general election.

"Knew all the time you would win. Love, Fiorello," wired Rankin's old friend LaGuardia from New York City. Another telegram of congratulations came from Thomas E. Dewey, a special prosecutor waging war on Mafia racketeering in New York City. Rankin wrote back: "My brother, Wellington Rankin, has been one of the greatest powers for good in the State of Montana for many years. His intelligent management of my campaign was the deciding factor in my election."[284] Wrote Shirlie Shunk Fenn of Kooskia, Idaho: "I hope that History will not repeat itself in regard to the necessity of voting for or against war. What a commotion was raised over your [1917] vote!"[285]

Jeannette Rankin, again a member of Congress after a twenty-two-year hiatus, spent most of Election Day at Avalanche Ranch where she and her mother shivered beside the fireplace as the temperature fell to twelve below zero. When the weather cleared, they loaded the car and hit the road for the long drive to Washington, DC. "Mother and I started East to avoid the storm, but I think we followed it along for it snowed everywhere we went," she wrote Ben Chestnut in Anaconda, Montana. When they got to Minneapolis they shipped the car via train to Pittsburgh, then drove to Washington to their small apartment at 2220 Twentieth Street. "The trip took twice as long as usual, and I have laid up with a cold most of the time since. It is hard to keep one's head with the warmongers down here," Rankin wrote.[286] To another Montana friend, she wrote, "I am just recovering from the strenuousness of it."

In 1940, Rankin remained the only women ever elected to Congress from Montana, but the world was different. No longer was she a frontier "slip of a girl" but instead a shrewd political veteran. Despite a sprinkling of news reports that she made many of her dresses and hats and was "famous as a good cook," especially those frosted lemon pies, the novelty of being a woman in Congress had faded. Ten women held seats in the winter of 1940, all of them in the House except for Senator Hattie Wyatt Caraway of Arkansas.

In 1916 Rankin had campaigned for suffrage, child labor laws, compulsory education and improved health care for women. By 1940 all those issues were enacted into law. Thirty million more people lived in the United States. Insulin and penicillin had been discovered, talking movies invented, and the first liquid-fueled rocket launched. Astronomers found a distant planet they named Pluto after the Greek God of the underworld. Congress approved *The Star Spangled Banner* as the national hymn. Conveniences such as sliced bread and car radios appeared on the market. Alcoholics Anonymous was founded in the midst of the Great Depression. The Dust Bowl emerged, Amelia Earhart vanished. Engineers built the Hoover Dam and the Golden Gate Bridge.

As war again shook Europe, Adolf Hitler turned his obsession away from Britain and approved *BARBAROSSA*, the invasion of Russia by three million soldiers. The United States was emerging from a decade of vigorous pacifism on the home front, but by 1940 the political drumbeats for war had killed much of the nation's enthusiasm for peace. "I remember your heroic stand which you took against our entry into the last war," wrote a constituent, Donald P. Wright. "Again the world is engulfed in a cataclysmic tragedy of even greater intensity and magnitude, and we need people like yourself who have the necessary courage to speak for peace as against a conflict whose only outcome, whichever side wins, will be almost complete destruction, devastation and demoralization."[287]

Still a familiar figure at the US Capitol, where she had testified relentlessly through the 1930s, Rankin again took a seat in the House. "The world was interested twenty-four years ago, but I am afraid only my personal friends and myself are going to get a real thrill out of this," Rankin wrote to her old friend Mary Stewart in San Francisco.[288] To Hugh Ronald of Portland, Indiana, Rankin wrote: "Isn't it a grand surprise for me to get back into Congress?" The National Council for the Prevention of War, pleased that the confirmed pacifist was back in the House, placed flowers on Rankin's desk on opening day. History indeed was repeating itself.

As a full-fledged pacifist, Rankin would resist any efforts by fellow representatives and President Roosevelt, serving an unprecedented third term after a decisive win over Republican Wendell Willkie, to push the United States into war. "In spite of all F.D.R's blustering confidence, I still feel sure that he can be bluffed out of going to war if women will do their part," Rankin told Jane Fenby Bausman from New Jersey. Hundreds of women wrote letters investing their faith in her. Mrs. O.G. Marksen asked: "By doing all in your power toward keeping the United States out of this tragic threatening war, we citizens here will back you up 100%. You can depend on us — can we depend on you?"

Public opinion polls by Gallup and Fortune in May 1940 before the presidential election showed an overwhelming desire to stay out of war, but also documented a creeping fear that England and France weren't doing well in their eight-month fight with Germany. Polls showed concern that the US Navy wasn't strong enough to withstand an attack. More than half of the respondents wanted a president who would "keep us out of war," a desire that ranked more important than balancing the federal budget. Asked to evaluate the European war, only eight percent of respondents thought the Allies were winning compared to 67 percent who saw Germany as the victor. A slight majority thought the United States would enter that war someday, but almost all respondents, ninety-three percent, opposed a war declaration on Germany that would involve sending American troops to Europe. When asked if the nation's military forces could fight off an attack by foreign powers, eighty-five percent said no. In another finding, a strong majority of survey respondents declared that President Roosevelt was doing a good job dealing with the war crisis in Europe.[289]

In January 1941, the Roosevelt Administration began promoting controversial legislation known as the Lend-Lease Act, which would permit the shipment of billions of dollars in war materiel to allied nations embroiled in a growing war with Germany. Congressional foes reacted bitterly, asking how the United States could presume to police the world's armory. Rankin joined her Montana colleague, Senator Burton K. Wheeler, in denouncing the bill. Wheeler testified that Lend-Lease would ensure a grave for every fourth American boy. Rankin fumed that the measure would bring the United States one step closer to war: "Mothers alone can prevent our entering the war if they will express their opinions now."

A month earlier, British leaders had told the Roosevelt Administration that their country faced bankruptcy because of the war and they no longer could pay cash for arms as the United States required. "We cannot, and we will not, tell them that they must surrender, merely because of present inability to pay for the weapons which we know they must have," Roosevelt told Congress. Elected isolationists, such as Hamilton Fish of New York and Dewey Short of Missouri, opposed Lend-Lease legislation because they believed, as Rankin did, that it shifted too much war power to Roosevelt and might hurl the United States into the conflict. "We have never been asked to consider anything like it," said former Representative James Wadsworth of New York. "The powers proposed to give to him by Congress are enormous."

Weeks of intense debate included testimony against Lend-

Lease by aviation hero Charles Lindbergh before the House Foreign Affairs Committee. Rankin had tried to amend the bill to read: "Nothing in this act shall be construed to authorize or permit the President to order, transfer, exchange, lease, lend, or employ any soldier, sailor, marine, or aircraft pilot outside of the territorial waters of the Western Hemisphere without specific authorization by the Congress of the United States." Her amendment ran into immediate opposition. "Under this amendment we could not send any troops to the Philippines, to Hawaii, or even to protect ourselves anywhere," retorted John McCormack, the House Majority Leader from Massachusetts.

"We can no more trust good intentions to keep us out of war today than we could in 1917," Rankin said on the House floor on February 8, 1941. "Many, who fallaciously believe that human relations can be adjusted by force and violence, also believe that the threat of violence is effective." Rankin's amendment died on a 137-82 vote.[290] That very day, after several other members failed to pass amendments, the House voted 265 to 165 to approve House Resolution 1776. Even as violence flared in Europe and Asia, Rankin continued to believe that broad oceans would prevent a surprise attack on the United States. Quoting the late US Senator Ernest Lundeen of Minnesota, killed in a plane crash in 1940, Rankin said no military officers would be willing to risk their reputations by speculating that the United States was vulnerable to attack. Like many other Americans, she just didn't think it comprehensible that a foreign army or navy could inflict harm on the United States, but she suspected FDR of beckoning it. "She sees in the leadership of Mr. Roosevelt a playwright designing scenes that lead to war as a climax," wrote journalist Ernestine Evans.[291]

That very month Rankin received a letter from her sister Hattie's second husband, Grant McGregor, from their home in London. "After enjoying the glamour of being America's first Congresswoman it must be a thrill to go back again after so many years," he wrote. "Harriet and I figure there is no reason why, now that you have got into your stride again, you should not go back for a number of Terms. You, of course, know of many things which are wrong and which should be corrected, but the first requirement for accomplishing your end is to keep in office. No doubt this will often require soft peddling on highly controversial questions until the right time." McGregor and Hattie witnessed, from their flat, German bombing attacks that destroyed several buildings. "The greater part of London, including our district, is protected by a balloon barrage which prevents any accuracy on the part of the enemy airmen," he wrote. "To say the people here are highly pleased with the policing President Roosevelt is pursuing with the predatory Axis Power is to put it mildly. Never before have such criminal gangsters gained so much headway in their efforts to put the world under their heel."[292]

Rankin's efforts to thwart war arrived on the desk of the politically paranoid J. Edgar Hoover at the Federal Bureau of Investigation. In a letter dated January 10, 1941, special agent R. G. Danner of Atlanta, Georgia, seized on Hoover's obsessive hatred of communists with a warning of Rankin's "possible Communist sympathies." Danner documented his conclusions on her affiliation with the "peace mobilization movement" in Georgia and his presumption that she was "closely associated" with Robert H. Hall, a journalist who had embraced communism during the Depression.

Meanwhile, war arrived into Rankin's life in a personal way when her beloved niece, Dorothy McKinnon, wrote in April 1941 that she had eloped with Walter Brown in hopes that he wouldn't be drafted. "I'm depending on you to keep us out of war," McKinnon wrote. For nine months preceding the Japanese attack on Pearl Harbor, Rankin tried to slow the momentum of military legislation. "I am still trying to keep our men from being sacrificed in the slaughter house across the ocean, but we seem to be going in the direction of war just the same," she wrote Joseph H. Griffin in Seattle. In May 1941 she introduced legislation imploring Congress to adopt a policy against sending armed forces outside of the Western Hemisphere or American territories. It was futile legislation, much like her other attempts to commit Congress to a defensive military position, but she didn't seem at all intimidated when the bill died for lack of support.[293]

A month later, she offered an amendment to an appropriations bill to combine all United States military operations into a single department. Her idea was to cut Congress out of war making. In essence, American voters would decide when and where wars were fought. "Public opinion demands everything necessary to protect our shores from invasion," she said in House proceedings. "Public opinion demands security against attack, and at the same time insists that we refrain from fighting foreign wars."[294] Rankin knew better than to expect miracles. Never would Congress relinquish its power to make war. Again, her amendment died for lack of support.

Even as Rankin and other pacifists held fast to their ideals, world aggression became impossible to ignore. Germany's reign of terror in Europe had reached alarming proportions. In the Pacific region, Japan was conquering neighboring countries. Rankin, early into her term in the House of Representatives, ridiculed the military chiefs of staff for what she called their "annual war scare for appropriations." Even FDR, in 1940, had vowed: "I have said this before, but I shall say it again and again and again: your boys are not going to be sent into any foreign wars."

While many Americans hoped that Roosevelt meant what

he said, the isolationist mood began to change after Hitler invaded Poland, Denmark, Norway, Belgium, Luxembourg and the Netherlands, crushed France, and gained Italy as an ally. CBS correspondent Edward R. Murrow shook Americans nightly with his sonorous on-the-spot coverage of Germany's bombing of London. In June 1941, Germany invaded Russia.

Pollster Elmo Roper reported in the autumn of 1941 that Americans had reversed their stand against war. A majority of poll respondents favored some form of US intervention to end German aggression. "The willingness to use our armed forces has increased even more than our nominal tendency toward intervention," he said. "Now you have big majorities for using all branches of the armed forces, if necessary." However, polls also showed what Rankin already was hearing from her constituents in Montana — that nearly all Americans said they opposed an outright declaration of war against Germany. It was a critical distinction. To Rankin, that public opinion would prevent American involvement in international bloodshed.

As Nazi Germany rampaged to the East, Japan continued to expand its empire in East Asia. Japan's invasion of China in 1937 led to its proclamation that it intended to dominate the region. By 1939, the United States withdrew from its commercial treaty with Japan. In August 1941, the United States initiated an oil embargo against Japan, blocking 80 percent of its oil imports. The embargo threatened to cripple the Japanese economy and its military strength. Tension had mounted rapidly between the two countries, starting with the Japanese sinking of *U.S.S. Panay*, an American gunboat. Rankin, watching the chain of events from Washington, encouraged stronger diplomacy. She said in the House: "I commend patience to them. If their talks serve to put off or avert a war, I hope they go on tirelessly. Here is an occasion for the much-derided diplomat tea sipping and cake pushing to vindicate himself."295

In retrospect, it was all so clear. A decade of isolationist debate in the United States had shone light on profits from war and flubs in diplomacy. Lessons of history were made public for everyone to see. Americans were painfully aware that the First World War didn't fulfill Woodrow Wilson's promise of "making the world safe for democracy," and most people seriously doubted it was "a war to end all wars," another fallacy. Instead, a series of events in the summer and autumn of 1941 suggested that all that was heard and said about pacifism in the 1930s was for naught. Soon the movement for peace would unravel and Jeannette Rankin would stand at the heart of a national crisis.

Incident by incident, the United States drifted toward war. American troops were sent to occupy Greenland and Iceland on the premise of occupying supply routes. By a 203-202 vote, the House of Representatives passed the extension of the draft service in August 1941 and approved any decision to send American combat troops to foreign nations. The United States and Japan, already drifted apart diplomatically by 1941, quickened their provocative behaviors. The Americans, having denied oil and scrap iron to Japan, awarded a $25 million loan to China. Japan opened air bases in northern Indochina and then signed a treaty of alliance, the Tripartite Pact, with Germany and Italy. The United States froze Japanese credits. Japan did the same with American dollars.

The Japanese ambassador, Admiral Kichisaburo Nomura, and special representative Saburo Kurusu met with US Secretary of State Cordell Hull in futile negotiations. In November 1941 the Japanese proposed that the United States loosen economic restrictions and recognize Japan's right to occupy the Asian mainland. Hull refused. In their final proposal, on November 20, the Japanese said they would withdraw forces from southern Indochina and refrain from further attacks if the United States, Britain, and the Netherlands stopped their aid to China and lifted sanctions against Japan. The Americans replied a week later, telling Japan to evacuate all of China unconditionally. On November 27, generals at the Pentagon sent warnings to commanders of American bases in the Pacific that war was imminent. Why no one took the warning seriously, especially American naval commanders at a faraway place in Hawaii known as Pearl Harbor, remains a great mystery in history.

In the months leading to the bombing, the America First effort endured. Celebrities such as novelist — and Rankin's friend — Sinclair Lewis, poet e e cummings, film producer Walt Disney and screen star Lillian Gish were active in the cause, as were student politicians like future President Gerald Ford. Charles Lindbergh issued inflammatory comments about how American involvement in the European war would hurt American Jews — and how a greater threat to the United States was influential Jewish ownership of the film industry, newspapers, radio and government. Rankin, in private letters, revealed her worry that a new war would exacerbate racial tensions:

"I feel that the colored people are in a tight spot right now," she wrote to Mary Church Terrill, a friend and president of the National Association of Colored Women. "We all appreciate the good things President Roosevelt has done, but if he takes us into war, the reaction that will come later against those groups who have supported him — the women, the colored people and the Jews — will be like the reaction in Germany, if not worse. For the protection of themselves, it seems to me that the colored people should take an open stand against war now. I know of nothing that is going to be so tragic as the race riots that will result from the hate generated if we go to war. This, to me, will be the most tragic part of the war."[296]

Rankin promised a negative vote if Congress considered a declaration of war. She was seemingly oblivious to the dramatic reversal of public opinion. She refused to believe that Americans desired war. Hundreds of letters from her Montana constituents crossed her desk, ninety-five percent of them asking her to prevent war. She forged ahead to commit women to her peace ideal through her example, despite the outbreak of world war. That worried J. Edgar Hoover. That very month, special FBI agent S.K. McKee had written Hoover to allege that Rankin insulted the son of a high-ranking Navy officer who had asked her for an appointment to the Naval Academy at Annapolis. McKee relayed a complaint from the officer that Rankin had inquired about the occupation of the young man's father, and after hearing he was a commander, replied: "He is one of those killers too." McKee's short letter to Hoover didn't speculate on the accuracy of third-hand information.

In mid-November 1941, Rankin pushed a resolution onto the House calendar calling for a national poll to determine opinions toward war. Japan's fierce attack on the US Pacific Fleet at Pearl Harbor, on December 7, rendered the poll useless. As news of the attack reached the mainland, people expressed disbelief. Many Americans heard the first reports broadcast on one of the nation's 45 million radios that afternoon. A news reporter standing on the roof of a building in Honolulu sent the first eyewitness report over the NBC Blue Network: "We have witnessed this morning ... a severe bombing of Pearl Harbor," the reporter said, background static punctuating his message. "The city of Honolulu has been attacked and considerable damage done. This battle has been going on for nearly three hours.... It's no joke, it's a real war." Just hours after the Sunday papers had been printed, newspaper presses roared to life in mid-afternoon as editors hastily compiled extras for shocked readers. A woman browsing at a newsstand at the corner of Michigan and Randolph avenues in Chicago locked her eyes on the headlines and asked, "What's this?"

The vendor erupted. "We're at war, lady, for crying out loud!"

She replied: "Well, what do you know? Who with?"

As the initial shock melted into deafening cries of outrage, much louder than the voices of pacifists had been, Americans prepared for war. Weeks and months would pass before the full extent of the Japanese attack was known, of how major battleships had exploded into infernos and sunk, of how men drowned in submerged hulls and burned to death in flaming oil slicks.

Rankin and her sister Edna were at home in Jeannette's apartment when they heard news of the attack on a broadcast from a Washington radio station. Jeannette refused to believe it. She would say later that she simply could not fathom such a tragic possibility, although for twenty years she had held the opinion that economic greed would be the foundation for another world war.

In the midst of national uncertainty about what really had happened at Pearl Harbor, in the American territory of Hawaii, Rankin defied the news as war propaganda. She tried in vain to reach somebody at the US Capitol to find out when the House would convene. Sunday evening, she boarded a train for Detroit where she had a speaking engagement. Edna, meanwhile, had planned a luncheon for the following day that was intended to encourage the chief of the US Children's Bureau to endorse birth control. First Lady Eleanor Roosevelt made sure the luncheon continued as planned, despite the frenzy in the nation's capital, although she didn't attend herself and the Children's Bureau didn't take up the cause of birth control.

Twelve hours after the Pearl Harbor attack, Wellington placed several telephone calls to Edna, wanting to find Jeannette. "Where is she? Are you hiding her from me? Edna, what is she going to do about this declaration of war?" Edna explained that Jeannette was on a train. "Well, keep her on that train or be sure how she's going to vote. She can't be for peace again — after Pearl Harbor!" he shouted over the fuzzy phone line.[297]

Resting in an upper berth, listening intently to a radio, Jeannette learned that Roosevelt would address a joint session of Congress at noon the next day to ask for a declaration of war against Japan. She left the train in Pittsburgh in the middle of the night and caught another back to Washington. As the train glided across the Pennsylvania countryside, passing peaceful meadows and forests, Rankin knew what awaited her. She, more than almost everyone else in Congress, understood the lonely life of a pacifist when war came knocking. In those quiet hours that she rode the rails she thought of all those years she had worked for peace. Now, this. Rankin knew what she would do.

When Rankin arrived at Union Station that morning she saw anger in the eyes of passengers rushing through the station. She sensed a grim intent. She drove home and climbed into bed and fell asleep. Jangling of her telephone awakened her. At the other end, her anxious brother muttered relief. Wellington knew his sister well. If President Roosevelt proposed a declaration of war, she would vote against it. Still, he pleaded with her, begging that she vote for the resolution to protect her political future. Wellington, thinking he had better vision of the voter landscape than his sister, tried to help her find a way out. He suggested she could rationalize a yes vote for the sake of national defense.

In 1917 Wellington was a young, strutting military patriot, consumed with traditional beliefs about the nation's honor and eager to protect his law reputation in Montana. Now, like Jeannette, he was much of a rebel himself. Although Jeannette never persuaded him with her arguments for why the country should stay out of war, family ties permitted his respect for her commitment to peace. However, he could better see the practical result of another vote against war than his idealistic sister, who had made it abundantly clear over the past twenty-five years where she stood. She also considered her election on a peace platform an irrefutable endorsement of her position, believing that Montanans remained entrenched in their opposition to war.

Rankin left her apartment, nudging her automobile into traffic pulsing with excited drivers. The city was alive with anticipation and anger. She drove for hours to avoid visitors and telephone calls, just as she had done by escaping on the train. When the Capitol dome popped into view she was reminded of a similar day in 1917. More than a coincidence, it was an eerie replay of history. She would describe her excursion through Washington, waiting for her second political execution in Congress, as one of the most terrible experiences of her life. Shortly before noon, Rankin went to her office at Room 110 in the House Office Building. She masked her mental anguish, giving Frances Elge, her personal secretary, the impression that the forthcoming vote hadn't ruffled her.

Elge had met Rankin years earlier during a casual conversation at the university women's dormitory in Missoula. After Elge finished law school and was admitted to the state bar association in 1930, she applied for a job with Wellington, then a US attorney in Helena. He had his offices in the imposing Pittsburgh Block where he also ran a private law practice. A strange and forbidding man named Abdo, either Turkish or Greek, ran a dilapidated and creaking elevator to Wellington's office. The dim hallway was cluttered with hay bales, saddles, barbed wire and other supplies from his ranches. Wellington, ever focused on legal matters and political maneuvers, appeared nonchalant to the mess around him. His rare concern over decor surfaced in peculiar ways, such as when he reserved a room for Jeannette in the nearby Placer Hotel, a 1913 building of extraordinary luxury for its time and a place where gathering politicians could hobnob over fine food and free drinks. Wellington was a partner in the hotel's ownership. Susan Eaker, a friend of the Rankins, recalled that Jeannette's room had red carpet. She shuffled her feet when walking on it. Wellington, annoyed, warned her not to wear out his carpet. Jeannette colored the worn spots with a red crayon so he wouldn't find out she had ignored him.

Elge, somewhat aware of Wellington's idiosyncrasies, nevertheless asked him for a job. Instead, Wellington encouraged her to open a law office. Feeling sanctioned into Helena's legal community by such an influential attorney, she did so in 1932. Wellington then arranged for a meeting when Jeannette came to Helena to visit, and when Jeannette filed for Congress in 1939, Wellington asked Elge to join her campaign. She became secretary-treasurer for the Jeannette Rankin for Congress Club, a statewide organization managed from Helena. Elge quickly learned that it was Wellington, not Jeannette, who masterminded the campaign. He was more politically astute in Montana, where he had legions of political contacts, while Jeannette was charming and clever and easily won over audiences with her charisma. Elge thought of her as exceedingly quick-witted. Jeannette and Wellington made a powerful team when they worked together. Anyone who knew the Rankin family well recognized that no two of them spent much time together without a clash of wills. Jeannette and Wellington had a deep affection for each other despite their differences. Mutual teasing continued throughout their lives.

Elge remembered Wellington as a benefactor to a good many people, including fellow attorneys down on their luck. At times he was generous with his money. Other times he walked past friends and acquaintances on the street, dressed in his familiar blue serge suit and Homburg hat, without acknowledging them. Elge's impression was that he had to work harder at being perceived as a successful political contender. He had the qualifications, the name recognition and extensive knowledge of party politics and precincts. He also could be quite good with people when he made an effort. To Elge he often seemed preoccupied and aloof. He fell to public criticism for leaving his vast cattle ranches in poor condition, rounding up parolees at the state prison to provide cheap labor and other faults, real or perceived, but he was a shrewd businessman who knew how to turn a profit by ignoring repairs and other needed expenses. Despite his skill in managing his substantial law business and land holdings, he often labored in managing Jeannette.

On Monday, December 8, President Roosevelt summoned his secretary, Grace Tully, into his study and dictated: "Yesterday comma December seven comma nineteen forty-one dash a date which will live in infamy dash." Roosevelt drafted the brief but emotional speech that would propel the United States into world war. The Secret Service, fearing that someone might try to assassinate him, drove the president to Congress in a bulletproof 1928 Cadillac that once belonged to Chicago gangster Alfonso "Scarface" Capone. The US Treasury Department had seized the car in 1931 when Capone was convicted on federal tax evasion charges. Roosevelt would give his address at midday.

In an uncanny repetition of her experience twenty-four years earlier, Rankin waited solemnly for the walk to the House chambers while friends whispered encouragement to her. Another of Rankin's secretaries, Sigrid Scannell, tried to console her when the bell rang. Defiantly, Rankin pushed herself away and walked to the Capitol, where she searched for a seat on the House floor, now crowded with outsiders who ignored chamber rules and pressed inside. Aides and messengers rushed about excitedly. Unlike the war vote of 1917, when the debate over whether to send American into war with Germany had been remorseful and indecisive, faces now reflected purpose and duty.

Grimly the senators and representatives quieted while the nation's ailing but patriarchal president entered the House chambers and approached the podium. It was twenty-nine minutes past noon. Roosevelt's son, James, helped the president lurch to the podium on dead, polio-stricken legs. Flanked by the stern faces of Vice President Henry Wallace and House Speaker Sam Rayburn, Roosevelt asked in an eight-minute address that Congress approve a state of war with Japan.

"December 7, 1941, a day which will live in infamy, the United States of America was suddenly and deliberately attacked by naval and air forces of the Empire of Japan.... It will be recorded that the distance of Hawaii from Japan makes it obvious that the attack was deliberately planned many days or even weeks ago," Roosevelt told Congress in his measured New York accent. "During the intervening time, the Japanese government has deliberately sought to deceive the United States by false statements and expressions of hope for continued peace. The attack yesterday on the Hawaiian Islands has caused severe damage to American naval and military forces. I regret to tell you that very many American lives have been lost. In addition, American ships have been reported torpedoed on the high seas between San Francisco and Honolulu."

Roosevelt revealed that Japan also had attacked Hong

Kong, Guam, the Philippines, Wake Island and Midway Island, succeeding in a surprise military offensive across the Pacific Ocean. Promising that the United States would gain an "inevitable triumph" against a "dastardly" attack, Roosevelt asked for a declaration of war. "I believe that I interpret the will of the Congress and of the people when I assert that we will not only defend ourselves to the uttermost, but will make it very certain that this form of treachery shall never again endanger us," he told assembled members of Congress, including the avowed pacifist, Jeannette Rankin. She sat silent and unsmiling as people around her roared their approval, clamoring for war.

18 ~ An eerie echo of history

'Miss Rankin is on her feet. She's asking to be heard'

The president left for the White House minutes after completing his short speech, heard on radio by eighty-one percent of Americans. While the Senate debated war, the House voted to suspend rules requiring that the war resolution be heard first in committee. Instead, leaders began to seek immediate passage of Joint Resolution 254.

After the resolution calling for a state of war with Japan was read, Rankin stood to object. "No objection is in order," replied McCormack, the majority leader. The first member to speak on behalf of the resolution was Joseph Martin Jr., of Massachusetts. "The attack on our territory will rally every patriotic American in support of the nation's needs," he told the emotion-charged assembly. "In shipyards, in factories, in mines, in blast furnaces, on farms, all over this broad land there will be one spontaneous response. The people of America will unanimously meet the attacks of the aggressor and join in an irresistible effort of increased production."

Representative John Gibson of Georgia called for Americans to unite in thought, purpose and determination to resurrect freedom that otherwise would perish "before the forces of cowards who do not feel the impulses of honor." Echoed Earl Wilson of Indiana, "We have done our best to avoid this war with Japan. Now she has asked for it. The only thing we can do is let her have it. By that I mean complete destruction of her war machine. Let us hope and pray that a minimum of lives will be lost."

Argued Chauncey Reed of Illinois: "America aroused will hesitate not an instant and will never rest until the world is rid of the monsters who planned and executed yesterday's dastardly outrage. Japan will rue the day that the fury of peaceful, liberty-loving people was unleashed."

If anyone remembered the legacy of the First World War, meaning that another world war would hasten a staggering human toll that would leave families crying all over the nation, little would be said of it. Roosevelt's abbreviated speech, deliberately kept short for dramatic appeal, finished off the American isolationist movement. Aggression would be met with aggression. Japan's bombing of Pearl Harbor, a faraway place in the South Pacific that was a mystery to most Americans, accomplished more than sinking battleships and killing and wounding thousands of American sailors. It drove a dagger of fury deep into the heartland. In their rage, Americans couldn't foresee ferocious Navy battles, an epic slaughter of US Marines at Iwo Jima, Air Force crews shot down in artillery barrages over Germany, Army and National Guard soldiers met with storms of gunfire at Normandy, the elite mountaineering First Special Services Forces losing half its men chasing the occupying German Army out of the Alps in Northern Italy, and banners of Gold Star Mothers dotting every American neighborhood.

Rankin tried to stop the House from voting without discussion. All too familiar with what she called "passion of the moment," she fought for an opportunity to move the war declaration to committee, off the House floor. McCormack quickly called for a vote, attempting to end forty minutes of speeches.

"Mr. Speaker...!" she called from the aisle, her purple dress starkly visible in the sea of black suits.

Sam Rayburn, frozen by the tidal wave of emotion around him, ignored the Lady from Montana.

"The gentleman from Massachusetts demands the yeas and nays," Rayburn roared. "Those who favor taking this vote by the yeas and nays will rise and remain standing until counted."

Rankin well remembered what followed when she failed to defend her first war vote on the House floor. She didn't want the nation to go to war. Standing and waving, she called for recognition a second time:

"Mr. Speaker! I would like to be heard!"

Evidently aware that Rankin would try to obstruct the resolution if she was allowed to speak, Rayburn ignored her again.

"The yeas and nays have been ordered," he said. "The question is, will the House suspend the rules and pass the resolution?"

For a third time, Rankin shouted to the podium. This time a radio newsman who had placed a microphone on the speaker's platform heard her clearly. Fulton Lewis Jr., a strong supporter of America First and its chief voice, Charles Lindbergh, told nationwide listeners: "Miss Rankin is on her feet. She's asking to be heard." Her pleading was broadcast into the packed antechambers surrounding the House floor. "Mr. Speaker, a point of order!" she called.

"Sit down, sister!" someone shouted.

Lewis, broadcasting the historic moment for Mutual Broadcasting System without knowing or caring that he was in violation of House rules for doing so, went into even more detail in his crisp radio voice. After reporting the Senate voted 82-0 for a war declaration, he turned to the House debate. "There was a considerable, a very very impressive and very dramatic occasion in there that I was telling you about," he told his listeners. "Miss Jeannette Rankin tried to the very bitter end to get recognition from the floor. She even made a point of order trying to get recognition from the floor. Whether or not she wanted to object to this resolution as she objected to passage of the resolution during World War Number One we do not know. But as a matter of fact it may turn out, sooner or later, that Miss Rankin actually wanted to, uh, to make a speech in favor of this resolution, but, as I say, we've been unable to tell."[298]

A congressional aide who realized that Mutual's broadcasts were being heard by a nationwide audience told Lewis to stop. After an argument, heard vaguely over a muffled microphone, Lewis returned with the news that the aide had no authority to shut down the broadcast.

Rankin, standing in the aisle of the chamber with her hand raised, tried again for Rayburn's attention. He turned to address her directly and was heard on the radio. "A roll call may not be interrupted by an emotion or a—!" Rayburn yelled out to Rankin, his voice fading over the airwaves.[299] More congressional aides confronted Lewis then, silencing his broadcast and driving him from the House chamber.

Quickly, as if the enthusiasm might fade, the roll call began. Allen, Anderson, Andrews, Arnold, all yes.... McLean, McMillan, Maciejewski, all yes...."

Rankin: "As a woman, I can't go to war and I refuse to send anyone else."

And so the roll call continued through the alphabet: Stratton, Sullivan, Sumner, Sutphin, yes.... From the NBC Blue Radio Network in New York came a bulletin: "The roll call is up to the letter S, and only Jeannette Rankin has voted no."

Minutes later, from Mutual: "We have a flash from the House that Miss Jeannette Rankin has voted no," intoned Fulton Lewis, now out of sight and earshot of the House floor, to his radio listeners. The roll call had started at what would be remembered as 2:05 Eastern wartime. Eight minutes later, the United States declared war with Japan.

As Rankin recorded her vote, boos rained on her from members on the floor and observers in the gallery. This time she was allowed no sympathy or compassion. The anger toward Japan for the destruction at Pearl Harbor was too great. Gone was her youthful curiosity of 1917 that had graced the House floor and caused such unflagging interest. She was no longer an innovation. Some congressmen complained that she was an undesirable fixture that should be placed in storage. NBC commentator Earl Godwin broke into the Blue Network's "Let's Sing and Swing" program with this observation: "... this thing that's happened up on Capitol Hill this afternoon is the fastest thing ever in American history. It certainly, certainly galloped this thing through. The fact that Jeannette Rankin would just as soon see the Japanese sweep over the country and kill everybody in the streets hasn't—." His passionate statement ended abruptly, leaving confusion whether Godwin was cut off because of what he said or because the network interrupted him to announce that the House had voted 388-1 in favor of the declaration.

From the moment the roll call ended, Rankin was alone. The war resolution swept through the House without another dissenting vote. Some of the members who also might have voted against the declaration instead abstained and fled the chambers, sensing that a neutral stand wouldn't arouse as much anger. Several solemn-faced colleagues walked up the aisle to her seat, among them George Bender of Ohio and Karl Stefan of Nebraska. As they bent over her, pleading that she change her vote, she shook her head in defiance. Rankin was the only member of the entire House who carried the banner for peace, but many saw her vote as akin to treason. "As soon as the vote was over, people just swarmed in everywhere and they started in on me. There I was in the center of a mob in the cloakroom where outsiders are never supposed to go."[300] Someone told her the Senate had voted unanimously for a declaration of war. She met a stunned Senator Everett Dirksen, from Illinois, who asked why she opposed the declaration. "I can't bear to be a worm," she informed him, using one of her favorite expressions.

From the NBC Blue newsroom in New York, commentator H.V. Kaltenborn mocked Rankin's vote as the flustered reaction of a weak woman. His ridiculing sing-song voice came over the crackling radio like this: "It's strange how history repeats itself. That same little woman, who on the occasion of the first world war faltered in her seat at the House, when that fateful roll call came, she, who had always believed in pacifism, always opposed war, broke down and wept as she whispered the word no...." Then Kaltenborn spoke of a new war, and a new vote: "As the roll call swept down the line, through the letters of the alphabet until it came to R, each member voiced a thundering Aye as his name was called. Then, this thin little woman, older now, but still completely devoted to her pacifism, utterly ignoring the facts of a situation in which we are not declaring war but which we are merely stating we are willing to fight when we are attacked, even so in her endeavor to be consistent once again, and once more, with faltering voice, she voted no."[301]

The vote in Congress, as the nation's newspapers reported that evening, was 470 to one: eighty-two in the Senate and 388 in the House. Rankin's isolationist colleague from Montana, the Democrat Burton K. Wheeler, wasn't present in the Senate when the vote was cast. Later that day he issued a statement that he would have voted yes and to "lick hell out of them" was the only recourse. Other opponents of international conflict, such as Senators Gerald Nye and Arthur H. Vandenberg, reversed course after the Japanese bombing of

Pearl Harbor. "That day ended isolationism for any realist," Vandenberg said. In the House, only Harold Knutson of Wisconsin remained from the fifty-six members who, like Rankin, had opposed a war declaration against Germany in 1917. Now, against Japan, he voted yes.

It made little difference that most Americans knew nothing about Pearl Harbor before it hit the headlines. They would learn that the United States concentrated its Pacific Fleet there, on the island of Oahu, and that a wave of Japanese planes laid waste to American ships. They would learn of a shocking loss of life, exceeding 2,400 American troops, and of nearly 1,300 wounded. Although the death toll was far less than any of ten major battles in the Civil War, it jolted Americans into understanding that their country was vulnerable to foreign aggression, however remote the location. The wave of retaliatory emotion that swept the country crushed the isolationist movement in a single day. The influential America First, once 800,000 members strong, dissolved four days after Pearl Harbor was attacked. Charles Lindbergh, tarred with accusations of Nazi sympathies, had delivered a speech in September 1941 that described Germany's army as superior to the United States. The public backlash included removal of his name from the city water tower in his hometown of Little Falls, Minnesota. Eventually Lindbergh would fly two dozen combat missions and shoot down a Japanese aircraft, but for his hero legacy, the bloom was off the rose.

Some of Rankin's colleagues left her stranded on an island of public condemnation. For reasons including abstentions and absenteeism, forty-one of her fellow House members didn't vote at all. Congressman Francis Walter of Pennsylvania rushed into House chambers to announce he had wanted to vote in favor of the resolution but a cordon of police and soldiers around the Capitol prevented his taxicab from parking closer than several blocks away. Representative Clyde Ellis of Arkansas complained that he was stranded in Tennessee and his chartered plane couldn't fly because of a Civil Aeronautics Authority order that grounded civilian aircraft. Bad weather hampered Samuel Dickstein of New York. A wife's illness delayed Beverly Vincent of Kentucky, who lamented missing the vote by a single minute, and Joseph McArdle of Pennsylvania said the Pearl Harbor attack surprised him during a vacation in Florida. At least three House members were ill and unable to vote.

Rankin stood alone. One small, lonely voice crying to be recognized. One black mark on the nation's war conscience. She was to learn anew the price of standing for an unpopular conviction. This time it would be worse.

Angry, unauthorized people crowded into the cloakroom, a private placed reserved for members of Congress. Among them were Capitol police reeking of liquor and burning with emotion. They swarmed Rankin. Some of them grabbed and pushed at her and demanded she change her vote. Afraid that she would get no help from the police and sure the situation was close to a riot, she escaped into a telephone booth and slammed the doors. A police officer pounded on the glass. Rankin thought he wanted to escort her to safety. She opened the door, smelling alcohol on his breath as he muttered incoherently. "You're drunk!" she shouted at the officer, who scurried away.

Rankin dialed the Capitol switchboard for help. Flashbulbs popped. Despite the hysteria, she was shown in newspapers across the country the next morning in a typically relaxed pose, cradling the telephone receiver conversationally. Sober Capitol police accompanied Rankin to her office and stood guard while she wrote a letter of explanation to constituents. She lacked sufficient facts about the Japanese attack on Pearl Harbor, she told them, to justify a hasty vote for war.

"While I believed that the stories were probably true," she penned, "still I believed that such a momentous vote, one which could mean peace or war for our country, should be based on more authentic evidence...." Reminding her constituents of her campaign pledges for peace, Rankin said she had voted her convictions. Years later, she would say, "Everyone knew I was opposed to war, and they elected me. I had to vote against war whether I wanted to or not because I had been instructed by my constituents to vote against war."[302]

Soon after the vote Rankin telephoned her brother in Montana. He snorted in disgust: "Montana is 110 percent against you." Later that night, Jeannette felt the despair of being shunned by almost everybody. "I have nothing left now except my integrity," she confided to a friend.

As Rankin began to feel the full measure of public anger, she went to stay with her sister Hattie and her nieces Mary Elizabeth and Virginia at their house. Jeannette had told Virginia, "I'm going to vote one vote for democracy," and now Jeannette again paid that price. Virginia, whose married name would become Ronhovde, remembered that Jeannette maintained a fearsome exterior until dinner one night when she told Jeannette about a song called "Well Done" that the family's housemaid sang at Negro funerals. The South Carolina girl sang over coffins to honor the dead for their efforts when alive. Tears came to Jeannette's eyes, the first flicker of the distress she was feeling. "God love you for a gal with guts," she whispered, leaving Virginia to wonder just who her aunt meant.[303]

Thousands of letters and telegrams of condemnation flooded Rankin's office. "You made an ass out of yourself trying to be like a man. Now, come home like a lady," snarled the Young Republicans of Harlem, Montana. "I hope a Jap bomb drops on your head or home," one man wired. A newspaper editor advised: "Though[t] you might be a woman instead of a mouse." Josephine Powell from Tulsa, Oklahoma, wrote: "I am shocked and ashamed that the only member of our sex in Congress showed to the world such a total lack of patriotism, courage and understanding as you did today when you voted 'NO.' You have certainly demonstrated in a most outstanding manner some most perverse qualities of character." John A. Motley of Albany, Oregon, advised: "When you come to your end you will go down as a blight upon the pages of American history and will be 'unwept, unhonored and unsung.'" Jane H. Partridge from Beaver, Pennsylvania, wrote the day of Rankin's vote: "I was never more ashamed of my sex or more utterly convinced of womens unfittness [sic] for public office than at the news of your traitorous and infamous vote." From Pittsburgh came a blazing condemnation from William F. Piper: "You are a cheap publicity seeker, the glamor girl of Congress, I suppose since Speaker Rayburn ignored you, you used your franchise, and would have sacrificed the nation, for it has been well said, 'Hell has no fury like the scorn of a woman.'" Withrow Morse, who said he was representing Rankin family clans in Ohio and Maryland, protested her perceived abuse of the family name. "You will search in vain among members of this old Scottish clan a Rankin who has exhibited such stupidity," he wrote from Philadelphia.[304]

Other correspondence accused Rankin of being a "pettycoated idiot," going down in history as another Benedict Arnold, called for her impeachment, said she was unworthy of her government paycheck, undeserving of any voice in the war decision because she had no sons to sacrifice. "Resign, you poor sissy," wrote a man from Lexington, South Carolina. "So you went and did it again, eh?" admonished Ethel Nye Sanborn of Lansdale, Pennsylvania. "I told my husband, when you went back to the House, that if the opportunity arose you would make just the same kind of a - er - 'jack' of yourself you did in 1917." One letter described Rankin's antiwar vote as "one of the most shameful and unpatriotic acts in American history," another accused her of having a pact with Hitler, and a third compared her with Judas. A man writing from a hotel in Wichita Falls, Texas, appealed to her conscience: "It is evident that you wish to see your fellow citizens bombed and machine gunned by your little yellow heroes — the Japanese. How do you think those good Americans in Montana must feel to find they have been betrayed and disgraced in the eyes of the country by you — their representative? How do you feel about it?" Wrote a resident of Virginia: "Montana certainly produces some queer specimens — you and Burton K. Wheeler, for instance." A letter even came from a former suffrage leader, Catherine G. Callanan of Roanoke, Virginia. "I am ashamed of my sex for your attitude today. why dont [sic] you skip politics and take a maids [sic] job?"[305]

Henry McLemore, a columnist for Hearst Newspapers, wrote that Rankin would make an ideal wife, for her pacifist qualities would prevent her from declaring war on her husband at home. "She dismissed the bombing as lightly as she would a run in her stocking," McLemore fumed. "The chances are she'll go on to even greater fame by being voted Miss Tokyo of 1941 by the Japanese."[306]

While Rankin peace vote of 1917 had been ridiculed as the weakness of a woman's heart, many people regarded her vote against war with Japan as treason. Even the pacifist Quakers, who had made a fuss on her behalf the first time, now were conspicuously silent. Only Emily Balch, an intimate friend and longtime Quaker, wrote Rankin to commend her courage. Rankin had lost respect for the Quakers, convinced that even Balch had turned her back on international peace because she supported the war to counter Nazi aggression.[307]

"What kind of creature can you be?" demanded a California woman. "In 1917 American women by thousands bowed their heads in shame because of you. Now every American mother must curse you for the shame you have brought upon our sex."

Outwardly Rankin maintained a cool demeanor, appearing undaunted by the criticism. Inside she was bewildered that she should be accused of rendering havoc with the pride of women considering her devotion to their behalf since the suffrage campaigns before World War I. While they complained that Rankin had brought shame to womanhood, she thought she was guiding them to liberation. For more than twenty years, peace had been her utopia. She never wandered from her argument that women could be free if they would rise as a political bloc to stop war.

While Rankin's vote against war with Germany in 1917 had been an interesting footnote in history, her lonely vote against war with Japan in 1941 lost meaning because it was a single incident in a lifetime of more extensive peace work. Rankin stated in letters that her vote had saved the nation from a totalitarian war regime, publicly acclaiming it as an example of democracy at work. The vote also proved to be nicely symbolic of the independence of womanhood, but Rankin regretted having gone on trial that way. She had vowed at least six years earlier that she would vote against war, "today — tomorrow — and forever" and she was disappointed and dismayed that Americans should awaken with hysteria to her work as if it were a completely new idea. She wrote Frederick Libby:

"What one decides to do in a crisis depends upon one's philosophy in life, and that philosophy cannot be changed by an accident. If one hasn't any philosophy, in crises others make the decision. The most disappointing feature of working for a cause is that so few people have a clear philosophy of life. We used to say, in the suffrage movement, that we could trust the woman who believed in suffrage, but we could never trust the woman who just wanted to vote."

This frustration with women who regarded the vote as a novelty but not a means to a greater end troubled Rankin, making her doubt at times that she had accomplished anything. Although believing she was fighting for the welfare of women everywhere, she often felt like an outsider, and she sometimes complained acidly that people refused to follow the path lighted for them. Three days after the United States went to war with Japan, on December 11, Germany and Italy declared war on the United States. Roosevelt asked Congress to reciprocate. When the time came in the House for a vote on war with Germany, silence fell on the chamber when the clerk called, "Rankin of Montana?" in the roll call.

"Present," she responded in a weak voice. The clerk, not understanding, asked her to repeat her vote. "Present," she said again, receiving scattered applause. She replied the same way in a vote against Italy later that day. As she nibbled on an apple and sipped milk in the cloakroom, the United States went to war with Germany and Italy. The nation had entered a world war that would engulf dozens of countries, cause as many as 85 million deaths from combat, famine and disease, and include Jewish genocide in the Nazi extermination camps. Millions of American men and women would flock to military uniforms and defense manufacturing plants in a mobilization of breathtaking proportions. The phenomenon of Rosie the Riveter would become legendary. Hundreds of popular songs would result from the war. No better example emerged than the legendary Andrews Sisters, who crooned romance into the Second World War with mega-hits such as *Boogie Woogie Bugle Boy* and *Don't Sit Under the Apple Tree*, a song about two young lovers pledging their fidelity while one is away at war.

As World War II began, Rankin endured one of the cycles of history that plagued her life's work, reminding her that while she campaigned for what she believed a perfectly sensible cause — peace — she again was branded as a radical as she had been in Georgia. National sentiment did not see merit in her cause.

The national mood swung like a yo-yo from conservatism to tolerance to liberalism through the decades while Rankin in her steady commitment to peace was thrown in and out of perspective. The public opinion makers, the historians, the preachers, most spoke of the obligation of war as a Biblical tradition; Rankin condemned anyone who favored a society founded on war. She was pushed aside as Americans ran to their guns. Yet, her message was always the same: war kills men, but it also kills a country's future. Little did Rankin's opinions matter after Pearl Harbor. She no longer was in vogue with many Americans. Letters were proof of that fact.

"Traitor Nazi."

"Jap."

"Skunk."

"Your half-baked idea is an insult to us," wrote a Montanan. "I was one of the fools who voted for you, but you may be sure of one thing, the people of this state will vote you out of office next fall so fast you will wonder what happened."

Wrote another: "I sincerely hope that your failure to stand by your people of Montana, and the United States, will cause you to send in your resignation immediately, and drop out of public life, where it is now apparent that you never belonged." Yet another constituent wrote: "Sentimentalism has no place in times of crisis when clear thinking is demanded."

The Cowpokes Union of Deer Lodge, Montana, telegraphed: "In view of the bad storms in the offing and the way you botched up the last branding we would like to have you saddle up your bronc, tie your bedroll on behind and just ride home. As we have decided it best to let the rest of our critters run as mavericks until we have a chance to send a new representative after the next election."

W.J. McMahon, writing from Montana's labor stronghold, summed up his reaction this way: "You had two guesses, both wrong. Look to the Japs and Germans for sympathy. None in Butte."

Rankin's worth to America was compared with droughts, grasshoppers and dust storms. She was encouraged to wrap herself in a bed sheet so she could look the part of Mahatma Rankin [a jibe directed at Indian pacifist Mahatma Gandhi]. She was ordered to hang herself. Some outraged observers merely questioned why Rankin had voted against war while others accused her of political grandstanding, and most of the "con" letters demanded that she resign from office.

All pacifists found themselves kicked off the national stage in those angst-filled days after Pearl Harbor. Nobody became a target of public hate and ridicule as much as Rankin. The grim letters and telegrams that poured into her office reminded her just how lonely dissent could be. A national committee member from her own Republican Party, Dan Whetstone of Cut Bank, Montana, notified her of widespread anger in her home state. Another Montanan, Julia Gumprecht of Helena, wrote to say she had voted for Rankin but, given the Japanese attack, her opinion had changed: "Oh! how ashamed I am to have to admit that you are my Representative in Congress." Robert J. Gorham of Oklahoma City asked Rankin to explain why she wasn't a "fanatic pacifist" as he had heard other people describe her, and to refute claims that she was "not a representative of the people, but as a representative of your own selfish interests and fanatic ideas." One anonymous letter recommended that she be spanked on the floor of the House: "That an old-fashioned hairbrush be used as per the good old days and be it specifically stipulated that there be no silk, rayon or any other fabric between the backside of the hairbrush and point of contact of Jeanette's [sic] anatomy."

She was called "Pig Rankin," told to pack her bags and go to Japan, and showered with oaths of fury in public places. She was accused of ignoring the murder of her own people. Cold and unfeeling. Delightfully unimpressed with such slaughter. A surrogate for Fascist and imperialist interests in the United States. "Never have I seen such a 'silly' looking person — and to think you really in our Congress. You look like a horse — with a hat on — you should jump in the nearest river," a woman from Houston, Texas, prattled two days after the bombing of Pearl Harbor. Another Texan wrote: "You will go down in history as a disgrace to the congress and set women in politics back a thousand years. Who can trust them — if you are an example?" So urgent and voluminous was the mail that Rankin's secretaries prepared more than 3,000 form letters to reply to everyone who had written her.

Despite the acrimonious anti-Rankin response, she would tell friends and relatives in private correspondence that letters from Montana slightly favored her vote against war with Japan and she would reiterate she had campaigned for peace. Wrote District Attorney W.E. Keeley from Deer Lodge: "I am satisfied that the great majority of your constituents were not in favor of the war and the only reason you might suffer some detriment with some of the voters was that Japan attacked this country. However, it is also realized that you voted in accordance with your declared platform, and when American boys begin to die on foreign fields, in large numbers, there is bound to be a great feeling of animosity toward those responsible for this country becoming involved."

Letters from a few other states and Canada and South America overwhelmingly were in favor — by ten to one — of her stand against war. "Our country is full of hysteria, and Hitleritis, if you choose to call it that.... I thought when we were in the last war, that we had learned a lesson that would remain with us for some time to come," wrote Dr. W. Randolph Angell of Boston. Helen Courtois of Los Angeles had heard the House debate for war on the radio: "No packs of hounds in chase at the moment of capture could be more vicious, as the procedures sounded to me."

Rankin found refuge with women who had stood with her for much of her life. "Your vote today should make you Montana's next senator," telegrammed Margaret Laughrin from Butte. "Montana women feel Japanese attack has long been administration provoked if not invited. Montana women will organize behind you to resent hoodlum hisses and boos on our woman leader. Montana women feel personally insulted. We are with you 100%."[308] Wrote another Montanan, Amanda Swift of Lewistown: "In all of history no man has done so brave, so commendable a thing, let alone a woman. So often I've regretted my sex, as I've contacted silly, shallow, chattering women. Today I feel that you've vindicated womanhood...."[309] One of Rankin's closest confidantes was Millacent Yarrow, a friend since her early involvement in suffrage. A month after the Pearl Harbor vote, Rankin drove alone to Montana, exchanging letters with Yarrow all the way. "Wish that I could look into your eyes," Yarrow wrote in one communication, suggesting the apparent depth of their emotional intimacy.

The *Evening Kansan-Republican* saw the vote as the work of a martyr to an eternal principle — throbbing in the hearts of women — to oppose bloodshed and war. Wrote Lillian Smith, editor of the *North Georgia Review* and author of the books *Strange Fruit* and *Killers of the Dream*: "That one little vote of yours stands out like a bright star in the dark night." A letter from Lavinia Dock — the last of the old suffragists of the Susan B. Anthony style — spoke the best for them:

"I can see the men crowding around you to urge your change from what appeared to them a hopeless and useless stand, but I can also look further and see that you were a symbol and type of the eternal hatred of war that is the heart and soul of downtrodden, oppressed, civilized, humane, forward-looking people of every nation, in every age, in every country."

Rankin's niece, Mary Jane Sedman, wrote two days after the vote to express her approval of the vote against Japan. "Everyone seemed to be saying that now that fighting has begun we can say nothing against it; but since your vote I see that one can be a consistent pacifist even now. Several friends have let us know that they are very glad you voted as you did. One of the teachers told Mother how much she approved."[310]

Rankin's votes on the war declarations unleashed a torrent of mail that kept her busy for more than two weeks. She had the presence of mind to bundle up the most vivid letters and mail them to her niece in Virginia for safekeeping. Rankin confided to her friend Ethel Bielenberg in Deer Lodge that she lost five pounds of weight from lack of sleep and good food and "I do not advocate this treatment for slimming." Rankin wrote Bielenberg, president of the Deer Lodge Republican Women's Club, that she had received "a good many more friendly letters from the District than critical" and said fourteen letters favoring her vote and one opposing were found in the mailbag opened that day. She said of the war declarations: "Except for the added dislocation and confusion at home and the tragic death of thousands of young men at sea, the situation will remain the same for a long time until, through exhaustion, we will achieve a victory, and then what remains of the dispute will be settled as it could have been settled six months ago."[311]

Wellington, forever the watchdog for a sister who sometimes seemed oblivious to threatening political winds, discovered shortly before the holidays that she had addressed 4,000 Christmas cards to her Montana constituents with the greeting "Peace on Earth" printed on the front and was ready to take them to the post office. Wellington suspected the irony of the Christmas greetings would arouse tremendous antagonism. He firmly told Jeannette to destroy the cards. "It was a great disappointment and came too late to make any substitutions," she wrote Bielenberg in the new year.

Soon after the war votes she traveled to New York to spend a few days with her old friends Katharine Anthony and Elisabeth Irwin, whom she had known from the early days of the Heterodoxy Club. Anthony and Irwin, a declared lesbian couple who spent summers in Connecticut, referred to themselves as the "gay ladies from Gaylordsville" to their friends. Anthony, by the onset of the war, had established herself as an author of substantial biographies of famous women. After her successful *Catherine the Great* had come biographies of Marie Antoinette, Louisa May Alcott and Queen Elizabeth. Irwin was founder of Little Red School House, an experimental school in Manhattan that applied many of the theories and beliefs from early Progressivism to the city's diverse ethnic students. Anthony and Irwin had raised two adopted daughters.

When Rankin arrived in New York early in 1942, she attended a few satirical Broadway plays with Anthony and Irwin to shut out the new war. She spent Christmas at her niece Virginia's home. From Montana, Ethel Bielenberg sent Rankin a traveling bag as a gift. In a thank you letter, Rankin said she had received "hundreds of Christmas greetings" and at least ten times more letters. "The number of approvals from [Montana] still outnumber the condemnations. Why people are so mad at me when they have the Japs to hate and are now at war, I cannot understand. Lots of love to you dear. I always feel your understanding and love. Devotedly, Jeannette."[312]

By February the flood of critical mail slowed, but an avalanche of unanswered letters remained. Rankin made Photostats of the best ones and sent them to Wellington. On the national front, Americans soon were too busy obliging the pressures of mobilizing a military to continue chastising what many of them thought was an aging and eccentric spinster from Montana.

Memories were longer in Montana, especially in the Western District where Rankin had campaigned in high schools that war was a foreign problem. "Do you realize that speeches such as you made before our high school two years ago confused many Americans, especially the young ones? 'No airplanes can cross the oceans.' 'The two oceans are sufficient defense,' etc.," wrote C.H. Scherf of Kalispell, where he was a high school science teacher. "Has that falacy [sic] not been demonstrated by what happened at Pearl Harbor and off the coast of California?" Rankin's brand of isolationism, Scherf wrote, described proper military preparedness that would hasten an end to war. Scherf and many other Montanans called for Rankin's resignation. "I voted for you (both times) and urged my friends to give their support to your election," wrote Murdock Macdonald of Missoula the day after Rankin's vote against war with Japan. "I have talked with several hundred people in the past few hours here in Missoula and I have yet to meet one who not feel bitterly over your action this morning." Wrote Cecilia H. Best, president of the Women's Republican Club in Dillon: "We wonder what alternative you would recommend after the wanton aggression and wholesale murder perpetuated by Japan on

American soil. We feel you were not given the privilege of registering the convictions of Jeanette [sic] Rankin in Congress, but the privilege of representing the wishes of the people of your state."

R.J. Bowers of Hamilton condemned Rankin for her eventual explanation that an opposing vote was necessary to avoid a totalitarian state. "It was a silly thing to do on your part and your hysterical explanation, when you sensed the temper of your constituents back here in Montana, might be considered a contemptable [sic] slap at our Congress of these United States — even seditious and traitorous — by many people."

With no little irony, Rankin's critics roundly accused her of reacting emotionally and failing to think through the consequences. One of them was Mrs. T.S. Benson of New York City, who advised Rankin: "You should put on a crying act. You should go out and hang yourself." Margaret Burkhart of Oakland, California, described herself as a "Real American" and commanded Rankin, as if nudging her from a deep sleep: "Woman, awaken."[313]

Rankin, eager to forget the angry mail, sought distractions of any sort. She complained sentimentally to her mother in a letter that the license plates her brother sent from Montana were not as colorful as the previous year. "I suppose we must not ask for pretty things in war time," she wrote two months after Pearl Harbor was bombed. She refused to take a government-issued gasoline rationing card, available to members of Congress, which would have ensured her preferential treatment.

Rankin viewed the new war no differently than the First World War. Her bitterness was grounded deep in twenty-five years of pacifism. She had ridden the crest of fame and fashion in her election to Congress in 1917 and she had plummeted into the canyon of despair in 1941 as her single protest was swept under the tide of a nation's shock.

No Christmas benevolence was found among editorial writers toward the wisdom of Rankin's vote, although a few praised her courage to stand alone. One of those was William Allan White of the *Emporia Gazette* of Kansas. "When in a hundred years from now," White wrote, "courage, sheer courage based upon moral indignation is celebrated in this country, the name of Jeannette Rankin, who stood firm in folly for her faith, will be written in monumental bronze not for what she did but for the way she did it."

Her contemporaries generally tried to banish her from the mainstream of the peace movement with eulogies for her tombstone, but she was not ready to quit. Rankin declared that she had spoken for American mothers who did not want their sons to go to war. She took the liberty to conclude that in her political involvements she had learned facts about government's intentional entanglement in war. These facts, she said, were hidden from public view.

During the days Rankin had invested with the National Council for Prevention of War, she suspected that if the United States could blunder into war through financial commitments to foreign belligerents, it soon would learn the value of making war for its own benefit. She broadened her viewpoint to include allegations that Franklin Roosevelt by the late 1930s had manipulated public opinion in favor of war. "This Administration would like nothing better than to have the country condemn Congress and consider it of no consequence," Rankin wrote to H.H. Hoppe of Victor, Montana, one of her critics. "The history of dictators shows that their first step is to nullify the representatives of the people."[314]

Rankin had nothing to lose in seeking the truth, or at least her interpretation of it, for her political future again was in danger. To her, the atrocity of Pearl Harbor had served to distract attention from the causes and reasons of the attack. The bombing, strafing and torpedoing had crippled a proud and democratic nation. More war resolutions followed. On June 5, the United States declared war on Bulgaria, Hungary and Romania. Rankin, absent from the chamber, didn't vote on any of them. Neither did about seventy other members. Her Democratic colleague from Montana, James O'Connor, voted in favor.

Rankin, trying to finish her term constructively, found her credibility shattered. The world that Jeannette Rankin the 1940s feminist and pacifist saw was very different from what it would become twenty-five years later under influence from Gloria Steinem and the women's liberation movement. Even as she stubbornly held onto hope that women would vote Roosevelt out of office in 1944, Rankin admitted:

"I am still convinced that the women can prevent war if they put their minds on it. If the mothers cared as much for their sons as they do for their social position, we would not have war. Alas, the parasitic life they have led has corrupted their emotional life."

American women disappointed Rankin when they reelected FDR, although they at least attempted to steer the nation away from war by discussing peace among other "gracious living" topics at the trendy women's clubs. Teenagers — including the young boys Rankin was trying to protect — were locked into a social phenomenon of Army boots, bobby sox, slumber parties and jukeboxes. Rankin, in her persistent dedication to pacifism, suffered bouts of futility and depression. She wrote her mother in Montana: "I am inviting a couple of Congressmen and their wives to dinner tonight.... I did not go to sleep until 4 a.m. so am feeling very dull and stupid and now have to have a party tonight. I set the table last night when I could not sleep, literally not figuratively. I served the dinner figuratively. I tried to get a girl to help me, but I do not know whether she is going to turn up or not, so I have to be prepared to do it myself."³¹⁵

At the Capitol, she required her staff to work long days. Occasionally McGillicuddy, a canary belonging to Olive Rankin, sang away until someone silenced the chatter by placing a cloth over his cage. Fond of growing things, Rankin kept potted plants everywhere in the office. She preferred geraniums as a source of inspiration. She kept a copy of Benjamin Kidd's *Science of Power* on her desk. Frances Elge, one of Rankin's administrative assistants, spent very little time in her rented room during daylight hours because Rankin kept her and the rest of their small staff working into the night answering correspondence. Rankin was excessively dependent on her staff, in their view, somewhat selfish in her demands for their attention, and often impatient if she didn't see business moving ahead at a brisk pace. On one occasion she chastised a secretary for losing a document — "I know I gave it to you!" — but later it was found on Rankin's desk. She hated stupid behavior, avoiding people who couldn't think and act as quickly as she expected. Elge worked Saturdays as well, sorting mail and organizing work for the following Mondays. It was on one of those Saturdays, as she collected mail from a basket outside Rankin's door in the House Office Building, that Rankin strolled in with Fiorello LaGuardia. "They were very close," Elge remembered some years later. Wellington took notice of his sister's affection for LaGuardia, but he never thought it would lead to love. "You know Jeannette, she has to be the boss, she has to dominate, she has to make the decisions, and any man would be scared to death of her." Her siblings understood Jeannette's passion for ideas and activism, but they also recognized that family circumstances might have swayed her from marriage. Their father had died young. Jeannette's leadership in the family in those years after John Rankin's death often included caring for her mother as she aged.[316]

Despite the hectic business at the Capitol, Rankin made accommodations for her friends from back home and sometimes in personal ways. One of them was Marguerite Marcum, from Helena, who came to the nation's capital for a visit. Elge informed her, apologetically, that Rankin was leaving by plane that very night for Montana during the Congressional recess. Elge promised Marcum a tour of the Capitol, consoled that the White House "does not allow visitors any more," but then promised to give her a key to Rankin's apartment. "There are two studio couches so move in if you would like. She told me to be sure to tell you this," Elge wrote.[317]

Even with the war commanding headlines every day, other major issues nudged their way into Rankin's office. One of them was an effort to abolish the poll tax in Southern states by expanding federal protection of voters' rights. By 1941 the coalition had become the National Committee to Abolish the Poll Tax. Supporters said states used the poll tax to discourage blacks and poor whites from voting. States assessing the tax countered that it was their right to do so. Labor organizations threw their support behind the federal effort. They flooded Rankin's office with inquiries.

Elge and Scannell struggled to stay current with stacks of mail. Rankin, trying to find a position she could support, debated aloud with her staff in their private moments. She told Elge that she thought the poll tax was a matter of regulation by individual states. Contrarily, if she voted against legislation opposing poll taxes, she would snub constituents in Montana all too aware of how Anaconda Copper had been accused of manipulating votes. If she voted for the legislation she would offend Southern lawmakers, who she strangely saw as allies despite her failed Georgia peace experiment. Like every other member of Congress,

Rankin paced the floor to find an answer. Politics was a stew of complications.

Much like her first term, she would leave Congress before the big action would occur. In World War I she was gone before the Twentieth Amendment ensured women in every state the right to vote. In World War II she left before the worst destruction ever known engulfed the world in its full fright, FDR died suddenly of a massive stroke, and new President Harry Truman dropped atomic bombs on Hiroshima and Nagasaki.

In the spring of 1942, as the United States began exporting troops to foreign battlefields, Rankin decided she wouldn't run for reelection. Through the summer she flirted with the prospect of reversing her decision. "I saw another dress in a shop and bought it and had lots of compliments on it, so I am pretty well decked out," she wrote her mother. "I think it will make a nice campaign dress in 1944, if the world is going at that time."[318] Wellington, meanwhile, decided to run for the US Senate. Having twice helped elect his sister to Congress, Montana's attorney general filed for office at the same time he summoned Jeannette to Montana because their mother had fallen ill. Jeannette often disclosed her fear that Wellington wouldn't be as happy in Congress as he thought he would. He was a prominent man in Montana. Jeannette shared her deepest worry that Wellington would run for the Senate and lose. "If Wellington lost an election, he could take that very hard," Jeannette told Elge. She also wrote her niece, Dorothy Brown: "I think this is his opportunity to get elected, and probably his only opportunity." In June 1942 she wrote to a friend: "While a few loud-talking people are going to say that they are opposed to him because of me, there are going to be hundreds of quiet mothers who, when they find my name absent, are going to vote for the Rankin name because he is my brother."[319]

Wellington Rankin, never comfortable on the campaign trail, nevertheless reached out to Montanans while disguising his legendary bluster. As Jeannette worked on legislative matters in the nation's capital, he toiled away in hopes of finally winning his own seat in Congress. One of his many strategies involved mailing at least 20,000 personal letters to Montanans. "He is conducting an excellent campaign with little noise and not attacking anyone," Mary O'Neill wrote Jeannette from Butte. "The girls all look worn out, especially Helena, she certainly is a trump card," O'Neill wrote of his campaign workers.[320]

That fall, during a break from House business, Rankin returned to Montana to help care for her mother at Avalanche Ranch. Olive shared Jeannette's apartment in Washington, DC, until Jeannette no longer could balance the demands of public office with caring for her ailing parent. Jeannette's arrival in Montana meant a respite for her sisters Edna and Grace. She quickly sent a letter describing the beauty of an October autumn to her friend and confidante Katharine Anthony. "Your description of the ranch makes me long to be there with you," Anthony wrote back, noting that longtime partner Elisabeth Irwin was recuperating in New York City Hospital with a broken leg. She would die in the hospital a week later, and Anthony's desire for Rankin's companionship would blossom in the following months and years.[321]

A month before Jeannette finished her term in Congress, in November 1942, Wellington narrowly lost the US Senate election to the popular incumbent Democrat, James Murray. Wellington lost by about 1,200 votes but might have won except that Murray and his son Charles smeared Wellington for Jeannette's antiwar record. Charles Murray asked voters to judge Wellington's "pacifist sister" for her "un-American" vote. "Nazi newspapers in Berlin would hail his victory," Charles Murray said of Wellington. "We can only judge him on his sister's record." James Murray carried the same message to radio. Burton K. Wheeler, who had been working hard for a Rankin victory, surmised Wellington would have won the election had he countered the Murray allegations with a strong response. "I don't think Rankin has shown as much courage and guts as he should have," Wheeler said. "He has been entirely too timid because of the severe criticism that Jeannette got."[322]

As Wellington tallied election returns and then dismally resigned himself to Murray's victory, Jeannette began the tedium of closing her office and resolving never-ending details. It was work she hated. Ever preoccupied with peace and other big ideas, she reacted with anger when one of her secretaries, Sigrid Scannell, refused to return to Washington. Rankin wrote: "I received your letter yesterday and am horribly inconvenienced and disappointed that you are not coming back. I don't know how we are going to close up the office, knowing as little as we do about the files and all the [West Point and Annapolis] appointments to manage." In mid-December, Scannell wrote Rankin from North Dakota: "I do not want to return to Washington to work unless I find it absolutely necessary, for a change from that unhappy environment appeals to me too strongly."[323]

Two days before Christmas in 1942, barely a year after her solitary vote against war with Japan, Rankin inserted a three-page statement, "Some Questions About Pearl Harbor," into the *Congressional Record*. Her remarks were the first attempt to explore the reasons behind the Japanese wave of death since sociologist Charles Beard in 1935 had forecast such an attack. Unencumbered by needing to line up votes for a second term, she let loose with a torrent of accusations against Franklin Roosevelt and Winston Churchill that echoed her antiwar speeches in the 1930s. Her essay was dated December 8, 1942.

"Astounding as the Pearl Harbor attack was to the

American public as a whole, if it was secretly anticipated and even played for, why did the President permit our forces at Pearl Harbor to be taken by surprise?" she wrote. Describing herself as a "belligerent pacifist" in an interview with *Associated Press* on the day she released the statement, she called into question Roosevelt's change in policy after his Atlantic conference with Winston Churchill. The British prime minister had persuaded Roosevelt to accept economic sanctions against Japan, Rankin contended, that Churchill knew would embroil the United States in a conflict with Japan and eventually led to Britain's defense in the European war.

"Was it not strange," she asked, "that Mr. Roosevelt, who, by refusing for years to enforce the Neutrality Act of 1936 to prevent shipments of war supplies to Japan despite popular demand, had largely contributed to supplying that nation with the raw materials for the armaments now being used against our own troops, after the Atlantic conference when an incident with Japan seems to have been desired, suddenly changed his policy and not only cut off war supplies, but virtually everything required by the civilian population of Japan as well?" Her lengthy examination of Roosevelt's presumed collusion with Churchill ended with this:

"A year ago, one of my congressional colleagues, having observed for months the adroitness with which President Roosevelt had brought us ever closer to the brink of war in the Atlantic only to be continually frustrated in the final step by a reluctant Congress, seeing fate present the President on December 7, 1941, with a magnificent moral categorical, right out of the blue, a *casus belli* beyond all criticism, exclaimed in despair, 'What luck that man has!' But was it luck?"

Other members of Congress joined her in asking for an investigation. The Naval Affairs Committee of the House of Representatives refused to discuss the issue while the nation was embroiled in world war. Rankin ignored accusations that criticism meant treason. She accused Roosevelt of a conspiracy with Churchill to deprive Japan of raw materials until its people were near starvation. She assembled documents proving that Japan, unable to survive the economic blockade, was compelled to fight.

Rankin alleged that the beleaguered Churchill had duped Roosevelt into war to protect British imperialist interests in the Orient. The ambitious Japanese government, also imperialist, had threatened British colonialism with its aggression in China. Rankin contended that Churchill was worried he would be robbed of Britain's Far East possessions while the Germans bombed England. In her view, Churchill had convinced Roosevelt that American embargoes of exports to Japan would stall the enterprising Japanese from invading China. In Rankin's opinion, Churchill had hoped the Japanese would retaliate and attack the United States, drawing the King of Capitalism into the war as an ally to the British and their sagging war economy.

Painstakingly, she substantiated her argument. She referred to sixteen published journals, comments or articles that pointed to a conspiracy. She insinuated that Roosevelt had expected an attack on Pearl Harbor, because for two weeks before the bombing the White House had sent almost daily warnings to the commander in chief of the Pacific Fleet that the Japanese were expected to strike. Rankin blamed the early morning attack on an unwillingness by naval commanders to take the cables seriously. The immoral implications of sacrificing innocent Navy men to influence public opinion was reprehensible, she wrote. To her, the severity of the attack was beyond Roosevelt's expectations and won his instant support for war.

Rankin's suspicion of American conspiracy with the British eventually won her acclaim as the first revisionist to contest the facts of Pearl Harbor. She considered any armed conflict a social crime. She might have tolerated war if the United States was surprised with an invasion of its continental shores, making immediate defense imperative, but she could not condone war as a method of economic aggression, feigned in the shroud of defense, as she interpreted the attack on Pearl Harbor. Strip the profits, she believed, and little appetite would remain for war.

Americans, preoccupied with a war drive that already engulfed millions of people at home and abroad, hardly stopped to listen. The White House avoided comment. Earl Godwin, a radio commentator on the Blue Network's *Ford Hour*, arose to President Roosevelt's defense. "I have no use for any woman who stands in the place where a man ought to be.... Seems to me that it is about as low down a state of American mind as you could get without excavating pretty deeply," he broadcast. Rankin was not without allies. One of them, Walter T. Koch of Merrill, Wisconsin, demanded an investigation into collusion preceding the Japanese attack on Pearl Harbor. "Do we want World War III? ... We investigate the cause of a train wreck, a plane crash, a mine disaster, therefore, in the name of common sense, let us demand a public, impartial investigation into the causes of this war." Frederick Libby, meanwhile, informed her that the National Council for Prevention of War had circulated 265,000 copies of "Some Questions About Pearl Harbor," an extraordinary volume in times of war.

Rankin got little credit her work, but within a decade, five major books would allege a conspiracy. Fiorello LaGuardia, as if sensing Rankin's mood and seeking to brighten it, wired her a day after Christmas: "With all your faults, I love you still."

As the year ended, Rankin left the closing of her office to her remaining secretary, Rosa Nell Spriggs, and drove back to Montana to the refuge of Avalanche Ranch. Sounding perturbed, Spriggs soon informed Rankin, "It has been hard work every single minute right up to the end to get the office cleared." Rankin's legendary disdain for preserving records wasn't lost on Spriggs, or anyone else who had worked for her, but Spriggs closed the letter as such: "I haven't seen anything of the new Member who is coming in this office — but understand he is from Maine."[324]

Exhausted and disillusioned, Rankin sensed she could offer nothing more to the peace cause that had commanded her life for so many years. "Perhaps some day the people will learn that every country loses every war, and then they will hang all the dictators, including Roosevelt and Churchill," she wrote in one instance.[325] While at Avalanche Ranch she traded a series of letters with Katharine Anthony, who was grieving over Elisabeth Irwin's death and fawningly asked Rankin to join her in New York. "I hope you are coming back soon and certainly by next winter. I would like you to be near," Anthony wrote in January 1943. The next week she wrote, "... the only work for you and me seems to be here." Rankin asked Anthony to accompany her on a trip to Mexico but Anthony inexplicably declined. "We must write to each other more often," she wrote. "We have to annihilate the distance." Rankin, forever a prolific author of personal correspondence, told Anthony how much she missed her. "I need you too, darling," Anthony responded. "You don't know how much I look for your letters. I depend on you and we will hang together." Rankin shared her desire for Anthony and other women to live with her in Georgia, to which Anthony responded: "I am interested in your daydreams. Your dreams of Georgia correspond with mine. I always have a picture of being there with you again." Increasingly, she signed her letters with heartfelt and provocative salutations. "Lots and lots of the most devoted and loyal love to you, dear," said one. Then, in April of 1943: "Here's all my love to you, my darling Jeannette. I think of you every day and every night. I lean on you in my thoughts and you help to pull me out of depression when it falls on me. You are true and solid and enduring and the part of me that is loyal to you just couldn't ever cave in."[326]

Even as Anthony poured out her deepest feelings, Rankin kept up a vigorous correspondence with other women essential to her life. To Flora Belle Surles and her partner Ann, Rankin issued an invitation to visit her Montana ranch. "From our window we can see 30 miles to the sunset, and on the north it is hard to see the top of the mountain from the window. On the south we slope down to Lake Sewell which is part of the Missouri River, where we have a darling cabin and lovely beach to swim. Alas, it is 5 miles from the house, all on the ranch, and we can coast most of the way down...." To writer Katherine Devereux Blake, a founding member of the Women's Peace Union, she expressed worry about the domestic fallout of war, "always a breeder of hate and prejudice. I certainly feel sorry for the poor Jews, Negroes and colored people after this war." To Rosalie Jones, her longtime suffrage ally, she revealed some apparent regret at her isolation from politics: "I am here with my mother trying to live out the war." Millacent Yarrow, always the flirt, addressed Rankin as "Girlie" in one letter.[327]

In the meantime, Rankin resisted Mary O'Neill's efforts to get her involved in Butte's contentious labor issues. She had committed to spending six months at the ranch alone with her mother, who by autumn was making six quarts of applesauce a day. "It has been something she can do and see real results," Jeannette wrote to a friend. Ollie by that time had stockpiled 200 quarts. She also canned jelly, pickles and apple butter. Before the first snow fell, Jeannette drove her mother to Idaho to spend the winter with Grace. She then returned to Georgia to move to her new tenant house near Watkinsville, which she remodeled under the "oaks of Shady Grove." Although she entertained thoughts of regaining public office, Wellington advised that her chances for reelection were nil. She told Frederick Libby: "It would take twice as much money as I have to make an easy race a hard one even more. Since there is no way to know about the war situation in the future im [sic] not willing to risk all I have.... I shall always feel that I could have won if I had had the money and could have reached the people." [328]

Rankin dwelled in comparative isolation in Georgia, appreciative of the solitude, while Wellington's secretary kept her informed about news in Montana. "I wish he could get more out of life, other than worrying constantly about his ranches," Helena Stillwell wrote, also sending news that "dear little blue-eyed" Mary O'Neill had died in Butte.

Toward the end of World War II, Rankin began a period of international travel that began with a Pan-American gathering of suffragists in Mexico. She accompanied Abby Crawford Milton, a one-time suffragist from Tennessee. In this period Rankin considered writing a book about peace organizations in America, but the truth was she never was inclined to document the past. More appealing to her sense of adventure was a trip to India, ostensibly to study that country's contribution to world peace. Weary from years of intermittent care for her mother, Rankin left the feeble matriarch with three nurses at Wellington's home in Helena. Ethel Bielenberg offered to oversee Ollie's care while Jeannette traveled. In 1946 she boarded the *Marine Carp* in New York to sail to Turkey, where her longtime friend Harriet Yarrow, Millacent's daughter, was a missionary.[329] Her intended destination was India, where she sought a greater truth in the teachings of Mohandas Gandhi.

19 ~ Learning from Gandhi

'India has much to give us in the way of inspiration'

During the summer of 1943, Jeannette Rankin contemplated writing a book she would name *India's Contributions to the Peace of the World*. She planned to use the example of India to demonstrate how her views of peace could be implemented in the United States. She outlined several chapters. In one she hoped to expose the reasons and causes of war, particularly how the American economy created a climate for it. Another would discuss the importance of public opinion in creating a state of neutrality. Other chapters included a review of United States defense strength and a lesson on how to organize a peace plan, using the famous Gandhi's protest tactics. Her friends, including Millacent Yarrow, encouraged continuing activism in politics. "Enough are dead now if only they cared," she wrote Rankin. "But the girls go on marrying the uniforms, sending them off with a tear dropped on their shoulder — and drawing the 'provision.' No, Jeannette, don't wait for that to wake up the women. You must wake them up. You <u>can</u>. You <u>must</u>. <u>You must</u>."330

Rankin scribbled extensive general notes in preparation for the book, but true to her character, failed even to write the first page. She wasn't a writer, but an orator, as experience had shown. She regarded Gandhi as the key to international understanding, believing his example of nonviolence to encourage change — *Satyagraha* in the Indian language — a flawless blueprint for world peace. She compared his teachings with the art of *jujitsu*, in which one opponent overcomes the other not by pushing harder but by yielding faster. "All the nice words about understanding and goodwill are accompanied by the parade of new engines of destruction," Rankin wrote. "The abyss between word and deed creates a problem for those who knew that real progress can only be achieved through their harmony."[331]

Mohandas Karamchand Gandhi was known as a man of inner peace, mental strength and spiritual vision. For this he was renamed Mahatma, meaning "Great Soul." Many people admired his passive resistance to violence and his studied independence from oppression. Gandhi was one of two primary influences — the other being British sociologist Benjamin Kidd — who dominated Rankin's quest for worldwide peace in the final decades of her life. Gandhi, born in 1869, experienced a mediocre childhood fraught with disappointments in school, sports and social circles. Even when he graduated from London University with a law degree, he withered from personal attacks common in the courtroom. He signed a year's contract as legal counsel to an Indian firm in Natal, South Africa. The oppression he observed toward Hindus there started a new life for him. He became an activist with a talent for inciting people to peaceful protest. In 1941, when Rankin cast her historic and controversial vote against war with Japan, he already had been jailed and ostracized for his beliefs, yet was considered the prophet of nonviolence in the twenty-first century.

This vegetarian Indian, dressed in a loincloth, showed how the public opinion of a nation could be vested against the government to secure a greater freedom. Personally, Gandhi's sacrifices were immense. He read deeply and compellingly, fasted, mediated, and circulated quietly among the Indian people, sharing his gospel of passive resistance. Rankin was in some ways Gandhi's western counterpart.

Rankin's voyage to India took six weeks. The fare was $400, which included meals. After a short visit in Turkey with Harriet Yarrow, Rankin entered India in the autumn of 1946 to seek out the famous Gandhi. She had great expectations of India. Because Wellington had paid for the trip — subsequently he would help her with six more trips to India and world tours that included Russia, South America and South Africa — Rankin could be frugal without being restrictive. She continued her appearance of poverty. The pursuit of knowledge was a pleasure she could enjoy. Education continued to be a high priority in the Rankin family.[332]

A week shy of Christmas that year, Rankin wrote Bielenberg: "I've thot [sic] of you so much and am so grateful to you for your care of mother. It was a great sacrifice I know but you will never say so for you are so good. I've felt all along that you were helping me take this trip which will mean so much to me." Rankin described travel difficulties including poor telephone, telegraph and mail service. Her reputation and political activism in the United States evidently opened doors for her abroad because she told Bielenberg she talked with the prime minister and members of Parliament in Turkey, army officers in Iraq, political leaders in Iran, and attended the All India Congress. She "saw enough of the masses, the poverty and the English and Anglo Indian to be able to picture the many complicated problems."[333]

When Rankin arrived in Delhi, she was told Gandhi was 1,000 miles away in Bengal, trying to calm rioting between Hindus and Muslims. The intrepid master of the Indian people was arising before dawn each morning to walk to nearby villages to teach. Fearing she would impose while he was preoccupied with peacemaking, she decided to wait until her next trip to India to visit him. She would regret that decision. In 1948 a Hindu newspaper editor shot Gandhi to death at his home of retreat and prayer — his *ashram*. Although saddened at his passing, Rankin found in his life an immutable dedication to freedom that did not differ much from her own.

In letters to friends and relatives the "Lady Rankin," as she was known in India, wrote about her desire that the United States look seriously at the best of Gandhi's attributes and apply them. Rankin thought that India, with its fierce desire for independence, could become a model for world peace. "Civilization can be saved only by new ideas," she wrote. "If India has much to give us in the way of inspiration, we should receive it gladly. There is a new awakening in those old countries with their long backgrounds and we can profitably share in it, if we have the will and the knowledge to do it."

Rankin, forging ahead in her purposeful desire to free American women from the slavery of war, considered the aging Indian pacifist the second inspirational hero of her life, after Kidd. He represented to her the ultimate quest: independence of the mind. Dutifully and nonviolently, he turned Indian public opinion against British colonial rule and was estranged as a criminal and branded a rebel for doing it. She talked often of Gandhi leading the "Salt March" in 1930 that unchained a series of events that eventually ended British colonialism in India.[334] Some people questioned her attempts to persuade men to repair disagreements through peace. How dare she suggest they become more excited about international diplomacy instead of new factory orders for fighter planes? Gandhi did it, she said. While Rankin had stood alone amid the popular outcry for blood after Pearl

Harbor, Gandhi was advocating passive resistance to the German and Japanese militaries. Rankin understood his lonely pursuit of peace.

Her burning desire to learn more about his teachings had smoldered since 1918, when in her second year in Congress she had urged that the United States recognize Irish independence from British rule. American leaders of the Indian community came to her office to inquire why she hadn't considered introducing a resolution to recognize India's struggle for independence. Rankin subsequently met an Indian author named Lala Lajpat Rai and read his books, *Young India* and *England's Debt to India*. They chatted about Gandhi for several hours until Rankin realized that Gandhi represented the power of one person using democratic rights for social change.

From that moment, she was sensitive to developments in India and was an avid student of Gandhi. The significance of her India experience was not because Gandhi did things that interested her, but how he did it. She once wrote: "Gandhi got England — then the biggest nation in the world — out of India without the loss of life. In my opinion he was the greatest philosopher of our time. He had two things he taught people: truth and nonviolence. If his philosophy doesn't hold, we are lost."

Otherwise they had little in common: Gandhi was a nationalist, Rankin a social revolutionary; he was deeply religious, she a political philosopher; he fasted and sipped fruit juice to sustain himself, she was a skilled cook when she put her mind to it; he supported the British in World War I while her anger toward her country's commitment to what she considered a European war persisted throughout her life. Although many fellow Americans over the years considered Rankin an authority on nonviolent social change, she had much to learn if she was to match the Gandhi ideal. She wrote from India: "One thing is certain. There will be ample opportunity for growth, and I hope I shall come back better prepared to face our own problems."

The Gandhi philosophy of passive resistance was conceived partly by Henry David Thoreau, who in checking out books on his Harvard University library card began an extensive reading of Indian teachings. From that literature, Thoreau developed his principles of civil disobedience: a moral consciousness higher than civil law. Gandhi integrated Thoreau's work into his philosophy of passive resistance, essentially a method by which Indian people could peacefully protest unjust laws. Rankin absorbed this knowledge as she brushed the lives of India's poor. She opened her eyes to the decadence of Indian society, where fourteen percent of the world's population was crammed into two percent of the world's land.

During Rankin's first visit to India, she went to Gandhi's school for basic education at Sevagram. To her the school was the most thrilling thing she saw in India, a living demonstration of Gandhi's work. Gandhi had seen that England was buying natural resources such as cotton for a low price in India, processing it into cloth in England, and shipping it back to India to sell at a higher price. To correct these economic inadequacies, he taught self-sufficiency in his school, stressing that to provide for one's life lessened the chances of autocratic rule.

Rankin saw in the school a reflection of Gandhi's love for ideas. Children were given many responsibilities considered premature by American standards although similar to her own childhood. The kitchen staff, for example, planned the menu, kept inventory of the pantry, and maintained a ledger of money spent. Children were encouraged to study in the library. They listened to the headmistress give an account of the current affairs at the end of the day. Teachers showed the children how to plant a cottonseed. Eventually through this saturated training, children were expected to become masters of their destinies, being suitably informed of the world and capable enough in their crafts to defy anyone wanting to enslave them. This self-sufficiency theme encouraged Rankin in her belief that humankind could learn how to shed the traditions of war.

While Gandhi's love of peace had origins in deep religious beliefs, Rankin was known to possess little patience with organized religion because she thought it interfered with free thinking and fostered war. It made no difference to her that many other pacifists had deep roots in religion. She ignored the role of religion in the peace movement, preferring instead to judge the sincerity of the pacifist.

Rankin seemingly remained agnostic throughout her life, although her brother Wellington and her sister Edna and their mother were strong Christian Scientists. Wellington and Edna differed on her work on behalf of international birth control. Wellington, who had a puritanical streak to him, was outraged that the topic should be discussed out loud. He felt personally embarrassed at the prospect of Edna campaigning for the issue in Montana and told her so. She left the state.[335] Jeannette took a different position. Personal correspondence revealed she was knowledgeable of religion. Sometimes she freely quoted the Bible in references to peace, yet she was known to publicly accuse the church of being a tool of war propagandists. Edna would recall that Jeannette commonly ridiculed people who called themselves Christians because she thought so few of them were willing to lobby against war. Despite that, she also had many friends who were devoted church workers.[336]

Throughout her life, she gave conflicting impressions of her beliefs to many people. At times she was mocking of religion. She once bought a magnifying glass for Wellington, who because of his devotion to Christian Science refused to admit that his eyes were failing and declined to wear glasses. In another instance, her niece Dorothy Brown wrote in a thank-you letter, "Merry unchristmas and suitable greetings to all us infidels and anti-Christians. I have my Mexican cigarette case and I thank you very much for thinking of me."[337]

Despite her many preoccupations, Rankin maintained a brisk correspondence with Bielenberg, a Montana pioneer whose greatest love was Christian Science. Many of Rankin's letters to her bore a spiritual tone, full of praise for Bielenberg's religion. Rankin took time after the Japan war vote in 1941 to extract religious quotations and send them to her old friend. "A moral issue is no longer moral when it requires force instead of spiritual power to uphold it," one quote said. "A candle beam is the most effective when the night is the darkest," said another. At least six letters from Rankin contained the quotation from Mary Baker Eddy: "One with God is a majority." Rankin left Bielenberg's son, Donald, with the impression that much of her pacifism was founded on religious beliefs.[338] To the contrary, Belle Fligelman Winestine, who had spent many weekends at the Rankin house in Missoula in the early years, recalled that nobody in the family went to church on Sundays. It's also possible that Rankin sought emotional refuge with her religious friends in times of personal crisis.

It appeared that for religion, Rankin substituted a worldwide search for knowledge. She was rewarded during her first trip to India when she met Prime Minister Jawaharlal Nehru. While traveling from America, she had talked with the young son of Nehru's doctor, who promised Rankin that he would try to get her an appointment with Nehru. She met him in his office in Delhi and left impressed with his thoughts on the role of women in the world. Rankin had read Nehru's autobiography, *My India, My America*, in 1942, and her meeting with him fortified her strong ties to India.

Nehru was more hawkish than Gandhi. Rankin persuaded him to talk of peace, and he talked with praise of the contributions of women to Indian life. Nehru's eyes assumed a distant flicker and he talked intensely, never glancing at Rankin. She watched him silently, absorbing his words. In mentioning contributions of India women to independence, Rankin had asked the appropriate question, and Nehru, who had reinforced her old beliefs about the role of women in social change, had given the appropriate answer. Rankin respectfully bowed out of his office, vowing to repeat his message that women made a difference in human equality.

Hearing that her mother was near death, Rankin left India and hurried back to Montana. Her mother died on a hot July day in 1947 after a stroke. Ollie, described in a newspaper obituary as "Mrs. John Rankin" despite her husband's death more than four decades earlier, was nearly 94 years old. Jeannette was there to comfort her mother as she slipped away, as were her sisters Mary, from California, and Edna, from Chicago. Ollie Rankin "had retained a high interest in all cultural and educational endeavors," said an obituary in a Helena newspaper the next morning. She had spent her final winters in Idaho, living with her daughter Grace, and her summers at Avalanche Ranch with Jeannette.[339] The old mother, a widow for forty-three years, finished her life in Wellington's home in the Berg Apartments where he read to her from Mary Baker Eddy's book. Ollie's body was shipped to Missoula for funeral services and burial.

Soon afterwards Jeannette planned another trip to India to polish her expectations of what the world could do with a leadership bent on peace rather than war. "Definitely the United States is going straight to war unless we change our course. It will be as soon as we get another crop of men ready," she said of deteriorating relations with Russia even as both countries remained emotionally devastated from World War II.

"India may yield a substitute for war," she said on the eve of her second departure in 1949. "Certainly the world needs one, in the face of the powerful weapons of destruction that are being developed." The trip coincided with the World Pacifist Meeting, envisioned before Gandhi's death to bring pacifists from East and West together for a month-long conference. Rankin got her first real taste of the rigors of Gandhi's lifestyle when she was assigned a bed of hard boards. "All I had was a cotton saree and a wool blanket," she informed friends. "Someone found me a thin quilt and mat. I wished I had more cushion on my bones."

Having taken her Ford automobile to India and hired a driver — whom she fired because he knew less than she — Rankin drove from Madras in southeast India to Lahore (now Pakistan) in the Northwest portion of the country to study the life of the common people. She was said to have a celebrity quality, always being met with humor, respect, sympathy and understanding from villagers and high officials alike. One of her favorite places to stay was the Taj Mahal Hotel in Bombay. She sipped tea and watched ships arrive on the Arabian Sea. She spent the summer at Almora in the Himalayas, sharing life with the natives. Much to her satisfaction, she found Gandhi's influence everywhere. She also found an opportunity to join her sister Edna and the legendary Margaret Sanger at an international birth control conference in India. Hearing delegates talk about the importance of blunt references to women's bodies, Jeannette delivered her famous line: "All you talk about is vaginas, vaginas, vaginas. I'm getting out of here!"

She met the 1950s with a worldly search for new knowledge about peace just as the United States entered the

Korean War. President Harry Truman issued a statement from the Oval Office observing that Russia had exploded an atomic bomb. Truman ordered development of a more powerful hydrogen bomb after discovery that German-born physicist Klaus Fuchs shared secrets of the first American atomic bomb with the Soviets. The Cold War had begun, beginning a powerful arms race unlike anything the world had seen. Americans who were infatuated with the threat of communism and terrified The Bomb would end the new prosperity hardly noticed the expenditure of 25,000 men in Korea, the "Forgotten War." Rankin wrote Frederick Libby: "To my great disappointment, the warriors have succeeded in getting a good war started. It is hard to see the sad faces of the young boys who are having to face this war."

Her admiration grew for Truman's successor, Dwight D. Eisenhower, whom she credited with having the common sense to recognize the futility of war. After Korea, Americans found new distractions in the glamor of sex symbol Marilyn Monroe, the commercialization of Davy Crockett, the Hula-Hoop fad and the Beat Generation's slang, guitars, poetry and coffee houses. The post-World War II economy produced staggering numbers of new houses, which Americans stocked with gleaming appliances and that catalyst of culture, the television set. Jonas Salk invented a polio vaccine. The Russians launched Sputnik 1, beating the first American trip to space by four months. Doo-wop groups and the King of Rock and Roll, Elvis Presley, replaced Big Band sounds of the 1940s with a hip-wagging beat. In the nation's capital, Joe McCarthy and other fanatics fearful of communism gained control of political discourse with their Red Scare.

Matching the country's lackadaisical political mood, Rankin faded entirely from public view. She was more than seventy years old. Despite her foreign travels she maintained a vigorous correspondence with her family and many old friends dating to the suffrage and Progressive reform eras. One of them was Katharine Anthony. In the ensuing years, Anthony's letters to Rankin insinuated lingering desire for a closer relationship, but neither woman seemed inclined to compromise their differing approaches to life to spend much time together. Rankin, forever on the move, invited Anthony to her house in Georgia. Anthony, still mourning over her lover Elisabeth Irwin's death and forever researching books, became a creature of public libraries.

In early 1951, Anthony rejected Rankin's request to travel to Georgia on the excuse that she had begun researching a new book about suffrage pioneer Susan B. Anthony. "Somehow or other I have got to make the lady human and interesting, something that nobody else has yet done for her," Anthony wrote. She then invited Rankin to come to New York to join a tour of Susan B. Anthony museums and homesteads. "How would you feel about coming up here and making that trip with me, though I can't see what you would get out of it to tell the truth. It was just a wild idea that struck me." Anthony closed her letter with, "Love to you, darling."

Rankin didn't go to New York. Instead she traveled to India that year, as she would do again in 1956 and 1959. She visited Africa and Indonesia in 1953, went to South America in 1956, and toured Ireland, Russia and Turkey in 1962. In these years of political exile, she absorbed the cultures and politics of those countries and expressed dismay at discovering American corporate influence everywhere.

Her international travel was sufficient cause, evidently, to revive interest at the FBI. Again, Rankin's name landed on the desk of J. Edgar Hoover. A bureau agent reported on April 9, 1952, that he had discovered a "photostat of a communication" from Rankin, a person of lingering interest in Hoover's mind because of her antiwar activities in the 1920s and 1930s, and her vote against war on Japan. Hoover viewed any protests against American policy as being tantamount to treason. While the point of the letter from the Central Intelligence Agency remains hidden under a censor's heavy black ink, the insinuation was that the intelligence agencies somehow saw Rankin's overseas travel as a threat to national security. "Please be assured that I am very grateful for your interest in bringing this information to my attention," Hoover replied.[340]

Even while Rankin traveled in India, she remained intensely interested in her brother's latest campaign for Congress. The Montana Republican Party had nominated him for the US House race in the Western District. The charismatic Mike Mansfield, a Democrat, was vacating the seat to run for the US Senate. Jeannette's letters to her sister Grace that summer showed deep skepticism Wellington would succeed. The letters also showed Jeannette's weariness toward her family's activism in politics more than forty years after she became involved in suffrage. Jeannette had just observed her seventy-second birthday when she got word of Wellington's filing. He was sixty-eight. "It worries me very much," Jeannette wrote Grace. "I do so want him to win but haven't any courage. I think it is wise that I'm so far away for I couldn't stand the physical strain of the campaign and I'd hate to announce that I'm 'too old'...."

It was Wellington's fifth attempt and, despite Jeannette's reservations that he was too aloof to win votes, he was heartened that President Eisenhower's popularity gave new hope to Republicans. Wellington cleared his first hurdle when he defeated his Republican opponent, Winfield Page, in the primary election. Now the upstart liberal Democrat, Lee Metcalf, stood in his way. The tone of a letter that Jeannette wrote to her sister showed her relief that Wellington had sent her a cable advising of his primary victory. "Thank goodness I asked him to send it if he won and am so glad I did for I was getting more depressed each hour thinking the worst," she wrote. Jeannette also described meeting four "men callers" for tea and said she was looking forward to their sister Edna's visit to India. "It will give me a marvelous excuse to stay over," Jeannette wrote, curiously revealing that she had bought fifty-six pounds of powdered skim milk just for the occasion.[341]

In subsequent letters that summer, Jeannette fretted over Anaconda Copper's role in the election and how that might hurt her brother's chances. She encouraged Grace to join her in India, traveling from her home in Coeur d'Alene, Idaho, because it "would be such fun to talk over India for the rest of our lives." She was certain Wellington would bankroll the trip. "I'm sure Wellington would love to send you if he doesn't feel too broke with taxes and campaign," Jeannette wrote. Her trip by that time had cost about $3,500, which presumably Wellington paid.

Over the years, Jeannette's mother sent money from stocks invested from their sale of the family home in Missoula. Once, when the Montana Flour Mill stock stopped paying dividends, Jeannette needed money, and it always came from Wellington. As an influential attorney and the largest landowner in Montana, he could afford to pay for his sister's world adventures, sometimes in $1,000 installments. Jeannette told Grace that she had nearly $2,000 deposited in a bank in Helena, hoped to receive $1,000 if she sold her car, and also had $1,000 in traveler checks. "You see I really am a rich lady so I may be able to help out on your trip." Still, Wellington's campaign troubled her: "I don't see how I'm going to wait until November for the returns. I think of myself as one of those people Wellington has always sneered at, one waiting for returns and doing no work."[342]

In the end, after a slugfest that fall, Wellington lost by a mere 1,500 votes in an election where Eisenhower and other

Republicans prevailed nationwide. How much of the defeat could be attributed to having a sister who cast controversial votes opposing two world wars was hard to measure. Acrimony over his years as Montana attorney general and trial attorney and his reputation as an inattentive ranch landlord didn't help, but Wellington also acknowledged that he didn't have the campaign skills of his famous sister. "If I'd called Jeannette to come back and put her on the road, I'd have won that," he told the young Fergus County attorney who soon would become his wife, Louise Replogle.

Privately, Jeannette fretted that while Wellington longed to become a US senator he could be personally abrasive and often deaf to the needs and opinions of the constituency he had hoped to represent. She suggested in a letter from India to her sister that she might upstage his performance if she helped with his campaigning. Jeannette also privately criticized Wellington's purchases of ranches and other real estate although, because of his generosity, she owned one herself.

Wellington had inherited his father's intuition for profit, amassing a fortune of nearly $10 million. Being a man of strong opinions and accustomed to courtroom banter, he occasionally embarrassed Jeannette. One day at Avalanche Ranch, when Wellington brought some business associates to visit, he decided to humor them at his sister's expense. He reportedly demanded of her: "Pull up your dress, Jeannette, and show my friends how bowlegged you are." He also thought she talked too much and made promises she couldn't keep.

Everyone who knew the Rankin siblings understood that while they pestered each other, family loyalty ran stronger than their fierce individualism. To tangle with one Rankin was to tangle with all of them. The epic rivalry between Jeannette and Wellington, very different people in most respects, persisted beneath an exterior of love and companionship. She was the philosopher, he the realist. He was a master in the strategy of law, real estate and money. She was drawn to ideas and people. Both had been influenced greatly by their father, although each reacted differently. Jeannette thought Wellington unnecessarily preoccupied with property. He found her style of living appalling.

For years she heated her living room in Georgia by twisting Sunday editions of the *New York Times* into logs that she rotated in the fireplace. The earth floor was covered with plastic, tarpaper and Oriental rugs. Indian memorabilia, much of it pertaining to Gandhi, cluttered the walls. She pumped water from a nearby well. Her end table was an orange crate. Wires from electric lights she installed for reading swarmed across the room. Indoor plumbing would cost as much as a one-way ticket to India, and she preferred the ticket. Wonder Robinson, a black sharecropper, and his wife Mattie lived in the comfortable brick house that was the main building on the property, but only because Rankin wanted it that way. The Robinsons helped with heavy chores.

Her illusion of poverty, however misleading in the context of family wealth, nevertheless fell in line with the teachings of Gandhi and Henry David Thoreau. She simply had little use for material possessions and shunned sentimentality. Her minimalist living became apparent to anyone acquainted with her long dedication to peace. One young fan thought that Rankin epitomized "in one personality what [Benjamin] Kidd is driving at for a coming generation of women who will allow the emotion of the peace ideal to totally possess them."

She had no practical reason for living so poorly, because Wellington would have paid handsomely for her to live in a modern house. She rejected his offers, however, continuing her love affair with the simple home life she had enjoyed in Georgia since 1926. Her indifference to material possessions and practical matters troubled her brother. After one summer in Montana, Rankin prepared to drive home to her farm. Wellington swiftly appraised her old Ford. "You can't drive that old wreck back to Georgia," he told her.

"Why not?" she replied. "There's nothing wrong with it. It's a perfectly good car." In a few days, her brother presented her with a new one.

In another instance, Jeannette baked a pecan pie for Wellington in a new stove he bought for her Georgia home. She carefully wrapped the pie and mailed it to him, forgetting that after eight days in the mail it hardly would be a culinary delight when it arrived in Montana. The pie was inedible. Wellington raved to his wife Louise about his sister's impractical thinking. Feeling sorry for Jeannette and realizing her good intentions, Louise wrote Jeannette that Wellington ate the pie and found it delicious. Jeannette was so happy that she baked another pie — and mailed it.[343]

Wellington persisted in ensuring his sister's financial independence. "She always took care of the mother, so Wellington took care of the two of them," Louise said. Although these strong-minded Rankins had battled philosophically for most of their long lives, Wellington gave her the money without reservation. By all accounts Jeannette used it judiciously, spending most of her income for study trips, books, magazine subscriptions, and bequests to needy friends or relatives. Family members considered Jeannette a hopeless manager of money. Wellington and wife Louise kept her informed how much money she had in her savings and checking accounts and filed her income tax returns.

Jeannette was a vagabond her entire life, changing addresses sometimes several times a year. Whenever in doubt, or in need, she returned to Avalanche Ranch, which Wellington had bought in 1927. It was her compass, but only for short periods of time. She rode horses at Avalanche Ranch well into her sixties and was known as a skilled rider. Her niece, Virginia Sedman Ronhovde, recalled how Jeannette, even in her fifties, could jump onto an unsaddled horse. She valued her privacy when she was at the ranch. Except for hosting guests Wellington entertained there, Jeannette cherished the solitude until she made yet another foray into the world of politics.[344] Ranch life could be lonely in Montana's great empty midsection. When visitors left and quiet fell, Jeannette began searching for the next brush with people. "Now I'm alone on the ranch with Mrs. Hammond, the cook," Jeannette wrote Ethel Bielenberg in 1954. Rankin again was planning to visit India. This time she would sail from Seattle with Lola Kerl, a friend of her sister Grace. "I'm planning to run off again," Rankin wrote.

Later that year, Grace died. "Dear, good, life-saving Jeannette. There are so many of us left still to love you," Katharine Anthony wrote after Grace's death, and soon after Rankin sent her a pair of slippers in a "gay color" as a Christmas gift. Rankin was in Idaho helping Grace's family with the aftermath when another letter from Anthony arrived there. "It is a trial, going through Grace's things," the grieving Anthony commiserated. "I just took Elisabeth's things and wore them, and it was quite an economy during those first years the kids were at school. It is a wrench to the heart to use them but one has to be practical."[345]

Katharine Anthony, in the midst of revising her biography of Susan B. Anthony, discouraged Rankin from making Montana her permanent home. Living there, Anthony wrote, "would be a very cold winter home for a solitary woman. I think you are better off in Georgia, where you have friends in Athens and where I can visit you."[346] In another letter that summer, Anthony again made overtures of concern to Rankin, an independent traveler: "I am so glad you have reached Montana safely. You have made the trip often before without the benefit of my brooding over your progress, step by step.... It wasn't so much that I was afraid of accidents and such, I hated to think of you alone all that time." Much of Anthony's letter was chatty, talking about needed repairs at her summer house and a surplus twenty-four dollars she found in her bank account after visiting Rankin at her Georgia farm. Anthony also mentioned the 71 Ranch, Wellington Rankin's latest land acquisition. "What did you think of it when you saw it?" Anthony asked in her closing sentence.[347]

The 71 was a 74,025-acre property on the South Fork of the Musselshell River in central Montana. Formerly known as the Smith Brothers Ranch, it had the largest acreage of contiguous deeded land of any ranch in Montana. That year, in 1954, Wellington married Replogle. He also acquired the 30,000-acre Lingshire Ranch on the lower Smith River and, for Jeannette, he bought the 1,280-acre Weiglow Ranch near the 71.[348] Those purchases hurried Wellington well on his way to becoming the largest landowner in Montana. He managed his ranches from the Pittsburgh Block in Helena, where much of his attention was consumed with his law practice. In time, Jeannette would make the Weiglow Ranch, which she called the Lazy 101, her private retreat for very occasional visits. She adorned a little 1870-era house with furniture that belonged to her mother and brought rugs from Georgia that she had collected on her world travels. The remote house became a beacon to thieves who stole most of the furnishings.[349]

Rankin, in an unconscious parallel to Gandhi's work ethic, preferred life's simple pleasures over modern leisures such as golf or tennis. This was an ideology rather than an old-fashioned notion. She believed hard work created an awareness of a person's independence in the purest democratic fashion. Her disinterest in money and material goods was more of a studied determination. She had proven early in life that her ingenuity for mechanical skills no doubt exceeded the interest of the average America woman. "If I haven't had anything else, I've had freedom," she told a visiting minister. She knew how to entertain but sometimes just didn't care, occasionally embarrassing her family, for example, by serving sheep liver to her dinner guests.[350]

Despite the Rankins' vast land holdings, Avalanche Ranch would remain the preferred family retreat. Jeannette often described large family gatherings at the ranch including one instance when sixteen people stayed over a few nights and twenty converged for a Sunday meal. "We would be riding somewhere, and see somebody, and she'd say, 'Come out and see me sometime,'" said Jeannette's sister in law, Louise. "And Wellington would say, 'My God, I just hope all these people come.'"[351]

In 1966, at age eighty-one, Wellington went to Mayo Clinic in Rochester, Minnesota, to repair a hernia that had bothered him for much of his adult life. After surgery, he died suddenly from a pulmonary embolism. His death left a huge hole in a family accustomed to his patriarchal, domineering nature. Jeannette lost the man closest to her. Wellington, although a strong and sometimes ruthless brother, never controlled Jeannette. They loved each other in good times and tolerated each other in troubled times. Wellington's death didn't set Jeannette free, as some observers would conclude, but deprived her of the strongest organizational force in her life. "I am so sorry that your beloved Wellington had to go before you. Such a joy and comfort and pillar of strength he was for us. It was a great comfort for me to know that you had him," Flora Belle Surles told Jeannette.[352]

Wellington had become one of the largest landowners in the entire country. He was a distinct millionaire at a time when most people only dreamed about such a thing.[353] His many public accomplishments included years as associate justice on the Montana Supreme Court. "He was a 190-pound dude with a hard fist, ready at any time to accept a physical challenge as he was to accept a court testimony of legal ability," wrote Great Falls Tribune reporter C.T. Sullivan after Wellington's death. Jeannette and her surviving sisters each inherited $100,000 from his estate, a small share of the fortune he had amassed through law and property ownership. Grace's share, postmortem, went to her three children. The money was more than enough for Jeannette, who gave some to the Robinson family at her farm and set aside the remainder for her survivors.[354]

The year of Wellington's death brought other troubles as well, signs of aging and family squabbles. Jeannette's sister Edna sent money a few weeks before Christmas that year for "extras" on Jeannette's upcoming trip to New York, and even to pay interest costs on money taken from her stock holdings. Edna also alluded to problems with Wellington's estate, ending the letter this way: "But I do want you to have the money which is rightfully YOURS from Wellington and you should have it now. I'm glad you wrote the letter and do hope it brings results, which I rather think it will."[355] A delay in executing the terms of Wellington's will apparently angered the Rankin sisters, portrayed in some accounts as being suspicious that his widow Louise was hiding money from them. Louise, Montana's first female county attorney who had risen to statewide repute for busting illegal slot machines, told a much different story. The delay, she said, resulted from a lack of cash flow despite Wellington's immense wealth. As executor of his will, she waited until cattle were sold that fall to pay his sisters.[356]

Edna's daughter Dorothy, meanwhile, wrote Jeannette a month before Christmas to report that she'd suffered a nervous breakdown caring for her mother. "Walter and the psych man both feel that it was her moving 'permanently' to

Missoula that unscrewed all my nuts and bolts," Dorothy wrote of Edna, who had spent much of her life on the road promoting birth control. "This is a difficult thing for any mother to swallow but she is trying hard."[357]

Despite family problems, events of the 1960s would rekindle Rankin's interest in politics, although her public emergence would wait until the feminist movement intersected with protests over the Vietnam War. In the presidential race of 1960, Rankin supported Richard Nixon, thinking that President Eisenhower's ideas about peace had influenced Nixon in eight years of the vice presidency. Nixon's opponent, Senator John F. Kennedy, had written *Profiles of Courage* to showcase achievements of American men. Embarrassed by public reaction that he had not included women, he quickly dashed off an article for *McCall's* magazine entitled "Three Women of Courage," one of whom proved to be Rankin. Although the article contained several errors, he did compliment her: "Few members of Congress have ever stood more alone while being true to a higher honor and loyalty." Rankin wrote Kennedy in 1958 to thank him. He responded that he was "very glad to hear of the cheering effect it had on you," and hoped they would meet someday.[358] That never happened in the remaining five years of his life.

Kennedy's article coincided with the buildup of American military advisers in South Vietnam. Rankin, who had been silent publicly for a decade, was aroused to anger. "My views on peace have never changed," she said in 1961. "I have always been an advocate of peace. I am fearful that warfare in this nuclear age will be the downfall of mankind." That was hardly a radical view during the Cold War years when millions of Americans considered building bomb shelters. Wars and threats of war came and went, but Rankin remained consistent in her opposition to international conflict. In August 1961 she was conferred with an honorary Doctor of Laws degree at Montana State College in Bozeman. President Roland Renne commended her "for the courage of your conviction that international difficulties should be settled by mediation rather than force."

Rankin, herself a living example of independence, told women the only discrimination they faced they had imposed on themselves. If women would not make decisions about their futures, how could they expect to overcome obstacles such as lower pay for equal work? Or, like Rankin, find themselves elected to public office? She admonished: "You can't throw out half the people of the country and say that their minds and feelings are inferior." Just when she thought no one was listening to her anymore she ascended, once again, to national prominence in the American peace movement.

20 ~ The Jeannette Rankin Brigade

'If I haven't had anything else, I've had freedom.'

For twenty-three years after Jeannette Rankin's second term in Congress ended, she disappeared from the peace movement, preferring to occupy herself with world travels and quiet summers at Avalanche Ranch. Many Americans had forgotten her. A national magazine referred to her as "the late Jeannette Rankin," supposing her absence from politics meant she was dead.

When she wasn't traveling, Rankin adhered to her self-imposed life of poverty in Georgia. At Shady Grove, an exile of her choosing, she combined humble living with an obsession for causes and ideas. Feeling renewal after the long war years, Rankin described to her World War II secretary, Sigrid Scannell, how daffodils bloomed early and fruit was appearing on her peach, plum and pear trees. Her friends joked about conditions at Shady Grove. Flora Belle Surles reminisced about taking a bath at the farm years earlier. "How dry we were, and even when we were wet in the little bitty tub, we weren't very wet," she wrote.[359] Rankin herself laughed about the bathtub, telling her peace march friend Vivian Hallinan, from the Jeannette Rankin Brigade, that she finally installed an avocado green tub. "I tried to be a modern woman," Rankin said.

In 1967, Rankin hired carpenters to build a communal

residence on her farm. She had long hoped to share her land with other older women, helping them remain independent, and she settled on an idea while sailing from Asia in the mid-1960s. She envisioned the communal nature of the place as helping women prosper as friends and allies. They would share costs to sustain themselves financially.

After returning to Georgia, Rankin designed what became known as the Round House, spending $13,000 to construct it from cement blocks on a hill overlooking her cottage. She referred to the house as a cooperative homestead for "unemployed homemakers" who had neither the means nor desire to live in rest homes. "It was my idea to offer a place to live for elderly women of small means in this area who do not wish to live alone or with their children," Rankin explained to one prospective tenant. Ten wedge-shaped bedrooms, each with a half-bath, surrounded a common living area with a kitchen. Three bathrooms were built to one side. Rankin planned a large vegetable garden and a lake for boating and swimming. Carloads of people came to witness the curious building, but nobody accepted a room.

Many women, among them longtime friend Elizabeth Winburn Sinclair, had good intentions of joining the commune, but their enthusiasm soon withered. Sinclair promised to come see "your Dream House" once she recovered from struggles with cataracts and arthritis. "I'd love to be connected with something that you advocate. But I'm not spry enough, really and truly, to share responsibilities with other old folk."[360] Two weeks earlier, Sinclair implored Rankin not to "let all of the rooms go" before she could make a commitment but then listed several reasons why she couldn't move to the Round House, including her grandchildren's impending graduations. Other women conceded to the pressures and responsibilities of their families, or admitted belatedly that they were afraid to trade the security of their homes for this new venture. Only after it stood empty for a few years did the Round House finally see a tenant when a man, separated from his wife, rented a room.

Dejected, Rankin turned her interest to other projects while the Round House subsequently suffered the indignities of a brawling fraternity party, a roaming gypsy band and a marijuana arrest. The house would remain mostly idle. Her last will and testament revealed that she still saw hope in the project. A clause read: "Five acres of said land, surrounding the round house for women workers and including said house, together with five acres surrounding my own home and residence, shall be distributed to such charitable foundation ... to be used for the benefit of unemployed mature women workers as a home...."

The Round House, although a monument to her faith in people, also demonstrated how her optimism for new ideas sometimes overreached financial and social realities. Rankin just couldn't accept that people might let her down. She thought her ideas hadn't won wide public acclaim only because they weren't in style.[361] Current affairs in later decades would prove her mostly right. "She was always impatient at women that they didn't do more," said Louise Rankin Galt, who recalled in particular Jeannette's exasperation over the Equal Rights Amendment debate. "She'd throw up her hands in despair. 'Fifty years ago we worked for this, and they don't even know it.' This was her philosophy: if women were concerned about equal rights, hire a lawyer and do something about it."

Rankin never conceded her expectation that women take command of their lives as she had done. They were too dependent on men to realize their full potential, she said, telling a friend: "Edna told me of your marriage. I suppose I should congratulate you and say nice things, but you know I don't believe in marriage."[362] However idealistic she was in her theories about women's contribution to the peace movement, she demonstrated the perseverance of one woman committed to a cause and a zest for attempting to stop the rambling cessation of war. As she neared her ninetieth birthday, people who knew her well understood the true milestone of her life was not her age, but her progressive thought.

Controversy over Vietnam would resuscitate Rankin's public life. It would be the last big event in a trilogy of American wars that would define her legacy. No longer politically dormant, Rankin again would find a cause, or the cause would find her. As the Vietnam casualty figures sailed upward, voices of female protest became louder. By the era of Rankin's Round House, targeted to a generation of her peers, a movement of young feminist women had blossomed. The new National Organization of Women (NOW), led by Betty Friedan, unveiled a Bill of Rights that stunningly paralleled Rankin's lifelong political agenda. NOW, a formidable equal rights organization, evolved from an attitude that only widespread activism would move women into equal positions in politics, economics and other aspects of the human condition. While NOW didn't expressly call for an end to war, its advocacy of government-funded child care, employment law and other issues to improve the lot of women and children hauntingly echoed Rankin's efforts in Progressive reform and woman suffrage. The chief objective of NOW, a federal Equal Rights Amendment, seemed to activists a natural successor to a federal amendment guaranteeing them the vote.

A new era of angry women emerged, finding common ground in the varied but mounting political and social protests of the 1960s. Their influence led President Johnson to issue an executive order extending affirmative action to women. Rankin's long history of activism would make her an icon of national proportions at a time when second-wave feminists were trying to impress on the American public how long the struggle for equality had endured. The ranch girl from the West, born nine years before Montana Territory became a state, supplied a rich and colorful history of determination. Her attempt to build a peace epidemic had fizzled. Too often, she had stood alone.

Women's power to embrace peace had proven little to Rankin in the years between the passing of the Nineteenth Amendment in 1920, which gave women the right to vote, and the Jeannette Rankin Brigade in 1968. Even in 1966, before widespread opposition to American intervention in Vietnam had taken hold, she urged women in Montana to vote against war. Rankin placed an advertisement in eight Montana newspapers with the message, "If any of your candidates for Congress are not opposed to war, protest by writing the names of persons who are opposed to war — your own, if necessary." In an interview with *Associated Press*, she alleged that the US military created enemies to build public opinion in favor of war. "To me, it isn't this war or that war. It's the war system. We've never settled any dispute by fighting." She also expressed her annoyance that women hadn't put their votes to use to stop war. "The reason women haven't done anything in the last fifty years is because they have lost their freedom," she said.

The Jeannette Rankin Brigade's march to the US Capitol was a small antiwar protest lodged in an era of huge ones, but it was notable for being a display of resistance by ordinary women. Despite the many celebrities involved — Rankin herself would qualify as one — most marchers were mothers and sisters and grandmothers who represented the heart of America. They were church women, volunteers, business owners, homemakers and teachers. Their mixture of skin colors infused the brigade with a reminder of the civil rights movement. Many of the women were new to public protest, possibly unfamiliar with protest of any kind, but they took their message to the nation's capital with diligence. Opposition to the Vietnam conflict was filtering into the nation's neighborhoods. That much was clear. The reality of as many as 10,000 women and children banded together to lobby for peace was an important milestone in Jeannette Rankin's turbulent life. She saw the brigade as a bellwether confluence that transcended age, race and philosophy, bringing a coalition of moderate and radical middle-class women together in common purpose. To her, the march symbolized her life's work. "This tremendous number of women, expressing their deep emotion against war, can't do anything but help," she said.

A few weeks after the Rankin brigade's antiwar protest, public opinion turned sharply against the war when the North Vietnamese and Viet Cong surprised American troops with the Tet Offensive. Just when many Vietnamese began their observance of the lunar new year, more than 100 attacks commenced throughout South Vietnam. Enemy soldiers attacked government buildings, military bases and even entire cities. American television crews showed Viet Cong invading the US embassy in Saigon and US Marines dying in a ferocious firefight in the city of Hue. The Tet Offensive proved that President Johnson's position that the United States controlled the war was a lie. General William Westmoreland, who commanded American troops in Vietnam, asked Johnson for an additional 200,000 soldiers. The president viewed the request as political suicide. Poll numbers after Tet revealed public opposition to what they saw as a futile war.

By March, new Defense Secretary Clark Clifford advised Johnson that the country lacked a plan for Vietnam and the war was at a crossroads. "The time has come to decide where we go from here," he told the president. Weeks later, Johnson announced he wouldn't run for reelection. He also reduced large-scale bombing and declared his intentions to negotiate peace. Despite Johnson's epiphany, the war would drag on for another five years as the United States fumbled to arrange a withdrawal that appeared victorious. The death toll would mount alarmingly, as would government spending. Antiwar protests would become angrier and more frequent, as if the Jeannette Rankin Brigade had lighted a fuse of broad dissent. Suddenly even more Americans demanded an end to the war. When Richard Nixon won the presidency in November 1968 and vowed to save the country's honor on behalf of what he called the Silent Majority, the nation fell into an uncomfortable conflict. A conservative resurgence held fast to the waning notion that the United States should fight to end communist aggression in foreign lands.

The old hot fire that stoked Jeannette Rankin's public activism in suffrage returned, this time with light. As President Nixon was calling for "peace with honor," Rankin reminded anyone who would listen that enthusiasm for war led to predictably tragic consequences. Probably more than most Americans, she had seen firsthand the blend of political arguments and military bravado required to enter wars, always times of fierce determination, and human ruin that followed. Rankin, hardly a government outsider, stood firm against arguments for military force that to her sounded identical to what she had heard in the US House of Representatives. Only enemies had changed. In the 1960s, she was the same Jeannette Rankin who had stormed the nation for suffrage and opposed declarations of war on Germany and Japan. In 1963, as President Kennedy widened American involvement in the Vietnam conflict, she reflected on her milestone election to Congress in 1916: "I've said a good many times that I never ran for Congress; I ran for women's suffrage and against war."³⁶³

It was with no little irony that Rankin devotee Katharine Anthony, a famous and prolific biographer of women, died in the midst of the Vietnam aggression without having documented Rankin's life. Anthony once told Rankin that she was casting about for another woman to feature in a book and was considering Jane Addams. "She is about the only American woman left who is worth all the time and trouble," Anthony told Rankin. In another instance, Anthony turned down an opportunity to write about Rankin. An author asked Anthony to collaborate on a biography, but Anthony sneered at the idea. "She wanted me to help and I told I would, but I wouldn't collaborate, as she suggested. I am not a good collaborator. But her idea of getting started — an idea which she seems to share with a group of her friends — was to give dinner parties for me and this group. To an old tread-mill horse like me, this doesn't seem to be the way to go about it."

One wonders if Anthony was so preoccupied with Rankin as a potential lover, which her letters strongly imply, that she was unable to see herself working at arm's reach in an objective treatment of Rankin's life. "This is just to tell you I love you and think of you almost constantly," Anthony wrote in one letter. In another, she expressed her dismay that she had repainted her kitchen in preparation for a Rankin visit that never came. "I don't believe any of those expenses kept you from coming up. I guess you lost the impulse before you acted on it," she wrote from Connecticut. Rankin, for her part, expressed no more interest in having a devotional relationship with Anthony than in delving into a long commitment to telling her life's story. She didn't have the patience, and when Anthony died from a heart attack in November 1965, Flora Belle Surles wrote Rankin: "I know you will miss Katharine — though your times with her were few and far between and of short duration." A few weeks later,

Surles observed: "I had hoped that among Katharine's publications would be a biography of you, for she must have known you better than any other person who could have done it."[364]

Had Anthony lived long enough to witness the Jeannette Rankin Brigade, she might have reconsidered. Issues under discussion that day supplied a bookend to Rankin's pacifism: war's brutality and profiteering, government reform to improve domestic standards, and compelling women to stop war. The march to the US Capitol revived Rankin's status as one of the nation's foremost pacifists. The second portion of the day's event, the "Congress of American Women," would call on lawmakers to "heal a sick society at home." Once the protest at the Capitol concluded, activist Marion Beardsley remembered, marchers boarded buses that ferried them to the Shoreham Hotel, the old suffrage headquarters. Chilled from temperatures hovering in the low thirties and their boots wet from snow, the women hurried into the warm ballroom. It was at the Shoreham where a faction of "several hundred self-styled radicals" broke away from the other women and convened a "Counter-Congress" in another room. "Their thesis was that the march was useless and that the government couldn't care less," Beardsley recalled. "They wanted to promote some illegal action to let the establishment know we meant business.... My own feeling as a pacifist is that militancy is an important ingredient in any movement but the thin line between militancy and violence must be heeded, for violence begets violence and we defeat our peaceful purpose in resorting to it."[365]

Leading the main meeting at the Shoreham were Pearl Willen, representing Jewish women; Mary Clarke of Women Strike for Peace, and Coretta Scott King, representing church and black women. First, Vivian Hallinan spoke about the origins of the Jeannette Rankin Brigade. Then Rankin talked about the history of war and why women must claim peace. The United States, she said, was "the biggest and strongest and most threatening country in the world ... if we disarmed all countries would disarm. They are all arming to protect themselves from us." The United States, she said, "could drift out of Vietnam just like we drifted in. Nobody invited us there and nobody declared war on us."[366]

Rankin held fast to her thinking that the march was intended more to embolden women than to intimidate Congress. It would broaden opposition to military involvement in Vietnam. As quietly as she had resisted opposing factions in the suffrage campaigns, she ignored the Sixties militants. Factional squabbles, she said, divided women. Arguments from the radical caucus that the brigade should break the law to influence public opinion failed to sway her. Rankin, a first-wave suffragist, reasoned that militant second-wave feminists should avoid violence.

One of those militants was Shulamith Firestone, cofounder of the radical feminist group Redstockings and eventual author of *The Dialectic of Sex: The Case for Feminist Revolution*. "It is naive to believe that women who are not politically seen, heard, or represented in this country could change the course of a war by simply appealing to the better natures of congressmen," she wrote afterwards. "That is, the Brigade was playing upon the traditional female role in the classic manner. They came as wives, mothers and mourners; that is, tearful and passive reactors to the actions of men rather than organizing as women to change that definition of femininity to something other than a synonym for weakness, political impotence, and tears."[367] The dissenting women staged a mock funeral procession in Arlington National Cemetery with a larger-than-life dummy that wore blonde curls, reclining on a bier. Hanging from the bier were S & H Green Stamps, curlers, garters and hairspray. Streamers floated off the bier and women carried large banners with messages such as "DON'T CRY: RESIST."

Kathie Amatniek, another radical feminist, delivered a eulogy that sounded closer to Rankin's lifelong pursuit of peace than she might have realized. "Yes, sisters, we have a problem as women all right, a problem which renders us powerless and ineffective over the issues of war and peace, as well as over our own lives. And although our problem is Traditional Manhood as much as Traditional Womanhood, we women must begin on the solution.... And that is why we must bury this lady in Arlington Cemetery tonight, why we must bury Submission alongside Aggression. And that is why we ask you to join us. It is only a symbolic happening, of course, and we have a lot of real work to do. We have new men as well as a new society to build."[368]

Radical women, passionate in their speeches, wanted a stronger expression of anger against men. They wanted more conspicuous protests. One participant of the Jeannette Rankin Brigade, Amy Swerdlow, thought their messages were more confusing than enlightening. Another participant, Charlotte Bunch, described the Jeannette Rankin Brigade and ensuing disagreements as "one of the early confrontations between feminists and peace women about women's priorities, relationships with men, and feminism."[369]

The Jeannette Rankin Brigade, despite its populist appeal, received ho-hum publicity. Editors acknowledged that it wasn't big enough, lacking conflict compared with other public demonstrations of the day, and therefore didn't merit heavy coverage. Rankin, forever at odds with a news media failing to explore her attitudes and opinions, accused newspapers and broadcasting of a "conspiracy of silence." The march coincided with the opening day of Lyndon Johnson's final Congress, but both print and broadcast media reported that Washington generated little news that day. The work of so many reporters who had covered the march was boiled into a few sketchy stories, although ultimately organizers would determine that 456 articles, photographs and editorials reached 31.2 million Americans. Most of that amounted to nothing more than frosting, however, and Rankin wanted the cake. Women who had participated began arguing among themselves. "The march was a farce," complained one black nationalist only hours afterward. "The only part that was worth anything was the [radical caucus after the march] because it made people think."

A few months later, the leftist *Ramparts* magazine featured a cover story that showed a shapely women's Barbie Doll torso wearing a button that read "Jeannette Rankin for President" pinned strategically close to her plunging cleavage. The editor and his wife panned the Jeannette Rankin Brigade as a "miniskirt caucus" and described as a "narrow-minded bitch" the early sister of the suffrage movement, Elizabeth Cady Stanton. Some readers saw the article as a spoof. Other condemned it as a travesty. "Any discussion which purports to deal with a woman as a person with full political dimensions and begins by showing her from the neck down is a fraud," wrote Barbara Dane of Brooklyn, New York.[370] However controversial with feminists, the *Ramparts* piece did its part to remind readers how long Rankin had lobbied for peace. "If only we could get more women to follow in your footsteps," wrote a New York woman, Mary Jane Hoffman, who had read the magazine. "Not merely to have won the vote is enough; that to take one's public stand for what is right and just is more important."[371]

The greatest legacy of the Jeannette Rankin Brigade wasn't its militant infighting, or its reputation of Main Street respectability, but that it contested the federal law restricting public demonstrations at the Capitol — and won. In

"Jeannette Rankin Brigade vs. Chief of Capitol Police," attorneys representing the women, including the legendary maverick William Kunstler, sought to have the law declared unconstitutional. Their legal filings described the Rankin Brigade as an "ad hoc coalition of women from all parts of the nation opposed to the country's involvement in Vietnam and inattention to domestic problems."

Fundamentally the case weighed constitutional questions such as rights of assembly and free speech versus the right of government to maintain its grounds. Section 193(g) of federal law read: "It is forbidden to parade, stand, or move in processions or assemblages in said United States Capitol grounds, or to display therein any flag, banner, or device designed or adapted to bring into public notice any party, organization or movement...." The Jeannette Rankin Brigade wanted repeal on grounds the law interfered with the First Amendment "right of the people peaceably to assemble, and to petition the Government for a redress of grievances."

Federal appeals judge Charles Fahy would agree. He wrote of the Capitol grounds as defined by law: "This spacious greensward studded with the mansions of government certainly sweep far beyond the 'immediate vicinity' of the Capitol, and encompasses areas where even the loudest hosanna of protest could scarcely distract a legislator from the task of legislating.... Congress may impose reasonable limitations upon the right of free assembly and free expression. But such restrictions must be whittled to the scale of the evil feared.... Consequently the court should declare the statute unconstitutional upon its face."[372]

Not until 1972 would a federal court rule that demonstrating at the Capitol is "an exercise of basic constitutional rights in their most pristine and classic form." The function of the First Amendment is to invite dispute, the court said, and "no government interest would justify the blanket prohibition of assembly contained in the words of section 193(g)." The US Supreme Court affirmed the decision on November 6, 1972, noting that the restrictive law unconstitutionally abridged rights to assemble and petition.[373] For the first time since the 1882 Act to Regulate the Use of the Capitol Grounds, peaceful demonstrations could be staged because of the efforts of the Jeannette Rankin Brigade.

From the instant Rankin conceived her ideal of peace decades earlier, she was unimpressed with every argument for war. She thought that logic and diplomacy should preempt the hotheaded emotionalism of slaughter. By 1969, she began a round of speeches in which she criticized the military as democracy's worst threat. She found large, accessible, sympathetic audiences eager to hear her condemnations of war. The escalating antiwar movement welcomed her, sustained her, even vindicated her for a lifetime of frustration. On October 15, national Vietnam Moratorium Day, she told 1,500 students at a University of Georgia rally that the Vietnam War was being kept alive by mercenary interest groups with tremendous influence on federal lawmakers. "We waste our money on the military," she complained. "We spend over half of our peacetime money getting ready for the next war. We give military aid to countries that have no need of it and say we're settling a dispute. Day after day ... we say that we've got to be strong enough to dominate the world, and the people do not have a vote."

Determined to exercise her constitutional rights, Rankin joined every antiwar demonstration she could find and eagerly ridiculed the military mind. "War is nonsense. Bring the boys back forthwith," she told a reporter from the *San Francisco Examiner*. The reporter asked if that meant surrender. Rankin replied, "Surrender is a military idea. When you're doing something wrong, you stop." The growing war protests intrigued, even captivated her. She was thrilled that many hundreds of thousands of Americans were expressing their convictions in street protests and public rallies, although she was sure their might was small compared with that of the military.

Youth in the peace movement found themselves drawn to Rankin's high profile. The elegant and dignified portrait of her that appeared in *Ramparts* was made into a color poster and hung in bookstores. One young fan, visiting a San Francisco shop full of peace literature, found her portrait framed, on the wall, and the owner told him why. The young man later wrote Rankin: "He has you serving as a 'Correct Example' to all the peaceniks who come into the shop by telling them how you worked for peace so hard all your life."[374] She, too, gained something new. She read current antiwar books, such as *Armies of the Night*, Norman Mailer's nonfiction account about peace demonstrations at the Pentagon, and called moratoriums "a marvelous expression of opinion ... the most spontaneous thing that has happened." Rankin was an old woman, a spinster in the midst of a Woodstock generation of vibrant youth, but she would discover in the final years that her ideas were considered forever young.

21 ~ Voice for women and peace

'I salute her for being the original dove in Congress'

In some respects, the first woman elected to Congress became a pathetic figure as death crept closer. Almost belligerently, she demanded of children: "Have you ever heard of Jeannette Rankin?" Predictably they replied no. She scanned the index pages of new reference, history and political books for her name. Mostly, it was absent. In her final years, Rankin sometimes regretted not documenting the historical value of her life. Had she kept a journal of her most private thoughts, Rankin the person would have endured long after Rankin the politician fell from the headlines. Had she not lent bundles of her political papers to graduate students who never returned them, a fuller political record of Jeannette Rankin the leader would remain in libraries all over the country. Publication of the book, *Ten Fighters for Peace*, profiled her pacifism with the likes of Leo Tolstoy, Abraham Lincoln and Mark Twain. Perhaps hoping that was her legacy, she bought dozens of copies that she distributed to willing readers.

But the equanimity of Rankin's personality made her an inspiring thinker to the last moments of her life. This was her public side. This Jeannette Rankin had waved banners for suffrage and weathered the hostility of a nation at war. This Jeannette Rankin had worked for peace. Much of her correspondence in her later years dealt with governmental reform or requests from student researchers. In some cases, younger Americans wrote to marvel at her contributions to the antiwar movement. One such letter came from a political science professor at Cerritos College in California: "You have never fallen prey to all of the nonsense that parades as truth," wrote Jeffrey Elliot.

Rankin kept up a ceaseless campaign to condemn war, telling one newspaper, "Little children don't make wars. Mothers don't make wars. Men in business, the professions, and private life don't make wars. But governments do. And it is only by becoming concerned, informed and active citizens that each of us can work together to prevent wars."[375]

Many people regarded her as one of the few great humanitarians of her age. Surely, many others remembered her as treasonous, viewing her as somehow siding with our country's enemies and showing contempt for government. She was obsessed with learning throughout her life and had earned her prestige. Letters, books and magazines littered her tables. Visitors who expected a teacup and small talk were surprised with her vigorous handshake and discussion of American foreign policy. With customary wit, she also reflected on the miracle of being the first woman elected to Congress, saying she received "crank letters from everyone who had a complaint and couldn't get a man to listen to it."

Rankin celebrated her 90th birthday on June 11, 1970. A celebration commensurate with her status was scheduled at the Rayburn House Office Building in Washington, DC. Hundreds of people waited for the invincible old suffragist to walk into the banquet room. Three months earlier, Rankin fell on the steps of a drug store in Watkinsville, Georgia, fracturing her hip. Family members expressed hope she would recover. "Mother said you were already up and walking when she called just before she left," Jeannette's niece, Dorothy Brown, wrote from Missoula, Montana. "So by now you should be ready for the track team. I hope the experience wasn't too painful. They do marvelous things now with bones and pins and plastic knobs."[376] Try as she might, Rankin was unable to regain her strength to walk. A fighter should stand, she had said so many times before. She felt some humiliation at having to use a wheelchair. Her peers, however, took no notice. This timeless woman was known among them as a person of dedication and conviction, a woman who had forged a path for peace and justice before many of them were born. Senator Margaret Chase Smith of Maine described Rankin as "ninety years young, tall as a giant in statesmanship that is unparalleled in American history. She broke the way for me by being elected in 1916. I salute her for being the original dove in Congress."

Wearing a gold-tinted silk dress she had sewn while living in India, Rankin was both a prominent and a curious presence in the room. Seated between Montana Senators Lee Metcalf and Mike Mansfield, both of whom had started their political careers on the heels of her election to Congress in 1940, Rankin saw decades of social change reflected in members of the audience. Representative Patsy Mink of Hawaii represented the continuing role of women in Congress. Former Senator Gerald Nye of North Dakota had fought vigorously against war profiteering in the 1930s. Former Senator Burton K. Wheeler of Montana, a lawyer, had championed labor rights. Inevitably, acknowledgments focused on Rankin's work for peace.

Metcalf, in speaking of her contribution to the human race, heralded her as one of the most prominent women in the world: a voice for peace, freedom and the consumer; for child welfare and industrial and labor problems, against economic maladjustments, social injustice and racial prejudice. This resembled the calendar of issues before Congress. Metcalf also mentioned some of her early proposals that by her ninetieth birthday had become American law: Suffrage for women, support for dependent families of enlisted men, free postage for members of armed forces, granting to American women married to foreign nations the right to retain their citizenship, and creation of a water board. He explained further:

"Such is only a bare outline of a truly incredible career, which has extended for sixty years.... I have dwelt on what Miss Rankin accomplished in her long life. They say, better than I can, what she is: a saver with a great heart, a builder, a trailblazer and an example to all legislators who would have the courage of their convictions.... I salute Jeannette Rankin for her effective interest in Western problems that have influenced global civilization. It was easier to represent the First District of Montana independently because of her example."

When Rankin was ninety years old, she contemplated running for Congress again. Had she won a seat she would have been the oldest person ever to sit in Congress, but the possibility of that did not excite her. She was more interested in the ideas she had to offer. Old age would render a political campaign impractical, but she occasionally documented on paper what she wanted to say in person, to crowds: "A person can be shot, but an idea cannot. Killing is the antithesis of life and negates the very possibility of growing into fullness. It is the same passion for the ideal, which a mother expresses in her love for her children, which we must achieve and maintain if we want our ideals to mature and flourish in society; self-control, compassion, honesty, integrity, and love must be conceived in our minds, incarnated through our daily actions and living, and patiently sustained in adversity. A dead enemy cannot become our friend. And — just as certainly — the idea dies within us when we violate it."[377]

In her final years, taking a summary of her life, she would conclude that her most important vote — and her most important accomplishment — was voting against World War I. "That was the beginning of our entering a military regime in this country," she told Montana historian John Board. "I think if we had won that vote that we would have had an entirely different country. We would have developed our democracy and shown by example to the rest of the world what could be done through a democracy. It would have stalled any possibility of other countries using us in violence to settle their disputes. Now, you can call that a victory or a defeat. It was both. We failed to stay out of war but I registered the protest of women."[378]

Death was promising to interfere with Rankin's plans. She faced the reality that her active involvement in American politics was limited to years, maybe months. Most of the women who had shared her life had died. The latest, in 1971, was Flora Belle Surles, who over the years had penned cheeky letters to Rankin in flowery script. In her later years Surles had written a biography of her partner, Anne King Gregorie, who was editor of *South Carolina History* magazine. Despite her relationship with Gregorie, Surles remained enchanted with Rankin until her death. Meanwhile, Rankin's sister Mary died that year also, leaving only Edna and Hattie from the original large Rankin family. Jeannette's world of social influence shrank as friends and family diminished in number. Correspondence arriving in her mailbox described onsets of the flu, broken hips, isolation, depression and other malaise associated with old age. Many people who knew her best and loved her most were gone, including Fiorello LaGuardia.

To many Americans, Rankin's advanced age remained invisible. "I nominate you for President of the United States. Your [sic] beautiful, I love you, God bless you," wrote Vernon

C. Runkel, a fan from Kansas. To the close observer, national politics teemed with new discoveries of the very old peace and war problem that Rankin had dedicated her life to exposing. Daniel Ellsberg slipped a copy of the 7,000-page "Pentagon Papers" to the *New York Times*, starting a chain of events that would lead to Richard Nixon's downfall. Much like Rankin's own testimony for most of her adult life, the top-secret government study of US involvement in Southeast Asia showed the fallacy of war, deception by presidents, and a military arrogance toward combat deaths and grief felt by ordinary Americans. Revelations that tumbled out in nine installments in the *Times*, despite the Nixon Administration's attempts to quiet them, affirmed what Rankin had argued all along about wars. She received a birthday card from President and Mrs. Nixon as the first revelations of the Watergate burglary hit the papers. "We want to add our warm good wishes that peace, joy, and contentment will always be yours," the president wrote, his greetings rich with irony.

Meanwhile, Vivian Hallinan wrote to express her surprise that litigation continued from the Jeannette Rankin Brigade protest. "Don't worry, if you go to jail, I'll go with you," Hallinan said. "Four more years of that evil Nixon, and I don't know what will happen to us." In another instance, a woman surfaced who had seen Rankin vote against war with Germany in 1917. "You don't know me but I was in the gallery when you voted against World War I and I was the girl who was arrested for making a speech on the Capitol steps in favor of woman suffrage," wrote Frances Gledhill, a member of Women Strike for Peace.[379]

Jeannette Rankin lived alone at her Shady Grove farm with a dachshund named Sam until a wayward law student arrived on a motorcycle in 1971 and pitched a tent in her yard. Soon John Kirkley cooked vegetarian meals and became her personal secretary. A blizzard of mail came to her door. Much of it contained requests for autographs, memberships, personal mementos, interviews, research materials, public appearances and participation in academic papers. One letter included a recipe for pumpkin nut bars because the author had read in the *New York Times* in 1916 that Rankin was a cook and a baker. It was maddening to her that so many letters asked for biographical details easily available in libraries, such as the year she was first elected to Congress.

She began a habit of scrawling notes on letters she received that Kirkley then typed into formal responses. One such letter, from the Women's National Abortion Action Council, sought her support as a "revered feminist" for a rally that would be held in Washington, DC, in late 1971. The letter took note of her long-standing — if hardly prominent — endorsement of women's right to choose and closed, "in hopes that we will someday be marching with you in a Jeannette Rankin brigade for the repeal of all the anti-abortion laws." Evidently uncomfortable with the implication, Rankin wrote on the letter: "Give support to march? NO!! Statement — but not name."[380]

Kirkley also made it possible for Rankin to travel to numerous national public appearances where she could share her pacifism. Kirkley assumed the role of agent; Rankin, of star guest. He managed transportation and lodging. Rankin paid repair bills for his car, named Moonshine. She also wrote checks for his law school tuition in Texas and Georgia, and other expenses. "He did this as well as any professional had ever done for me," she would recall, fending off friends' concern that he was taking advantage of her hospitality and bank account. "Of course he's using me, but I'm using him, too," she told one of them. "At 91 I do as I please with my money."[381]

Those national appearances, in the winter and spring of

1972, began when feminist Gloria Steinem asked Rankin to appear on the *David Frost Show* in New York. Rankin found herself very much in demand again and seized on the opportunity to showcase her favorite quotes about the futility of war. "We must have absolutely unilateral disarmament," she told a *New York Times* reporter. "If we disarmed, we would be the safest country in the world. After all, you have to have a worthy adversary to fight. Would Cassius Clay fight a Boy Scout?"[382]

One morning in February, Rankin carried her mail into the living room of her Georgia cottage and tore open an envelope from the National Organization for Women. She was asked to board a plane for New York. She had been chosen the first member of the Susan B. Anthony Hall of Fame, established to recognize the superstars of women's rights. At the presentation, with 1,500 women in attendance, she was recognized as "the world's outstanding living feminist." They rose to their feet in thunderous applause. Among them were other famous sisters of the cause: Steinem, Bella Abzug, Betty Friedan and Shirley Chisholm. This honor came at a time in Rankin's life when she needed help with her mood, because of her fear she would leave the mortal earth without having left an impression in American history.

"Women must devote all their energies today in gaining enough political offices to influence the direction of government away from the military industrial complex and toward solving the major social disgraces that exist in our country," Rankin told the audience. "We are here together to work together for the elimination of war.... My dream has always been that women would take this responsibility.... We have to gather women from every walk of life, starting with the precinct."[383]

Public appearances continued into spring. An interview as a "principal performer" on the *Merv Griffin Show* paid $290.

Rankin and Kirkley traveled to colleges and universities where she spoke about women and peace. Kirkley described her appearance on the *Today* show: "Jeannette had a way of saying the most devastating things in a most disarming manner. The hosts of the *Today* show were absolutely floored when they announced the time was up and Jeannette said, 'They're always cutting me off. They never let me say all I have to say.'" Her comment drew laughs but everyone knew it was a poignant reference to her failed attempt to speak against the war declaration against Japan in 1941.[384]

Rankin felt obliged to leave Americans with a legacy of hope. In a flurry of public appearances, she presented her principles of people power during national television appearances that included meetings of women's political caucuses in Georgia, New York, Arkansas and Tennessee. She also appeared on the *Dick Cavett Show*, where she told her host that her election to Congress in 1916 wasn't premature but belated because women had been trying to vote since 1848. "Do you mind my mentioning that you never married? Was that an early decision in your life?" Cavett asked her. "That's a personal thing," she responded. "Of course, I can say I had so many suitors I couldn't choose."

When she wasn't giving interviews she distributed information sheets nationwide that told of her ideas on democratic reorganization. Radio broadcasts and newspaper columns were filled with her ideas. National news magazines heralded Rankin as the Grand Dame of the feminist movement. With Kirkley's help, she wrote an essay on why she had voted against war, one of her many attempts in old age to restore lost history: "We did not labor in suffrage just to bring the vote to women, but to allow women to express their opinions and become effective in government. Men and women are like right and left hands. It doesn't make sense not to use both."[385]

In a rare historical footnote, Rankin addressed the Montana Constitutional Convention in Helena in 1972, sixty-one years after she first spoke at the State Capitol to argue favor of woman suffrage. Her appearance at a debate over a proposed minimum age to hold public office didn't persuade delegates to remove an age limit altogether, but attorney Bob Campbell, a delegate from Missoula, made the case that Montanans used the same argument against women seeking the right to vote during statehood proceedings in 1889. *LIFE* magazine's Elizabeth Frappollo wrote: "In a national election year, Jeannette Rankin's political experience and phenomenal energy are helping to make her one of the most popular — and surprising — figureheads of the women's movement."

Kirkley, well aware of Rankin's national profile and historic accomplishments, marveled at her simple life. Her idea of a shopping spree, he wrote, was buying a package of rubber bands at Woolworth's, her favorite store. Evidence of her Mother Earth existence was found in her Shady Grove cottage, which Kirkley described like this: One water faucet — cold water tap in the bathtub in the kitchen; double-burner hot plate and electric skillet in the "cook room," entertainment in the "fireplace living room" which opened into her bedroom; no doors inside the house but instead tapestries from India and Mexico; a pedal-flush toilet in the bedroom which Rankin refilled with water by dipping from a five-gallon urn. No stove.[386]

Vicariously, Rankin was the prime of youth. Her mind had resisted the stereotypes of old age, although she was wrinkled, had trouble seeing, and wore wigs to cover thinning of her once-abundant hair. She had lived through five American wars. Her mind was fresh and searching, always seeking new knowledge.

She hated sexist titles, despising in particular the timeworn "Lady from Montana," which she thought should be "Woman from Montana." She preferred "men and women" rather than "ladies and gentlemen," and thought the salutation Mrs. implied, "You're married, too bad, sex." As early as 1918, Rankin had been asked whether women's status should change after marriage, to which she replied: "That marriage should change a woman ... is inconsistent and absurd. It is a relic of the old common law idea that held woman to be man's property."

Despite her advanced age, she continued to devote more thought to the role of women in the peace movement than to the prospect of losing her physical capabilities. Her cottage and her new retirement apartment in Carmel, California, were decorated with anti-war posters, Indian tapestries, and magazines of every description. She poked fun at newspapers, sticking to her distrust that started after her election to Congress. She couldn't bear the "so cutesy, upsy" *Christian Science Monitor* because of her brother's lifelong devotion to Christian Science. By the 1960s Rankin sometimes expressed enormous contempt for organized religion. She didn't like the pressures of Christianity — that people should be coerced into believing a religious theme. History, she was fond of pointing out, showed religious strife caused wars.[387]

Wellington's wife, the former Louise Replogle, held a different point of view. She never saw evidence of a common public perception that Jeannette was a hard-headed atheist. Jeannette often was first to ask for a prayer at family dinners, Louise said, and despite her independent spirit she savored time spent with her nieces and nephews and could be quite accommodating in the presence of family.[388]

As the Vietnam War stumbled toward a conclusion and Rankin neared the end of her life, she found allies among youth who faced the prospect of other wars. The long view of history might have eased any surprise over Rankin's public acceptance. Beginning with those early days at the School of

Philanthropy in 1908 and her friendship with settlement worker Jane Addams, her position on the American political economy was based on the principle that human rights transcended property rights. Of the humanitarian's contribution to peace through reform, Rankin noted:

"I am sure that if she were living today she would recognize how important it is to perfect the machinery through which the people may voice their wishes. It is difficult for me to see what one can accomplish for peace unless one recognizes that even in times of peace one half of our tax money is spent to promote the war establishment. Day by day we become aware of the fact that our government is not carrying out promises to curb the war machinery." Rankin thought that if war was eliminated, taxes could be cut drastically and people would have more money to spend, stimulating the economy. She figured that a liquid money system would redistribute wealth and lessen the struggles and misery that class consciousness caused.

In truth, Rankin's belief that women could save the nation from future wars was enormously popular with doves who shared her point of view but rejected by hawks who fully supported God, country and the American homemaker as a single political force. The rise of Phyllis Schlafly and eventually, her ultraconservative *Eagle Forum*, echoed opposition to woman suffrage six decades earlier. Known as "the Gloria Steinem of the Right," Schlafly built a strong political base of women who fought the Equal Rights Amendment as a desecration of home and family. One objection warned that men and women would share public bathrooms, another that a new amendment would ruin traditional families. Schlafly also had written books critical of American foreign policy for, in her view, failing to arrest the spread of communism.

However radical she was perceived by feminists, Schlafly

had the ear of women who had no intention of rocking the domestic boat much less join a campaign to promote international peace. To Rankin, these arguments sounded all too familiar. She had no patience for such hesitation. She even needled her more liberal counterparts, accusing them of working only microscopically for women's rights because they did not consider the oppression of war a major issue. Rankin was ambivalent toward this sudden popularity among some women to consider themselves liberated, believing the mechanics of the movement were good but the goals were excessively timid. "I've been talking about these same things for fifty years," she often remarked.

Change didn't occur fast enough for her. She could not fathom dying without seeing her life's goals achieved. After six decades of political activism, Rankin still viewed war as woman's greatest hindrance. To her, women had failed to subdue the male arrogance and brute force found in war and sublimated in sex. She said the relationship between fear and procreation was shown in the substantial number of "war babies" of the 1940s. "The modern male looks too much at woman as a sex object," she told feminists gathered on the steps of Georgia's Capitol in 1970. "In the animals, sex is a matter of procreation." Rankin viewed sex as the only creative pleasure remaining for those Americans who, she contended, had resisted change for most of the century. "Most of it is for enjoyment," she observed in an interview in 1971. With a smile, she added: "How would I know?"

During a cross-country tour, Rankin jokingly complained to a Tacoma, Washington, reporter: "If they're independent, talkative, and say what they think, they can't get a job or a husband. Look at me — unmarried and unemployed most of my life." Newspapers snapped up her pithy quotes. "I find you in the press more often than a promising starlet," wrote Rankin's niece, Dorothy Brown, who implored Rankin to preserve records of her lifelong work and to summarize her ideas about preferential voting on index cards. Dorothy's husband Walter wrote to Rankin about an upcoming appearance in Philadelphia: "Don't forget to smile, even if somebody does mention FDR."

Born into a close and proud political family, Rankin reacted with dismay to modern American families who relied on material goods, television and machines to entertain themselves while the Vietnam War remained unsettled. Although a woman without a son, she argued that war was ruining the American family. Rankin in a single-minded sense slipped past — without great commitment — many other facets of American culture. She detested football, but loved baseball, Wellington's favorite sport. He never missed a game during the World Series, which uncharacteristically beckoned him home from his law office in downtown Helena. Jeannette often came to visit him during the World Series. Wellington was a New York Yankees fan, and when they played, Jeannette became a fan too.

She thought light reading and movies were mostly a waste of time. In her last years she grew fond of the bigoted Archie Bunker in *All in the Family* because, like many Americans, she applauded the strength of the television program's satire. Rankin's appreciation for the show probably related as well to its connection with her hometown of Missoula, Montana, where Archie actor Carroll O'Connor had obtained degrees from the university.

Rankin thought the family to be the mainstay of American living, but unlike Schlafly, she saw it as the human institution on which war inflicted the most harm. Every American soldier killed on foreign soil meant grief for a family. Rankin pleaded with women to spend less money for electrical conveniences such as can openers and dishwashers and contribute the dollars they had saved to the peace movement.

She said modern appliances had made housework less challenging, depriving the woman of her purpose in life by devaluing her role as wife and mother. Rankin told one interviewer: "It isn't a question of what she does. It's what she contributed to society as a whole."

President Nixon had condemned day care centers as a threat to the family, but Rankin shot back: "I don't think being separated from the children hurts them. I think it's what the mother does when she is with the child." Clearly, she believed the first responsibility of a mother was to teach her children the attributes of peace and the truth about war. Sometimes her optimism faded, for in 1969 she said bluntly: "Women still raise the boys and men take them off to war and kill them."

Rankin related two anecdotes to illustrate her concern of military propaganda on women and children. First, some children visited her home in Georgia and alarmed her when they began singing about wanting to be soldiers. Sensing that they did not understand military life beyond the romanticism of the uniform, Rankin had them substitute "slave" for "soldier," explaining that a soldier knew no glamor because he did only what he was ordered. The children sang the tune with "slave" as briskly as they had sung with "soldier." In another instance, Rankin had seen a kindergarten teacher telling children to march with the instructions, "Raise your knees like soldiers." In complaining that in a peaceful environment children should not learn the indoctrination of war, she condemned the kindergarten lesson as "the most awful propaganda you could think of."

Rankin was popular with children. Bursting from her wrinkled exterior was an incarnate childishness shining in a disarming smile. Her charm with young people was shown in a letter from youthful Jennifer Robinson, the black girl who lived over the hill from Rankin's Shady Grove:

Dear Jeanette Rankin
You is coming home tonight   I did miss you and I no you miss me   Stanley Wonder and Mattie Jeff and me miss you   We wrote you a letter   did you Right us a letter   We send you some picture and we send you a letter   Miss Rankin I did miss you   I love you all of us Love you
From Jennifer
Love you

In a telegram congratulating Rankin on her birthday, Loretta Scott King observed: "Your dauntless courage as a leader for equal rights for women and as a champion of peace have immortalized you in the hearts of millions at home and abroad. It has been a privilege to support your efforts and to have my efforts supported by so great a woman. You have brought honor to yourself, America, and womanhood."[389]

The accolades sketched a portrait of an American woman who had defied convention to make her appeals heard, but Rankin wasn't finished with her blueprint for peace. One major segment remained. She wanted to see American people more in control of their government. Doing so, she reasoned, would steer the nation away from a powerful union that lawmakers in Congress had struck with war makers in industry. Rankin's view of war as a threat to democratic government hardly was radical. President Eisenhower, in 1961, warned of dangerous connections between legislators and war contractors in what he called a military-industrial complex. Rankin had promoted her ideas about government through decades of outrage toward the war establishment, but only during the protests of the late 1960s did she unveil a campaign to alert voters to what she thought was a deliberate military takeover of the United States. She was convinced that a military-induced conspiracy already was planning a sequel to the Vietnam War. Anticipating that her life had nearly run its course, she frantically and elaborately outlined the methods she thought would be most helpful to bring Americans closer to democracy.

By 1972, consumer advocate Ralph Nader had concluded that her ideas were sound and prophetic. "Miss Rankin is a future directed person who throws herself into her cause. If aging is the erosion of one's ideals, then Jeannette Rankin is young forever," he said of the 92-year-old pacifist. "Her stamina behind her ideals is absolutely staggering."[390] Nader was engaged in a yearlong study of Congress. Rankin, although struggling with her voice, flew to Washington to confer with him and his student aides about the benefits of multimember districting. She would refer to her admiration of Nader as "a love affair," but soon after meeting with him her throat constricted and she began to lose weight. She thought of studying Spanish as therapy but abandoned the idea as she became sicker. Famous for her pithy quotes, Rankin never let her physical decline interfere with her life's mission. "The minute someone on the television starts talking about war, I turn it off," Rankin told her friend Hannah Josephson. "I never read about it in the papers. I haven't any time for it. I would much rather pull weeds."

22 ~ Government by the people

'May I stand? I fight better standing.'

By 1968, Jeannette Rankin had taken a fresh look at the role of the presidency. As the United States deepened its involvement in the Vietnam War, she threw her support behind the Democratic populist Eugene McCarthy. After McCarthy was destroyed in the primary, she cast her vote for Richard Nixon, resurrecting her belief that he had learned the value of peace from being vice president to Dwight D. Eisenhower. "Ike seems to be really ernest [sic] about preventing war," she had written during the 1950s. "It is the only way his name can live in history and he knows it." Rankin's regret for her choice in 1968 became apparent in the election of 1972, when she voted for George McGovern and his antithesis of Nixon's war policy and his personal and presidential styles.

She lost faith in Nixon early. Her interpretation of his statement "peace with honor" was that it revealed his allegiance to the military-industrial complex. She thought that while a nation sick of war stampeded Lyndon Johnson out of the Oval Office, outdated election machinery prevented Americans from carrying their will further. "The 1968 political year demonstrated ... we can throw a President out, but we cannot elect one," she said. In the midst of the Vietnam controversy she wrote Belle Fligelman Winestine and her husband Norman at their home in Helena, Montana, to tell them she was thinking of running for Congress.[391] Even as an old woman, Rankin saw herself as a reckoning force in politics.

Rankin thought the only way Americans could escape presidential misconduct and corporate influence was to elect a president truly representative of the people. First, the Electoral College must be abolished. Rankin regarded it as an archaic ritual that went against the will of the people. Previous presidential elections, such that of Benjamin Harrison in 1888, substantiated this contention. President Grover Cleveland had won more of the popular vote but Harrison had the benefit of the Electoral College.

Her solution in its purest form was to return government to the people. Although her ideas about direct democracy were embedded in the history of Twentieth Century America, only in the 1960s and 1970s with a new awareness in politics did they become popular. She found herself more publicly useful in the final eight years of her life, enabling her to teach the lessons of the past. As a democratic, future-oriented person, Rankin believed she should speak loudly and forcefully about inequities in American government. The idea of philosopher John Stuart Mills that a true democracy is "a government of the whole people by the whole people represented," was a favorite with her.

Because Rankin's call for broader representation endangered special interest groups and the congressmen they had elected, she was not popular with the conservative business-oriented sector. Among progressive legislators, however, she found new friends and allies. One of them was Representative Emanuel Celler, a New York Democrat who had been in Congress when Rankin was elected in 1940. He invited her to testify about election reform before the House Committee on the Judiciary in February 1969.

She was a big attraction. The mysticism that had drawn thousands of people to her lectures in 1917 found a revival. People praised and were awestruck by this old suffragist and pacifist. As she entered the committee room on Capitol Hill, she again discovered such an atmosphere. Several men rushed to the door to escort her to a chair. She indignantly brushed past them. Despite her age she was remarkably energetic. A wide leather watchband was strapped to her right wrist and a string of "hippie" beads encircled her neck. As she spoke, she rose out of her chair. But Chairman Celler interrupted her and urged her to sit, fearing she thought she was obliged to stand despite her age. Rankin was unimpressed. "May I stand?" she asked him. "I fight better standing."

Anyone knowledgeable in the issues of election reform knew where Rankin stood. She advocated, supported and pursued the principle of "people power," which in her humanitarian ideal meant a voice for everyone. They weren't just the rich, intelligent, influential and inspiring, but the poor, ignorant, apathetic and innocent. "I can trust the people," she told the committee. When Rankin plunged into Progressivism in 1910, she mocked the thinking of President William Howard Taft and other big-money advocates who believed an uneducated strata of Americans was incapable of running the government and needed the guidance of wealthy industrialists. To her, lobbyists regulated the intent and direction of legislation, depriving ordinary Americans of their voice in government. If Congress wanted to propel them into war, how could they stop the momentum? If social legislation was shelved, who would help them get it back?

Her timeless ideology of "people power" in governmental affairs proved as apropos fifty years later, when she revived old ideas to crest a new movement. Rankin considered her vision of people power a final effort for peace, for it involved the rudiments of democracy in their purest form. She simply wanted to restore government to the people. She had proposed such principles before ninety percent of today's Americans were born. To Rankin, the question of election reform was simple: either elected representatives supported democracy, or they did not.

She sought several democratic changes through her lifetime. They included the initiative, which enabled voters to petition to put legislation on the ballot; the referendum, to repeal legislation undesirable to voters; the recall, providing a chance to end the poor performance of an elected official by voting him or her out of office; multi-member congressional districts, to place more candidates before the electorate; a unicameral Congress to better represent voters and prevent gerrymandering of districts; and the preferential direct election of President, to downplay the presidential primary, remove candidate selection from the power of the two major parties, and provide the voters with a broader selection of candidates. "What good is the vote if you have no one to vote for?" she asked, regarding preferential voting as a natural extension of suffrage.

Under Rankin's plan, abolishing the Electoral College would make presidents more dependent on public opinion and less on corporate money to win. A popular vote also would better serve ordinary Americans. Some people challenged these ideas as subversive, but Rankin argued that the Constitution implied the power of Americans to determine their destinies through election reform. "People can generally be divided into two groups: those who want to be ruled by a good king or a benevolent dictator or a great president, and those who believe in the sovereignty of the people and feel they should have the opportunity to govern themselves," she wrote to the author of a *New Republic* article that examined concentration of power in the United States.[392]

Rankin believed, as many Americans did, that the military-industrial complex controlled the balance of power in the legislative and executive branches. "The military governs us today because they have the organization, the money, and they have developed the technique of making the opposition feel unpatriotic," she wrote in the same letter. To her, the consequence of industrial control of government was war. If federal time and money were devoted to economic investments abroad — and huge sums of money were appropriated to a questionable defense plan — Americans would suffer. In a nation of plenty, people would go hungry. "With all our ingenuity, skill and devotion to progress, why have we hungry people in the United States?" she had asked the congregation of the Prince Avenue Baptist Church in Athens, Georgia, in 1932. "Is it because we don't care? Is it because of our inability to overcome the obstacles? Is it because of failures in the past?"[393]

She remembered well when the United States was in the midst of the Great Depression and unemployment caused unprecedented numbers of broken homes and unhappy people. She regarded the Depression as the unsavory aftermath of American investments in World War I. Economic suffering would provoke other aspects of social misbehavior, such as crime and welfare abuse, and in Rankin's belief, the government would find difficulty policing the problems it caused by its negligence.

In her golden years, Rankin campaigned especially hard for preferential voting. This idea was linked to her premise that political parties did nothing useful; her intermingling attitudes on economics and politics made her less than a party advocate. She detected no major differences between the Republicans and the Democrats. To her they adopted platforms only to entice the mood of the people they were trying to sway without taking a firm stand on any issue.

In the months before Rankin entered Congress for the first time, Theodore Roosevelt wrote from Sagamore Hill to encourage her to make and keep the Republican Party loyal to the spirit of Abraham Lincoln. Roosevelt thought Rankin symbolized the power of change and innovation. He asked that she always be conscious of the rights of each American and that she remember that the Republican Party must "make this nation the land where love and justice go hand in hand; which stands for fair play...." By the time she celebrated her ninetieth birthday, she had little regard for Roosevelt's worship of the Republican ideal, but she had heeded his advice on democracy.

Political parties to her were nothing but roadblocks to real issues. She had proven in both of her elections to Congress that only the issues on which she campaigned made the difference in her being elected. In 1916, she was elected as a Republican in a Democratic landslide, although she resembled more of an independent candidate without party affiliations. As Woodrow Wilson was elected president, he carried the Democratic tide almost to the precincts, but Rankin had been elected on the nonpartisan issue of equal suffrage. In 1940, she was elected to Congress when Montana Democrats swept the state with huge pluralities; a blatant peace candidate shadowed by war. With the inhibiting threat of party politics removed, Rankin argued, candidates could pursue their beliefs.

She viewed the ideal presidential election as a horse race in which each participant in the field had widely varying abilities. Her plan was to circumvent the primary elections where party politics flattened minority candidates. On the general election ballot would be names of every candidate who legitimately desired to become president. Candidates would be required to prove a genuine following to prevent the list from becoming outrageously lengthy. The ballot might contain the names of several Democrats, several Republicans, and a handful of minority candidates, but they would not be designated as such.

Following Rankin's vision, a voter in the 1972 presidential election — and this is the author's interpretation — could have had a choice among Shirley Chisholm, representing blacks and women; Henry Jackson, a Western financial conservative; George Wallace, representing the white South; Edmund Muskie, a New England liberal with a respected congressional background; George McGovern, an antiwar candidate with Populist leanings; Richard Nixon, a domestic conservative with friendly ties to the military and industrialists, but with a strong foreign relations portfolio; Hubert Humphrey, a liberal champion of labor; Fred Harris, an antiwar liberal representing the poor and the Indians; and Eugene McCarthy, representing students, the poor, the working class and the antiwar movement.

Rankin said names should be rotated on the ballots among states, as psychology revealed that people often voted alphabetically. The order of the candidates' names in Montana, for example, would differ from the order on the Minnesota ballot or the New Mexico ballot. The essence of the open ballot was twofold, in Rankin's opinion. Anyone with a large following could be a candidate, through petitions or preferential primaries.

Rankin anticipated that voting would be more complex but not beyond any American's intelligence. A ballot sheet would list all candidates. Voters would mark the order of their preference. A voter who wanted Richard Nixon as president, for example, would mark a blank after Nixon's name as his first choice. If Henry Jackson were the voter's second choice, he would mark it accordingly.

Computers would tabulate votes. A person with a majority of first place votes would become president. Lacking a first place majority, the candidate with a majority of second-place votes would become president. The counting would continue in this manner until a candidate won. Votes for the vice president — ensuring a candidate properly prepared for office, unlike the old system of party politics — would be conducted likewise.

Rankin justified the direct preferential vote as the method of election most in accord with American democracy, believing it returned to the American people the sovereign power of choice and made the president more responsive to the voters. "It would increase the possibility of each vote having the same value," she had said at Carnegie Hall. "True democracy demands that each man has a vote and one man one vote."

Anticipating an outcry from party convention-goers that she was destroying the two-party system, Rankin footnoted her overtures by assuring them that they still could wave their banners and balloons. By 1972, American concern for the environment, the Vietnam War, alternative lifestyles and new forms of energy had revived interest in greater voter influence. Jeannette Rankin appealed to national public opinion makers to explore these surfacing ideas. She urged *CBS News* commentator Mike Wallace, who had reported on the issue of voter dissatisfaction, to air some of the constructive alternatives. To David Brinkley, the *NBC News* anchor who mentioned the crying need for election reform as he covered the 1968 Democratic convention, she proposed the same. Walter Lippmann, who wrote a story about election reform entitled "The American Predicament" in *Newsweek* magazine, was told the fundamental idea of "people power" represented progress. Ralph McGill, publisher of the *Atlanta Constitution*, was informed that change was not new to the election process. Rankin reminded him that the US Senate once was a "rich gentleman's club" of men chosen by state legislatures. She appealed to pollsters George Gallup and Lou Harris to conduct a scientific analysis of voter habits and the voters' opinion of preferential voting, and she asked them whether she could adapt such a polling technique to the national peace organizations.

Rankin's plan for multiple-member districts in electing members of Congress was only a more sophisticated method of taking the profits out of war. More congressional candidates on a state ballot meant less inclination to align with special interest groups, presuming financial backing would not be required for success. This proposal was reminiscent of her suffrage work, decades earlier, when she had argued to convince men of the power of their vote and the significance of extending it to women.

To gain a broader representation of talents, backgrounds and viewpoints in Congress and to teach candidates to govern on behalf of voters, Rankin proposed to pare to a minimum the number of congressional districts in each state. New York, for example, which had forty-one districts in 1972, could have six districts with forty-one members. This meant each voter could cast more votes for representatives, ensuring in her view a greater base of loyalty among congressmen. Therefore, special interest groups whose desire was to control the behavior of members of Congress, could not gerrymander one district.

By 1972 Rankin had become a staunch proponent of a unicameral legislature, which she had admired and witnessed during her visits to India. She questioned why the United States should duplicate the expense of elections, research, salaries and committees in the Senate if the House of Representatives consciously responded to the needs of the electorate. Controversy, she argued, had been incompatible with traditional American politics because elected officials were too preoccupied with the procedures of being reelected.

"When I went to Congress in 1917, a kindly old hand asked me if I knew what my concern should be," she said. "Before I could open my mouth to tell him what I felt to be the burning issues, he smiled and said, 'Working for your next election.' The implication was that I should remain passively placid and not stir up any bears. Unfortunately for my Congressional career he was right."

In Rankin's love for the emotion of an ideal, she had outlasted many of the "old hands." In a lifetime of work, she had stated her case for freedom. As she contracted a throat ailment and began to lose her voice, she involuntarily stopped her public appearances. She kept her farm in Watkinsville but rented a studio apartment in Carmel, California. She planned to spend a few months a year at Carmel Valley Manor with her sister, Edna McKinnon. Interviewer Malca Chall wrote of Rankin this way when meeting her for an oral history project: "Miss Rankin belied in almost every way her ninety-two years. She had a small trim figure and always wore handsome tailored dresses in becoming colors of blue, yellow, or gray, and low-heeled dress shoes. A soft brown wig framed her expressive, not deeply lined face. Her eyes, behind glasses, were bright and alert, and twinkled when she was amused. Her throaty laugh was a joy to hear. The only outward sign of age was her halting walk, for support of which she used as a cane.... During that first meeting I had gained certain impressions about Miss Rankin which never altered. She was immediately friendly, open and direct; she made me feel truly welcome. She was very intelligent, had a good memory, a keen wit and enjoyed a certain amount of sharp banter. In the course of time I also came to see that she was strong-willed and deeply committed to democratic principles."[394]

Despite Rankin's continuing popularity as a political figure at a time when Watergate was unraveling Richard Nixon's presidency, one nagging question remained. Decades of work had shown one woman's proposal for a path to peace. Now, Rankin's blueprint was complete. True fulfillment would come in recognition of her work. History would judge her. Would she be remembered, or had she struggled in vain?

23 ~ Jeannette Rankin's legacy

'She stood her ground and gave an example of moral courage'

In 1910, Jeannette Rankin asked herself, "What can I, one person, do?" She was under the auspices of the Washington Equal Suffrage League when she apprenticed the painstaking task of learning how to seek change when people resisted. In 1973, Rankin knew the answer. Seeking change was tedious, unrewarding work, but she never lost sight of the emotion of her ideal: Pacifism. Her work was the example to Americans of all beliefs; no less to men than to women, no less to hawks than to doves, no less to conservatives than to liberals. "I tell these young women that they must get to the people who don't come to the meetings," she said in 1972. "It never did any good for all the suffragettes to come together and talk to each other. There will be no revolution unless we go out into the precincts. You have to be stubborn. Stubborn and ornery."[395]

Throughout her often stormy life, she remained a free thinker who made an example to women everywhere. She said of her first congressional vote for peace: "I had not planned to make that speech. All my life, I have worked harder for freedom than the average person, but I knew that the first woman in Congress had to vote against war."

After that brief moment in 1917, when an epiphany guided her onto a lighted path of peace, Rankin found her calling.

Most people shun dissent because it's an uncomfortable role, thick with controversy. Rankin never saw herself as a martyr who was sacrificing romance and family for causes. She rarely spoke of personal sacrifice. To her, woman suffrage, pacifism and government reform were civic responsibilities. She deeply understood how dissent often angered people, but she also knew that dissent and reform brought them hope. "I believed then as I do now that women are the ones who must be concerned with the needs and development of the human race," she noted in a self-produced pamphlet. "I have always fought for the dignity of all human beings — for those of the present as well as those of future generations. I will continue to struggle as long as I live."

Over nearly six decades of social activism, Jeannette Rankin avoided a life of gender stereotypes. She had proven by her own life that a loud stir could be made by one woman who raised her voice. Privately she sometimes lost hope that American women could end war if they joined in the same dedication for peace and freedom, but she rarely wavered publicly. "The women's movement is going to take forward steps beyond anything we envision today," she told the *Spokesman Review* of Spokane, Washington. "I'm quite thrilled with what they're doing."

For better or worse, Rankin's contribution to humanity was etched in history. It was the work of an inspired woman committed to dreams of international peace. Rankin's mission was complete. Now history would judge her — or, she feared, forget her. "I am much impressed by the fact that you have not lost sight of what really matters in life," a California political science professor wrote her in 1971 in a letter typical of commendations she received toward the end of her long life. "You are an idealist, an independent, a fighter — a woman of deep conviction, rare courage, and unquestionable honesty."[396] Rankin was disappointed that her work for peace showed few results as the world's superpowers competed in a maddened race for nuclear superiority and greater military sophistication. Privately, she blamed herself that she didn't cut deeper with her peace plan.

Such self-degrading thinking was futile. Rankin had sacrificed every moment of her adult life to the pursuit of peace. She had avoided marriage, a family and the kind of personal anonymous contentment that comes with a nonpublic life. She wanted Americans to better understand causes and antecedents of war and the sweetness of peace. If Jeannette Rankin gained anything in her tenure as a feminist and pacifist, she carried a message that freedom and justice were not empty words. To her, war was not the glorious and patriotic institution it was portrayed but instead a social problem that thrived on ignorance and lies to survive.

Rankin reflected that as the first woman who had the opportunity to vote against war, she had an obligation to do so because that was a key position in the suffrage campaigns. History delivered her that opportunity. "It wasn't a question of the dispute between countries. The question was the method of settling those disputes. War is a method which has nothing whatever to do with the dispute. It wasn't so long ago we were sending arms to Russia to protect ourselves from the Germans. Today we are sending arms to Germany to protect ourselves from the Russians.... It is very evident that most people today realize that there is a choice between using violence or using some other method to save our civilization."[397]

Only months before Rankin's death, *LIFE* magazine published a cover story about the "unprovoked" sinking of the British ocean liner RMS Lusitania in 1915, which "dragged us toward war." Rankin read the story with fascination because of her own belief, more than 50 years earlier, that Americans had been duped into declaring war on Germany.

"I was there. See, I told you," she said to her niece, Dorothy Brown. "That's what I tried to tell them at the time."[398] Brown knew her aunt could sniff international conflict like a bloodhound: "She could see war coming. She was very instinctive about the chicanery that goes on in high public office."

Rankin believed peace was an attainable goal because it appealed to the progressive nature of humanity. Unfortunately, she had no measuring stick to gauge the effect of her work. She was greatly disappointed she did not witness the signing of a world peace pact and the abolition of war as a means to settling disputes. To her critics this seemed farfetched and even foolish, but to Rankin it was a matter of common sense.

While Rankin preferred to see her efforts come to a supreme conclusion, many of her contemporaries recognized her as a flesh-and-blood statue of human progress, to whom the American people could look for guidance when they truly decided to pursue the peace ideal. Presidential peace candidate George McGovern, for example, piloted a bomber plane during World War II, yet he became a strong admirer of Rankin for her "absolute devotion to principle and for her rare courage."

Even in the final years of Rankin's life, people asked her why she didn't abstain from voting on the war declaration with Japan in 1941. Doing so, they argued, would have spared her the pain of being the only member of Congress to vote no. She might have been reelected and risen to prominence in Congress. "You know, there is no such thing as compromise," she told Dorothy Brown. "Once you have compromised, then, whatever ideals you believe in, you've compromised away. You are not fit to carry those attitudes anymore. You don't belong in the club."

Despite Rankin's appearances of poverty in Georgia and

her seeming indifference to money, she had accumulated significant wealth. After Wellington died, his longtime partner Arthur Acher continued to supervise Jeannette's investments. There were many. Just how much she knew or cared about these financial transactions was never clear, even to her closest relatives. It's entirely likely that Wellington bought them for her because she had a reputation for being inattentive to her finances. He could afford to do it, as the value of his estate attested. When he died, he owned 22,000 head of cattle in addition to his investments and vast land holdings.

Acher, with help from Wellington's widow, Louise, sold oil properties at Kevin, Montana, and deposited $59,020 into Jeannette's bank account in Helena. Another $10,000 went into a certificate of deposit in her name. Within a month after the Jeannette Rankin Brigade dispersed and went home in 1968, she began receiving $285.32 a month in annuity payments from Equitable Life Assurance Society. That summer, Acher announced a "ranch and cattle deal" that eventually would lead to the sale of her Weiglow Ranch in central Montana. She began receiving rental checks right away and the 320 head of cattle would bring a handsome price. Jack Galt, who eventually would marry Louise Rankin, paid Jeannette $30,000 in five payments.

Money came from stocks. Acher placed ninety shares of United Aircraft and 1,569 shares of Helena Hotel Company, one of Wellington's corporations, in her bank safety deposit box. She owned 1,180 shares of Montana Flour Mills stock. Then, Nebraska Consolidated Mills bought Montana Flour Mills, bringing a windfall of $43,424 for Rankin. That was invested in a time savings certificate at five percent interest. Until her 91st birthday she received $147 a month from Social Security.[399] The extent of Rankin's financial wellbeing contradicted her image of a penniless life. If there was a convenience in appearing poor, it emerged in her politicking, but her bank account told a much different story. There's little evidence that Rankin paid much attention at all to the wealth created on her behalf, although it surely helped fund her world travels. Some of her investments, had they been known publicly, would have cost her considerable embarrassment and dearly in her credibility as a pacifist.

Just why she owned stock in three aircraft companies that had histories of producing war planes remains lost in history. United Aircraft was sixth among American corporations for dollars earned from wartime contracts. She also received dividends from stock in Fairchild Hiller Corporation and Boeing Corporation. She must have been aware of her investment in companies that profited from war, because Acher advised her of transactions, but it's difficult to decipher the implied hypocrisy. Did Rankin pay attention? Protesters would have been outraged to hear that she owned stock in weapons-producing companies during the Vietnam War. The very idea of it ran so counter to her lifelong hatred of war profiteering that it's probable she would have demanded that Wellington take her name off the stock.

In January 1973, when the sale of the Weiglow Ranch was completed, Acher deposited $60,000 in her checking account. She distributed some of the profit in $3,000 installments to thirteen family members, including her sister Hattie and nieces and nephews. "The gift had particular meaning coming from you; as you have been a source of admiration and inspiration to me for as long as I can remember," wrote Ann Ronhovde.[400] Some members of the Rankin family, possibly out of favor with Jeannette, didn't receive any money at all.

Rankin thrived on conversations about ideas and causes until the last months of her life. She struggled with dizzy spells. Then a stroke stole her voice altogether. She felt truly alone. Viewing news programs and documentaries on television wasn't enough. Her friends, bewildered at the garble and drool from her mouth, couldn't understand what she was saying. In her final six months, her weight dropped to eighty pounds. She remained in spirit the "slip of a girl" notably chronicled in national newspapers after her election to Congress in 1916. Now she was nothing more than a slip of that woman who had resisted war. "I am worried about your health and state of mind," Rankin's first biographer and close friend, Hannah Josephson, wrote her. "You must not think you are either powerless or forgotten. You would be disabused of such notions if you could only see how people's faces light up when I say I am trying to write a book about you."[401]

Frustrated and alone, Rankin begged her doctor to withdraw her medicine and let her die.[402] Talking and ideas were the bread and milk of her existence. "She really wanted to get off this earth more than anybody I have ever seen," said Dorothy Brown. "She was raging because nobody would help her." The doctor refused a mercy killing. Soon after, Rankin died in her sleep in her California apartment. It was May 18, 1973, a few weeks short of her 93rd birthday.

When news of her death reached the wire services, Teletype click-clacked in newsrooms across the world. Her passing aroused ambivalent memories as her body was prepared for cremation. A small service, attended by a few family members, was held at Little Chapel by the Sea in Pacific Grove. A month after her death, Paul Mortuary delivered her remains to pilot Frank Moody, who boarded his plane with a funeral attendant, Terese Moroney. They scattered the ashes of the nation's first congresswoman at sea, three miles west of Point Lobos, near Carmel, California.

Her death was a blessing, said longtime friend Belle Fligelman Winestine, because everyone could see Rankin's failing health. "At the end of one's life, you realize that death isn't a terrible thing, it's like a graduation, you've finished with life, and you've done the best you could," Winestine said four years after Rankin died.

Her voice silenced, Jeannette Rankin now stands before the nation, awaiting judgment. Would it be as John Hurt of Woodstock, New York, had described the day after Pearl Harbor? "In the history of our nation there are a few men who are remembered in disgrace. I for one can assure you that in their [sic] category you will never be forgotten. ... Please reconsider and if possible change your vote to keep your name from being remembered as that of the only woman who so delights in blood and slaughter that she voted in favor of no resistance to the murder of her own people."[403]

Or, would it be as the old Woman's National Party suffragist Lavinia Dock had written in 1941 in utter contrast: "You represented then not only the protest of women against the war system, but of the whole human race, and some day this will be universally recognized and you will stand high in memory — perhaps after you are dead."[404]

To some people, Rankin's solitary vote opposing war after the Pearl Harbor fiasco would freeze her in history. TV newsman Walter Cronkite observed on the fiftieth anniversary of the vote that she was "remembered as the one Member of Congress paralyzed by principle in the face of an enemy attack in 1941."[405] In broader context, he also observed that the nation's best-known isolationists in Congress dropped that cause in a heartbeat that day, leaving Rankin to stand alone in a barrage of national criticism. She would be ignored, he reasoned, for the remainder of her term.

"She had such charm and a special style of beauty that her opponents respected, even loved her," remembered American Civil Liberties Union founder Roger Baldwin in 1978. The spunky Baldwin, himself a vigorous opponent of war, believed Rankin's sense of humor, her wit and her common sense appealed to everybody, whether conservative or liberal, man or woman. "Miss Rankin's special distinction was her political courage, her fidelity to a pacifist conviction..., her integrity, her courage, her charge, and her broad appeal to women especially."

As a dissenter, Rankin realized she never would command widespread public interest that once surrounded ideologues such as George Wallace and establishment liberals like John Kennedy. Instead, she hoped Americans would remember her contributions to women and peace. She was certain her ideas were unbound by time or incident. They eventually would become relevant to growing numbers of Americans.

Rankin often resorted to homespun anecdotes when trying to convince people that peace was a simpler pursuit than they might realize. She viewed war much like the predicament faced by a mentally challenged child, tested for his learning ability by dipping water out of a barrel being filled from a faucet. "How do you know when he is feeble-minded?" someone asked Rankin. "They who aren't feeble-minded turn off the spigot," she replied. In this example she tried to convey that when Americans awake to the simplicity of peace they will shut off the spigot of war.

To Rankin, peace was the ultimate recognition by civilization that humankind could exist in harmony and understanding without the influence of hate and discord. Problems could be shared and solved. Hungry people could be fed. Ignorant people could be taught. Pacifism truly was Rankin's "emotion of an ideal," as the British sociologist Benjamin Kidd had written, for in her opinion human rights superseded all other commitments. She said in a prayer in 1942: "God grant us the courage and wisdom to insist that the abundance we have here today may be shared with all mankind; that freedom, justice, righteousness, brotherhood and everlasting peace be established throughout the world."

Contrary to Rankin's hope that she would be remembered for what she had done, her public records and personal papers were in disarray, scattered across the country. Close friends struggled with how to document her place in history. What could be done to commemorate a controversial social and political activist who had stormed through the Twentieth Century? In Georgia, where Rankin had begun her "peace epidemic" experiment fifty years earlier, Nan Pendergrast and other women who had joined her to oppose the Vietnam War held a simple memorial remembrance a few days after her death. "How we shall miss her!" Reita Rivers, a friend, wrote to Jeannette's sister, Edna. "And how responsible we felt, having known her, to try to measure up as best we can to her courage, integrity, and concern for others."[406]

The Shady Grove farm remained a concern because "things there of real historical value" sat behind flimsy doors, Rivers wrote Edna. The caretaker, Wonder Robinson, was in the hospital. Several women went to the farm to cut grass and give the place a lived-in look to discourage thieves and vandals. Rankin, in her will, left twenty acres of her farm to her niece Brown, and five acres to the Robinsons, including the house where they lived. Wonder's children, Jeff, Jennifer and Stanley, each received $2,000. Five nieces and nephews, including Brown, received $10,000 each, as did a grandniece. Rankin's estate was valued at $162,000, equivalent to more than $865,000 in 2016. Money from stocks, bonds, bank deposits and 1,280 acres of land in Montana would be divided evenly among nieces and nephews. Edna McKinnon sniffed at how Jeannette had disguised her wealth. "Jeannette had a particular sort of neurosis of wanting to appear poor," Edna related to writer Susan Brownmiller.[407] Contrary to that perspective, there was no evidence Jeannette had invited her moderate wealth. Had Wellington not invested money in her name, it wouldn't have existed.

As Rankin's assets were being distributed, other practical matters emerged as well. Dorothy Brown appealed to Dr. George Thorngate, who had been Rankin's physician in the final years of her life, to help the Internal Revenue Service understand that she hadn't distributed earnings from the sale of her Montana ranch "in anticipation of death." The IRS, Brown wrote, might think wrongly of Rankin as trying to defraud the government of inheritance taxes. "Over the years she has been very generous with me and with many others and I have never felt that she was doing in it anticipation of death," Brown wrote. "I don't think she minded dying; in fact I think she dreaded living as long as her mother, but I'm quite sure that she did not feel near the end in spite of the frustrations of drooling and losing the faculty to speak."[408]

Friends, relatives and acquaintances said they knew no weak side to Rankin, except for an occasional flaming temper that showed when the work of other people failed to meet her expectations. Private letters would betray her occasional emotional hurt and fear of rejection, but most people knew her as self-assured and confident, fearless toward the possibility that someone opposed to her views might try to injure or assassinate her. She believed that the power of progressive ideas transcended other earthly considerations. "To my mind, she believed in a fairy tale, that people were capable of greater intelligence and kindness," Dorothy Brown said a few years after Rankin's death.

Rankin would not be forgotten. Four years after she died, Ambassador to Japan and former Senate Majority Leader Mike Mansfield wrote: "She was a remarkable woman who has left her imprint upon history and who strove consistently to achieve a more peaceful world. We will miss her, but she has made her contribution and she will be remembered for decades to come."

She was driven by despair, by a yearning to make the world right, and yet her work was so infinitely hopeless, so much a lamb's peep among the roar of lions. That we should find the pacifist Jeannette Rankin among citizens of a nation built on military pride; the feminist Rankin calling for equal rights when women traditionally were relegated to second-class citizenship; the social reformer Rankin struggling to protect women and children when industry was plunging full bore onto the conscience and backbone of America; that is the anomaly. She was out of step with time and destiny, more of an icon in history than someone who had shaped it, both mercilessly earnest and perilously self-destructive. Just a few months before her long life ended, she acknowledged she would do it all again "but this time I'd be nastier."

Jeannette Rankin was a leader in troubled times, drifting forth when the world was not ready for her message. She was a prophet of peace. She resisted violence and regret, disappointment and despair, chasing a dream she found so simple and attainable. "History seldom repeats itself with the cruel symmetry it conferred on Jeannette Rankin," concluded Susan Brownmiller, adding tongue in cheek: "She was a sidebar disgrace to the rally 'round the flag for Roosevelt, democracy and country, the little old lady who was so out of touch that she voted no to the two great wars, a laughing stock who was 'just like a woman.'"[409]

A century later, Rankin remains the only woman ever elected to Congress from Montana. Even more significant, history confirms her as the only Member of Congress to oppose both world wars. "Yet for all of the prominence those two antiwar votes brought her, it remains difficult to piece together how she transformed a basically timid and insecure personality and several early career setbacks into a charismatic public personage," Montana scholar Joan Hoff Wilson observed. "The pioneer ideals she accepted in her

Montana youth — hard work, honesty, perseverance — blended with her perceptions of women, international conflict and the destructiveness of war to make Jeannette Rankin one of the most unique female figures in American political history."[410]

In 1974, Montana State Representative Ora Halvorsen of Kalispell introduced a bill in the Montana Legislature to commission a statue of Jeannette Rankin that would stand in the State Capitol. The completed work by artist Terry Mimnaugh stood seven feet tall. A few years later came another decision to place a statue of Jeannette Rankin in the United States Capitol, and again Mimnaugh fashioned her likeness. Rankin remains there now in Statuary Hall, sharing the privilege of representing Montana alongside the brilliant western artist Charles Marion Russell, her eyes still drifting beyond the nation's great arena of government to a vision of peace for all Americans.

Acknowledgements and Sources

A few years after Jeannette Rankin died, I met Belle Fligelman Winestine. Belle was living in Helena, Mont., where I was a reporter for the local newspaper, the *Independent Record*. Like Rankin, Belle was an early suffragist. As a born campaigner and diligent political activist, Belle helped elect Rankin to Congress in 1916. She so inspired me to write about Rankin's life that I decided on the spot, on that day in 1977, to write a biography. Weeks later, by happenstance, I met Oregon publisher Oral Bullard. He had come to Montana to sell books. I pitched the biography, Oral embraced it, I researched and wrote it, he published it, and in 1980 I became the author of *Flight of the Dove: The Story of Jeannette Rankin*. Belle was especially proud of my book. She was by then an old woman who had traveled a long political road, a historical figure herself who trusted an untried young man to get the story right. Oral was much the same. Although several years younger than Belle, he knew life's hard road well and found solace in words. I credit both of them for inspiring this biography, both my first book and the new and expanded edition that you, dear reader, now hold in your hands. Belle and Oral are gone now but their collective spirit remains very much alive in me.

The first biography introduced me to new friends and colleagues who joined my quest to write the second one. Much gratitude to actors and writers Jeanmarie (Simpson) Bishop and Allyson Adams, my "sisters" in all things

Jeannette Rankin. Their insight into Rankin's life and times, their encouragement and friendship and collaboration, speaks loudly in this new edition, *One Woman Against War*. Thanks as well to the Porch Party circle of friends who endured (and encouraged) my frequent descriptions of the Rankin biography, the many sources who guided my research in libraries, and to the miracle of the internet. Every word spoken, every word written, helped tell Rankin's story.

Thanks to Rankin family members who shared what they knew about Jeannette in letters, phone calls and personal interviews. Notable among them were Dorothy "Mackey" Brown, Edna Rankin McKinnon, Louise Rankin Galt and Virginia Ronhovde. A close friend of the Rankin family, Frances Elge, offered considerable insight into the dynamics between Jeannette and her brother Wellington. Elge was one of Rankin's congressional secretaries during her World War II term.

Which brings me to my family. Thanks to my daughter Hillorie Giles-Brauch for inspecting my manuscript for errors and repetitions, to my daughters Heather Peacock and Harmony MacDonald for their unconditional support and love, to son in laws Jim, Jim and Dwayne, and to my seven grandchildren: Haylie, Kazin, Kimberly, Seanna, Liam, Kyleigh and Kayde. Especially, thanks to my wife Becky, who understands and encourages my innate desire to write and tell stories. You are my world, all of you.

Information about Jeannette Rankin lies in the hands and minds of widely dispersed sources. The Jeannette Rankin Collection at the Arthur and Elizabeth Schlesinger Library on the History of Women at Radcliffe College in Cambridge, Mass., includes correspondence and other documentation highlighting her Congressional years. A substantial collection of her work in the peace movement can be found in the files of the National Council for Prevention of War in the peace collection at Swarthmore College in Pennsylvania. A smaller but growing collection at the Montana Historical Society Library in Helena includes notes and papers of Belle Fligelman Winestine. The Society's collection of Jeannette's late brother, Wellington Rankin, also was useful. Documents and photographs related to Rankin's peace work in Georgia can be found at the University of Georgia in Athens. A small number of documents are listed under Rankin's name at the Library of Congress.

Selected Bibliography

BOOKS
Addams, Jane, *Twenty Years at Hull House* (N.Y., MacMillan, 1938)
Beard, Charles A., *The Devil Theory of War* (N.Y., Vanguard, 1936)
Catt, Carrie Chapman and Schuler, Nettie Rogers, *Woman Suffrage and Politics* (N.Y., Charles Scribner's Sons, 1926)
Chamberlain, Hope, *A Minority of Members: Women in the U.S. Congress* (N.Y., Praeger, 1973)
Chatfield, Charles, *For Peace and Justice, Pacifism in America* (Knoxville, University of Tennessee Press, 1971)
Dykeman, Wilma, *Too Many People, Too Little Love: Edna Rankin McKinnon, Pioneer for Birth Control* (N.Y., Holt, Rinehart and Winston, 1974)
Glasscock, C.B., *The War of the Copper Kings* (N.Y., Grosset and Dunlap, 1935)
Engelbrecht, H.C., and Hanighen, F.C., *Merchants of Death* (N.Y., Dodd and Mead, 1934)
Fleming, Alice, *Ida Tarbell: First of the Muckrakers* (N.Y., Crowell, 1971)
Flexner, Eleanor, *Century of Struggle, the Women's Rights Movement in the United States* (Cambridge, Belknap Press, 1959)
Fox, Mary Virginia, *Pacifists, Adventures in Courage* (Chicago, Reilly and Lee, 1971)
Grimes, Alan P., *The Puritan Ethic and Woman Suffrage* (N.Y., Oxford University Press, 1967)
Harper, Ida Husted, editor, *History of Woman Suffrage* (N.Y., National American Woman Suffrage Association, 1922)
Hofstadter, Richard, *The Age of Reform* (N.Y., Alfred A Knopf, 1955)
Josephson, Hannah, *Jeannette Rankin: First Lady in Congress* (N.Y.,

Bobbs-Merrill, 1974)
Karlin, Jules A., *Progressive Politics in Montana* (N.Y., Lewis, 1956)
LaGuardia, Fiorello, *The Making of an Insurgent* (N.Y., Capricorn, 1961)
Lawson, Don, *Ten Fighters for Peace, an anthology* (N.Y., Lothrop, Lee and Shephard, 1971)
Libby, Frederick J., *To End War* (N.Y., Fellowship Publications, 1969)
Lopach, James J. and Luckowski, Jean A., *Jeannette Rankin: A Political Woman* (Boulder, University Press of Colorado, 2005)
Malone, Michael P. and Roeder, Richard B., *Montana: A History of Two Centuries* (University of Washington Press, 1976)
Melosi, Martin, *The Shadow of Pearl Harbor: Political Controversy over the Surprise Attack, 1941-1946* (Texas A and M University Press, 1977)
Millis, Walter, *The Road to War: America 1914-17* (Boston, Houghton Mifflin Co., 1935)
Norris, Frank, *The Octopus* (N.Y., Bantam, 1901)
Park, Maud Wood, *Front Door Lobby* (Boston, Beacon Press, 1960)
Richey, Elinor, *Eminent Women of the West: Jeannette Rankin, Woman of Commitment* (Berkeley, Howell-North, 1975)
Riis, Jacob A., *How the Other Half Lives* (N.Y., Hill and Wang, 1957)
Rutland, Robert A., *The Newsmongers: Journalism in the Life of a Nation* (N.Y., Dial Press, 1973)
Sinclair, Upton, *The Jungle* (N.Y., Heritage Press, 1906)
Slayden, Ellen, *Washington Wife, Journal of Ellen Maury Slayden from 1897-1919* (N.Y., Harper and Row, 1962)
Smith, Norma, *Jeannette Rankin: America's Conscience* (Helena, Montana Historical Society Press, 2002)
Solomon, Louis, *America Goes to Press* (London, Crowell-Collier, 1970)
Spargo, John, *The Bitter Cry of the Children* (N.Y., Garrett, 1970)
Steele, Volney, *Wellington Rankin: His Family, Life and Times* (Bozeman, Bridger Creek Historical Press, 2002)
Toole, K. Ross, *Twentieth-Century Montana: A State of Extremes* (Norman, University of Oklahoma Press, 1972)
Waldron, Ellis, *An Atlas of Montana Politics Since 1864* (Missoula, MSU Press, 1958)

Wheeler, Burton K., *Yankee from the West* (N.Y., Doubleday, 1962)

PERIODICALS
American Historical Review, July 1920, "New Light on the Origins of World War," Sidney Fay.
_____, October 1970, "Preparing the Public for War: Efforts to Establish a National Propaganda Agency, 1940-41."
Atlanta Constitution and Journal Magazine, June 21, 1959, "Rebel with a Cause," Gregory Favre.
_____, May 7, 1967, "First Woman in Congress Still a Pacifist," Lucy Justus.
_____, Feb. 13, 1972, "She Campaigns for Change," Lucy Justus.
Atlanta Journal and Constitution, Nov. 24, 1953, "Pioneer Lady Solon a Georgian," Frank Daniel.
Brenau Bulletin, February 1935, "The Chair of Peace."
Bulletin of Friend's Historical Association, 1954, "An Early Example of Political Action by Women," E.B. Bronner.
Christian Century, Sept. 4, 1940, "First Congresswoman Seeks to Return."
_____, Nov. 20, 1940, "Congresswoman Rankin Returns to House."
Christian Science Monitor, April 15, 1932, "Women to Put Masses Power Back of Peace."
Collier's Weekly, April 21, 1917, "Jeannette of Montana," Peter Clark MacFarlane.
Commercial West, July 27, 1918, "Worthy Tribune to Miss 'Congressman' Rankin."
Current History, July 1924, "American Women's Ineffective Use of the Vote," M.W. Willey.
Current Opinion, December 1916, "Portrait."
Fortune, March 1934, "Arms and the Men."
Georgia Historical Quarterly, Spring 1974, "Jeannette Rankin in Georgia," Ted C. Harris.
Harpers, Dec. 5, 1914, "Motherhood and War," F.W. Pethick-

Lawrence.

_____, May 1933, "Our Quarreling Pacifists," Marcus Duffield.

Independent, Nov. 20, 1916, "Portrait."

_____, April 2, 1917, "Lady from Missoula," Donald Wilhelm.

Independent Woman, December 1940, "Who's Who in Elections."

Journal of Modern History, March 1951, "The War-Guilt Question and American Disillusionment."

Life, March 3, 1972, "Feminists' New Heroine," Elizabeth Frappollo.

Literary Digest, Nov. 18, 1916, "Portrait."

_____, Nov. 25, 1916, "Member from Montana."

_____, Aug. 11, 1917, "Our Busy Congresswoman."

McCall's, April 1917, "Our First Woman Congresswoman," Bertha Filer.

_____, 1917, "What Women Should Do," Jeannette Rankin (ghosted by Katharine Anthony).

_____, January 1958, "Three Women of Courage," John F. Kennedy.

Montana Business Quarterly, Autumn 1971, "Montana's First Woman Politician: A Recollection of Jeannette Rankin Campaigning," Dorothy Brown.

Montana: The Magazine of Western History, July 1967, "The Lady from Montana," John Board.

_____, Winter 1973, "Montana Women and the Battle for the Ballot," T.A. Larson.

_____, "Mother Was Shocked," Belle Fligelman Winestine.

Nation, May 31, 1917, "Lady from Montana," The Tattler.

_____, Nov. 2, 1918, "Politics in Montana," Louis Levine.

New Outlook, November 1933, "Deaf and Dumb Ships," Wayne Francis Palmer.

New Republic, Mar 9, 1918, "The Legal Status of War," S.O. Levinson.

_____, Nov. 18, 1936, "Pacifism: Its Rise and Fall," Bruce Bliven.

Newsweek, Feb. 14, 1966, "Woman Against War."

Outlook, Nov. 22, 1916, "First Woman Elected to Congress."

Pacific Northwest Quarterly, January 1964, "The Montana Woman

Suffrage Campaign, 1911-1914," Ronald Schaffer.
Peace Action, March 1936, "Emergency Peace Campaign Is Planned."
Public Opinion Quarterly, April 1937, "Organizing American Public Opinion for Peace," Elton Atwater.
_____, March 1940, "Influences of World Events on U.S. Neutrality Opinion," P.E. Jacob.
_____, September 1940, "America Faces the War: A Study in Public Opinion."
_____, December 1940, "The Peace Groups Join Battle."
Ramparts, February 1968, "History of Rise of the Unusual Movement for Women Power in the United States, 1961-68," W. and M. Hinckle.
Scribner's Magazine, February 1935, "National Politics and War."
Suffragist, Jan. 16, 1915, "Woman's Movement for Constructive Peace."
_____, March 31, 1917, "An Impression of Jeannette Rankin," Winifred Mallou.
Sunset, November 1916, "First Woman Elected to Congress," Belle Fligelman.
Survey, July 21, 1917, "Political Power in the Hands of a Woman."
_____, Feb. 1, 1919, "Federal Mothers' Aid."
_____, December 1920, "National Consumers League."
Survey Graphic, February 1937, "Who Wants Peace?" Dorothy Thompson.
Union Printer, May 5, 1945, "Social Progress Moves on the Feet of Women."
Woman Citizen, July 2, 1917, "What a Congresswoman Has Done for Working Women," Ethel Smith.
Woman's Home Companion, July 1926, "Our Gypsy Journey to Georgia," Katharine Anthony.
_____, August 1926, "A Basket of Summer Fruit," Katharine Anthony.
_____, September 1926, "Living on the Front Porch," Katharine Anthony.
Woman's Journal, Nov. 11, 1916, "Miss Rankin Gives New Turn to Old Ideas," p. 365.

_____, Nov. 25, 1916, "The Press on Jeannette Rankin," p. 384.
_____, Dec. 23, 1916, "G.O.P. Bowed to Woman's Spirit," p. 415.
_____, Jan. 6, 1917, "Quiet Life for Congresswoman."
_____, March 10, 1917, "Jeannette Rankin Addresses 3000," pp. 55-56.
_____, March 17, 1917, "Breezy Bits from the Capitol," p. 4.
_____, March 17, 1917, "Miss Rankin Aids Suffrage Hearing," p. 63.
_____, March 24, 1917, "Miss Rankin Speaks in N.J.," p. 67.
_____, March 31, 1917, "Congresswoman Opens Office in Washington," p. 73.
_____, April 7, 1917, "Jeannette Rankin Takes Place in House," p. 79.
_____, April 14, 1917, "Miss Rankin Kept Busy," p. 89.

UNPUBLISHED MANUSCRIPTS

Board, John C., *Jeannette Rankin: The Suffrage Years and Before*, graduate paper, undated.

Board, John C., *The Lady from Montana: Jeannette Rankin*, master's thesis, University of Wyoming, Laramie, 1964.

Harris, Ted Carlton, *Jeannette Rankin, Warring Pacifist*, master's thesis, University of Georgia, 1969.

Harris, Ted Carlton, *Jeannette Rankin: Suffragist, First Woman Elected to Congress, and Pacifist*, doctoral dissertation, University of Georgia, 1972.

Lindquist, Adah Donovan, *A Study of Jeannette Rankin and Her Role in the Peace Movement*, (Hanover, Ind., 1971), Honors Paper, Swarthmore College, Pa.

Oral History Project, The Bancroft Library, University of California, Berkeley, *Jeannette Rankin Transcript*.

Schaffer, Ronald, *Jeannette Rankin, Progressive Isolationist*, doctoral dissertation, Princeton University, 1959.

Ward, Doris Buck, *Winning of Woman Suffrage in Montana*, master's thesis, Montana State University, June 1974.

Wilson, Joan Hoff, *Peace is a Woman's Job ... Jeannette Rankin's Foreign Policy*, fellowship paper, Arizona State University, 1977.

MANUSCRIPT COLLECTIONS

Belle Fligelman Winestine Papers, Montana Historical Society Library, Helena.

Jeannette Rankin Papers, Montana Historical Society Library.

Jeannette Rankin Papers, National Council for Prevention of War files, Swarthmore Peace Collection, Swarthmore College, Pa.

Jeannette Rankin Papers, Arthur and Elizabeth Schlesinger Library on the History of Women in America, Radcliffe College, Cambridge, Mass.

Jeannette Rankin Papers, Richard B. Russell Library for Political Research and Studies, University of Georgia, Athens.

Wellington D. Rankin Papers, Montana Historical Society Library.

PUBLIC DOCUMENTS

House Journal of the Twelfth Session of the Legislative Assembly of the State of Montana. Helena, Mont., Independent Publishing Co., 1911.

Senate Journal of the Thirteenth Session of the Legislative Assembly of the State of Montana. 1913, pp. 110, 138, 159.

National American Woman Suffrage Association, 45th Annual Report, 1913, p. 80.

U.S. Congressional Record, 65th Congress, First Session, 1917.

U.S. Congressional Record, 65th Congress, Second Session, 1918.

Hearings, "Rights of Suffrage to Women," House Committee on Women Suffrage, 65th Congress, Second Session, on H.J. Res. 200, Washington, 1918.

Report of the International Congress of Women, Zurich, 1919, Women's International League for Peace and Freedom, 1919.

U.S. Congressional Record, 67th Congress, Vol. 61, 1921, pp. 3141-3146, 4206-4217, 7926-7950, 7979-8014, 8034-8037.

Hearings, "Public Protection of Maternity and Infancy," House Committee on Interstate and Foreign Commerce, 66th Congress, Third Session, on H.R. 10925, Washington, 1920.

Hearings, "Exportation of Arms or Munitions of War," House Committee on Foreign Affairs, 72nd Congress, Second Session, on H.J. Res. 580, Washington, 1933.

Hearings, "Construction of Certain Naval Vessels," Senate Committee on Naval Affairs, 73rd Congress, Second Session, on S. 2493, Washington, 1934.

Hearings, "Taking the Profit Out of War," House Committee on Military Affairs, 74th Congress, First Session, on H.R. 3 and 5293, Washington, 1935.

Hearings, "American Neutrality Policy," House Committee on Foreign Affairs, 75th Congress, First Session, on H.J. 147 and 242, Washington, 1937.

U.S. *Congressional Record*, 77th Congress, First Session, 1941.

U.S. *Congressional Record*, Vol 87, Part I, 77th Congress, First Session, pp. 791-793, 813-814, 9520-9530, Washington, 1941.

U.S. *Congressional Record*, "Some Questions About Pearl Harbor," 77th Congress, Second Session, Dec. 8, 1942.

Hearings, Joint Committee on the Pearl Harbor Attack, 79th Congress, First Session (38 parts), Washington, 1946.

Report of the Joint Committee on the Pearl Harbor Attack, 79th Congress, Second Session, Senate Document 244, Washington, 1946.

U.S. *Congressional Record*, 91st Congress, Second Session, Vol. 116, Parts 15-16, June 22, 1970.

ORAL INTERVIEWS

Brown, Dorothy McKinnon, personal interviews with the author, Jan. 29, 1978 and July 5, 1978, Del Mar, Calif.

Elge, Frances, personal interview with the author, Oct. 6, 1978, Helena, Mont.

Galt, Louise Rankin, personal interviews with the author, Oct. 6, 1978 at Helena, Mont., and Oct. 14, 2012, at 71 Ranch, Martinsdale, Mont.

Rankin, Jeannette, interview with John Board, Aug. 29-30, 1963,

Missoula, Mont.
Rankin, Jeannette, television interview with Dick Cavett, April 17, 1972, Los Angeles, Calif.
Ronhovde, Virginia, personal interview with the author, Oct. 11, 1978, Helena, Mont.
Winestine, Belle Fligelman, personal interviews with the author, Aug. 17, 1977, Dec. 14, 1977, July 21, 1978, Helena, Mont.
Winestine, Belle Fligelman, interview with George Cole, undated, Lewis and Clark Public Library, Helena, Mont.

PERSONAL CORRESPONDENCE

Baldwin, Roger, personal letter to the author, Aug. 23, 1978.
Mansfield, Mike, personal letter to the author, Sept. 18, 1978.
McGovern, George, personal letter to the author, Nov. 1, 1978.
McKinnon, Edna Rankin, personal letter to the author, Oct. 10, 1977. (Mrs. McKinnon, Jeannette's sister, died in 1978.)
Ronhovde, Virginia, personal letter to the author, Nov. 1, 1978.

NEWSPAPERS

Anaconda Standard (Montana), Aug. 15, 1917, pp. 1,7.
Athens Banner-Herald (Georgia), Feb. 10, 1928, p. 4; Sept. 28, 1934, p. 1; Oct. 18, 1934, p. 1; Oct. 26, 1934; Dec. 8, 1941.
Athens Daily Times (Georgia), Nov. 4, 1934, p. 5; Dec. 20, 1934; Jan. 28, 1972, p. 1.
Bismarck Tribune (North Dakota), May 19, 1967.
Boston Advertiser, March 9, 1925.
Butte Daily Bulletin (Montana), Oct. 24, 1918.
Butte Daily Post (Montana), Oct. 30, 1940; Nov. 4, 1940; Nov. 7, 1940.
Chicago Evening News, May 19, 1919.
Chicago Sunday-Herald, Jan. 9, 1917; Feb. 11, 1917; Feb. 18, 1917; May 13, 1917; May 27, 1917; June 3, 1917; June 10, 1917; June 17, 1917; June 24, 1917; July 8, 1917; Aug. 5, 1917; Oct. 21, 1917; Nov. 11, 1917; Dec. 3, 1917; Dec. 10, 1917; Dec. 17, 1917.
Cleveland News, March 27, 1925.
Cleveland Plain Dealer, March 26, 1925.
Daily Missoulian (Montana), Jan. 15. 1914, p. 6; Feb. 15, 1914, p. 1;

March 23, 1914, p. 3; April 3, 1914, p. 4; May 26, 1914, p. 1; Nov. 6, 1914, pp. 1,7; Nov. 8, 1914, p. 8; Nov. 14, 1914, p. 1; May 18, 1916, p. 2; July 9, 1916, p. 2; July 29, 1916, p. 5; July 30, 1916, p. 2; Aug. 23, 1916, p. 1; Aug. 24, 1917, p. 4; Aug. 30, 1916, p. 4; Sept. 27, 1916, p. 8; Oct. 23, 1916, p. 8; Nov. 2, 1916, p. 1; Nov. 6, 1916, p. 1; Nov. 7, 1916, p. 12; Nov. 10, 1916, p. 1; Nov. 18, 1916, p. 10; Jan. 12, 1917, p. 5; March 31, 1917, p. 1; April 6, 1917, p. 1; April 17, 1917, p. 8; June 4, 1917, p. 1; Aug. 22, 1917, p. 1; Aug. 23, 1917, pp. 1,5; Jan. 6, 1918, editorial p. 1; April 20, 1918, p. 6; July 6, 1918, p. 1; Aug. 29, 1918, p. 1; Nov. 3, 1918, p. 8; Nov. 6, 1918, p. 1; Nov. 7, 1918, p. 6; Oct. 22, 1940, p. 5; Oct. 23, 1940, p. 6; Nov. 6, 1940, p. 1; Jan. 4, 1941, p. 3; Dec. 11, 1941, pp. 1,4,5.

Des Moines Register (Iowa), April 15, 1917, p. 4.

Emporia Gazette (Kansas), Dec. 10, 1941, p. 4.

Gainesville News (Georgia), Oct. 31, 1934.

Great Falls Tribune (Montana), June 20, 1934; April 6, 1937; July 7, 1940, p. 5; July 12, 1940, p. 1; July 19m, 1940, p. 1; Nov. 7, 1940; July 12, 1941; Dec. 12, 1941, p. 7; Sept. 29, 1949; June 3, 1951; June 6, 1951; Oct. 5, 1959.

Helena Independent (Montana), Feb. 2, 1911; April 3, 1917, p. 4; April 26, 1917, p. 4; Aug. 9, 1917, p. 6; Oct. 5, 1917; Jan. 17, 1918, p. 4; Jan 22, 1918; April 18, 1918; April 19, 1918; May 21, 1918, p. 4; June 23, 1918; June 26, 1918; July 7, 1918; Nov. 3, 1918, p. 4; July 16, 1940; Dec. 9, 1941.

Helena People's Voice (Montana), Oct. 30, 1940; Dec. 10, 1941, p. 1; Aug. 11, 1967.

Knoxville News-Sentinel (Tennessee), Feb. 13, 1972.

Louisville Courier-Journal (Kentucky), April 8, 1917, p. 4.

Macon Evening News (Georgia), Feb. 11, 1930, p. 1; Dec. 10, 1934, p. 4; Oct. 10, 1935, p. 4.

Macon Telegraph (Georgia), June 2, 1928, p. 4.

Minneapolis Tribune, Dec. 10, 1941, p. 4.

Montana Progressive, Jan. 14, 1915.

Montana Record-Herald, July 12, 1916, p. 2; March 3, 1917, p. 7; April 11, 1917; Aug. 16, 1917; Sept. 12, 1918, p. 1.

Montana Standard, Dec. 10, 1941, p. 4.

Nashville Tennessean, Feb. 13, 1972.

New York American, Jan. 10, 1918; Jan. 11, 1918; March 17, 1918.
New York Herald-Tribune, Jan. 24, 1947.
New York Times, Aug. 14, 1913, p. 6: Nov. 18, 1916, p. 10; Nov. 21, 1916, p. 10; Feb. 21, 1917, p. 14; March 3, 1917, p. 4; April 3, 1917, p. 4; April 6, 1917, p. 1; April 7, 1917, p. 4; April 8, 1917, II, p. 2; April 14, 1917, p. 12; May 29, 1917, pp. 1,4; July 2, 1917, p. 7; July 16, 1917, p. 9; Aug. 3, 1917, pp. 3.16; Aug. 31, 1917; Nov. 9, 1917, p. 13; Nov. 17, 1917, p. 4; Dec. 13, 1917, p. 19; Aug. 3, 1918, p. 16; Aug. 10, 1918, p. 5; April 10, 1919; May 18, 1919; Dec. 16, 1934, IV, p. 6; Feb. 10, 1938; Feb. 6, 1940; June 9, 1940, IV, p. 2; Dec. 9, 1941, p. 8; Dec. 12, 1941, p. 8; Jan. 16, 1968; Jan. 24, 1972, L, p. 24; May 20, 1973.
New York Tribune, Feb. 25, 1917, p. 7.
St. Louis Post-Dispatch, Dec. 10, 1941, p. 2C.
Washington Daily News, April 6, 1937.
Washington Evening Star, Dec. 8, 1941; Jan. 16, 1968.
Washington Post, May 6, 1917, p. 3; April 2, 1917, p. 1; April 8, 1917, p. 4; Dec. 12, 1941; Jan. 12, 1968.
Washington Times, April 2, 1917, p. 3; Aug. 8, 1917, p. 2.

FILM

Adams, Allyson, writer and actor, "Peace is a Woman's Job," independent film, Moment of Peace Productions, filmed in Montana.

Bishop, Jeanmarie (Simpson), writer and actor, "A Single Woman," Nevada Shakespeare Co. and Heroica Films, 2008. (Bishop also has performed the stage version hundreds of times.)

Fisher, David, "Jeannette Rankin: First Lady of Peace," a film produced for WGTV in Athens, Ga. On file at the Schlesinger Library on the History of Women in America, Radcliffe College, Cambridge, Mass.

Citations

[1] Linda Goodman to Jeannette Rankin (JR), May 21, 1967, JR MSS, Schlesinger Library, Radcliffe Institute, Harvard University.
[2] Author interview with Nan Pendergrast, March 25, 2013.
[3] "Women Power," Warren Hinckle and Marianne Hinckle, Ramparts Magazine, February 1968, pp. 22-31.
[4] JR interview with Malca Chall, University of California-Berkeley oral history, 1974, pp. 22-23.
[5] An account of Jeannette Rankin Brigade organizing can be found in "Women Strike for Peace: Traditional Motherhood and Radical Politics in the 1960s," Amy Swerdlow, University of Chicago Press, 1993.
[6] Katharine Anthony to JR, Feb. 7, 1954, JR MSS, Schlesinger.
[7] The March on the Pentagon, including acts of civil disobedience, later was portrayed in Norman Mailer's critically acclaimed book, "The Armies of the Night," New American Library, 1968.
[8] Federal Bureau of Investigation files, "Jeannette Rankin," Jan. 16, 1968.
[9] Marion D. Beardsley, "Report on the Jeannette Rankin Brigade March," JR MSS, Schlesinger.
[10] Video clip interview with Jeannette Rankin at US Capitol, Jan. 15, 1968.
[11] JR interview with Malca Chall, Suffragists Oral History Project, University of California, Berkeley, 1974, p. 95.
[12] Ibid, Hannah Josephson, p. 207.
[13] John C. Board, "The Lady from Montana: Jeannette Rankin," MA thesis, University of Wyoming, 1964, p. 6.
[14] Author interview with Dorothy McKinnon Brown, Helena, Mont., July 5, 1978.
[15] Wellington Rankin interview with John C. Board, "The Lady from Montana: Jeannette Rankin," MA thesis, University of Wyoming, 1964, page 12.
[16] JR interview with Malca Chall, University of California-Berkeley oral history, p. 191.
[17] Author interview with Dorothy McKinnon Brown, Helena, Mont., July 5, 1978.
[18] JR interview with Malca Chall, University of California-Berkeley oral history, p. 95.
[19] Ronald Schaffer, "Jeannette Rankin: Progressive Isolationist," PhD dissertation, Princeton University, 1959, p. 6.
[20] "Wellington Rankin: His Family, Life and Times," Volney Steele, Bridger Creek Historical Press, 2002, Bozeman, Mont., p. 47.
[21] E.T. Devine, "The New View of Charity," Atlantic Monthly, Dec. 1908, vol. 102, p. 739.

[22] "America 1908," Jim Rasenberger, Scribner, 2007, page 100.
[23] JR to Mary Rankin, Feb. 1909, JR MSS, Schlesinger.
[24] Collier's Weekly, April 21, 1917, p. 7.
[25] "Our First Woman Congressman," McCall's Magazine, April 1917, volume XVI, p. 95.
[26] Naval Postgraduate School Officer Student's Wives Club Magazine, Volume II, No. 8, pp. 140-41.
[27] JR interview with John Board, Missoula, Montana, Aug. 29-30, 1963.
[28] "Sex in Education or, A Fair Chance for Girls," James R. Osgood and Co., Boston, 1875.
[29] JR interview with John Board, Missoula, Montana, Aug. 29-30, 1963, p. 21.
[30] Details of New York's Heterodoxy are covered in "Radical Feminists of Heterodoxy: Greenwich Village, 1912-1940," Judith Schwartz, New Victoria Publishers, 1982, Lebanon, N.H.
[31] Peter Clark MacFarlane, Collier's Weekly, April 21, 1917, p. 37
[32] JR interview, Suffragists Oral History Project, p. 185.
[33] JR to Harriet Laidlaw, May 11, 1912, Harriet B. Laidlaw MSS, Schlesinger.
[34] JR interview with Ted C. Harris, Jan. 16, 1969, p.5.
[35] Flexner, Eleanor, "Century of Struggle, the Women's Rights Movement in the United States," (Cambridge: Belknap Press, 1959)
[36] Florida Times Union, April 18 and May 4, 1913.
[37] Ted C. Harris, "Jeannette Rankin: Suffragist, First Woman Elected to Congress, and Pacifist" (PhD dissertation, University of Georgia, 1972), pp. 75-76.
[38] JR interview with Hannah Josephson, Suffragists Oral History Project, p. 209.
[39] Mary O'Neill to JR, 1913, JR MSS, Schlesinger.
[40] "Jeannette Rankin: America's Conscience," Norma Smith, (Helena: Montana Historical Society Press, 2002) p. 93.
[41] Mary O'Neill to JR, JR MSS, undated, Schlesinger.
[42] Great Falls Daily Tribune, July 29,1914; Great Falls Leader, July 22, 1914.
[43] Suffragists Oral History Project, University of California at Berkeley, Aug. 2, 1972, pp. 47-48.
[44] JR interview with Harris, Feb. 14, 1969, p. 8.
[45] "Washington Daily News," April 6, 1937.
[46] JR interview with Board, p. 9.
[47] Ibid, p. 9.
[48] Ibid, p. 10.
[49] "What They Do with the Vote When They Get It," The Woman Citizen, Volume 1, Aug. 25, 1917, p. 234; "Jeannette Rankin: Suffragist, First Woman Elected to Congress, and Pacifist," Harris, pp. 91-92.
[50] Antoinette Funk to JR, April 2, 1915, General Correspondence and Papers, Series II, JR MSS, Schlesinger.
[51] "First Lady in Congress: Jeannette Rankin," Hannah Josephson, (Indianapolis and New York: Bobbs-Merrill, 1974), p. 49.
[52] Author interview with Belle Fligelman Winestine, Helena, Mont., Dec. 14, 1977.
[53] "Wellington Rankin: His Family, Life and Times," Steele, pp. 82-85.

⁵⁴ Helena Daily Independent, July 11, 1916, p. 8
⁵⁵ Author interview with Belle Fligelman Winestine, Helena, Mont., Aug. 17, 1977.
⁵⁶ Ibid.
⁵⁷ "Godfrey Favors Jeannette Rankin," Helena Daily Independent, Aug. 9, 1916, p. 3.
⁵⁸ JR interview with Board, p. 17.
⁵⁹ JR campaign letter to Montana farmers, Oct. 31, 1916, JR MSS, Schlesinger.
⁶⁰ Campaign cards, JR MSS, Schlesinger.
⁶¹ JR interview with Board, p. 15.
⁶² Wellington Rankin interview with John Board, undated.
⁶³ Philadelphia Evening Ledger, Nov. 11, 1916, p. 6.
⁶⁴ Ellis Waldron, "An Atlas of Montana Politics since 1864," p. 155.
⁶⁵ JR letter, Nov. 13, 1916, JR MSS, Schlesinger.
⁶⁶ "Miss Rankin's Vote a Personal Triumph," New York Times, Nov. 12, 1916, p. 4.
⁶⁷ New York Times, letter to the editor, Nov. 18, 1916, p. 10.
⁶⁸ Rosalie Jones letter to JR, Nov. 12, 1916, JR MSS, Schlesinger.
⁶⁹ Charles F. Easton letter, Nov. 30, 1916, JR MSS, Schlesinger.
⁷⁰ New York Times Magazine, Nov. 19, 1916, p. 15.
⁷¹ Louis Levine, "First Woman Member of Congress Well Versed in Politics," New York Times, Nov. 19, 1916.
⁷² Daily Missoulian, Nov. 18, 1916.
⁷³ "The Lady from Montana," Chicago Sunday Herald, Dec. 19, 1916.
⁷⁴ Book referenced was written by Lynn Haines, National Voters' League, 1915.
⁷⁵ John Board interview with Wellington D. Rankin, March 23, 1964.
⁷⁶ New York Tribune story reprinted in the Missoulian, "Jeannette Movie Fan She Tells New York," March 4, 1917, p. 2.
⁷⁷ New York Times, March 3, 1917, p. 4.
⁷⁸ Collier's Weekly, April 21, 1917, p. 7.
⁷⁹ "Miss Rankin Makes Speech," Montana Record-Herald, March 3, 1917, p. 3.
⁸⁰ Board interview with Wellington Rankin, p. 38.
⁸¹ Ibid.
⁸² Anna Howard Shaw to JR, March 20, 1917, JR MSS, Folder 5-13, Montana Historical Society.
⁸³ Chattanooga News, March 22, 1917.
⁸⁴ "Miss Rankin Going East to Fight," Minneapolis Morning Tribune, Nov. 12, 1916, p. A11.
⁸⁵ "The Evening Mail," March 1, 1917.
⁸⁶ "The Lady from Missoula," Donald Wilhelm, "The Independent," April 2, 1917, p. 25.
⁸⁷ "The Member from Montana," The Literary Digest, Nov. 25, 1916, p. 1417.
⁸⁸ "The Capitol Welcomes Jeannette Rankin," The Suffragist, V, April 7, 1917, p. 7.
⁸⁹ JR quoted in Montana Progressive, Oct. 12, 1916.
⁹⁰ JR in a letter to "men and women" of Montana farms, Oct. 31, 1916, JR MSS, Schlesinger.
⁹¹ "The Suffrage Planks," JR MSS, Schlesinger.
⁹² Winestine, "Lady in Congress" manuscript, p. 4, Montana Historical Society.

[93] Ibid, p. 6.
[94] JR interview with Hannah Josephson, Suffragists Oral History Project, p. 196.
[95] "Washington Wife, Journal of Ellen Maury Slayden from 1897 to 1919, (N.Y: Harper and Row Publishers, 1962) pp. 298-99.
[96] New York Times, April 3, 1917.
[97] Maud Wood Park, "Front Door Lobby" (Boston: Beacon Press, 1960) pp. 72-73.
[98] US Congressional Record, 65th Congress, First Session, 1917, LV, Part 1, p. 214.
[99] US Congressional Record, 65th Congress, First Session, April 5, 1917, LV, p. 332.
[100] Winestine, "Lady in Congress" manuscript, p. 11, Montana Historical Society.
[101] Ibid, p. 13.
[102] Author interview with Belle Fligelman Winestine, Helena, Mont., 1977.
[103] Helena Independent, April 26, 1917, p. 1.
[104] Author interview with Virginia Ronhovde, Oct. 11, 1978.
[105] JR to Stephen J. Stillwell, Dec. 14, 1914, Ronald Schaffer, "Jeannette Rankin: Progressive-Isolationist," p. 82.
[106] Peter Clark MacFarlane, Collier's Weekly, April 21, 1917, p. 7.
[107] Congressional Record, 65th Congress, first session, April 5, 1917.
[108] Fiorello H. LaGuardia, "The Making of an Insurgent: An Autobiography" (N.Y.: J.B. Lippincott Co., 1948), p. 141.
[109] Kate O. Hegeman, New York Times, April 8, 1917, II, p. 2.
[110] "The Lady from Montana," The Nation, Volume 104, May 31, 1917, p. 667.
[111] Maud Park Wood, "Front Door Lobby," p. 78.
[112] New York Times, April 7, 1917, p. 4.
[113] New York Times, April 10, 1917.
[114] New York Times letters to editor, April 14-16, 1917.
[115] Imojean Earl Younger to JR, April 30, 1917, Folder 5-13, JR MSS, Montana Historical Society.
[116] Suffragists Oral History Project, University of California at Berkeley, Malca Chall, June 8, 1972.
[117] Dorothy Brown McKinnon letter to the author, 1978.
[118] Author interview with Belle Fligelman Winestine in Helena, Mont., July 21, 1978.
[119] Inez Haynes Irwin, "The Story of the Woman's Party" (New York: Harcourt, Brace, 1921), p. 300.
[120] "Miss Rankin's Rival at Polls a Suicide," New York Times, May 6, 1917, p. 15.
[121] Constituent letters, General Correspondence, Folders 40-48, JR MSS, Schlesinger.
[122] Hannah Josephson, "First Lady in Congress: Jeannette Rankin," (N.Y.: Bobbs-Merrill, 1974), p. 85.
[123] Belle Fligelman Winestine MSS, Montana Historical Society.
[124] Correspondence concerning the Bureau of Printing and Engraving investigation is contained in Folders 1-7 of the JR MSS, Montana Historical Society.
[125] Letters concerning medications dated July 7, 1917, and Sept. 15, 1917, JR MSS, Folder 5-13, Montana Historical Society.
[126] Jeannette Rankin interview with Board, p. 36.
[127] Wellington Rankin interview with Board, undated, p. 24.

128 Mrs. H.N. Kennedy to JR, June 26, 1917, JR MSS, Folder 1-8, Montana Historical Society.
129 Montana Record-Herald, March 3, 1917.
130 K. Ross Toole, "Twentieth-Century Montana: A State of Extremes" (Norman, University of Oklahoma Press, 1972), p. 146.
131 Chicago Sunday Herald, July 22, 1917.
132 JR to Joe Kennedy, Aug. 17, 1917, JR MSS, Folder 2-8, Montana Historical Society.
133 JR to John D. Ryan, telegram dated Aug. 4, 1917, Folder 2-8, JR MSS, MHS.
134 Wellington Rankin to JR, August 7, 1917, JR MSS, MHS.
135 Mary O'Neill to JR, Aug. 6, 1917, Folder 2-8, JR MSS, MHS.
136 Great Falls Daily Tribune, Aug. 9, 1917, Folder 2-8, JR MSS, MHS.
137 Mary Stewart to Belle Fligelman, JR MSS, Folder 5-13, MHS.
138 Wellington Rankin interview with Board, p. 23.
139 Helena Independent, Aug. 9, 1917.
140 JR quoted in Buffalo Evening News, Aug. 8, 1917, JR MSS, Folder 2-8, MHS.
141 Belle Fligelman to JR in Butte, Montana, undated, JR MSS, Folder 2-8, MHS.
142 Belle Fligelman Winestine MSS, MHS.
143 Will Campbell to JR, Aug. 19, 1917, Folder 2-8, JR MSS, MHS.
144 Elizabeth Watson to JR, JR MSS, Folder 5-13, MHS.
145 JR interview with Board, 1963, p. 39.
146 These and dozens of other letters of support are found in Folder 2-8, JR MSS, MHS.
147 O'Neill's communications with JR are found in Folder 1-10, JR MSS, MHS.
148 House of Representatives, 65th Congress, 2nd Session, Dec. 7, 1917, Congressional Record, LVI, Part I, p. 98.
149 Author interview with Belle Fligelman Winestine, Helena, Mont., Dec. 14, 1977.
150 Belle Fligelman Winestine letter to Hannah Josephson, 1972, BFW MSS, MHS.
151 Ibid.
152 Ibid.
153 BFW MSS, Montana Historical Society.
154 JR to G. Stelljes, Jan. 2, 1918, JR MSS, Folder 5-13, MHS.
155 Ted C. Harris doctoral thesis, University of Georgia, 1972, p. 138.
156 New York Tribune, Oct. 7, 1917.
157 JR interview with Board, p. 26.
158 Ibid.
159 "Miss Rankin Beaten for Committee Head," New York Times, Dec. 13, 1917, p. 19.
160 Hearings, US House Committee on Woman Suffrage, 65th Congress, Second Session, Jan. 3, 1918.
161 US Congress, House of Representatives, 65th Congress, Second Session, Jan. 10, 1918, Congressional Record, LVI, p. 771.
162 JR interview with John Board, Missoula, Montana, Aug. 29-30, 1963, p. 22.
163 US Congress, House of Representatives, 65th Congress, Second Session, Jan. 10, 1918, Congressional Record, LVI, p. 771.
164 "Front Door Lobby," Maud Park Wood, p. 144.
165 Congressional Record, Jan. 10, 1918.

166 Survey Journal of Public Social Policy, Feb. 1, 1919, p. 640.
167 Wellington Rankin interview with John Board, undated, p. 17-18.
168 Jules A. Karlin, "Progressive Politics in Montana," essay in the book "A History of Montana," ed. M.G. Burlingame and K. Ross Toole (N.Y., Lewis Historical Publishing Co., 1957), p. 260.
169 Toole, "Twentieth-Century Montana: A State of Extremes," pp. 179-80.
170 Carrie Chapman Catt in Helena Independent, April 18, 1918, JR MSS, MHS.
171 Harriet Rankin Sedman to Rosalie Whitney, July 26, 1918, JR MSS, Folder 1-8, MHS.
172 Letter of Annabel M. Rooney to Thomas J. Walsh, Aug. 7, 1918, T.J. Walsh MSS, MHS.
173 JR interview with Board, p. 41.
174 Carrie Chapman Catt to Harriet and James Laidlaw, Sept. 11, 1918, JR MSS, Schlesinger.
175 Helena Independent editorial republished in Commercial West, July 27, 1918, MHS.
176 Norman Winestine. "The Lady from Montana," JR MSS, 1918, Schlesinger.
177 Butte Daily Bulletin, Oct. 24, 1918.
178 Ibid, p. 263.
179 Eleanor Flexner, "Century of Struggle, the Women's Rights Movement in the United States" (Cambridge: Belknap Press, 1959).
180 Ted C. Harris, "Jeannette Rankin in Georgia," Georgia Historical Quarterly, Spring 1974, p. 1.
181 JR interview with Harris, May 24, 1969, pp. 1-2.
182 Author interview with Dorothy McKinnon Brown, Helena, Mont., July 17, 1978.
183 Harris, "Jeannette Rankin in Georgia," pp. 5-7.
184 Boston Advertiser, March 9, 1925.
185 Florence Kelley, "Congress and the Babies," The Survey, May 14, 1921, p. 200.
186 Report of the Fourth Congress of Women's International League for Peace and Freedom, Washington, 1924, p. 51.
187 "Peace and the Disarmament Conference," undated, Box 3, JR MSS, Schlesinger.
188 Cleveland Plain Dealer, March 26, 1926.
189 Dorothy Detzer to JR, March 18, 1925, General Correspondence, Folders 40-48, JR MSS, Schlesinger.
190 "Schedule for Miss Rankin," Women's International League for Peace and Freedom, JR MSS, Schlesinger Library.
191 Robert T. Kerlin to JR, March 16, 1925, JR MSS, Schlesinger.
192 Flora Belle Surles to JR, April 3, 24, 1925, General Correspondence, Folders 40-48, JR MSS, Schlesinger.
193 J.P. Nunnally letter to JR, April 27, 1925, JR Papers, Schlesinger.
194 JR to Josephine Wilkins, April 18, 1925; Dorothy Detzer to JR, April 20, 24, 1925, JR MSS, Schlesinger.
195 Katharine Anthony, "Living on the Front Porch," Woman's Home Companion, September 1926, pp. 32, 34.
196 Ibid.

197 Author interview with Dorothy McKinnon Brown, Helena, Mont., July 5, 1978.
198 Description in "Jeannette Rankin: America's Conscience," Norma Smith, Montana Historical Society Press, 2002, pp. 152-53.
199 JR, draft of speech, circa 1926, JR MSS, Schlesinger.
200 "War and Human Nature," Georgia Peace Society folder, Swarthmore College Peace Collection.
201 Athens Banner Herald, June 1, 1928.
202 "Peace Through Political Action," 1928, JR MSS, Swarthmore.
203 Macon Telegraph, June 2, 1928.
204 National Education Association, Proceedings and Addresses, 1929, p. 324.
205 Harris, "Jeannette Rankin in Georgia," p. 10.
206 Described in "Jeannette Rankin, Progressive-Isolationist," Ronald Schaffer, PhD dissertation 1959, Princeton University, page 177.
207 Edna Rankin McKinnon, letter to the author, Oct. 10, 1977.
208 "Another Washington Gadabout," Good Housekeeping, July 1934, p. 108.
209 Wellington Rankin to Jeannette Rankin Fields, July 3, 1931, JR MSS, Schlesinger.
210 Harry L. Allen to Dr. J.J. Handsaker, Dec. 18, 1933, JR MSS, Schlesinger.
211 Belle Fligelman Winestine to Frederick Libby, Jan. 13, 1934, National Council for Prevention of War MSS, Swarthmore.
212 Helen Kerr Maxham to NCPW, Nov. 25, 1933, Swarthmore.
213 Selma M. Borchardt to JR, Feb. 21, 1933, JR MSS, Schlesinger.
214 Eleanor Roosevelt to JR, Nov. 13, 1933, JR MSS, Schlesinger.
215 "Membership Drive," Georgia Peace Society, JR MSS, Swarthmore
216 JR to Mary Ida Winder, Sept. 6, 1930, JR File, NCPW, Swarthmore.
217 JR to friends of the Georgia Committee on the Disarmament Conference, March 27, 1934, NCPW, Swarthmore.
218 "Outlaw War Constitutionality," JR speech, Women's Peace Union, 1929, Box 19, Swarthmore.
219 "Peace and the Disarmament Conference," JR, written from Consumer League headquarters, New York City, undated, JR MSS, Schlesinger.
220 Athens Daily Times, Nov. 4, 1934.
221 Hearings before the US Senate Committee on Naval Affairs, 76th Congress, third session, on H.R. 8026, 1940, Congressional Record, pp. 13-14.
222 Wayne Francis Palmer, "Deaf and Dumb Ships," New Outlook, November 1933.
223 NCPW, Box 6, 1930-38, Swarthmore.
224 D.P. McGeachy to JR, Nov. 15, 1934, NCPW, Swarthmore.
225 "A Student's Answer," Student Union newspaper, undated, NCPW, Swarthmore.
226 The New Republic, LXXXI, Dec. 26, 1934, p. 177.
227 JR to H.J. Pearce, Nov. 22, 1934, NCPW, Swarthmore.
228 JR to Mrs. Haywood J. Pearce Jr., Gainesville, Ga., Dec. 29, 1934, NCPW, Swarthmore. In a subsequent letter, written to JR from Robert O. Grady on September 25, 1935, he wrote: "...you seem really to epitomize in one personality what Kidd is driving at for a coming generation of women who will allow the emotion of the peace ideal to totally possess them."
229 Atlanta Post No. 1 vs. Brenau College, February 1935, NCPW, Swarthmore.

[230] Macon Evening News, Dec. 10, 1934.
[231] Veterans Corner, Bill Janes, Macon Evening News, Oct. 10, 1935.
[232] Roger Baldwin letter to H.J. Pearce, April 19, 1935, NCPW, Swarthmore.
[233] Walter G. Cornett letter to Harry F. Ward, ACLU, Nov. 4, 1935, NCPW, Swarthmore.
[234] Jeannette Rankin letter to W.G. Cornett, 1936, NCPW, Swarthmore.
[235] W.T. Anderson statement, November 1936, NCPW, Swarthmore.
[236] Charles Penrose interview with Ted C. Harris, Jan. 29, 1972, author's personal files.
[237] JR letter on behalf of NCPW, May 15, 1936, NCPW, Swarthmore.
[238] Mrs. C.A. VerNooy, JR "commendations," NCPW, Feb. 6, 1930, Swarthmore.
[239] "Hearing on Taking the Profit out of War," on H.R. 3 and H.R. 5293, 74th Congress, 1st Session, pp. 307-308.
[240] "Jeannette Rankin, Progressive-Isolationist," Schaffer, p. 224.
[241] "Ballots or Bullets?" Radio interview with JR by Sylvia Press, May 14, 1939, NCPW, Swarthmore.
[242] Ibid.
[243] News release, April 15, 1935, NCPW, Swarthmore.
[244] John T. Flynn, Washington Daily News, April 29, 1935, pp. 3-4, Swarthmore.
[245] Jeannette Rankin interview with John Board, Missoula, Montana, Aug. 29-30, 1963, p. 56.
[246] "Military Discipline a Moral Asset," 1916, General Correspondence, Series II, JR MSS, Schlesinger.
[247] "Taking the Profits Out of War," Hearings before the Committee on Military Affairs, House of Representatives, Seventy-fourth Congress, first session, 1935.
[248] US House Committee on Judiciary, hearings on amending the Constitution with Respect to Declaration of War, HJ Res. 217 and 218, 73rd Congress, second session, sub-committee No. 1, Congressional Record, pp. 10-11.
[249] Undated 1930s Rankin speech, "During the discussion of the war resolution ...," NCPW, Swarthmore.
[250] "I Would Vote No Again," JR radio speech, 1935, NCPW, Swarthmore.
[251] "Jeannette Rankin: Suffragist, First Woman Elected to Congress, and Pacifist," Harris; "Jeannette Rankin: First Lady in Congress," Josephson, p. 148.
[252] "Twenty Years After!", Christian Herald, April 1937, JR MSS, Swarthmore.
[253] Historians later debated whether Rankin was a true isolationist or only appeared so because of the times. One of them, Joan Hoff Wilson, wrote that JR was more of an internationalist who used the isolationist argument to further her goals of international peace.
[254] "Do You Know," flyer describing costs of war, undated, JR MSS, Swarthmore.
[255] "Miss Rankin Makes a Fine Impression," Fulton, Missouri, Daily Sun-Gazette, Nov. 6, 1937, JR MSS, Swarthmore.
[256] "Speech of Jeannette Rankin," September 1934, NCPW, Swarthmore.
[257] "World Outlook," November 1938, p. 12.
[258] "Twenty Years After!", Christian Herald, April 1937, JR MSS, Swarthmore.
[259] JR public letter on NCPW letterhead, Sept. 25, 1937, JR MSS, Swarthmore.
[260] Gaylord W. Douglass to Frederick Libby, June 26, 1936, NCPW, Swarthmore.

261 Frederick L. Libby to Ernest Briggs, promotional flyer, April 1, 1932, JR MSS, Schlesinger.
262 "Prospectus for Acquainting the Public with the Plans and Objectives of the National Council for the Prevention of War via Jeanette [sic] Rankin," 1937, NCPW, Swarthmore.
263 JR testimony, 1936, NCPW, Swarthmore.
264 "Congress Is Considering Important Military Economies," Frederick J. Libby, undated, NCPW, Swarthmore.
265 JR to Clara Park Oliver, May 6, 1936, General Correspondence, Folders 40-48, JR MSS, Schlesinger.
266 "Europe Doesn't Want War," Sept. 7, 1937, JR MSS, Schlesinger.
267 Suffragists Oral History Project, University of California at Berkeley, Malca Chall, June 8, 1972.
268 "Between War and Peace," JR speech on Inter-City Network, Dec. 29, 1937, NCPW, Swarthmore.
269 "Peace is a woman's job: Jeannette Rankin's Foreign Policy," Joan Hoff Wilson, Arizona State University, p. 25.
270 JR to "Georgia Committee on the Disarmament Conference," Jan. 17, 1933, NCPW, Swarthmore.
271 Author interview with Dorothy McKinnon Brown, Helena, Mont., July 5, 1978.
272 JR to Frederick Libby, March 25, 1938, NCPW, Swarthmore.
273 "Statement of Miss Jeannette Rankin," Hearings before Committee on Foreign Affairs, House of Representatives, on proposed amendments to Neutrality laws, April 11-28 and May 2, 1939.
274 Undated speech, "During the discussion of the war resolution ...," NCPW, Swarthmore.
275 "Democracy and Women," comments by JR inserted into Congressional Record, 76th Congress, Third Session, Jan. 16, 1940.
276 JR interview with John Board, Missoula, Montana, Aug. 29-30, 1963, p. 44.
277 Suffragists Oral History Project, University of California at Berkeley, Malca Chall, Aug. 2, 1972.
278 Gerald P. Nye, Committee on Military Affairs, US Senate, June 22, 1940.
279 Author interview with Belle Fligelman Winestine, Helena, Mont., July 21, 1978.
280 Author interview with Dorothy McKinnon Brown, Helena, Mont., July 17, 1978.
281 Author interview with Virginia Ronhovde, Oct. 11, 1978.
282 July 22, 1940, NCPW, Swarthmore.
283 JR interview with Board, p. 49.
284 JR correspondence with LaGuardia and Dewey, General Correspondence, Folders 40-48, JR MSS, Schlesinger.
285 Ibid.
286 JR to Ben Chestnut, Dec. 14, 1940, JR MSS, Schlesinger.
287 Donald P. Wright to JR, Nov. 7, 1940, JR MSS, Schlesinger.
288 JR to Mary Stewart, Dec. 28, 1940, General Correspondence, JR Collection, Schlesinger.

[289] "Gallup and Fortune Polls," Public Opinion Quarterly, September 1940, pp. 533-553.
[290] Congressional Record, 77th Congress, First Session, Feb. 8, 1941, p. 814.
[291] "Woman Against War," Scribner's Commentary, Nov. 7, 1941, p. 30.
[292] Grant McGregor to JR, Jan. 10, 1941, JR MSS, Schlesinger.
[293] Congressional Record, 77th Congress, First Session, May 7, 1941, p. 3687.
[294] Congressional Record, 77th Congress, First Session, p. 4380.
[295] Congressional Record, House of Representatives, 77th Congress, Second Session, p. A4439.
[296] JR to Mary Church Terrill, June 16, 1941, JR MSS, Library of Congress.
[297] Students Union newspaper, 1974, p. 84-85.
[298] "Jeannette Rankin Against War" (1941), Fulton Lewis Jr. on Mutual Broadcasting Network:
[www.albany.edu/talkinghistory/archivalaudio/mutual_broadcast_congressional_debates_pearl_harbor_jeannette_rankin(december_1941).mp3
[299] Congressional Record, 77th US Congress, Dec. 8, 1941, pp. 9536-9537.
[300] JR interview with Board, p. 58.
[301] H.V. Kaltenborn, NBC Blue, "Let's Sing and Swing," Dec. 8, 1941, 1:15 p.m. EST.
[302] JR interview with Board, p. 59.
[303] Author interview with Virginia Ronhovde, Oct. 11, 1978.
[304] Letters protesting JR's antiwar vote can be found in General Correspondence, Folder 153, JR MSS, Schlesinger.
[305] Ibid.
[306] "Ideal Wife for a Wild Man," Henry McLemore, JR MSS, Schlesinger.
[307] Suffragists Oral History Project, University of California at Berkeley, Sept. 12, 1972.
[308] Margaret Laughrin telegram to JR, Dec. 8, 1941, JR MSS, Schlesinger.
[309] Amanda Swift to JR, Dec. 10, 1941, JR MSS, Schlesinger.
[310] Mary Jane Sedman to JR, Dec. 9. 1941, JR MSS, Schlesinger.
[311] JR to Ethel Bielenberg, Dec. 19, 1941, Bielenberg family private papers.
[312] Ibid., Jan. 8, 1942.
[313] Letters reacting to Rankin vote are held in JR collections at the Montana Historical Society and Schlesinger Library and in the author's private files.
[314] JR to H.H. Hoppe, Feb. 4, 1942, JR MSS, Schlesinger.
[315] JR to Olive Rankin, Feb. 10, 1942, JR MSS, Schlesinger.
[316] Author interview with Louise Rankin Galt, Oct. 6, 1978, Helena, Montana.
[317] Frances Elge to Marguerite Marcum, Aug. 22, 1941, JR MSS, Schlesinger.
[318] JR to Olive Rankin, July 1, 1942, JR MSS, Schlesinger Library.
[319] JR to Gladys Knowles, June 24, 1942, General Correspondence, Folders 161-165, JR MSS, Schlesinger.
[320] Mary O'Neill to JR, July 4, 1942, General Correspondence, Folders 161-165, JR MSS, Schlesinger.
[321] Katharine Anthony to JR, Oct. 10, 1942, General Correspondence, Folders 161-165, JR MSS, Schlesinger; Elisabeth Irwin died Oct. 16, obituary Oct. 17, 1942, New York Times, p. 15.

322 "Wellington Rankin: His Family, Life and Times," Steele, pp. 139-40.
323 Letters found in General Correspondence, Folders 161-165, JR MSS, Schlesinger.
324 Rosa Nell Spriggs to JR, undated, General Correspondence, Folders 166-172, JR MSS, Schlesinger.
325 JR to Gerald F.M. O'Grady, Aug. 16, 1943, JR MSS, Schlesinger.
326 Letters to and from Katharine Anthony and others found in General Correspondence, Folders 166-172, JR MSS, Schlesinger.
327 Ibid.
328 Ibid.
329 Ted C. Harris, University of Georgia doctoral dissertation, 1972.
330 Millacent Yarrow to JR, March 30, 1943, JR MSS, Schlesinger.
331 "Why I Am Going to India," JR MSS, undated, Schlesinger.
332 Author's personal interview with Dorothy McKinnon Brown, Helena, Mont., July 17, 1978.
333 JR to Ethel Bielenberg, Dec. 19, 1946, Bielenberg family private papers.
334 Author interview with Dorothy McKinnon Brown, Helena, Mont., July 5, 1978.
335 Author interview with Belle Fligelman Winestine, Helena, Mont., Dec. 14, 1977.
336 Edna Rankin McKinnon, letter to the author, Oct. 10, 1977.
337 Dorothy Brown to JR, Dec. 17, 1968, Edna Rankin McKinnon Papers, Folders 32-34, Schlesinger.
338 Donald Bielenberg interview with author, Deer Lodge, Mont., 1978.
339 "Mrs. John Rankin Dies Here," Independent Record, July 27, 1947, p. 1.
340 Federal Bureau of Investigation files, "Jeannette Rankin," April 17, 1952.
341 JR letter to Grace and Tom Kinney, July 19, 1952, JR MSS, Schlesinger.
342 Ibid, Aug. 30, 1952.
343 Author interview with Louise Rankin Galt, Helena, Mont., 1978.
344 Author interview with Dorothy McKinnon Brown, Helena, Mont., July 17, 1978.
345 Katharine Anthony to JR, Jan. 16, 1955, JR MSS, Schlesinger Library.
346 Ibid, Feb. 7, 1954.
347 Ibid, June 16, 1954.
348 "Wellington Rankin: His Family, Life and Times," Steele, p. 161.
349 Author interview with Louise Rankin Galt, 71 Ranch in Montana, Oct. 19, 2012.
350 Author interview with Louise Rankin Galt, Helena, Mont., 1978.
351 Ibid, Oct. 6, 1978.
352 Flora Belle Surles to JR, General Correspondence, Folders 166-172, JR MSS, Schlesinger.
353 Several judges and lawyers drafted a fawning resolution commending Wellington D. Rankin "as one of Montana's great jury lawyers" and for his service on the Montana Supreme Court. The resolution, dated Feb. 21, 1967, also spoke in awe of Rankin's accumulation of wealth.
354 Author interview with Louise Rankin Galt, 71 Ranch in Montana, Oct. 19, 2012.
355 Edna Rankin McKinnon to JR, Dec. 11, 1966, JR MSS, Schlesinger Library.
356 Author interview with Louise Rankin Galt, 71 Ranch, Oct. 19, 2012.
357 Dorothy McKinnon Brown to JR, Dec. 1, 1966, Edna Rankin McKinnon MSS, Schlesinger Library.

[358] John F. Kennedy to JR, April 15, 1958, JR MSS, Schlesinger.
[359] Flora Belle Surles to JR, April 1, 1967, General Correspondence, Folders 166-172, JR MSS, Schlesinger.
[360] Elizabeth Winburn Sinclair to JR, May 23, 1967, JR MSS, Schlesinger.
[361] Author interview with Dorothy McKinnon Brown, Helena, Mont., July 17, 1978.
[362] JR to Peter Besag, undated, General Correspondence, Folders 166-172, JR MSS, Schlesinger.
[363] JR interview with Board, p. 12.
[364] Letters from Katharine Anthony, General Correspondence, Folders 166-172, JR MSS, Schlesinger.
[365] Marion D. Beardsley, "Report on the Jeannette Rankin Brigade March," JR MSS, Schlesinger.
[366] Los Angeles Times, Jan. 7, 1968.
[367] Documents from the Women's Liberation Movement, Special Collections Library, Duke University.
[368] "Funeral Oration for the Burial of Traditional Womanhood," Herstory Project, Special Collections Library, Duke University.
[369] Amy Swerdlow, "Women Strike for Peace: Traditional Motherhood and Radical Politics in the 1960s" (University of Chicago Press, 1993), p. 140.
[370] "Marginalia," Ramparts Magazine, May 1968, p. 4.
[371] Mary Jane Hoffman to Jeannette Rankin, Feb. 26, 1970, JR MSS, Schlesinger.
[372] "Jeannette Rankin Brigade vs. Chief of Capitol Police," US Court of Appeals District of Columbia Circuit, argued Dec. 9, 1968; Decided June 20, 1969.
[373] Jeannette Rankin Brigade vs. Chief of Capitol Police, US District Court, May 9, 1972.
[374] Dan Hueni to JR, July 2, 1969, Edna Rankin McKinnon correspondence, Folders 32-34, Schlesinger.
[375] JR letter to editor, Athens, Ga., Banner-Herald, Nov. 9, 1971.
[376] Dorothy McKinnon Brown to JR, May 22, 1970, JR MSS, Schlesinger.
[377] "Jeannette Rankin: Why I Voted Against War," circa 1972, JR MSS, Schlesinger.
[378] JR interview with John Board, Missoula, Montana, Aug. 29-30, 1963, p. 33.
[379] Letters from MC246, Folder 185, JR MSS, Schlesinger.
[380] Sherry Smith to JR, Nov. 8, 1971, JR MSS, Schlesinger.
[381] Norma Smith, "Jeannette Rankin: America's Conscience" (Helena: Montana Historical Society Press, 2002), p. 220.
[382] Nadine Brozan, "Crusading Forerunner of Women's Lib," New York Times, Jan. 24, 1972, p.18.
[383] Quoted in, "First Lady in Congress: Jeannette Rankin," Josephson, pp. 204-205.
[384] Chall and Josephson, Suffragists Oral History Project.
[385] "Why I Voted Against War," Jeannette Rankin and John Kirkley, undated, JR MSS, Swarthmore.
[386] John Kirkley, "An Afternoon with Jeannette Rankin," Georgia Advocate, August 1971.
[387] Author interview with Dorothy McKinnon Brown, Helena, Mont., July 17, 1978.
[388] Author personal interview with Louise Rankin Galt, 71 Ranch, Oct. 19, 2012.

[389] Coretta Scott King telegram to JR, June 13, 1970, JR MSS, Schlesinger.
[390] Washington Star, September 1972.
[391] Belle Fligelman Winestine interview with the author, Helena, Mont., Dec. 14, 1977.
[392] JR to Professor Henry Steele Commager, May 1, 1971, JR MSS, Schlesinger.
[393] JR speech to Prince Avenue Baptist Church, Athens, Georgia, September 1932, NCPW, Swarthmore.
[394] Suffragists Oral History Project, University of California at Berkeley, Sept. 12, 1972.
[395] JR, quoted in Life magazine, March 3, 1972.
[396] Jeffrey Elliot to JR, July 19, 1971, MC 246, Folder 185, JR MSS, Schlesinger.
[397] Jeannette Rankin interview with John Board, Missoula, Montana, Aug. 29-30, 1963, p. 34.
[398] Author interview with Dorothy McKinnon Brown, Helena, Mont., July 5, 1978.
[399] Financial statements found in MC 246, Folder 185, JR MSS, Schlesinger.
[400] Ann Ronhovde to JR, Feb. 26, 1973, JR MSS, Schlesinger.
[401] Hannah Josephson to JR, Jan. 17, 1973, JR MSS, Schlesinger.
[402] Author interview with Dorothy McKinnon Brown, Helena, Mont., July 5, 1978.
[403] John Hurt to JR, Dec. 8, 1941, JR MSS, Schlesinger.
[404] Lavinia L. Dock to JR, Dec. 18, 1941, JR MSS, Schlesinger.
[405] Cronkite, Walter, The Lone Dissenter: Walter Cronkite Remembers Pearl Harbor, Jeannette Rankin. Radio address first aired December 7, 2001: "All Things Considered". National Public Radio Digitized Archive.
[http://www.npr.org/template/story/story.php?storyid=1134462.]
[406] Reita Rivers to Edna Rankin McKinnon, May 29, 1973, JR MSS, Schlesinger.
[407] Susan Brownmiller, New York Times, Nov. 3, 1974.
[408] Dorothy McKinnon Brown to Dr. George Thorngate Sr., Dec. 20, 1973, Edna Rankin McKinnon MSS, Folders 32-34, Schlesinger.
[409] "Jeannette Rankin," Susan Brownmiller, New York Times, Nov. 3, 1974, p. F14.
[410] Joan Hoff Wilson, "Jeannette Rankin and Foreign Policy: The Origins of Her Pacifism," Montana, the Magazine of Western History, Winter 1980, pp. 29-40.

Index

A

Abolition of War, 225
Abzug, Bella, 394
Acher, Arthur, 421
Addams, Jane, 36, 40, 41, 83, 149, 223, 276, 277, 378, 398
Amatniek, Kathie, 381
America First, 259, 284, 303, 315, 319
American Civil Liberties Union, 248, 249, 424
Anaconda Copper, 56, 83, 86, 101, 105, 152, 161, 171, 174, 180, 181, 199, 202, 205, 207, 337, 360
Anthony, Katharine, 11, 62, 123, 185, 216, 331, 339, 344, 358, 364, 378, 438, 439, 447
Anthony, Susan B., 61, 189, 210, 275, 330, 358, 364, 394
Ashe, Elizabeth, 39
Atlantans for Peace, 6
Avalanche Ranch. *See* Rankin, Jeannette
Averbach, Ida, 65

B

Bacorn, Frank, 173
Baldwin, Roger, 249, 424
Beardsley, Marion, 14, 379
Bielenberg, Ethel, 330, 331, 346, 364
Board, John, 391, 438, 443
Boeckel, Florence, 267, 279
Brenau College controversy, 243, 244
Brown, Dorothy "Mackey", 338, 354, 389, 399, 420, 423, 427, 438
Brownmiller, Susan, 426, 428
Bunch, Charlotte, 381
Burnet, Inez, 229

C

Campbell, Will, 161, 179, 202, 207
Cannon, 'Uncle Joe', 143, 160
Catt, Carrie Chapman, 59, 67, 114, 123, 125, 136, 150, 159, 191, 203, 205, 208
Cause and Cure of War, 230, 231, 235
Chair of Peace, 243, 245, 247, 437
Children's Home Society, 47
Chisholm, Shirley, 394, 411
Christian Science, 42, 354, 397, 437
Clark, Champ, 144, 145, 160, 289
Clarke, Mary, 379
Collins, Judy, 19
Cronkite, Walter, 424

D

Daly, Marcus, 57, 86
Detzer, Dorothy, 224, 226
Devine, Edward T., 43
DeVoe, Emma Smith, 50
Dick Cavett Show, 395
Dixon, Joseph, 37, 93, 227
Dock, Lavinia, 330, 424
Dodge, Mrs. Arthur M., 60
Douglass, Frederick, 194
Douglass, Gaylord, 268

E

Eaker, Susan, 308
Early days in Missoula, Mont., 26
Early suffrage movement, 36
Eastman, Crystal, 62, 188
Eddy, Mary Baker, 354, 355
Eisenhower, Dwight D., 357, 405
Electoral College, 406, 408
Elge, Frances, 292, 307, 336, 432
Equal Franchise Society, 52
Ethridge, Willie Snow, 235
Evans, John, 105, 129

F

Fahy, Charles, 383
Farr, George W., 99
Federal Bureau of Investigation, 13, 299, 447
Felton, Rebecca Latimer, 214
Firestone, Shulamith, 380
Fligelman, Belle, 93, 95, 98, 103, 129, 134, 135, 137, 146, 158, 161, 167, 177, 178, 183, 185, 188, 204, 208, 236, 273, 290, 354, 405, 423, 431, 433, 438, 439, 441, 443
Fligelman, Frieda, 84
Friedan, Betty, 374, 394
Funk, Antoniette, 88

G

Gandhi, Mohandas K., 164
Gay ladies from Gaylordsville, 331
Georgia Peace Society, 229, 231, 235, 237, 238, 240, 243, 248, 249, 274, 280
Goodman, Linda, 5
Great Depression, 233
Greenwich Village, 52, 62
Gregorie, Anne King, 391
Griffith, Alice, 39

H

Hallinan, Vincent, 7
Hallinan, Vivian, 7, 371, 379, 392
Haltigan, Patrick J., 144
Halvorsen, Ora, 429
Hegeman, Kate, 150
Hensen, Capt. A.L., 247
Heterodoxy Club, 62, 63, 84, 188, 203, 216, 331
Hinchey, Margaret, 81
Hoover, J. Edgar, 13, 299, 304, 358
Hubert H. Humphrey, 4
Huck, Winnifred Sprague Mason, 214
Hull House, 36, 40, 41, 149, 276, 277, 435
Hull, Cordell, 302
Humphrey, Hubert H., 4

I

India's Contributions to the Peace of the World, 347
Irwin, Elisabeth, 62, 331, 339, 344, 358

J

Jeannette Rankin Brigade, 2, 3, 8, 13, 14, 15, 16, 18, 371, 375, 377, 379, 381, 382, 383, 384, 392, 421, 447
Jeannette Rankin Brigade vs. Chief of Capitol Police, 383
Johnson, President Lyndon, 2, 4, 18, 381, 405
Jones, Rosalie, 81, 97, 108, 345

K

Kaltenborn, H.V., 318
Kelley, Florence, 43, 220
Kellogg-Briand Peace Pact, 230, 231, 249, 265, 282
Kelly, Cornelius. *See* Anaconda Copper
Kennedy, Joe, 173
Kennedy, John F., 368, 438
Kennedy, Robert, 4
Kerlin, Robert T., 225
Kidd, Benjamin, 9, 164, 247, 336, 348, 425
King, Coretta Scott, 1, 15, 19, 379
King, Martin Luther, Jr., 2, 3
Kinney, John, 262
Kirkley, John, 392, 393, 395, 396
Kitchin, Claude, 134, 215
Kurusu, Saburo, 302

L

Lady from Montana. *See* Rankin, Jeannette
Laidlaw, Harriet, 58, 80, 89, 113, 123, 136, 151, 203
Laidlaw, James, 80
Lanstrum, Oscar M., 204
Laughrin, Margaret, 329
Lee Keedick Agency, 113
Leech, Florence, 128, 134, 183, 185
Lever Bill legislation, 164, 165
Lewis, Fulton, Jr., 315
Libby, Frederick, 234, 249, 268, 271, 277, 279, 284, 293, 324, 343, 346, 357
Liberty Bonds, 161, 162, 165, 169
Lindbergh, Charles, 228, 284, 298, 303, 315, 319
Linderman, Frank Bird, 222
Lindfors, Viveca, 15
Little, Frank, 174, 178, 207
Loyall, Camilla, 40
Lundeen, Ernest, 298

M

Maddox, Lester, 4
Management Ernest Briggs Inc., 268
Mansfield, Mike, 20, 359, 389, 427
March to the Pentagon. *See* Jeannette Rankin Brigade
Markeson, Clara, 82
McAdoo, William, 166
McCarthy, Eugene, 17, 405, 411
McCormack, John, 19, 298
McGovern, George, 411, 420; Rankin's vote, 405
McKinnon, Edna, 414, 426

McReynolds, Sam D., 266
Merchants of Death, 270
Merv Griffin Show, 394
Metcalf, Lee, 359, 389
Militant protest groups, 4
Millis, Walter, 270
Milton, Abby Crawford, 346
Mimnaugh, Terry, 429
Montana Council of Defense, 202
Montana Equal Suffrage Association, 74
Montana Protective Association, 82
Montana Territory, 21, 23, 25, 27, 97, 375
Montana votes for suffrage, 85
Mott, Lucretia, 36, 61
Murray, James, 339, 340
Mutual Broadcasting System, 315

N

National American Woman Suffrage Association, 59, 68, 71, 85, 88, 167, 435, 441
National Consumers League, 43, 167, 220, 221, 222, 439
National Council for Prevention of War, 234, 235, 236, 237, 238, 242, 249, 250, 256, 266, 267, 268, 269, 270, 276, 279, 280, 281, 334, 343, 432, 441
National Organization of Women, 374
Nehru, Jawaharlal, 354
New Basis of Civilization, 44
Nixon, Richard, 4, 368, 377, 392, 405, 411, 414
Nolan, Cornelius, 53, 57
Nolan, Mae Ella, 214

Nomura, Admiral Kichisaburo, 302
Nonpartisan League, 200, 206, 209
Nye Committee, 257, 270, 278, 280, 281
Nye, Gerald, 264, 318, 389

O

O'Connell, Jerry J., 293
O'Neill, Mary, 74, 76, 79, 172, 174, 181, 339, 345, 346

P

Park, Maud Wood, 123, 149
Patchin Place, 61
Patten, Simon N., 44
Paul, Alice, 68, 69, 70, 83, 123, 124, 143, 148, 187
Peaceful demonstrations at US Capitol, 383
Pearce, H.J. Jr., 243
Pearce, H.J. Sr., 244, 251
Pearl Harbor, 300, 303, 304, 305, 306, 314, 317, 319, 320, 326, 327, 328, 329, 332, 333, 334, 340, 342, 343, 351, 424, 436, 442
Pendergrast, Nan, 6, 8, 426, 447
Printing and Engraving investigation, 165, 166, 168, 203
Progressive reform, 7, 35, 43, 66, 68, 77, 78, 82, 86, 92, 94, 95, 97, 125, 138, 163, 185, 190, 206, 358, 374, 436, 440, 444, 447
Puffer, Louise, 185

R

Raker, John E., 190
Ralph, Joseph, 166
Rankin ranches, 365
Rankin, Edna. *See* McKinnon, Edna Rankin
Rankin, Grace: as a child, 21; as family caregiver, 339; death, 364; inheritance, 367; letters from Jeannette, 359; living in Idaho, 292
Rankin, Hattie: 1918 Senate campaign, 203; as Jeannette's sister, 291; as office manager, 204; husband dies, 42; London bombing, 299
Rankin, Jeannette. *See* Nader, Ralph, *See* Fiorella LaGuardia, *See* Georgia Peace Society; ' little black pills', 168; 1916 primary election, 99; 1918 campaign for US Senate, 207; American Legion, 244; antiwar support, 5; appeal to Montana legislators, 53; as a girl in Montana, 21; as Aspasia, 216; as feminist leader, 396; as pacifist, 15, 311; as Progressive, 35; as reformer, 135; Austria-Hungary war declaration, 181; Avalanche Ranch, 285, 287, 294, 339, 343, 344, 355, 361, 363, 366, 371; birth, 23; campaigning for Congress, 91, 96; campaigning for Congress, 1940, 283; casting first antiwar vote, 145; Chair of Peace, 245; congressional salary, 128; death, 423, 424; declaration of war, 315, 317; defends antiwar vote, 334; direct preferential voting, 412; election to Congress, 103; first day in US House, 129, 131; first woman in US House, 114; ideas for peace in Georgia, 229; in Boston, 37; in Georgia, 213; in New York, 58; in New Zealand, 88; in San Francisco, 40; India and peace, 347; introduced to suffrage, 49; investments, 421; Ireland's independence, 198; Jeannette Rankin Brigade. *See* Jeannette Rankin Brigade; leading Montana suffrage, 67; legacy, 387, 390; march on US Capitol, 1; marketing image, 160; Montana home, 24; muckrakers, 41; national reaction to election, 107; NCPW, 268; Nez Perce war, 32; on feminism, 418; opposing Vietnam war, 377; outlawing war, 266; parents, 25; radio addresses, 257; reaction to first antiwar vote, 152; relationship with Katharine Anthony, 358; relationship with Wellington, 42; 'rustling card' practice, 171; second election to US House, 294; Shady Grove farm, 392; siblings, 25; speech to Butte miners, 178; statues, 429; symbol of suffrage, 108; travels to India, 349; vote totals, 105; war profiteering, 44; 'Win the War First', 200

Rankin, John, 10, 25, 26, 27, 28, 29, 31, 32, 34, 37, 336, 355
Rankin, Mary: as a child, 25; death, 391; dying mother, 355; letters from Jeannette, 44
Rankin, Olive, 10, 22, 24, 25, 28, 102, 130, 183, 184, 223, 336
Rankin, Philena, 25, 28
Rankin, Wellington: 1916 campaign, 92; antiwar vote, 136; as campaign manager, 101; as Christian Scientist, 353; as family benefactor, 227; as investor, 360; as The Boy, 28; at Harvard, 37; close to Jeannette, 42; criminal trial lawyer, 137; death, 366; influential politician, 93; landowner, 365; managing Jeannette's campaigns, 294; meeting Theodore Roosevelt, 117; Pearl Harbor, 306; relationship with Jeannette, 308; suffrage leader, 96; trying for Congress, 339
Rankin-Robinson legislation, 197, 220
Rankin-Sheppard legislation, 188
Rayburn, Sam, 310, 315
Replogle, Louise, 361, 397
Reynolds, Minnie J., 58
Rivers, Reita, 426
Robertson, Alice Mary, 214
Robinson, Wonder, 362, 426
Roosevelt, Eleanor, 237, 305
Roosevelt, Franklin D., 64, 233, 293
Roosevelt, Theodore, 34, 38, 103, 114, 117, 118, 193, 410
Round House, 372, 373, 374

Ryan, John D., 174, 176, See Anaconda Copper
Ryan, William Fitts, 19

S

Scannell, Sigrid, 310, 340, 371
Schlafly, Phyllis, 398
Science of Power, 9, 10, 247, 336
Sedman, Ellis, 37, 42, 169
Shaw, Anna Howard, 61, 85, 87, 119, 150, 191
Sheppard-Towner legislation, 197, 220
Shoreham Hotel, 122, 127, 379
Shusterman, Rabbi Abraham, 243
Sinclair, Elizabeth Winburn, 372
Sirhan Sirhan, 4
Slayden, Ellen Maury, 129, 149, 436
Some Questions About Pearl Harbor, 343
Spriggs, Rosa Nell, 343
Stanton, Elizabeth Cady, 61, 189, 210, 382
Stanton, Lucy, 229
Starr, Ellen Gates, 36
Steinem, Gloria, 335, 394, 398
Stellway, Helena, 191
Stewart, Mary, 177, 203, 296
Stewart, Sam V., 67
Stout, Tom, 66, 79, 91
Surles, Flora Belle, 225, 345, 366, 371, 378, 391
Swerdlow, Amy, 381, 447
Swinnerton, Cornelia, 61

T

Telegraph Hill settlement, 39, 40, 41, 62
Terrill, Mary Church, 303
Tet Offensive, 4, 376
The Devil Theory of War, 270, 278, 435
The Red Network, 251
The Road to War, 270, 436
Thoreau, Henry David, 6, 164, 352, 362
Thorkelson, Jacob, 287
Thorngate, Dr. George, 427
Triangle Shirtwaist fire, 58
Truman, Harry, 338, 357
Tully, Grace, 309

V

VerNooy, Mrs. C.A., 253
Vinson, Carl, 237, 252, 274

W

Wallace, George, 4, 411, 425
Walsh, Joseph, 190
Walsh, Thomas J., 53, 130, 205, 222
Washington, Booker T., 22, 43
Watson, Elizabeth, 62, 166, 179
Wheeler, Burton K., 203, 207, 297, 318, 323, 340, 389
Willen, Pearl, 379
Willkie, Wendell, 296
Wilson, Woodrow, 68, 89, 94, 105, 113, 140, 179, 184, 193, 244, 246, 263, 302, 410; war message, 132
Wobblies, 173, 174, 178, 207
Women Strike for Peace, 8, 13, 14, 379, 392, 447
Women's Christian Temperance Union, 36, 82, 208
Women's International League of Peace and Freedom, 224, 225
Women's Peace Union, 231, 240, 345

Y

Yarrow, Harriet, 346, 349
Yarrow, Millacent, 329, 345, 347

Z

Zimmerman, Arthur, 116

Printed in the USA
CPSIA information can be obtained
at www.ICGtesting.com
LVHW091728200824
788771LV00010B/76